The Experience of Thinking

When retrieving a quote from memory, evaluating a testimony's truthfulness, or deciding which products to buy, people experience immediate feelings of ease or difficulty, of fluency or disfluency. Such "experiences of thinking" occur with every cognitive process, including perceiving, processing, storing, and retrieving information, and they have been the defining element of a vibrant field of scientific inquiry during the last four decades.

This book brings together the latest research on how such experiences of thinking influence cognition and behavior. The chapters present recent theoretical developments and describe the effects of these influences, as well as the practical implications of this research. The book includes contributions from the leading scholars in the field and provides a comprehensive survey of this expanding area. This integrative overview will be invaluable to researchers, teachers, students, and professionals in the field of social and cognitive psychology.

Christian Unkelbach is Professor of Experimental Psychology at the University of Cologne, Germany. He is currently Associate Editor of the journals *Experimental Psychology* and *Social Psychology*. His research focuses on processing fluency, valence asymmetries, prejudice against Muslims, and sport psychology. He has authored numerous articles in international journals covering these topics.

Rainer Greifeneder is Professor of Social Psychology at the University of Basel, Switzerland. His research focuses on experiences of thinking, affective feelings, intuitive decision making, consumer choice, and ostracism. He has authored numerous articles in international journals covering these topics.

The Experience
of Thinking

How the fluency of mental processes
influences cognition and behavior

Edited by
Christian Unkelbach and
Rainer Greifeneder

Psychology Press
Taylor & Francis Group

LONDON AND NEW YORK

First published 2013
by Psychology Press
27 Church Road, Hove, East Sussex, BN3 2FA

Simultaneously published in the USA and Canada
by Psychology Press
711 Third Avenue, New York, NY 10017

*Psychology Press is an imprint of the Taylor & Francis Group, an informa
business*

British Library Cataloguing in Publication Data
A catalogue record for this book is available from the British Library

Library of Congress Cataloging in Publication Data
The experience of thinking: how the fluency of mental processes influences
cognition and behavior / edited by Christian Unkelbach and Rainer
Greifeneder.
   p. cm.
Includes bibliographical references and index.
1. Thought and thinking. 2. Cognition. 3. Social interaction.
I. Unkelbach, Christian. II. Greifeneder, Rainer.
BF441.E92 2013
153.4'2—dc23   2012021725

ISBN: 978-1-84872-065-7 (hbk)
ISBN: 978-1-84872-130-2 (pbk)
ISBN: 978-0-203-07893-8 (ebk)

Typeset in Times
by Cenveo Publisher Services

Contents

Contributors

Adam L. Alter, New York University, United States
Email: aalter@stern.nyu.edu

Pablo Briñol, Universidad Autónoma de Madrid, Spain
Email: pablo.brinnol@uam.es

Herbert Bless, Universität Mannheim, Germany
Email: bless@uni-mannheim.de

Heather M. Claypool, Miami University, United States
Email: claypohm@muohio.edu

Klaus Fiedler, Universität Heidelberg, Germany
Email: klaus.fiedler@psychologie.uni-heidelberg.de

Leonel Garcia-Marques, Universidade de Lisboa, Portugal
Email: garcia_marques@sapo.pt

Teresa Garcia-Marques, Instituto Superior de Psicologia Aplicada, Portugal
Email: teresa.marques@ispa.pt

Rainer Greifeneder, Universität Basel, Switzerland
Email: rainer.greifeneder@unibas.ch

Michael Häfner, Universiteit Utrecht, the Netherlands
Email: m.hafner@uu.nl

Jamin Halberstadt, University of Otago, New Zealand
Email: jhalbers@psy.otago.ac.nz

Jochim Hansen, Universität Salzburg, Austria
Email: jochim.hansen@sbg.ac.at

Ralph Hertwig, Max Planck Institute for Human Development, Berlin, Germany
Email: hertwig@mpib-berlin.mpg.de

Stefan M. Herzog, Max Planck Institute for Human Development, Berlin, Germany
Email: herzog@mpib-berlin.mpg.de

Daniel M. Oppenheimer, Princeton University, United States
Email: doppenhe@princeton.edu

Diane M. Mackie, University of California at Santa Barbara, United States
Email: mackie@psych.ucsb.edu

Richard E. Petty, Ohio State University, United States
Email: petty.1@osu.edu

Rolf Reber, Universitetet i Bergen, Norway
Email: rolf.reber@psysp.uib.no

Sabine G. Scholl, Universität Mannheim, Germany
Email: sabine.scholl@uni-mannheim.de

Sascha Topolinski, Universität Würzburg, Germany
Email: sascha.topolinski@psychologie.uni-wuerzburg.de

Zakary L. Tormala, Stanford University, United States
Email: tormala_zakary@gsb.stanford.edu

Christian Unkelbach, Universität zu Köln, Germany
Email: christian.unkelbach@uni-koeln.de

Michaela Wänke, Universität Mannheim, Germany
Email: michaela.waenke@uni-mannheim.de

Piotr Winkielman, University of California at San Diego, United States
Email: pwinkiel@ucsd.edu

1 Experiencing thinking

Rainer Greifeneder and
Christian Unkelbach

What could be more rational than thinking? Thinking, the act of reasoning, of gauging and weighing arguments, of considering and re-considering, is generally regarded as solid and factual. It is celebrated as the latest gain in evolution, separating homo sapiens from its predecessors. It is the supreme discipline higher education aims for. And it is almost antagonistic to the notion of feelings, which are often perceived as erroneous and fallible—think of Mr. Spock's condescension for Captain Kirk's often feeling-based decisions. When societies invest in and cherish the intellectual capabilities of their members, it is thinking based on logic and rationality that they aspire to. SATs (in the US) or large-scale scholarly research projects such as PISA in Europe focus on knowledge, logic, and deduction, following the implicit assumption that there is nothing more to thinking than thought content and declarative rules applied to this content. And yet, research during the last four decades has poignantly demonstrated that what is prized as rational is closely intertwined with feelings. In fact, every act of thinking is associated with experiences. Consider naming ten reasons why thinking and feeling have nothing in common. Even if you manage (and we think you will not), the mere attempt of naming these reasons likely *felt* difficult. Likewise, consider reading the non-word "ndoetvio" compared to the word "devotion"—most likely the process of reading the former *felt* more difficult than reading the latter. Such examples illustrate that despite the rational pedestal thought is put on, every mental process comes with an experiential component. These "experiences of thinking" influence judgments, decisions, further cognition, and behavior, and some even argue that it is the feeling component of thinking that constitutes the true adaptive advantage of human cognition.

The present volume puts the spotlight on these experiences accompanying thought and their consequences for cognition and behavior. Not from the standpoint of a biasing influence or unrequested fail-out of what seemingly pure thinking is about—but from an integrative standpoint that considers both the process of thinking itself and how this process *feels*. Thinking is thereby meant in its broadest sense, encompassing all kinds of mental processes, including, for instance, perceiving, categorizing, storing, retrieving, or generating information. Taking a similarly broad perspective, all experiences or feelings accompanying mental operations are jointly referred to as "experiences of thinking." As these experiences can be located on a continuum of easy to difficult, fluent to disfluent, they are also referred to as "ease of processing" or "fluency" in the literature. In what follows, we use these termini interchangeably, but emphasize what is likely the term most researchers can subscribe to, "fluency." We define this fluency as the subjective experience of ease or difficulty associated with mental processing. Note that fluency is used in the literature both to denote a specific (fluent) experience and the abstract concept, which encompasses the full continuum from *disfluency* to *fluency*. To increase reading flow, we follow this lead and refrain from separately referring to disfluency and fluency when talking about the abstract concept.

While phenomenological experiences of the kind discussed here were a central part in early theories about cognitive and mental processes (e.g., Wundt, 1862), psychology soon abandoned its experiential and phenomenological roots: initially, in the rise of behaviorism, which treated everything *inside* the human being as part of a black box that is beyond scientific investigations, because it is too unreliable and too subjective; later, during the cognitive revolution, which conceptualized humans as pure information processors, guided by computer metaphors of human cognition. It must have been against this background that Gerald Clore wrote: "We are better prepared to study the content of thought than the experience of thinking" (Clore, 1992: p. 133), mercilessly exposing a one-sided approach to research on cognitive and thinking processes. Today, 20 years after this assessment, we believe that psychological science is well-prepared to study the experience of thinking, and the present book is a strong testimony to the advances that psychological research has made in this respect. This volume brings together research findings and conceptualizations about how the experience of thinking, and more specifically, the fluency and disfluency associated with mental processing, influences judgments, decisions, and behavior. To lay the foundation for these contributions, in what follows, we delineate what we mean by "experiences of thinking" or "fluency."

What is fluency?

If you venture an experiential peek into your cognitive control room, no doubt you can *feel* what this book is about. Some operations are easy or fluent (like reading this sentence), other mental operations may be difficult or disfluent (for various reasons such as font size). Fluency experiences are common, but people do not always focus on them. Yet, if people attend to their mental processes, the feeling component tied to all thinking can be experienced. Nevertheless, although people are familiar with fluency experiences, what exactly fluency is as a scientific concept may still be blurry. Sharpening the concept is not an easy endeavor because fluency is intangible and by the definition of an experience, highly subjective, just like "love" or "Schadenfreude." With such intangible concepts, the solution is often to recruit descriptive features such as "Love is when you cannot be without the other person" or "Love is, when the world is colored purple." None of these "pseudo-definitions" exactly says what love is, but together they trace a picture of essential features that allows for gaining a better understanding what love must be about. Here we follow a similar approach and attempt to triangulate the fluency concept by means of five core components.

First, fluency is a *feeling*. It provides experiential information about otherwise inaccessible mental processes (e.g., memory retrieval) and thus feedback about the state of the cognitive system. By defining fluency as a feeling, we suggest that fluency is experienced the same way people experience emotional or bodily feelings, like appetite or hunger (which provide feedback about the state of the digestive system and nutrition level of the bloodstream, although people are largely agnostic as how these experiences are generated). By the same token, we suggest that fluency is available to conscious deliberation the same way that emotional or bodily feelings are. While it is not necessary that the fluency experience is always conscious, it should be consciously available if the attention is placed on it; a state termed pre-conscious (Dehaene et al., 2006: pp. 206–207).

Second, fluency arises as a by-product from mental operations. It has been characterized as the experiential output of an internal monitoring system that constantly screens how mental processing proceeds (Whittlesea & Williams, 2000). Note that this second component sets the fluency concept apart from perceptions of fluency resulting from other sources such as coordinated action or speech, which may also be termed as "fluent" but do not result from internal cognitive processes.

Third, fluency is informative about the ease or difficulty with which some mental operation is executed. This feature places the fluency concept on an easy-difficult dimension. While there are other possible dimensions, such as intensity, the easy-difficult distinction would appear to be the most defining one.

Fourth, the subjective location of a specific experience on the easy-difficult dimension is a function of prior experiences. That reading this subordinate clause feels subjectively difficult reflects the existence of (many) prior reading experiences that were easier to decipher. More generally, whether a specific mental operation is *experienced* as easy or difficult depends also on comparisons with prior processing experiences. This reflects the general law of relativism (Parducci, 1968; Mussweiler, 2003) applied to the experience of performing mental operations.

Finally, fluency is an integrative experience that summarizes ongoing mental activity. For instance, having difficulty in retrieving a specific word from memory summarizes the process of finding this word in the associative network structure; how this search proceeds is a function of, for instance, the information previously stored in the associative network structure, previous activation of the searched or related information, concurrent processing demands, and so forth. The experience associated with retrieving summarizes all these contributing aspects in one feeling. At least two critical consequences ensue: on the hand, for fluency to be informative, it needs to be attributed to a specific source and interpreted in its context (see Unkelbach & Greifeneder, Ch. 2). On the other hand, this summarizing function allows fast and efficient information processing when relying on fluency in further downstream cognition (Koriat & Levy-Sadot, 1999, coined the term "meta-summary").

These aspects tie fluency experiences to the realm of meta-cognition, that is, thinking about thinking (Nelson, 1996). This becomes evident, for instance, when considering that one can deliberate about the meaning of a given experience and its implications.

Just because fluency experiences are subjective and not easy to pinpoint, there is not always consensus about the right definition or its essential components, or in case of experimental psychology, the right manipulation to create fluency experiences. Therefore, across the book, there will be deviations from the components outlined here: for example, the consciousness component will be challenged (Oppenheimer & Alter, Ch. 6), or the idea that fluency is a by-product of mental activities (Topolinski, Ch. 3). Nevertheless, we believe that these five characteristics offer a good starting point and a refined picture of what we mean by fluency (and what not). It is obvious that this perspective encompasses a wide array of phenomena, all of which, however, are characterized by these five fundamental building blocks. Therefore, although labeled differently in the literature, we treat classic thinking experiences such as the tip-of-the-tongue phenomenon (e.g., Schwartz, 2002) or the feeling-of-knowing (e.g., Koriat, 1993) as fluency experiences, too (see also Alter & Oppenheimer, 2009; Topolinski & Reber, 2010).

Why are fluency effects interesting?

Research on fluency and thinking experiences has reclaimed the feeling component for modern cognitive psychology. This constitutes an important advancement beyond the long-time dominant computer metaphor and enriches psychological research—in fact, it makes the pure information-processing approach to scientific psychology again human. As Ch. 4 aptly states: "Once more with feeling!" This contribution to scientific research will be presented, for example, in the chapters on how fluency experiences emerge (Topolinski, Ch. 3), how fluency relates to emotional feelings (Garcia-Marques, Mackie, Claypool, & Garcia-Marques, Ch. 4), or if scientists investigate this topic in the proper manner (Fiedler, Ch. 14).

Yet, investigating fluency is not only important for propelling scientific knowledge, but has direct practical implications for everyday life, too. For example, it is known since the 1930s that the legibility of an essay has a potent influence on how the essay is evaluated, averaging up to one letter grade (James, 1929). This legibility effect may have serious consequences for those who do not write legibly, for instance, with respect to university acceptance. By uncovering the mechanism underlying this effect, fluency research explains a long acknowledged source of error in performance evaluation (Greifeneder et al., 2010). Relatedly, fluency has been shown to determine how deeply information is encoded and which information therefore is likely to be recalled later (Oppenheimer & Alter, Ch. 6). Contrary to many contemporary accounts in school and university didactics, fluency research shows that rendering learning ever easier may have detrimental consequences (see also Fiedler, Ch. 14). Fluency research also uncovered cognitive mechanisms that are critical in the courtroom. When evaluating eyewitness testimonies, for instance, it is important to know that statements that are easily processed are believed more (Unkelbach, 2007), and that people tend to identify fluently processed faces as "seen before" (Kleider & Goldinger, 2004). Among others, fluency research may help to create better settings for eyewitness line-ups (Fiedler, Ch. 14) and thus to increase fairness in the legal system. As final examples, consider that the ease or difficulty with which commentaries in evaluation forms can be given has been shown to affect final course evaluations (Fox, 2006). Moreover, it has been reported that non-native speakers appear less credible because processing their language output is less fluent (Lev-Ari & Keysar, 2010). Again, fluency research may help to understand how such biasing influences come about, and how they may be cured.

Curiously, the above examples suggest that fluency provides not veridical information but is rather a source of error. Yet, as often in psychology, the answer is not that simple. The contributors to this book will also present evidence that fluency is often a valid source of information and people seem to have learnt to draw correct inferences from fluency (Herzog & Hertwig, Ch. 12; as well as Greifeneder, Bless, & Scholl, Ch. 13). Thus, the question is not if people should use their cognitive feelings in judgments and decisions, but when they should use them and when not. Fluency may lead us astray in some contexts, but is a highly beneficial and adaptive cue in other contexts, for example, because fluency experiences provide directly accessible information about otherwise inaccessible properties of the world (see also Koriat & Levy-Sadot, 1999): When more fluently read names are judged to be famous, when companies with fluently processed abbreviations are evaluated as more successful, or when more fluently remembered instances are estimated to be more frequent, fluency influences are not undue, but they represent an adaptive and rational usage of the processing-by-product.

The above examples illustrate that research on thinking experiences has a descriptive and prescriptive side. Researchers can show that people have and use fluency experiences, resulting in fascinating and sometimes baffling effects (the descriptive part). Yet, when are people entitled to use fluency experiences? And if they are not, what are proper means to avoid undue fluency effects (the prescriptive part)? By covering both the descriptive and the prescriptive aspect of fluency research, the present book offers an innovative perspective and propels fluency research in a new direction. Without hesitation we therefore state that the "experience of thinking" is a fascinating topic, not for purely scientific reasons in an *ars gratia artis* sense, but for its ever-present justified or unjustified influences on the real world.

How to read this book?

The full scope of this book will likely become evident and the most fluent experience will emerge if one indulges in the pleasure to read the whole book from front to back, thereby benefitting from comparing different approaches in the chapters on the use and conceptualization of fluency, the cross-references between the chapters, and the agreements and disagreements between the authors. However, the book can also serve as a handbook on processing or cognitive fluency, as each chapter is self-contained. As the chapter titles and abstracts cover all important aspects, we refrain from providing a synopsis of each chapter here, but refer to the individual chapter outlines and the subject index at the end of the book. Whichever way you choose: have a pleasurable experience reading the book!

References

Alter, A. L., & Oppenheimer, D. M. (2009). Uniting the tribes of fluency to form a metacognitive nation. *Personality and Social Psychology Review, 13*, 219–235.

Clore, G. L. (1992). Cognitive phenomenology: Feelings and the construction of judgment. In L. L. Martin & A. Tesser (Eds.), *The construction of social judgments* (pp. 133–163). Hillsdale, N.J.: Erlbaum.

Dehaene, S., Changeux, J., Naccache, L., Sackur, J., & Sergent, C. (2006). Conscious, preconscious, and subliminal processing: A testable taxonomy. *Trends in Cognitive Sciences, 10*, 204–211.

Fox, C. R. (2006). The availability heuristic in the classroom: How soliciting more criticism can boost your course ratings. *Judgment and Decision Making, 1*, 86–90.

Greifeneder, R., Alt, A., Bottenberg, K., Seele, T., Zelt, S., & Wagener, D. (2010). On writing legibly: Processing fluency systematically biases evaluations of handwritten material. *Social Psychological and Personality Science, 1*, 230–237.

James, H. W. (1929). The effect of handwriting upon grading. *The English Journal, 16*, 180–185.

Kleider, H. M., & Goldinger, S. D. (2004). Illusions of face memory: Clarity breeds familiarity. *Journal of Memory and Language, 50*, 196–211.

Koriat, A. (1993). How do we know that we know? The accessibility model of the feeling of knowing. *Psychological Review, 100*, 609–639.

Koriat, A. & Levy-Sadot, R. (1999). Processes underlying metacognitive judgments: Information-based and experience-based monitoring of one's own knowledge. In S. Chaiken & Y. Trope (Eds.), *Dual-process theories in social psychology.* (pp. 483–502). New York, NY: Guilford Press.

Lev-Ari, S., & Keysar, B. (2010). Why don't we believe non-native speakers? The influence of accent on credibility. *Journal of Experimental Social Psychology, 46*, 1093–1096. doi:10.1016/j.jesp.2010.05.025

Mussweiler, T. (2003). Comparison processes in social judgment: Mechanisms and consequences. *Psychological Review, 110*, 472–489.

Nelson, T. O. (1996). Consciousness and metacognition. *American Psychologist, 51*(2), 102–116.

Parducci, A. (1968). The relativism of absolute judgments. *Scientific American, 219*, 84–89.

Schwartz, B. L. (2002). *Tip-of-the-tongue states: Phenomenology, mechanism, and lexical retrieval.* Hillsdale, NJ: Lawrence Erlbaum.

Topolinski, S., & Reber, R. (2010). Immediate truth – Temporal contiguity between a cognitive problem and its solution determines experienced veracity of the solution. *Cognition, 114*, 117–122.

Unkelbach, C. (2007). Reversing the truth effect: Learning the interpretation of processing fluency in judgments of truth. *Journal of Experimental Psychology: Learning, Memory and Cognition, 33*, 219–230.

Whittlesea, B. W. A., & Williams, L. D. (2000). The source of feelings of familiarity: The discrepancy-attribution hypothesis. *Journal of Experimental Psychology: Learning, Memory and Cognition, 26*, 547–565.

Wundt, W. (1862). *Beiträge zur Theorie der Sinneswahrnehmung.* Leipzig: C.F. Winter'sche Verlagshandlung.

Part I

Principles of fluency

2 A general model of fluency effects in judgment and decision making

Christian Unkelbach and
Rainer Greifeneder

Abstract

Processing or cognitive fluency is the experienced ease of ongoing mental processes. This experience influences a wide range of judgments and decisions. We present a general model for these fluency effects. Based on Brunswik's lens-model, we conceptualize fluency as a meta-cognitive cue. For the cue to impact judgments, we propose three process steps: people must experience fluency; the experience must be attributed to a judgment-relevant source; and it must be interpreted within the judgment context. This interpretation is either based on available theories about the experience's meaning or on the learned validity of the cue in the given context. With these steps the model explains most fluency effects and allows for new and testable predictions.

Processing fluency is the experienced ease of ongoing mental processes; when people perceive, process, store, retrieve, and generate information, they experience the ease or difficulty of these cognitive operations (cf. Chapter 1). This experience has profound influences on judgments and decisions: fluently perceived names are judged as famous; fluently read statements are evaluated as true; and fluently retrieved instances from memory are estimated to be likely and frequent. In addition, fluency is manipulated in many ways: repetition, perceptual clarity, font type, priming, rhyming, semantic coherence, and so forth (see Chapter 1 for examples, and Alter & Oppenheimer, 2009, for an overview). The scope of these manipulations and effects (which we will discuss in greater detail below and the following chapters will add some items to the list) begs three important questions: First, is fluency indeed a unitary construct, or are there different and varying explanations for what researchers call "fluency effects," depending on specific manipulations? Second, if fluency is indeed the theoretical construct that explains all these effects, how does fluency influence such a wide range of variables? And third, if fluency is indeed the explanation for these influences, why are these effects in the observed direction? Why are fluently perceived names judged as famous instead of non-famous, why are fluently read statements evaluated as true and not false, and why are fluently retrieved instances from memory estimated to be likely and frequent, and not improbable and rare?

While Chapter 1 aimed to introduce the construct and give a sense of what processing fluency is, the present chapter aims to delineate a model of fluency effects that answers these three questions and provides a general framework for fluency effects. And although this will be a "fluency" model, we believe that similar basic parameters as we discuss here apply to thinking experiences or cognitive feelings in general, including, for example, the tip-of-the-tongue phenomenon (Brown & McNeill, 1966; Schwartz, 2002), feelings of knowing (Hart, 1965; Koriat, 1993), or the "eureka" experience (Metcalfe & Wiebe, 1987; Topolinski & Reber, 2010).

Range of fluency effects

In this section, we provide a cursory overview of fluency effects. This overview serves to illustrate the phenomenon's richness and to motivate a general model, guided by the three questions outlined in the introduction.

The probably most famous example of fluency effects in judgments was provided by Tversky and Kahneman (1973). In one experiment, participants judged the frequency of English words starting with the letter "r" compared to words with "r" in the third position. Although words with "r" in the third position are factually more frequent, participants judged words starting with the letter "r" to be more frequent. Supposedly this is because words starting with "r" come to mind more fluently and are more fluently generated. While it seems almost self-evident to judge frequency by the fluency with which instances are retrieved from memory, other influences of fluency are less intuitive, and many of these influences have far-reaching consequences.

Besides this classic example how retrieval fluency influences frequency judgments (Tversky & Kahneman; 1973), the experience of fluency influences judgments and decisions regarding liking of stimuli (Reber, Winkielman, & Schwarz, 1998), familiarity of names (Whittlesea, 1993), fame (Jacoby, Kelley, Brown, & Jasechko, 1989), ability of persons (Greifeneder et al., 2010), size and duration (Reber, Zimmermann, & Wurtz, 2004), truth of statements (Hasher, Goldstein, & Toppino, 1977), perceptions of fairness (Greifeneder, Müller, Stahlberg, Kees van den Bos, & Bless, 2011), the economic value of stocks (Alter & Oppenheimer, 2006), or the gross value of companies (Hertwig, Herzog, Schooler, & Reimer, 2008).

For instance, Reber and colleagues (1998, Exp. 1) asked participants to judge the prettiness of slightly distorted pictures of neutral objects (e.g., a horse or a plane). All pictures were preceded by another picture that was only presented for 25 ms. This "prime" either was the contour outline of the following picture (i.e., a matching prime) or of another picture (i.e., a non-matching primes). As previous exposure facilitates processing (Feustel, Shiffrin, & Salasoo, 1983), participants should process the following picture more fluently when it is preceded by its contour. In line with this argument, participants judged pictures that were preceded by matching primes (and were therefore more fluently perceived) as prettier compared to those that were preceded by non-matching primes.

As a second example, consider again Tversky and Kahneman's (1973) finding that people estimate categories frequencies as being higher when instances from that frequency come easily to mind. In addition to laboratory results such as the letter frequency experiment detailed earlier (see also Greifeneder, Bless, & Scholl, this volume), Combs and Slovic (1979) provided a naturalistic example by showing that people grossly overestimated the likelihood of causes of death in relation to their availability from newspaper coverage; because these well-covered causes of death are easily and fluently available, people overestimate their frequency.

Finally, consider work by Begg, Anas, and Farinacci (1992) on the influence of fluency on judgments of truth. The authors reported that participants believed more in previously presented statements than new ones, even though participants could not remember having seen those statements before. Supposedly, this is because previous exposure renders later processing of the same stimuli more fluent, and this fluency is then used in judgments of truth.

Again, for a general model to explain these effects, it is necessary that providing contour outlines of pictures, featuring death-causes in newspapers, and encountering statements in previous sessions, influences the same psychological construct, processing fluency. We will save this question for the end, but already on a mere structural level, the common denominator of these examples is that people use the fluency of their ongoing mental processes (e.g., perceiving, retrieving) to judge an otherwise unknown or uncertain property, such as liking, frequency, or truth. This structure is at the heart of Brunswik's lens-model (1952), and we will apply this model to the question of how fluency influences judgments and decisions.

How fluency is used as information in judgment—a Brunswikian explanation

As stated, the present argument is inspired by Brunswik's (1952, 1955) lens-model, which we depict schematically in Figure 2.1 (see Karelaia & Hogarth, 2008, for an overview of lens-model applications in human judgments and decision making). For the present argument, the most important model feature is the distinction in *distal* properties of the environment and *proximal* cues to infer these properties. The lens model assumes that an organism (e.g., a human judge) uses proximal cues to infer a distal criterion that is not directly accessible (Hammond, 1955). A good illustration of these abstract concepts is intelligence; it is impossible to see, hear, feel, or assess a person's intelligence directly; it is a distal property. To judge intelligence, people must use available information, that is, proximal cues; for example, a person's performance in an intelligence test or her grades in school. None of this information perfectly predicts intelligence, but there should be some relation between school grades and intelligence, or between intelligence and school grades. Here, we assume that individuals use fluency in a similar way as a proximal cue to form judgments about distal criteria – such as liking, frequency, or truth.

The extent to which cues correlate with criteria (e.g., grades with intelligence) is referred to as "ecological correlations;" the weight assigned to a specific cue when forming a judgment is referred to as "cue utilization" (cf. Figure 2.1). These termini are best illustrated by the example of depth perception. Although humans readily experience a visual sense of depth, human eyes are actually not equipped to convey visual depth directly. Rather, depth is a distal criterion that people infer from proximal visual cues to create three-dimensional representations from the two-dimensional pictures on the retinas. Prominent cues in vision to infer depth are overlap (objects that hide other objects are closer to the perceiver), motion parallax (when perceivers move, objects that are closer seem to move faster than far away objects), and texture gradients (distant objects have denser textures than close objects). By using these cues and by combining them in a linear weighted fashion, people are able to infer depth from strictly two-dimensional sensory input.

The principle of "ecological correlations" suggests that cues vary in the extent to which they correlate with the criterion. For example, overlap is perfectly correlated with the distance of the perceiver to objects: An object overlapping another object will always be closer to the perceiver. In contrast, texture gradients are influenced by factors other than distance, and thus, the cue's relation to the criterion is proba- bilistic. And this probabilistic relation is certainly true for school grades and intel- ligence. Applying this reasoning to fluency, the ecological correlation is the fluency cue's validity with respect to the judgmental criterion (e.g., truth or frequency).

The principle of "cue utilization" suggests that people place differential weight on specific cues when forming judgments. For example, in a moving train, people usually weight motion parallax more strongly than texture gradients to judge visual depth. Similarly, some people and institutions use test scores as the sole

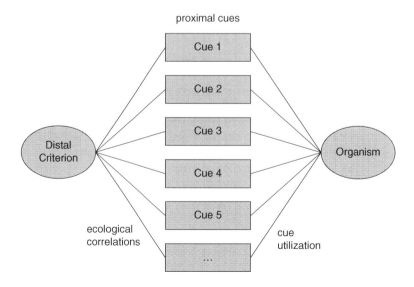

Figure 2.1 A "lens-model", illustrating how organism judge distal criteria by proximal cues.

cue for intelligence, while others scorn them completely. Applying this reasoning to fluency, cue utilization is the weight judge places on given cues when forming judgments in a specific situation. This also implies that judges use other available information as well (e.g., factual knowledge about truth), and the judgment output is a weighted function of the available cues.

Ideally, a cue's ecological correlation (i.e., its validity) determines the cue's utilization (i.e., its weight in a judgment). However, in many cases, ecological correlation and cue utilization do not match (Karelaia & Hogarth, 2008); for the fluency case, these are the instances when the influence of fluency is rightfully termed a bias or an unwanted influence; for example, when statements are believed because one has heard them before (e.g., Begg, Anas, & Farinacci, 1992), or when stocks are rated higher because their names are easy to pronounce (Alter & Oppenheimer, 2006).

Again, most, if not all, judgments that are influenced by fluency refer to distal properties of the environment, such as liking, fame, truth, ability, justice, or economic value. And people have no directly available informative about these properties—in contrast, for example, to the criterion "temperature," for which people have directly available sensory input. Distal properties defy almost by definition exact quantifications; so people *must* infer them from proximal cues. We believe that is very helpful to conceptualize fluency as such a proximal cue when modeling the influence of fluency on judgments. We suggests that this proximal cue (a) is readily and easily available from ongoing mental processes (see Greifeneder, Bless, & Scholl, this volume) and (b) is not a perfect cue but in a probabilistic relation with ecological criteria, just as texture gradients are not perfect cues for depth perception and school grades are not perfect cues for intelligence. In the following model, we will implement the suggested notion of fluency as a proximal cue in a comprehensive model with three distinct steps: experiencing, attributing, and interpreting fluency.

A process model

In the introductory passage, we have sketched that fluency may influence a multitude of very different judgments. This is precisely because fluency is a probabilistic cue that people use to judge otherwise inaccessible distal criteria. The Brunswikian lens-model presents a formal theoretical framework for this influence. In the following, we discuss the necessary process steps for this influence. People must have a feeling of fluency or ease (i.e., experiencing fluency), they must identify the proper cause for the feeling (i.e., attributing fluency), and they must infer what the feeling means in the given context (i.e., interpreting fluency). These steps are illustrated in Figure 2.2 and we will explain them in what follows.

Experiencing fluency

We start by postulating that people experience the working of ongoing mental processes, and that this working is reflected in feelings of fluency. Although people have little conscious access to what our mind really does (or does not) when performing mental operations such as accessing memory (Nisbett & Wilson, 1977), people experience the ease or difficulty of these operations. A parallel process is the experience of hunger when blood glucose level is low; albeit the level itself is not directly accessible (and hunger may stem from other sources as well), the experience itself is readily available. Similarly, feelings of fluency grant a window to otherwise inaccessible processes (Koriat & Levy-Sadot, 1999).

Two interesting questions directly ensue from this postulate: First, how do mental processes translate into perceptions of fluency? One possible answer is that all cognitive processing is continuously monitored, and that the output of this monitoring is fluency (Whittlesea & Leboe, 2000; see also Whittlesea & Price, 2001; Whittlesea, 2002). Koriat and colleagues (Koriat, 1993; Koriat & Goldsmith, 1996) have used the term "parasitic" to describe the effect that cognitive processes cause subjective experiences as by-products. Although describing feelings of fluency as parasitic might carry some negative connotations, it captures nicely the fact that the feeling emerges without need for attention or resources. The continuous monitoring function seems more problematic in that respect, but the analogy of cognitive with biological functions helps to illustrate the idea. The human body's biological systems monitor dozens of homeostatic variables such as body temperature, hormone concentrations, heart beat frequency, or again, blood glucose levels. These monitoring functions also work without attention and awareness. It is not too far-fetched to assume a similar monitoring function for cognitive functions.[1]

The second question pertains to *when* fluency is experienced and influences judgments and decisions? This question has been thoroughly investigated and we believe there is a clear answer: People experience fluency when there are processing differences compared to what is expected or compared to what has appeared

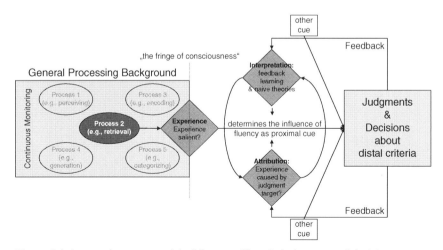

Figure 2.2 A general process model of fluency effects in judgments and decisions.

previously (Whittlesea & Williams, 1998; Hansen & Wänke, 2008; Hansen & Wänke, this volume). Deviation detection in monitoring is a well-established principle: for example, in a series of numbers, the deviating letter will stand out and vice versa (e.g., 2-6-7-K-8 vs. K-L-T-4-W). Similarly, unfamiliar names will stand out in a series of familiar names and vice versa (e.g., Bach, Beethoven, Weisdorf, Mozart vs. Weisdorf, Miller, Beethoven, Brown); or, as Whittlesea and Williams (1998) have argued, people will not detect how fluently they can process the faces of their family members during breakfast, but they will immediately detect the stranger at their table. Likewise, people will detect the deviating fluently processed face of a friend in a crowd of strangers.

In biological monitoring processes, people will for example notice when they are hungry and they will notice when they have eaten too much. Yet, most of the time the stomach does not provide a noticeable experience, although monitoring is going on continuously; it is when there are deviations from the norm that an experience becomes salient and is noticed. We have incorporated this principle in Figure 2.2, left side. For reasons of illustration, we assume that there are currently five cognitive processes going on (e.g., perceiving one stimulus, categorizing another stimulus, etc.). Of those five, only Process 2 deviates strongly enough from the processing background to be perceived or experienced. For example, when the retrieval of a certain memory is particularly easy, this retrieval process is noticed. This perceptual process takes place on the "fringe of consciousness" (Reber, Wurtz & Zimmermann, 2004).

It is important that the deviation does not have to between multiple ongoing processes, but can also result from expectancies, baselines, or prior experiences. Otherwise the model would not predict fluency effects when there is no variation in a given situation—for example, when people are asked to estimate the frequency of words having the letter "r" at the third place. Nevertheless, our model posits that for the underestimation effect reported by Tversky and Kahneman (1973), the retrieval should be difficult to some baseline (e.g., how easy/difficult is it in general to recall words from memory), to what is expected (e.g., are people being told that this is an easy or difficult task), or to comparable other processes (e.g., how easy/difficult is it to recall words from memory *starting* with the letter "r").

An experimental test that the impact of fluency depends on processing differences was provided by Dechêne, Stahl, Hansen, and Wänke (2009). In a first experiment, they presented participants with new and repeated statements, thereby manipulating how fluently participants could read these statements. Participants' task was to judge the truth of these statements. As discussed, the standard result is that people rate the truth of repeated statements higher compared to new statements (Hasher, Goldstein, & Toppino, 1977; Reber & Schwarz, 1999). To show the importance of processing differences, participants either judged mixed lists containing old and new statements (thereby creating fluency differences in statement processing), or lists of only new/only old statements (thereby eliminating fluency differences in processing). The higher rated truth for old statements only appeared when the lists were mixed, that is, when there were notable differences in experienced fluency across the presented statements. In a second experiment, the authors showed the same pattern for the greater liking of repeated stimuli. When participants judged how much they liked Kanji characters, they only preferred old stimuli when old and new Kanjis were mixed in a list. When participants judged old and new Kanji separately, no fluency effect on liking emerged.

Hence, the answer to the question *when* people actually experience fluency (or disfluency) seems indeed to be: The fluency of mental operation is experienced when the associated experience of fluency deviates markedly (a) from a baseline, (b) from what is expected in a given context, or (c) from comparable other processes.

A supplementary possibility is that fluency influences judgments when attention is drawn to the experience, for example, when people are asked how they feel about something. Just as people can tell that their stomach is full or empty when asked for it, they probably can assess whether cognitive processes are going fluently or disfluently, even when there is no immediate variation. However, in most cases, as the experiments by Dechêne and colleagues (2009) show, the experience should have no detectable impact on judgments when fluency experiences does not vary, for example, between to-be-judged objects. In other words, although family members at the breakfast table should be perceived more fluently than a crowd of strangers, judgments about family or strangers should not vary within the respective groups (Whittlesea & Williams, 1998).

Attributing fluency

The second step is that people need to draw an association between a particular fluency experience and a given stimulus for fluency to be informative about this stimulus. Let us illustrate this again with Tversky and Kahneman's problem of word frequency estimation: To judge words with the letter "r" at the third position as less frequent, people need to draw an association between the experienced disfluency and the mental process of retrieving the words—and not, for instance, an association between disfluency and background noise or splitting headaches. If fluency is attributed to the mental process of memory retrieval, it is informative about the word retrieval task. If fluency is attributed to background noises or headaches, fluency is not perceived as being caused by the task, and hence, the experience is uninformative about the task.

We assume that the attribution of feelings and experiences to possible causes are determined by salience—a salient cause stands out in some way. In Gestalt-Psychology terms, a cause is salient when it stands out as a figure stands out against the background. As this figure-ground principle also applies to the deviation idea we have introduced as one of the pre-conditions to experience fluency, it follows that attribution processes will result in the possibly correct ascription of fluency to the relevant mental process. From this, it seems likely that fluency is attributed to the correct cause in most situations (see Greifeneder, Bless, & Scholl, this volume).

However, there are classic demonstrations that fluency is not used in judgments and decision when another source is identified for the fluency experience. Probably the most direct test of this notion was provided by Schwarz and colleagues (1991; but see also the overview by Wänke, this volume). In one of their experiments (Experiment 3), people retrieved from memory six or 12 instances of either assertive or unassertive behaviors. The idea was that it is easy to retrieve six but difficult to retrieve 12 instances. Based on the fluency of this retrieval process, people should infer that there are few (difficult retrieval) or many (easy retrieval) instances of these behaviors and judge their own assertiveness accordingly. However, when participants were told that the ease/fluency experiences were caused by music in the background, the effects on judgments vanished (for a review, see Greifeneder, Bless, & Pham, 2011).

Interpreting fluency

When people experience fluency, and the experience is attributed to the ongoing mental process, the important last step is to identify the meaning of the experience. This last step explains why fluency is able to influence judgments of liking, frequency, truth, and many other domains. The word frequency estimation task again illustrates this point. If retrieving words having "r" as third letter is difficult and people attribute this difficulty correctly to the retrieval process, why does it follow that these words are rare (in comparison to words starting with "r")? Another interpretation could be that a person's verbal ability is low. Similarly, if people experience that they can read a name fluently, and they attribute fluency to reading the name, there are several interpretations of the experience. It could be that it is a famous name, a frequent name, a recently encountered name, and so forth.

How the experience is interpreted is central for the influence on judgments. In one experiment relevant for this point, Oppenheimer (2004) asked people to judge the frequency of surnames. Usually, one would expect that people judge more fluently processed names as more frequent—however, when the names were fluent because they belonged to famous persons (such as Nixon, Bush, or Lennon), participants did not use fluency to form frequency judgments. Rather, they even judged these famous names as less frequent compared to non-famous names. Thus, people interpreted fluency as fame, and not as frequency, and accordingly, fluency was discounted as a cue for frequency.

Similarly, if people experience memory retrieval as fluent, fluent retrieval can inform many judgments: Maybe the memory was significant, or it was particularly happy, or particularly painful. The interpretation of the experience determines the influence on subsequent judgments.

Direct evidence of interpretation was provided by Mandler, Nakamura, and Van Zandt (1987). In their experiment, people had to judge two grey-colored geometric shapes. One of the two shapes had been presented previously while the other was a new shape. Some participants were asked which of the two shapes they liked better. For these participants, a standard fluency effect emerged: participants preferred, on average, previously presented shapes over new shapes.

A second group of participants was asked which of the shapes were brighter (or, in another condition, darker). Interestingly, these participants also chose the old and hence fluently processed shapes to be lighter (or darker). This pattern of results suggests that the same cue—fluency—may be interpreted very differently (here, as indicating liking, brightness, or darkness).

The question is then, how do people know the meaning of fluency? One direct answer is that people use fluency in accordance with the task context—if they are asked "how frequent?", "how famous?", or "how true?", more fluently processed names are rated as more frequent, people as more famous, or statements as more true, compared to less fluently processed statements. This is equivalent to stating that people notice a difference (e.g., one name is read more fluently than the other) and translate this difference on the available judgment dimension. However, this answer is unsatisfactory, because it does not explain the direction of the effect. In other words, why do people judge the fluently processed name as more frequent, more famous, and more true, and not *less* frequent, *less* famous, or *less* true?

There are two ways to solve this important problem. The first is that people *learn* via feedback the interpretation of fluency in a given context (cf. Figure 2.2). This explanation is directly derived from the Brunswikian framework. People learn the validity of a cue by feedback from the environment. If a jury member believes a testimony that is easily processed, and she gets later feedback that the witness was indeed truthful (e.g., due to other evidence), she may learn that fluency is a cue to truth. While this explanation assumes a very basic, perception-like process, there is a second possibility (also depicted in Figure 2.2), involving higher cognitive processes, namely that people have naïve theories about the meaning of fluency. This explanation applies to the discussed results by Oppenheimer (2004). If people *know* that fame leads to fluent processing, they will not interpret fluency as frequency for famous names. Let us discuss the evidence for these two explanations.

Feedback learning

Again, this explanation follows directly from the Brunswikian framework. The analogy is apparent by using the perception example: Why do people use overlap in perception to judge distance? First, because haptic feedback from reaching out to objects shows a perfect correlation between distance to objects and their overlap—the object hiding the other object is closer. Second, because overlap correlates with other cues that indicate distance, that is, motion parallax, pattern density, and so forth. We assume that the same feedback-learning and inter-cue correlations allow people to use fluency in judgments: People have *learned* that categories from which instances are easily retrieved have indeed more members, and statements that are easily processed have a higher probability to be factually true. This assumption of learned ecological validity also explains why the same experience can have such differential influences. The fluency influence depends on the ecology in which a judgment is made; in experimental tasks, the ecology is often provided by the questions researchers are asking. And the influence should always be in the direction that people have learned from their experiences. Figure 2.2 includes this aspect in the feedback loop from judgments and decisions.

Direct evidence for the importance of feedback learning stems from experiments by Unkelbach (2006, 2007). In one experiment (Unkelbach, 2006, Exp. 1), participants indicated in a test phase whether they had seen a name before in a presentation phase. Processing fluency was manipulated by color contrast: low contrast names were difficult to read and high contrast names were easy to read. Importantly, before this test phase, there was a learning phase that conveyed correlations between fluency and recognition. Previously presented names were either shown in high contrast (i.e., a positive correlation between fluency and previous occurrence) or in low contrast (i.e., a negative correlation between fluency and previous occurrence). Participants made old-new judgments for each name and received feedback about the correctness of their judgment. In other words, some participants learned by feedback that fluent processing indicated that a name was new and for others fluent processing indicated that a name was false. In the test phase, the names' contrast and old-new status were not correlated. Nevertheless, given that people had received feedback that fluent processing indicated that a name was new, they judged the high contrast names as new. When they had received feedback that fluent processing indicated that a name was old, they showed the standard pattern and judged the high contrast names old.

The same pattern occurred for truth judgments (Unkelbach, 2007, Exp. 2). People learned that high fluency (due to color contrast) correlates with statements' falseness, and accordingly, judged in a test phase easy-to-read statements as false. For both these experiments, the clear critique is that there is no evidence that processing fluency was actually involved. People could simply have learned color contrast as a direct cue to judge the old/new status of a name or the truth of a statement. This point was addressed in another experiment (Unkelbach, 2007, Exp. 3; see also Unkelbach, 2006, Exp. 2). Participants initially saw statements in a presentation phase. Then, in a learning phase, they judged the truth of statements that varied in color contrast and accordingly, in processing fluency. As before, there were two conditions: Either high or low fluency correlated with truth and participants received feedback for their judgments. In the test phase, all statements were presented in black on white background, but half the statements were old and half were new (and this old/new status was orthogonal to factual truth). Thus, the statements did not vary in processing fluency due to color contrast, but varied in fluency due to prior exposure. When high contrast correlated with truth in the training phase, they showed the standard pattern and judged old statements as "true" with greater probability. However, when low contrast correlated with truth in the training phase, they showed the reversed pattern and judged new statements as "true" with greater probability (and old statements as "false"; see Olds & Westerman, 2012, for a replication).

These data provide good evidence that the interpretation of processing fluency changes depending on the learning history in a given context. In most cases, fluently processed statements are indeed true, simply because the factors influencing fluency also correlate with factual truth (for a complete discussion, see Reber & Unkelbach, 2010); for example, when people hear a statement from different sources, it is processed more fluently and the probability that it is true increases. Similarly, when a statement is consistent with known facts, it is also processed more fluently and also more likely true. And the same holds for other judgments—but the interpretation is not fixed and the meaning of the experience does not come out of the blue. In this explanation, it is the adaptive usage of a cue that has been learned via feedback to judge otherwise inaccessible distal criteria.

Naïve theories

An alternative reason why people use fluency the way they do are naïve theories about the meaning of the experience (Schwarz, 2004). Evidence for this theoretical position stems from experiments that show differential fluency effects on judgments when participants are informed about the meaning of fluency in this context. For example, Winkielman and Schwarz (2001) had participants retrieve four or 12 instances from their childhood. Participants should experience the former retrieval process as easy and the latter as difficult. Importantly, instructions provided participants with an interpretation of this experience: Half were told that happy memories fade quickly from memory (making them difficult to retrieve) and half were told that unhappy memories fade quickly. Then, participants judged the pleasantness of their childhood. In line with the idea of naïve theories, participants who were told that happy memories fade quickly and could retrieve memories easily (four instances) and judged their childhood not as happy as participants for whom retrieval was difficult (12 instances). However, the reverse pattern occurred when participants were told that sad memories fade quickly.

Briñol, Petty, and Tormala (2006; see also Briñol, Tormala, & Petty, this volume) reported similar effects on attitude judgments when participants were given theories that retrieval fluency is good or bad, that is, standard effects when fluency had positive implications and reverse effects when fluency had negative implications.

Disentangling naïve theories and feedback learning

These experiments illustrate the importance of naïve theories or lay beliefs for fluency influences on judgments. The important difference to the Brunswikian learning account is that providing naïve theories does not change the experience *per se*. People still experience easiness or fluency, but they use this experience differently depending on the provided information. Put differently, with the provision of naïve theories, the effect is located in the output stage; in contrast, the learning account assumes that the experience takes on a different meaning in a given context. The experience immediately means something different. Let us illustrate this with an example: Imagine you are reading your first crime mystery and all clues so far point to suspect X as the culprit. The provided information gives you the distinct feeling that X is guilty. However, you are also *told* that crime novel authors never give away solutions so easily—rather, they use obvious "red herrings" to lure you away from the factual and hopefully surprising solution. Thus, in the context of the crime novel, when you are asked if you believe whether X is guilty, you can judge that X is not guilty, *because* you have the clear feeling that X is guilty, which makes the person a red herring (and thus, not guilty). Yet, if you have read many crime novels and you have learned from experience that the obvious solution is never true (and the murderer is never the gardener), your feeling will directly tell you that X is not guilty. The effect is not located at the output stage of the judgment but rather on the experience stage. Thus, naïve theories conceptualize the fluency experience as input to a metacognitive judgment, while learning approaches conceptualize the fluency experience as a perception-like cue in judgments.

On an operational level, the two explanations are also easy to distinguish: Naïve theories are communicated in a top-down fashion; for example, participants are given *a priori* explanations about the meaning of their experiences. Accordingly, participants should be able to verbalize the theory. Contrary, for learning approaches, the meaning of the fluency experience is communicated in a bottom-up fashion, for example, by providing feedback about decisions. Participants are not necessarily able to verbalize what they have learned. Further on an operational level, for naïve theories, judgments are mostly done on the summary of the experiences (e.g., after participants retrieve four instances from their childhood). For learned interpretations, the judgments are made immediately, for example, when perceiving a stimulus or reading a statement (Reber et al., 1998; Unkelbach, 2006).

Yet, the explanations of naïve theories and learning are not in competition, they rather complement each other. This is the reason why Figure 2.2 features only one process—interpretation—that can be informed either by naïve theories or feedback learning. One can construe naïve theories as consciously available rules about correlations between fluency and a criterion. In our crime novels example, the experienced reader does not only have the feeling that X is not guilty, but also the available theory that authors use red herrings. Conversely, one can see theories and beliefs about a correlation as the enabling conditions for successfully learning of given fluency correlations. As recent research on learning and conditioning shows, successful learning depends not only on the environments' stimulus-relations, but also on attention, awareness, and goals on the learner's side (e.g., Mitchell, De Houwer, & Lovibond, 2009; Shanks, 2010). By acknowledging both the bottom-up component (i.e., learning) as well as the top-down component (i.e., theories and beliefs), we have a complete picture how people interpret fluency experiences.

Disentangling attribution and interpretation

Often, what we refer to as interpretation is referred to as one "attribution" step. We suggest that attribution and interpretation processes are separate rather than amalgamated within one process step. When amalgamated, the term attribution is used in a distal or ultimate sense, such as in "Fluency is attributed to the fame of a person/the truth of a statement/the falseness of the statement…". In this case, fluency is not attributed to a specific mental process (e.g., perceiving a stimulus), but directly to a distal criterion that *causes* fluency, in the best sense of attribution as perceiving causes. That is, it is not the stimulus that is said to cause the experience, but the underlying property of the stimulus (e.g., frequency, truth, or fame). If attribution is understood in this ultimate way, it encompasses the interpretation step. This appears tempting from many experimental setups that mix attribution and interpretation, especially when the task settings presuppose attribution and interpretation ("Please indicate the word frequency" vs. "Please indicate your verbal ability"). While attributions of the experience place constraints on the kind of fluency interpretations that are possible, we firmly believe it to be preferable to discern (a) attribution of perceived fluency to a cause, and (b) interpretation of fluency with respect to a criterion.

The conceptual need to keep these processes separated is shown when attributed fluency is interpreted very differently. Specifically, although the fluency source was clear in the experiments illustrating interpretation reviewed above (Unkelbach, 2006; Winkielman & Schwarz, 2001), participants used this fluency differentially—something that is difficult to explain with a pure attribution processes.

Word frequency estimation again illustrates this point; let us assume that people retrieve words starting with "r" easily. In a single-step frame, when attribution and interpretation are amalgamated, the ultimate cause for this fluent retrieval could be, for example, the absolute frequency of words starting with "r" in the English language (a distal criterion). In this case, fluency can only be used to judge this distal criterion, because the attribution to the criterion constrains the interpretation.

In contrast, in a two-step frame, people first attribute fluency to the process of retrieving words starting with "r", a very specific mental process. Only in a second step would individuals interpret retrieval fluency as indicative of word frequency. The same fluency experience could also be used to form many other judgments, including having a high verbal ability that facilitates word retrieval, or having recently read a list with "r" words. As the example illustrates, the attribution of fluency to a mental process in a two-step process does not (or at least less) constrain possible interpretations. Note that, compared to the one-step account which amalgamates attribution and interpretation, the present two-step account is much more in line with the empirical evidence on the many possible interpretations of one fluency experience discussed above.

Model summary and open questions

We have discussed three steps of perceiving, attributing, and interpreting fluency experiences, and provided a conceptual background (i.e., Brunswik's lens-model) for how fluency, as well as cognitive feelings and experiences in general, influence judgments and decisions. Figure 2.2 presents a summary of these steps: First, some deviation or difference in processing is necessary to experience a cognitive feeling (here, a deviation from the general processing background). Second, the model assumes a unitary experience and the multitude of fluency effects comes about by the interpretation of that experience, or, in Brunswikian terms, by the ecological validity of the fluency cue. This validity is conveyed by feedback from the actual judgments and decisions and the intercorrelation of the fluency cue with other available cues; or, people have naïve theories about the meaning of the experience. Third, attribution and interpretation determine reciprocally the impact of experienced fluency on subsequent judgments and decisions. While attributions constrain the interpretations that are allowed, interpretations also feed back into the attribution process by making possible causes salient. Finally, consequences from the judgments feed back into the ecologically validity of the cue. If interpretations of fluency lead constantly to wrong decisions, this interpretation must change or people should not use the cue anymore. Based on this summary, we now turn to what we believe to be intriguing open questions worth of future research.

Automaticity of the process?

A topic that is not featured in Figure 2.2 is the consciousness or automaticity issue. While the distinction of automatic and controlled, implicit and explicit, or conscious and unconscious processes has a long tradition in psychology (e.g., Chaiken & Trope, 1999), we avoided this point deliberately for the present discussion as it carries two problems: At present, there is no good criterion for defining consciousness in fluency research that can be tested experimentally. This lack of a criterion is pointedly apparent when fluency is localized at the "fringe of consciousness" (James, 1890; Reber, Wurtz, & Zimmermann, 2004), which we have incorporated as the threshold at which fluency experiences are perceived. Without such a criterion and resulting theoretical implications, it is not useful to discuss whether the postulated processes are controlled or automatic, conscious or unconscious. Second, we believe that processes can move along the scale from unconscious to conscious. Attribution processes can be highly controlled, deliberate, and conscious—especially when the source of a strong experience is not clear. However, attribution can also be automatic and follow a default (Weiner, 1991). Similarly, people can interpret their experiences controlled and with effort. Imagine you are wearing prism glasses that distort your vision—in the beginning, you must correct for the distortion with great effort, but after a relative short time period, you adapt to the distortion and the correction becomes effortless and automatic (see Redding, Rossetti, & Wallace, 2005, for an overview). Given these two problems, we believe it is not meaningful to incorporate assumptions about automaticity or consciousness into a fluency model.

Positivity of the experience?

Another feature not included is the positivity of the experience. Many authors assume and present strong evidence that fluency feels good (Garcia-Marques and colleagues, this volume; Winkielman & Cacioppo, 2001; see Reber, Schwarz, & Winkielman, 2004, for a review), or leads to positive affect (Topolinski & Strack, 2009).

And across many judgments tasks, it seems that fluency influences are biased toward the positive: statements are judged to be true, faces to be familiar, and people to be famous. The reverse is not often observed, and if so, under very specific circumstances; for example, when people are told that everything they heard before is false (Unkelbach & Stahl, 2009, Exp. 2). However, whether the experience is inherently positive or neutral to begin with is of no consequence for the present model, as we have stressed the interpretation of the experience as one of the critical variables for fluency effects. The model is about the meaning of the cue; whether this cue is generally positive or negative poses to begin with is largely inconsequential. On the contrary, if the fluency experience is inherently positive, then it allows for new and testable hypotheses within this model; for instance, it should be easier to learn that fluency correlates with positive distal variables than with negative distal variables. Interestingly, this is exactly what Mandler and colleagues (1987) found in the experiment described previously: while fluency led participants to judge geometric shapes as preferable, brighter, and darker, the fluency manipulation failed to influence judgments of disliking.

Another theoretical possibility is the path chosen by Weiner (1991) for his attribution theory of emotions. Supposedly, there is a very basic emotional positive-negative dimension that is not subject to other cognitive processes. For any other emotion, though, attribution processes play a role. The same could be true for fluency experiences, namely, that they can be used directly in judgments as a positive evaluation, but for more complex tasks, the steps depicted in our model are necessary. However, at present, there is no data on such a theoretical conceptualization.

Another intriguing possibility is given by the overall faster processing of positive information (Unkelbach et al., 2008), suggesting a reverse pathway from positivity to more fluent processing. Thus, people might also learn that fluency is highly correlated with positivity, leading to the observed positivity-fluency effects. However, similar to the argument above, there is no data yet available to support this conception of a reversed fluency-positivity pathway.

Fluency sources

We have stressed cognitive processes such as categorization, retrieval, or generation, as sources for fluency experiences; however, as the overview by Alter and Oppenheimer (2009) shows, there are many ways to create and manipulate fluency (for example, fluency resulting from motor movements, see Topolinski, this volume). Such multiple sources of fluency are compatible with our model, as long as the fluency experience feeds into the judgmental process. Whether we can summarize all these experiences and manipulations under the fluency label or more general, under the label of cognitive feelings, is a question we will discuss below.

Fluency and thinking styles

Another interesting aspect of the fluency experience is omitted in Figure 2: fluency also changes thinking styles (Oppenheimer, 2008). For example, Alter, Oppenheimer, Epley, and Eyre (2007) found that participants who experienced tasks as difficult switched from intuitive to more analytic thinking styles. The idea that fluency also influences thinking styles, for example, analytic vs. intuitive reasoning, adds another layer to research on fluency effects. At present, the interaction of such thinking styles with the present cue framework are not fully clear, and thus, we have omitted this interesting aspect from the model. We refer the interested reader to the chapters by Alter and Oppenheimer, as well as by Garcia-Marques and colleagues in this volume.

Theoretical restrictions

The way we present the model, it seems to account for most, if not all, fluency effects on judgments and decisions. However, this poses a problem for the logic of science (Popper, 1959), because it might be impossible to falsify the model. A model that allows for everything has no scientific value for experimental psychology and applied issues. We believe this is not the case and we want to present the model's theoretical restrictions for fluency effects that are testable in experiments. First, the model clearly implies that there is only one attribution and interpretation of the experience. These two process steps explain the experience. Thus, it should not be possible that an easily-read statement is judged to be true and to be liked more. Fluency influences judgments of remembrance ("old/new"), liking ("good/bad"), or truth ("true/false"); but once such judgments are made, fluency should not influence judgments about other distal variables.

Second, feedback should change the interpretation and this change should be specific to one context. People should be able to re-learn the usage of the cue (as shown in Unkelbach, 2006, 2007). And *if* people learn that fluency indicates, for example, a statement's falseness, they should not generalize this to judgments of fame, that is, that fluently processed names are non-famous.

Third, if other cues correlate negatively with the experience (e.g., when a known-to-be-unreliable witness gives a vivid and coherent testimony), the ecological validity or the cue weight determines the influence on the judgment/decision. Such a situation is often used to illustrate dual-process models of decision-making, but in the present framework, there is no need for such a duality. Imagine you have to choose between two cars; a friend tells you that car A is better, but you have a positive feeling about car B (e.g., the driving feels fluent). Whether you choose A or B depends heavily on the cues' validities—if your friend is a reliable expert for cars, you will follow her advice. Yet, if you have learned that following your feelings leads usually to good outcomes, you likely discard her opinion. These kinds of cue competitions are currently investigated in our research group and clearly illustrate that our proposed model is falsifiable.

A unitary construct?

We have saved one important point up to the end: It is the question if all the different manipulations used to cause fluency, including repetition, color contrast, priming, logical consistency, and so forth really result in one unitary experience. The alternative hypothesis is that fluency is not a unitary construct at all, but that there are multiple distinct experiences that have an inherent meaning which influences judgments the same way affective feelings influence judgments (e.g., Schwarz & Clore, 1983). If a stimulus makes you happy, it is a good stimulus and if it makes you sad, it is a bad stimulus—the meaning is inherent in the feeling and does not need further interpretation to influence judgments. If cognitive feelings are similar to emotional feelings, their meaning is distinct—it might be the set-up of all the experiments that leads to the illusion of one unitary experience. For example, Reisenzein (2000) discusses "surprise" as such a cognitive feeling that has a distinct meaning. So can we build our research on a unitary construct?

Aware of this question, Alter and Oppenheimer (2009) made a case for a unitary construct in an overview of methods to manipulate fluency. The central premise was that: "…the degree to which diverse instantiations of fluency converge to produce consistent outcomes […] implies that they share a common mechanism" (p. 227). However, this notion implies that if manipulation X leads to outcome Z, and manipulation Y also leads to outcome Z, X and Y must be the same. Logically, this inference is not valid and the evidence, albeit highly suggestive, remained inconclusive.

However, there is experimental evidence that people have the same experience from different fluency manipulations, and it is based on the idea of changing the interpretation of the experience. Remember that our model forbids generalizations of newly learned interpretations across different contexts (that is, from fluency implying falseness to fluency implying non-fame). Another generalization, however, must be possible: If people learn that fluency implies statement falseness, and fluency is a unitary construct, this must hold true independent from the specific statement fluency manipulation. For the learning account, we already discussed the data by Unkelbach (2007, Exp. 3), when participants learned that fluency indicates falseness. During learning, fluency varied due to color contrast. At test, fluency varied due to repetition. Nevertheless, the learning effect occurred although different fluency manipulations were used. This result is most likely when both manipulations influence the same experience, that is, the theoretical construct of fluency.

A similar effect was shown by Unkelbach and Stahl (2009; Exp. 2; see also, Unkelbach, Bayer, Alves, Koch, & Stahl, 2011) using naïve theories. They first showed that people process a set of factually true statements more fluently than factually false statements. Then participants saw true and false statements in a presentation phase. After some delay, participants saw true and false statements; half of those were old and half were new. Importantly, instructions informed participants that *all* statements from the presentation phase were false. Using this information, participants judged the old and easy-to-process statements as false, but also the new, factually true and easy-to-process statements. In other words, they applied the naïve theory about the meaning of fluency due to prior exposure ("all false") to fluency due to factual truth; again, this is only likely when repetition and truth result in the same fluency experience.

These experimental data are best explained by assuming that fluency is a unitary construct. Accordingly, a general model of fluency effects is a helpful requisite to understand the full scope of fluency effects.

Conclusion

We have presented a general model of fluency effects in judgments and decisions, based on the lens-model by Brunswik (1955, 1957). This model conceptualizes fluency as an experience resulting from ongoing cognitive processes (perception, retrieval, generation, etc.), and the experience is used as a cue in judgments and decisions. This conceptualization shows that we conceive fluency both as a metacognitive experience (Koriat, 2008) and the influence on judgments and decisions as a perception-like process (Whittlesea, 1993). The important steps in this model are experiencing fluency (i.e., when processes stand out as figures before a ground), attributing fluency (i.e., when mental process are salient and applicable causes of the experience), and interpreting fluency (i.e., when the process is given meaning by the context, learning history, or naïve theories and lay beliefs).

This model answers the three questions posed in the beginning that arise from standard fluency research: First, fluency is a unitary construct, thereby justifying a general model. Second, the processes of experiencing and attributing fluency allow one unitary construct to influence diverse judgments and decisions. And third, the process of interpretation determines the direction of observed fluency effects. By answering these questions, the model presents a comprehensive account of fluency effects so far; it organizes the available research in one coherent framework and clarifies assumptions and pre-conditions. Most importantly, it allows for new and interesting hypothesis (cue competition, salience manipulations, feedback learning), that will lead into further insight how the experience of thinking guides people's judgments and decisions.

Note

1 In addition to purely cognitive experiences of fluency, embodied sources of fluency have come into focus within the last years. Topolinski (this volume) provides an overview of this particular fluency source.

References

Alter, A. L., & Oppenheimer, D. M. (2006). Predicting short-term stock fluctuations using processing fluency. *Proceedings of the National Academy of Sciences, USA, 103*, 9369–9372.

—— (2009). Uniting the tribes of fluency to form a metacognitive nation. *Personality and Social Psychology Review, 13*, 219–235.

Alter, A. L., Oppenheimer, D. M., Epley, N., & Eyre, R. N. (2007). Overcoming intuition: Metacognitive difficulty activates analytic reasoning. *Journal of Experimental Psychology: General, 136*, 569–576.

Begg, I. M., Anas, A., & Farinacci, S. (1992). Dissociation of processes in belief: Source recollection, statement familiarity, and the illusion of truth. *Journal of Experimental Psychology: General, 121*, 446–458.

Briñol, P., Petty, R. E., & Tormala, Z. L. (2006). The Malleable Meaning of Subjective Ease. *Psychological Science, 17*, 200–206.

Brown, R., & McNeill, D. (1966). The "tip of the tongue" phenomenon. *Journal of Verbal Learning Behavior*, *5*, 325–337.

Brunswik, E. (1952). *The conceptual framework of psychology.* Chicago: University of Chicago Press.

—— (1955). Representative design and probabilistic theory in a functional psychology. *Psychological Review*, *62*, 193–217.

—— (1957). Scope and aspects of the cognitive problem. In H. Gruber, K. R. Hammond, & R. Jessor (Eds.), *Contemporary approaches to cognition* (pp. 5–31). Cambridge: Harvard University Press.

Chaiken, S., & Trope, Y. (Eds.), (1999). *Dual-process theories in social psychology.* New York: Guilford Press.

Combs, B., & Slovic, P. (1979). Newspaper coverage of causes of death. *Public Opinion Quarterly*, *56*, 837–843.

Dechêne, A., Stahl, C., Hansen, J., & Wänke, M. (2009). Mix me a list: Context moderates the truth effect and the mere-exposure effect. *Journal of Experimental Social Psychology*, *45*, 1117–1122.

Feustel, T. C., Shiffrin, R. M., & Salasoo, A. (1983). Episodic and lexical contributions to the repetition effect in word identification. *Journal of Experimental Psychology: General*, *112*, 309–346.

Greifeneder, R., Alt, A., Bottenberg, K., Seele, T., Zelt, S., & Wagener, D. (2010). On writing legibly: Processing fluency systematically biases evaluations of handwritten material. *Social Psychological and Personality Science*, *1*, 230–237.

Greifeneder, R., Müller, P., Stahlberg, D., Van den Bos, K., & Bless, H. (2011). Guiding trustful behavior: The role of accessible content and accessibility experiences. *Journal of Behavioral Decision Making*, *24*, 498–514.

Greifeneder, R., Bless, H., & Pham, M. T. (2011). When do people rely on affective and cognitive feelings in judgment? A review. *Personality and Social Psychology Review*, *15*, 107–141.

Hammond, K. R. (1955). Probabilistic functioning and the clinical method. *Psychological Review*, *62*, 255–262.

Hansen, J., & Wänke, M. (2008). It's the difference that counts: Expectancy/experience discrepancy moderates the use of ease of retrieval in attitude judgments. *Social Cognition*, *26*, 447–468.

Hart, J. T. (1965). Memory and the feeling-of-knowing experience. *Journal of Educational Psychology*, *56*, 208–216.

Hasher, L., Goldstein, D., & Toppino, T. (1977). Frequency and the conference of referential validity. *Journal of Verbal Learning and Verbal Behavior*, *16*, 107–112.

Hertwig, R., Herzog, S. M., Schooler, L. J., & Reimer, T. (2008). Fluency heuristic: A model of how the mind exploits a by-product of information retrieval. *Journal of Experimental Psychology: Learning, Memory, and Cognition*, *34*, 1191–1206.

Jacoby, L. L., Kelley, C., Brown, J., & Jasechko, J. (1989). Becoming famous overnight: Limits on the ability to avoid unconscious influences of the past. *Journal of Personality and Social Psychology*, *56*, 326–338.

James, W. (1890). *Principles of psychology (Vol. 2).* New York: Holt.

Karelaia, N. & Hogarth, R. (2008). Determinants of linear judgment: A meta-analysis of lens model studies. *Psychological Bulletin*, *134*, 404–426.

Koriat, A. (1993). How do we know that we know? The accessibility model of the feeling of knowing. *Psychological Review*, *100*, 609–639.

—— (2008). Easy comes, easy goes? The link between learning and remembering and its exploitation in metacognition. *Memory and Cognition*, *36*, 416–428.

Koriat, A., & Goldsmith, M. (1996). Monitoring and control processes in the strategic regulation of memory accuracy. *Psychological Review, 103,* 490–517.

Koriat, A., & Levy-Sadot, R. (1999). Processes underlying metacognitive judgments: Information-based and experience-based monitoring of one's own knowledge. In S. Chaiken & Y. Trope (Eds.), *Dual-process theories in social psychology.* (pp. 483–502). New York: Guilford Press.

Mandler, G., Nakamura, Y., & Van Zandt, B. J. (1987). Nonspecific effects of exposure on stimuli that cannot be recognized. *Journal of Experimental Psychology: Learning, Memory, and Cognition, 13,* 646–648.

Metcalfe, J., & Wiebe, D. (1987). Intuition in insight and noninsight problem solving. *Memory & Cognition, 15,* 238–246.

Mitchell, C. J., De Houwer, J., & Lovibond, P. F. (2009). The propositional nature of human associative learning. *Behavioral and Brain Sciences, 32,* 183–198.

Nisbett, R. E. & Wilson, T. D. (1977). Telling more than we can know: Verbal reports on mental processes. *Psychological Review, 84,* 231–259.

Olds, J. M., & Westerman, D. L. (2012). Can fluency be interpreted as novelty? Retraining the interpretation of fluency in recognition memory. *Journal of Experimental Psychology: Learning, Memory, and Cognition, 38,* 653–664.

Oppenheimer, D. M. (2004). Spontaneous Discounting of Availability in Frequency Judgment Tasks. *Psychological Science, 15,* 100–105.

Oppenheimer, D. M. (2008). The secret life of fluency. *Trends in Cognitive Sciences, 12,* 237–241.

Popper, K. R. (1959). *The logic of scientific discovery.* Oxford, England: Basic Books.

Reber, R., & Schwarz, N. (1999). Effects of perceptual fluency on judgments of truth. *Consciousness and Cognition, 8,* 338-342.

Reber, R., & Unkelbach, C. (2010). The epistemic status of processing fluency as source for judgments of truth. *Review of Philosophy and Psychology, 1,* 563–581.

Reber, R., Schwarz, N., & Winkielman, P. (2004). Processing fluency and aesthetic pleasure: Is beauty in the perceiver's processing experience? *Review of Personality and Social Psychology, 8,* 364–382.

Reber, R., Winkielman, P., & Schwarz, N. (1998). Effects of perceptual fluency on affective judgments. *Psychological Science, 9,* 45–48.

Reber, R., Wurtz, P., & Zimmermann, T. D. (2004). Exploring "fringe" consciousness: The subjective experience of perceptual fluency and its objective bases. *Consciousness and Cognition, 13,* 47–60.

Reber, R., Zimmermann, T. D., & Wurtz, P. (2004). Judgments of duration, figure-ground contrast, and size for words and nonwords. *Perception and Psychophysics, 66,* 1105–1114.

Redding, G. M., Rossetti, Y., & Wallace, B. (2005). Applications of prism adaptation: A tutorial in theory and method. *Neuroscience and Biobehavioral Reviews, 29,* 431–444.

Reisenzein, R. (2000). The subjective experience of surprise. In H. Bless & J. P. Forgas (Eds.), *The message within: The role of subjective experience in social cognition and behavior.* (pp. 262–279). London: Psychology Press.

Shanks, D. (2010). Learning: From association to cognition. *Annual Review of Psychology, 61,* 273–301.

Schwartz, B. L. (2002). *Tip-of-the-tongue states: Phenomenology, mechanism, and lexical retrieval.* Mahwah, NJ: Lawrence Erlbaum Associates Publishers.

Schwarz, N. (2004). Meta-cognitive experiences in consumer judgment and decision making. *Journal of Consumer Research, 14,* 332–348.

Schwarz, N., & Clore, G. L. (1983). Mood, misattribution, and judgments of well-being: Informative and directive functions of affective states. *Journal of Personality and Social Psychology, 45*, 513–523.

Schwarz, N., Bless, H., Strack, F., Klumpp, G., Rittenauer-Schatka, H., & Simons, A. (1991). Ease of retrieval as information: Another look at the availability heuristic. *Journal of Personality and Social Psychology, 61*, 195–202.

Topolinski, S., & Strack, F. (2009). The architecture of intuition: Fluency and affect determine intuitive judgments of semantic and visual coherence and judgments of grammaticality in artificial grammar learning. *Journal of Experimental Psychology: General, 138*, 39–63.

Topolinski, S., & Reber, R. (2010). Gaining insight into the "Aha" experience. *Current Directions in Psychological Science, 19*, 402–405.

Tversky, A., & Kahneman, D. (1973). Availability: A heuristic for judging frequency and probability. *Cognitive Psychology, 5*, 207–232.

Unkelbach, C. (2006). The learned interpretation of cognitive fluency. *Psychological Science, 17*, 339–345.

—— (2007). Reversing the truth effect: Learning the interpretation of processing fluency in judgments of truth. *Journal of Experimental Psychology: Learning, Memory and Cognition, 33*, 219–230.

Unkelbach, C., Fiedler, K., Bayer, M., Stegmüller, M., & Danner, D. (2008). Why positive information is processed faster: The density hypothesis. *Journal of Personality & Social Psychology, 95*, 36–49.

Unkelbach, C., & Stahl, C. (2009). A multinomial modeling approach to dissociate different components of the truth effect. *Consciousness and Cognition, 18*, 22–38.

Unkelbach, C., Bayer, M., Alves, H., Koch, A., & Stahl, C. (2011). Fluency and positivity as possible causes of the truth effect. *Consciousness and Cognition, 20*, 594–602.

Weiner, B. (1991). Metaphors in motivation and attribution. *American Psychologist, 46*, 921–930.

Whittlesea, B. A. (1993). Illusions of familiarity. *Journal of Experimental Psychology: Learning, Memory, and Cognition, 19*, 1235–1253.

Whittlesea, B. W. A. (2002). False memory and the discrepancy-attribution hypothesis: The prototype-familiarity illusion. *Journal of Experimental Psychology: General, 131*, 96–115.

Whittlesea, B. W. A. & Leboe, J. P. (2000). The heuristic basis of remembering and classification: Fluency, generation, and resemblance. *Journal of Experimental Psychology: General, 129*, 84–106.

Whittlesea, B. W. A. & Price, J. R. (2001). Implicit/explicit memory versus analytic/ nonanalytic processing: Rethinking the mere exposure effect. *Memory & Cognition, 29*, 234–246.

Whittlesea, B. W. A., & Williams, L. D. (1998). Why do strangers feel familiar, but friends don't? A discrepancy-attribution account of feelings of familiarity. *Acta Psychologica, 98*, 141–165.

Winkielman, P., & Cacioppo, J. T. (2001). Mind at ease puts a smile on the face: Psychophysiological evidence that processing facilitation elicits positive affect. *Journal of Personality and Social Psychology, 81*, 989–1000.

Winkielman, P., & Schwarz, N. (2001). How pleasant was your childhood? Beliefs about memory shape inferences from experienced difficulty of recall. *Psychological Science, 12*, 176–179.

3 The sources of fluency

Identifying the underlying mechanisms of fluency effects

Sascha Topolinski

Abstract

Processing fluency has pervasive effects on human attitudes and judgments; and the literature is full of fascinating demonstrations across a variety of domains. The question remains where the feeling of fluency originates. The present chapter explores the sources of fluency for several prominent phenomena in the literature—namely mere exposure effect, false fame, the truth effect, and aesthetics—by identifying the specific processes that exhibit fluency variations in each of these phenomena and by reviewing recent evidence that experimentally manipulated these fluency sources. For example, it is shown that the mere exposure effect is driven by covert oral motor-simulations and can be prevented by oral motor-interference. It is argued that identifying the underlying procedural sources of fluency effects not only permits experimentally switching fluency-effects on or off without conventional correction or debiasing methods, but also allows a deeper insight into the causal architecture that drives fluency effects. Also, a variety of future research questions is outlined.

Processing fluency has become a powerful explanation tool for a wide range of psychological phenomena (for a review, see Reber, Schwarz, & Winkielman, 2004), ranging from classical gems in social cognition, for instance, the feeling of familiarity (e.g., Jacoby, Kelley, Brown, & Jasechko, 1989), in cognitive psychology, for example, intuitions concerning hidden coherence (e.g., Topolinski & Strack, 2009d, Topolinski, 2011) and in memory research, such as the mere exposure effect (Zajonc, 1968); to even applied issues in persuasion and consumer psychology (e.g., Novemsky, Dhar, Schwarz, & Simonson, 2007). Actually, the whole present book is a remarkable illustration of the pervasive psychological effects of the experience of fluency. The specific contribution of the present chapter is to trace back the origins of this experience. We know that once the feeling of fluency emerges, it influences our attitudes and judgments. But how does this experience come about in the first place?

There is a general consensus among researchers concerning the basic principle how fluency works (e.g., Bornstein & D'Agostino, 1992; Reber et al., 2004): if a stimulus is processed with a relatively high efficiency or speed—for instance faster than other stimuli (Dechêne, Stahl, Hansen, & Wänke, 2009; Hansen, Dechêne, & Wänke, 2008; Hansen, Dechêne, & Wänke, 2008)—this increase in processing fluency is experienced as something positive (Topolinski, Likowski, Weyers, & Strack, 2009; Winkielman & Cacioppo, 2001; see also Garcia-Marques, Mackie, Claypool, & Garcia-Marques, this volume) and used as a cognitive feeling (cf., Clore et al., 2001; Schwarz & Clore, 2007), or a feeling-as-information (Schwarz, 2002) to guide judgments for which no other reliable cue is available (Unkelbach & Greifeneder, this volume).

For example, consider these two names of ostensible food additives, MAGNALROXATE, and HNEGRIPITROM (Song & Schwarz, 2009). Although they both sound exotic, the former is a bit easier to read than the latter; a fluency advantage that feels good. If being asked which of these substances is safe and not harmful to our health, individuals have no other cue than this fluency-triggered positive affect and more likely choose the former than the latter name (cf., Song & Schwarz, 2009; Topolinski & Strack, 2010).

In general, this causal logic is sufficient and explains many effects: high fluency in processing feels positive and is used as a judgmental cue. However, because stimuli are processed multi-modally and simultaneously on many parallel levels (see Borowsky & Besner, 2006; Kliegl, Nuthmann, & Engbert, 2006, for the example of simply reading words), the question emerges which fluency variations of which processes trigger the effects? In the case of the above examples, the question is in which modalities, or processing stages, is MAGNALROXATE more efficiently processed than HNEGRIPITROM? Is it in perceptually processing the visual appearance of the two words, in lexically identifying the single letters, in retrieving semantic associations, or even in sub-vocally whispering them?

The question where fluency gains reside targets on filling a substantial explanatory gap; and identifying these actual procedural sources would foster our understanding of the mechanisms that drive fluency effects, thus elucidating the *secret life of fluency* (Oppenheimer, 2008). Moreover, this question can be asked anew for each fluency effect in each stimulus domain, since the respective processes and modalities are highly stimulus-specific. The present chapter describes several lines of recent work that were conducted to identify the causal precursors of fluency effects in several stimulus domains and fluency effects, constituting a starting point in exploring the causal niches of fluency.

First, in the three main sections of the present chapter, I will review three different lines of research, regarding fluency-effects on attitudes and memory for words, on problem solving, and on visual aesthetics; and will then outline perspectives for future work in this area.

Oral motor-fluency drives fluency-effects in verbal stimuli

Surely the most extensively researched fluency phenomenon is the effect of presenting words repeatedly. For instance, in the classical work on *mere exposure*, Zajonc (1968; for a review, see Bornstein, 1989) presented nonsense words to participants, some of these words several times, and asked for liking ratings for these words. It turned out that old, i.e. repeated words, were liked more than novel words, i.e. words that had not been presented before. Likewise, in another classical study concerning the *false-fame effect*, Jacoby and colleagues (1989) presented names that were labeled as being non-famous persons, with some of the names being repeated. The result was that if participants forgot about the initial labeling of the names as being non-famous, they judged repeated names more likely to be famous than novel names.

For these effects of word repetition, a fluency account was proposed (Bornstein & D'Agostino, 1992). The repeated presentation of some of the target words or names, i.e. the old targets, rendered their processing more efficient (cf., Jacoby & Dallas, 1981; Jacoby & Whitehouse, 1989). This fluency advantage in reading words felt positive (e.g., Topolinski et al., 2009) and thus drove preference and attribution of fame.

However, this chain of causal mechanisms leaves open the question which processing stages, or modalities, were actually trained via repetition and thereby showed fluency gains, because a multitude of processes are automatically running simultaneously during the reading of words (Borowsky & Besner, 2006; Kliegl et al., 2006), such as visual, lexical, and motor processes. Identifying those processes that yield fluency variations would advance our understanding of the core mechanisms of those absolute classics of modern psychology.

Most recently, Fritz Strack and I have developed an account of the procedural fluency sources in this realm, which proposes motor processes to be the essential driving force behind these effects. In the following, this account will be outlined, and then, evidence supporting it shall be reviewed.

Embodied words: motor processes during reading

Among the processes that run during reading, some are obvious and come easily to the researcher's mind as being possible fluency sources, for instance, sensory and memory processes such as visual and lexical identification. However, there are also other, less obvious, processes that run during reading, such as covert simulations of pronouncing the read words (e.g., Stroop, 1935). That such a simulation of simply uttering the words may indeed play an important role even during silent reading is strongly suggested by embodiment theory (Barsalou, 1999).

This theory states that we represent stimuli by covertly simulating those actions that are usually associated with those stimuli (e.g., Glenberg & Robertson, 2000; Hommel, Müsseler, Aschersleben, & Prinz, 2001; Semin & Smith, 2008; Schubert & Semin, 2009), as is supported by a large amount of evidence. For instance, it was shown that passive viewing of graspable objects activates those brain regions that are responsible for actually grasping them (e.g., Craighero, Fadiga, Umiltà, & Rizzolatti, 1996), or hearing a piano sound triggers motor activity in the fingers of piano players (e.g., Haueisen & Knösche, 2001). Also, in typists, merely seeing letters triggers the motor programs to type them (Van den Bergh, Vrana, & Eelen, 1990).

Applying this embodiment hypothesis to the exposure of words, it can be hypothesized that merely seeing a word automatically triggers the covert motor simulation to pronounce them, as is illustrated in the classical Stroop-effect (Stroop, 1935). The crucial point is that those covert pronouncing-simulations may be the actual source of fluency gains during word repetition. From the literature, we know that overt, but also covert, pronouncing of words becomes more fluent with repeated reading of those words (e.g., Ehri & Wilce, 1979; Scarborough, Cortese, & Scarborough, 1977). Thus, it is possible that this increase in motor-fluency for repeated words compared to novel words might drive the effect of word repetition.

A simple test of this embodied account of word repetition is to block covert pronouncing simulations during the presentation of words. This can easily be done by engaging the oral muscles, which are responsible for pronouncing, in a secondary task, such as simply chewing gum (e.g., Campbell, Rosen, Solis-Macias, & White, 1991). This concurrent task would interfere with pronouncing simulations of the target words, which might prevent training and gains in motor-fluency for repeated compared to novel words. Consequently, if such gains are actually the driving force behind fluency-effects in word repetition, then oral motor-interference should substantially reduce fluency-effects. This was tested most recently, both in the domain of the mere exposure (Zajonc, 1968) and the false-fame effect (Jacoby et al., 1989).

Mere exposure

Testing whether the classical mere exposure effect for words (Zajonc, 1968), i.e. the preference for repeated compared to novel stimuli, is driven by oral motor-fluency, Topolinski & Strack (2009a) presented nonsense words as well as visual characters as targets to participants under oral, and manual, motor interference, and asked for preference ratings concerning these targets. Specifically, in a study phase, we presented nonsense words and visual characters while participants either chew gum (oral motor-interference), or moved a ball in their nondominant hand (manual motor-interference). Then, in a subsequent test phase, we presented the old words and characters from the study phase again intermixed with novel words and characters; and participants should indicate their liking of these target stimuli. Note that this set-up is a replication of a usual mere exposure study, only adding motor interference tasks.

The logic behind this set-up was the following: if mere exposure effects for words are driven by oral motor-fluency, then exclusively the oral, but not the manual, motor-interference should reduce mere exposure effects for words. The visual characters served as a stimulus control condition and were expected to exhibit mere exposure effects both under oral and manual interference, because processing visual characters is mediated by neither of these motor domains.

We found exactly this pattern of results. While participants liked old characters more than novel characters both under oral and manual motor interference, they preferred old over novel words only under manual motor interference, but not under oral motor interference (Topolinski & Strack, 2009a, Experiment 1; see also Topolinski, 2012). This pattern was replicated with other oral motor-interference tasks, namely whispering a task-irrelevant word (Experiment 2) and tongue tapping (Experiment 3). Most interestingly, in all these experiments, the crucial condition of oral motor-interference during word repetition, the mere exposure effect was not only reduced, but attenuated to such a degree that even descriptively no differences in preferences for old compared to new targets could be found.

This evidence shows that mere exposure effects for words being verbal stimuli are driven by the oral muscle system, presumably by gains during the repetition of covert pronouncing simulations (cf., Ehri & Wilce, 1979). In a further step, we tested whether oral motor-fluency may also mediate the false-fame effect (Jacoby et al., 1989).

False fame

Another classical fluency effect by word repetition is the false-fame effect (Jacoby et al., 1989). Here, repeated names of target persons are more likely to be judged as being famous than names that had not been presented before. To test whether also this effect draws on oral motor-fluency, we replicated the false-fame paradigm under concurrent oral and manual motor-tasks (Topolinski & Strack, 2010, Experiment 1).

Specifically, we presented names of actually existing Bollywood actors (e.g., *Aishwarya Rai*) first in a study phase. Then, in a later test phase that followed after one minute of relaxation, these already presented names re-appeared randomly mixed with novel names; and participants were asked to indicate how famous these actors were. Crucially, in this test phase we asked some participants to move a ball in their hand (manual motor-interference), and other participants to simply eat popcorn (oral motor-interference).

As a consequence, we found that old names were rated higher in fame than novel names in the manual motor-group; but no such false-effect was evident in the oral motor-group. Again, oral motor-interference did not only reduce the original fluency-effect, but completely destroyed it.

Conclusion on oral motor-fluency

The evidence reviewed in the preceding sections shows that oral motor fluency is the driving causal force behind fluency effects in word repetition, since oral motor-interference completely neutralized fluency effects. It is important to note that the old targets in the reviewed experiments (Topolinski & Strack, 2009, 2010) were perceptually similar both in the study and in the test phase. Thus, participants under oral motor-interference could have easily used the visual fluency as a cue for their preference, or fame judgments. However, they did not, which renders visual fluency a minor candidate for driving the original effects (see also the discussion below).

From this discovery also follows that mere exposure effects might not only be diminished, but also enhanced experimentally. For instance, reading words aloud compared to silent reading, or open the mouth while silent reading compared to keeping the mouth shut might facilitate the activity of the oral muscles and may thus lead to increased mere exposure effects; a prediction still to be tested.

These studies also illustrate how worthwhile a thorough investigation of the causal undercurrent of fluency effects is, because they demonstrate how easily two of the most robust and replicable effects in the psychological literature can be neutralized without any stimulus manipulation or strategic instructions. This could only be achieved by precisely identifying and blocking the underlying fluency sources of these effects. In the next section, we continue the search for fluency precursors in the domain of experienced truth.

Temporal contiguity drives fluency-effects in problem solving

Fluency has been shown to be genuinely linked to the experience of validity thought content (for succinct reviews, see Oppenheimer, 2008; Topolinski & Reber, 2010a). Many examples for this can be found in the domain of *retrieval fluency*, which is the speed and easiness with which certain contents come to mind, or can be retrieved from memory (Schwarz et al., 1991). Generally, the easier and faster an answer is retrieved from memory, the stronger people belief in the validity, i.e. correctness, of this answer (Kelley & Lindsay, 1993). As a consequence, people rely more readily on information that they have retrieved easily from memory than on information that was relatively hard to retrieve (e.g., Schwarz et al., 1991). Also, people are more confident in their capability to answer a general knowledge question correctly if this question is processed easily, independently of their actual capability (Koriat & Levy-Sadot, 2001); and they are more confident in their general memory content if they have retrieved an answer to a general knowledge question easily (Benjamin, Bjork, & Schwartz, 1998). Finally, the suddenness and fluency of ideas popping into mind determine the peculiar "Aha!"-experience, in which solutions to hard cognitive problems are experienced as insights with great confidence in their truth (Topolinski & Reber, 2010a, 2010b).

The common denominator of all these effects is that the fluency of retrieving answers to questions, or solutions to problems, determines the experienced validity of these answers, or solutions. Although the evidence for this link between subjectively-felt fluency and judged validity is abundant, the psychological question remains how this link comes about psychologically (see, Reber & Unkelbach, 2010; Unkelbach & Stahl, 2009, for the ecological question how the link between fluency and objective truth comes about in the first place). Most recently, Rolf Reber and I (Topolinski & Reber, 2010a) have proposed and tested a temporal contiguity-hypothesis for this relationship, which is described in the following.

Temporal contiguity and experienced validity

Expressed in abstract terms, the fluency-validity link is the basic relation that the faster a cognitive problem (e.g., a question, a riddle) is followed by a solution (e.g., an answer, an insight), the stronger that solution is experienced to be the correct solution for this problem (cf., Deleuze, 1990, for the epistemological relation between a problem and its solution), presumably because high thought speed again feels positive (cf., Pronin & Wegner, 2006). Thus, the mere temporal contiguity between a cognitive problem and its solution, i.e. how closely in time they are experienced, may be the mediating mechanism of the fluency-truth link.

A straightforward test of this hypothesis would be to manipulate the temporal contiguity between a cognitive problem and its solution independently from any processing fluency manipulation. In a most recent work, this was done by Topolinski and Reber (2010b). There, we presented problems and solutions to participants and manipulated the immediacy with which a solution followed a problem, namely for anagrams, mathematical equations, and insight problems.

As an example of the specific manipulations, a study involving anagrams should be described (Topolinski & Reber, 2010b, Experiment 1). There, participants received nonsense letter strings that either could be re-combined to form a proper German word (e.g., GEWIKITE, resulting in EWIGKEIT, which means *eternity*), or could not be re-combined into a German word (e.g., GELIKITE). These letter strings were presented for 1,500 ms only, followed by a blank screen. Then, a possible solution for these anagrams was presented and participants should spontaneously judge whether the solution candidate was the correct solution for the previous anagram. Crucially, the delay between the anagram and the solution candidate was either 50 ms or 150 ms. Note that this manipulation was very subtle and hard to recognize for the participants, because relatively to the duration of 1,500 ms of the anagram presentation, the crucial difference of 100 ms in the delay between anagram and solution was rather small. Furthermore, this manipulation did not entail any fluency manipulation in the conventional manner.

We found that solutions presented with a delay of 50 ms were more likely to be endorsed as being correct than solutions shown after 150 ms, independently of whether the solutions to the anagrams were actually correct or not. Furthermore, we could replicate this finding also for mathematical equations (cf., Reber, Brun, & Mitterndorfer, 2008), and remote-associate insight problems (cf., Topolinski & Deutsch, 2012; Topolinski & Strack, 2008, 2009a, 2009b, 2009d). For the latter, we even found a linear decrease in the likelihood of endorsing a solution as being correct with the delay between problem and solution increasing from 50 ms to 150 ms and 300 ms.

Thus, mere temporal contiguity in experiencing a cognitive problem and its solution influences the experienced validity of the solution, independently of any conventional fluency manipulation. This evidence renders temporal contiguity a plausible mediating mechanism also for other retrieval-fluency effects (see Topolinski & Reber, 2010a, for a discussion of possible underlying neuropsychological and affective mechanisms), but also beyond, which is outlined in the following.

Implications for the truth effect

Another prominent case where experienced fluency determines subjectively felt validity is the so-called *truth effect*, which is the classical finding that repeated statements are more likely to be judged as being correct or valid than novel statements (e.g., Bacon, 1979; Hasher, Goldstein, & Toppino, 1977). In recent years, this effect also was conceptualized to draw on processing fluency (Hansen, Dechêne, & Wänke, 2008; Reber & Schwarz, 1999; Unkelbach, 2007), with repeated statements exhibiting greater fluency than novel statements, which signals validity (Reber & Schwarz, 1999). For instance, the statement "Osorno is in Chile" is more readily accepted as being correct both if presented repeatedly and if printed with a higher figure-ground contrast, which increases visual fluency (Reber & Schwarz, 1999). However, again the question remains which exact processes exhibit fluency variations; and how fluency actually drives the effect.

There is no doubt that through repeated exposure and increased visual fluency the very process of reading a particular statement is executed faster (cf., Jacoby & Dallas, 1981). Applying the temporal-contiguity hypothesis (Topolinski & Reber, 2010a) to this, it might be argued that faster reading of a statement leads to an increased temporal contiguity between the different arguments within a statement. For instance, if the whole proposition "Osorno is in Chile" is read faster, the subject "Osorno" and the nominal subject "Chile" are processed closer in time. This temporal contiguity between the two arguments of the proposition may be the actual driving force behind the truth effect, which is still to be tested. A direct prediction from this account would be that a statement, if its constituents are presented one by one, is more likely to be accepted if the constituents follow each other with faster succession than with slower succession, above and beyond repeated exposure or conventional visual fluency manipulations. In the next session, we will turn over to yet another domain for which the sources of fluency shall be investigated.

Ocular motor fluency and visual aesthetics

Sometimes, the search for the specific sources of fluency effects can lead to surprising results. One such case shall be described as a final example in this chapter, namely fluency effects on visual aesthetic judgments. Applying our quest for the sources of fluency in the domain of vision, the question what processes exhibit fluency variations driving visual judgments seems easy to be answered: it must be some perceptual mechanism, specifically, some visual process between the retina and the brain. This guess is also supported by the idiom "Beauty lies in the eyes of the beholder."

However, independently of these possible perceptual sources of fluency during vision, a recent line of research identified another source of fluency variations that influences visual judgments to some extent, a source that is not located in visual, and not even in perceptual processing at all, which is outlined in the following.

Vision does not only entail sensory processes, i.e., merely seeing, but also subsidiary motor components, namely moving the eyes (Palmer, 1999). For most objects to watch, eye movements are necessary, because those objects move: for instance, a ballet dancer, the moves in a baseball game, or the gestures of a person we familiarize with. It is conceivable that also these subsidiary motor components can exhibit variations in fluency, for instance if being trained, and might feed fluency-triggered affect into vision-related judgments. A crucial prediction from this speculation would be that artificially increasing oculomotor fluency independently from visual input might shape judgments concerning this input.

This was tested in a recent work (Topolinski, 2010) by addressing the extra-ocular muscles (EOMs), the muscles that are responsible for moving the ocular bulb (Palmer, 1999). Using EOM-kinematics, I trained participants to follow the movements of a stimulus without actually seeing this stimulus by the following means. The extra-ocular muscles are not only responsible for moving the eyes while the head is held stationary, but also for compensating head movements while the eyes are gazing on a fixed point. For instance, the EOM-activity is the same if an individual is watching a stimulus moving to the *left* without moving the head as if an individual is gazing on a fixed point while moving the head to the *right*.

Exploiting this bio-mechanical fact, participants executed certain head movements while gazing on a fixation point before watching a target stimulus moving on a screen. In some trials, the resulting eye movements were the same both during gazing while moving the head and subsequently watching the target stimulus moving; while in other trials the eye movements did not match. For instance, in a matching trial, the participants moved their head *first downwards and then to the left* while focusing on the fixation cross; and then subsequently watched the target stimulus moving *first upwards and then to the right* on a PC screen (note that matching trajectories must have opposite directions because of the compensatory nature of EOM kinematics during head movements). In contrast, in a mismatching trial, participants moved the head *first downwards and then to the right* before watching the dot moving *first upwards and then to the right*. By this means, participants trained their eyes to follow a stimulus movement without actually seeing it.

As a dependent measure, participants were asked to indicate their liking for the stimulus movements, thus providing an aesthetic judgment concerning this visual input. Although participants were not aware of the oculomotor relation between their head movements and the stimulus movements, I found in three experiments that participants liked the stimulus movements more if they had trained exactly the same eye movements that were required to visually follow the stimulus movements than if they had trained different eye movements (Topolinski, 2010).

Thus, completely independently from visual input, the execution fluency of subsidiary motor components during vision substantially shaped the aesthetic experience of visual input. This surprising result illustrates how fluency may work in surprising ways, affecting perceptual judgments from non-perceptual sources.

Although the reviewed experiments only showed an experimental increase of fluency effect, experimentally interfering with visuomotor activity would also be a valid prediction for future research (similar to the verbal motor-tasks described above). For instance, moving the head in circles while watching a moving target might feed in interfering motor noise and destroy increased preference for repeatedly seen targets. Although speculative in nature, it is conceivable that future research may discover similar fluency-effects for other motor-components in perceptions, for instance the ear muscles for auditory judgments, or the muscles in the nose for olfactory judgments.

In sum, the research reviewed in the preceding sections shows that the causal underlying mechanisms for fluency effects can be identified and experimentally tested (Topolinski & Strack, 2009a, 2009d), sometimes with surprising findings (Leder, Bär, & Topolinski, in press; Sparenberg, Topolinski, Springer, & Prinz, 2012; Topolinski, 2010). Furthermore, it was illustrated that experimental manipulations of these mechanisms can be used to diminish and increase default fluency-effects (e.g., mere exposure) or even create novel fluency-effects. In the concluding section, future research questions pursuing this search for fluency sources as well as the benefits of this search will be outlined.

Chopping through the undergrowth of fluency

The lines of research that were described in the previous sections are only a starting point in identifying the processing undercurrents of fluency effects. Future research shall seek out the locations of fluency variations also for other domains. For instance, the question remains which exact stages of processing merely visual information exhibit fluency gains, such as in the classical case of repeated exposure of Chinese ideographs (Zajonc, 1968), but also in perceptual fluency manipulations (e.g., Reber et al., 1998; Reber, Wurtz, & Zimmermann, 2004). If it is merely visual processing, then a mental imagery task might interfere with visual fluency; if again oculomotor components are involved, such as reviewed in the preceding sections (Topolinski, 2010), then specific head movements might interfere with these effects; predictions still to be tested.

A pragmatic and meta-scientific objection, however, may ask for the benefit of such an extensive search. The above demonstrations may be already sufficient to illustrate the general notion that fluency effects may reside in very specific processing niches. However, identifying these procedural undercurrents yield interesting psychological insights beyond merely blocking established effects, some of which shall be sketched out in the remainder of this chapter.

Judgmental decontamination

Concerning the ecological validity in correctly predicting a judgmental criterion, fluency has both merits and discredits (Greifeneder, Bless, & Scholl, this volume; Herzog & Hertwig, this volume). In some domains, fluency was shown to be a valid cue to the objective judgmental criterion, for instance pertaining to familiarity (e.g., Jacoby & Dallas, 1981), or hidden semantic meaning (Topolinski & Strack, 2009a, b, d). In other domains, however, fluency is an irrelevant yet often used cue that biases judgments notoriously, such as in consumers' choices (e.g., Novemsky et al., 2007).

Thus far, preventing fluency effects was only possible by elaborate judgmental correction (for reviews, see Larrick, 2004; Schwarz, Sanna, Skurnik, & Yoon, 2007; Wilson & Brekke, 1994), that is, by actively discounting or re-attributing the fluency feeling from the judgment at hand (e.g., Greifeneder & Bless, 2007; Schwarz et al., 1991). For this decontamination strategy, however, individuals must be aware of the biasing fluency effect and must know in what way to correct their judgment (Strack & Hannover, 1996); conditions that are rarely met (Wilson & Brekke, 1994).

Providing a new answer for these classical judgment formation dilemmas in social psychology, procedurally blocking the causal undercurrents of fluency allows judgmental decontamination that is independent from elaborate correction strategies. For instance, cinema audiences may prevent themselves from being biased by repeated exposure to brand names during advertising by simply eating popcorn; a decontamination they are not even aware of.

Unexpected fluency sources

The evidence on oculomotor fluency reviewed in the earlier section (Topolinski, 2010), namely that beauty may not only reside in the eyes of the beholder, but also in the eyes' muscles, gives a nice example of how surprising the findings of a closer investigation of fluency sources may be. Evidence like that changes our view concerning the interplay between different modalities and mental domains, in this case perception and motor systems (cf., Cannon, Hayes, & Tipper, 2009). Further findings of domain-specific fluency variations that exert an impact on other, thus far theoretically separated, domains (e.g., perceptual, motor, memory, or even humoral levels) would substantially further our knowledge of how different mental realms are intertwined.

Fluency-specificity

Finally, and most importantly, identifying fluency-sources may yield important insights into the basic issues of stimulus processing and metacognition. Most stimuli are processed multi-modally. For instance, when we meet and familiarize with persons we process information from various sensory modalities, such as visual (looking at them), auditory (hearing their voice), and maybe haptic processing (shaking their hand). The question here is which fluency gains from which modalities drive the process of getting familiar: is it the more fluent processing in the visual, acoustic, or haptic domain? The first guess would be that the processing dynamics of all, or at least many, of the engaged modalities jointly contribute to fluency effects in some additive fashion; possibly with weighted impact depending on how salient the respective domain is (e.g., vision is more salient than haptics), or how strong the processing fluency might vary in the respective domains (e.g., vision being very fast exhibiting only small fluency gains due to a ceiling effect). A hint for this hypothesis is the finding by Reber and colleagues that different stages of a single perceptual domain, namely visual processing, jointly contribute to visual fluency effects (Reber, Wurtz, & Zimmermann, 2004). However, a re-occurring pattern in the studies on oral motor-fluency reviewed above provides an alternative view, which is developed in the following.

Consider the above case of oral motor-interference during the repeated exposure of nonsense words (Topolinski & Strack, 2009a). Many researchers would have predicted that participants chewing gum, who had no longer available the experience of pronunciation fluency as a cue for their preference judgments, would have switched to merely visual fluency (cf., Reber, Wurtz, & Zimmermann, 2004) as a judgmental cue, i.e. how the words looked. This flexible use of another stimulus-related fluency source would have led to possibly reduced, but still clearly emerging exposure effects: old nonsense words would have been liked more than novel ones because they simply *looked* more familiar, although the easiness of pronouncing them was no longer available. In contrast, it was found in several experiments involving different stimuli and different dependent measures that a concurrent oral motor-task did not diminish, but actually completely destroyed exposure effects (Topolinski & Strack, 2009a, 2010). This evidence makes the case that fluency effects for this stimulus domain, i.e. verbal stimuli, draw exclusively on oral motor-processing, and not on visual fluency.

This *fluency-specificity* may be found also for other multi-modally represented stimuli. One interesting fluency induction in this realm is typing font (e.g., Song & Schwarz, 2008). Concerning easy- or hard-to-read fonts, the respective contributions of the visual, oral, or semantic level (cf., Kliegl et al., 2006) to fluency effects should be tested by appropriate interference tasks.

A closer investigation of *fluency-specificity* may reveal how different stimulus properties and dynamics of the own processing of these properties are differentially exploited as judgmental cues, and how flexibly these cues can be used (cf., Unkelbach, 2007). To tap into this promising new research question more thoroughly, the causes for stimulus-fluency specificity should be explored. A first simple hypothesis may be mere *stimulus-modality dominance*: words, for instance, as verbal stimuli may be processed predominantly by the oral motor-system, because this domain is responsible for representing verbal information (cf., the *Stroop effect*, Stroop, 1935); while the visual system is irrelevant for verbal information. Consequently, fluency variations in the oral-motor, but not in the visual, domain influence heuristic judgments concerning words. However, this logic is flawed because words must first be visually processed to allow a motor-representation. Thus, of course words are also visually processed; and an exclusive link between words and the oral motor-domain cannot be hypothesized. However, other, more differentiated possible mechanisms for a fluency-specificity might be plausible, among them the following.

Fluency variability

Different processing domains may differ in the extent to which their processing efficiency can vary (see Topolinski & Strack, 2009d, for a thorough discussion of this). For instance, visual processing may be so efficient (Palmer, 1999) that it only exhibits small processing gains and thus triggers only subtle fluency feelings—similar to a ceiling effect. Relative to more substantial fluency gains in simultaneously available other domains, such as motor fluency, subtle fluency variations may not exceed the threshold of awareness (cf., Topolinski & Strack, 2009d) and thus do not influence judgments.

Modality salience

Also, different modalities of processing may vary in the extent to which individuals are aware of them or their processing dynamics (cf., Reber, Wurtz, & Zimmermann, 2004). Concerning words, the merely visual appearance of the letters might be less salient than the verbal information how easy they are pronounceable.

Attributional use of modalities

Finally, the fluency signals from different modalities may differ in the extent to which they are generally used as judgmental cues, or how likely they are (re-) attributed to the stimulus or the judgmental criterion, especially if several modalities are available. In the case of words, it is possible that the more fluent covert pronunciation of old compared to new words was used by the participants uncritically whenever available, while the more familiar visual appearance of old compared to new words was often recognized as being caused by previous exposure and thus discounted from the preference judgment (cf., Jacoby et al., 1989).

Stimulus-modality interaction

Finally and most probably, these mechanisms may be additionally moderated by an interaction between stimulus type and domain in the way that those modalities contribute more substantially to fluency signals that are more closer related to the particular stimulus (which is a differentiated version of the above hypothesis of simple stimulus-domain dominance). For instance, for verbal stimuli oral fluency signals may be more salient, or are more readily used as heuristic cues, than for visual stimuli.

Theoretically, each of these mechanisms, and also other mechanisms, or any combination of them can account for stimulus-fluency specificity. A future investigation of these underlying effects of fluency-specificity would reveal how flexibly we use the dynamics of our own processing in gaining meta-cognitive information (cf., Reber, Wurtz & Zimmermann, 2004; Schwarz et al., 2007; Topolinski & Strack, 2009d).

Conclusion

The present chapter features the search for the underlying psychological mechanisms that produce variations in processing fluency and are thus the causal undercurrents of fluency effects in general. Reviewing most recent research that investigated these procedural niches of fluency in the domains of mere exposure, false fame, truth, and aesthetics, the present approach shall serve as a starting point for future research elucidating the *secret life of fluency* (Oppenheimer, 2008).

References

Bacon, F. T. (1979). Credibility of repeated statements: Memory for trivia. *Journal of Experimental Psychology: Human Learning and* Memory, *5*, 241–252.

Barsalou, L.W. (1999). Perceptual symbol systems. *Behavioral and Brain Sciences*, *22*, 577–660.

Benjamin, A. S., Bjork, R. A., & Schwartz, B. L. (1998). The mismeasure of memory: When retrieval fluency is misleading as a metamnemonic index. *Journal of Experimental Psychology: General*, *127*, 55–68.

Bornstein, R. F. (1989). Exposure and affect: Overview and meta-analysis of research, 1968–1987. *Psychological Bulletin*, *106*, 265–289.

Bornstein, R. F., & D'Agostino, P. R. (1992). Stimulus recognition and the mere exposure effect. *Journal of Personality and Social Psychology*, *63*, 545–552.

Borowsky, R., & Besner, D. (2006). Parallel distributed processing and lexical–semantic effects in visual word recognition: Are a few stages necessary? *Psychological Review*, *113*, 181–195.

Campbell, R., Rosen, S., Solis-Macias, V. & White, T. (1991). Stress in silent reading: Effects of concurrent articulation on the detection of syllabic stress patterns in written words in English speakers. *Language and Cognitive Processes*, *6*, 29–47.

Cannon, P. R., Hayes, A. E., & Tipper, S. P. (2009). An electromyographic investigation of the impact of task relevance on facial mimicry. Cognition & Emotion, *23*, 918–929.

Clore, G. L., Wyer, R. S. J., Dienes, B., Gasper, K., Gohm, C., & Isbell, L. (2001). Affective feelings as feedback: Some cognitive consequences. In L. L. Martin & G. L. Clore (Eds.), *Theories of mood and cognition: A user's guidebook* (pp. 27–62). Mahwah: Lawrence Erlbaum Associates Publishers.

Craighero, L., Fadiga, L., Umilta, C. A., & Rizzolatti, G. (1996) Evidence for visuomotor priming effect. *Neuroreport: An International Journal for the Rapid Communication of Research in Neuroscience*, *8*, 347–349.

Dechêne, A., Stahl, C., Hansen, J., & Wänke, M. (2009). Mix me a list: Context moderates the truth effect and the mere-exposure effect. *Journal of Experimental Social Psychology*, *45*, 1117–1122.

Deleuze, G. (1990). *The logic of sense*. New York: Columbia University Press.

Ehri, L. C., & Wilce, L. S. (1979). Does word training increase or decrease interference in a Stroop task? *Journal of Experimental Child Psychology, 27*, 352–364.

Glenberg, A. M., & Robertson, D. A. (2000). Symbol grounding and meaning: A comparison of high-dimensional and embodied theories of meaning. *Journal of Memory & Language*, *43*, 379–401.

Greifeneder, R., & Bless, H. (2007). Relying on accessible content versus accessibility experiences: The case of processing capacity. *Social Cognition, 25*, 853–881.

Hansen, J., Dechêne, A., & Wänke, M. (2008). Discrepant fluency increases subjective truth. *Journal of Experimental Social Psychology, 44*, 687–691.

Hasher, L., Goldstein, D., & Toppino, T. (1977). Frequency and the conference of referential validity. *Journal of Verbal Learning and Verbal Behavior, 16*, 107–112.

Haueisen, J., & Knösche, T. R. (2001). Involuntary motor activity in pianists evoked by music perception. *Journal of Cognitive Neuroscience, 13*, 786–792.

Hommel, B., Müsseler, J., Aschersleben, G., & Prinz, W. (2001). The Theory of Event Coding (TEC): A framework for perception and action planning. *Behavioral & Brain Sciences, 24*, 849–937.

Jacoby, L. L., & Dallas, M. (1981). On the relationship between autobiographical memory and perceptual learning. *Journal of Experimental Psychology: General, 110*, 306–340.

Jacoby, L. L., Kelley, C. M., Brown, J., & Jasechko, J. (1989). Becoming famous overnight: Limits on the ability to avoid unconscious influences of the past. *Journal of Personality and Social Psychology, 56*, 326–338.

Jacoby, L. L., & Whitehouse, K. (1989). An illusion of memory: False recognition influenced by unconscious perception. *Journal of Experimental Psychology: General, 118*, 126–135.

Kelley, C. M., & Lindsay, D. S. (1993). Remembering mistaken for knowing: Ease of retrieval as a basis for confidence in answers to general knowledge questions. *Journal of Memory and Language, 32*, 1–24.

Kliegl, R., Nuthmann, A., & Engbert, R. (2006) Tracking the mind during reading: The influence of past, present, and future words on fixation durations. *Journal of Experimental Psychology: General, 135*, 12–35.

Koriat, A., & Levy-Sadot, R. (2001). The combined contributions of the cue-familiarity and accessibility heuristics to feelings of knowing. *Journal of Experimental Psychology: Learning, Memory, and Cognition, 27*, 34–53.

Larrick, R. P. (2004). Debiasing. In D. J. Koehler & N. Harvey (Eds.), *Blackwell handbook of judgment and decision making.* (pp. 316–337). Oxford: Blackwell Publishing.

Leder, H., Bär, S., & Topolinski, S. (in press). Covert painting simulations influence aesthetic appreciation of artworks. P*sychological Science.*

Novemsky, N., Dhar, R., Schwarz, N., & Simonson, I. (2007). Preference fluency in consumer choice. *Journal of Marketing Research, 44*, 347–356.

Oppenheimer, D. M. (2008). The secret life of fluency. *Trends in Cognitive Sciences, 12*, 237–241.

Palmer, S.E. (1999). *Vision science: Photons to phenomenology*. Cambridge, MA: MIT Press.

Pronin, E., & Wegner, D. M. (2006). Manic thinking: Independent effects of thought speed and thought content on mood. *Psychological Science, 17*, 807–813.

Reber, R. & Schwarz, N. (1999). Effects of perceptual fluency on judgments of truth. *Consciousness and Cognition, 8*, 338–342.

Reber, R., & Unkelbach, C. (2010). The epistemic status of processing fluency as source for judgments of truth. *Review of Philosophy and Psychology, 1*, 563–581.

Reber, R., Brun, M., & Mitterndorfer, K. (2008). The use of heuristics in intuitive mathematical judgment. *Psychonomic Bulletin and Review, 15*, 1174–1178.

Reber, R., Schwarz, N., & Winkielman, P. (2004). Processing fluency and aesthetic pleasure: Is beauty in the perceiver's processing experience? Personality *and Social Psychology Review, 8*, 364–382.

Reber, R., Winkielman, P., & Schwarz, N. (1998). Effects of perceptual fluency on affective judgments. *Psychological Science*, *9*, 45–48.

Reber, R., Wurtz, P., & Zimmermann, T. D (2004). Exploring "fringe" consciousness: The subjective experience of perceptual fluency and its objective bases. *Consciousness and Cognition*, *13*, 47–60.

Scarborough, D. L., Cortese, C. & Scarborough, H. S. (1977). Frequency and repetition effects in lexical memory. *Journal of Experimental Psychology: Human Perception and Performance*, *3*, 1–17.

Schubert, T., & Semin, G. R. (2009). Embodiment as a unifying perspective for psychology. *European Journal of Social Psychology*, *39*, 1135–1141.

Schwarz, N. (2002). Feelings as information: Moods influence judgment and processing style. In T. Gilovich, D. Griffin, & D. Kahneman (Eds.), *Heuristics and biases: The psychology of intuitive judgment.* (pp. 534–547). Cambridge: Cambridge University Press.

Schwarz, N., & Clore, G. L. (2007). Feelings and phenomenal experiences. In E. T. Higgins & A. Kruglanski (Eds.), *Social psychology. A handbook of basic principles (2nd ed.).* (pp. 385–407). New York: Guilford Press.

Schwarz, N., Bless, H., Strack, F., Klumpp, G., Rittenauer-Schatka, H., & Simons, A. (1991). Ease of retrieval as information: Another look at the availability heuristic. *Journal of Personality and Social Psychology*, *61*, 195–202.

Schwarz, N., Sanna, L., Skurnik, I., & Yoon, C. (2007). Metacognitive experiences and the intricacies of setting people straight: Implications for debiasing and public information campaigns. *Advances in Experimental Social Psychology*, *39*, 127–161.

Semin, G. R., & Smith, E. R. (Eds.), (2008). *Embodied grounding: Social, cognitive, affective, and neuroscientific approaches.* New York: Cambridge University Press.

Song, H., & Schwarz, N. (2008). If it's hard to read, it's hard to do: Processing fluency affects effort prediction and motivation. Psychological *Science*, *19*, 986–988.

—— (2009). If it's difficult-to-pronounce, it must be risky: Fluency, familiarity, and risk perception. *Psychological Science*, *20*, 135–138.

Sparenberg, P., Topolinski, S., Springer, A., & Prinz, W. (in press). Minimal mimicry: Mere effector matching induces preference. *Brain and Cognition*, *80*, 291–300.

Strack, F., & Hannover, B. (1996). Awareness of influence as a precondition for implementing correctional goals. In P. Gollwitzer & J. Bargh (Eds.), *The psychology of action: Linking cognition and motivation to behavior.* (pp. 579–596). New York: Guilford.

Stroop, J. R. (1935). Studies of interference in serial verbal reactions. *Journal of Experimental Psychology*, *12*, 242–248.

Topolinski, S. (2010). Moving the eye of the beholder: Motor components in vision determine aesthetic preference. *Psychological Science*, *21*, 1220–1224.

Topolinski, S. (2011). A process model of intuition. *European Review of Social Psychology*, *22*, 274–315.

Topolinski, S. (2012). The sensorimotor contributions to implicit memory, familiarity, and recollection. *Journal of Experimental Psychology: General*, *141*, 260–281.

Topolinski, S. & Deutsch, R. (2012). Phasic affective modulation of creativity. *Experimental Psychology*, *59*, 302–310.

Topolinski, S. & Deutsch, R. (in press). Phasic affective modulation of semantic priming. *Journal of Experimental Psychology: Learning, Memory, and Cognition.*

Topolinski, S., Likowski, K. U., Weyers, P., & Strack, F. (2009). The face of fluency: Semantic coherence automatically elicits a specific pattern of facial muscle reactions. *Cognition and Emotion*, *23*, 260–271.

Topolinski, S., & Reber, R. (2010a). Gaining insight into the "Aha"-experience. *Current Directions in Psychological Science*, *19*, 402–405.

—— (2010b). Immediate truth – Temporal contiguity between a cognitive problem and its solution determines experienced veracity of the solution. *Cognition*, *114*, 117–122.

—— (2008). Where there's a will - there's no intuition: The unintentional basis of semantic coherence judgments. *Journal of Memory and Language*, *58*, 1032–1048.

—— (2009a). Motormouth: Mere exposure depends on stimulus-specific motor simulations. *Journal of Experimental Psychology: Learning, Memory, and Cognition*, *35*, 423–33.

—— (2009b). Scanning the "fringe" of consciousness: What is felt and what is not felt in intuitions about semantic coherence. *Consciousness and Cognition*, *18*, 608–618.

—— (2009c). The analysis of intuition: Processing fluency and affect in judgements of semantic coherence. *Cognition and Emotion*, *23*, 1465–1503.

—— (2009d). The architecture of intuition: Fluency and affect determine intuitive judgments of semantic and visual coherence, and of grammaticality in artificial grammar learning. *Journal of Experimental Psychology: General*, *138*, 39–63.

Topolinski, S. & Strack, F. (2010). False fame prevented - avoiding fluency-effects without judgmental correction. *Journal of Personality and Social Psychology*, *98*, 721–733.

Unkelbach, C. (2006). The learned interpretation of cognitive fluency. *Psychological Science*, *17*, 339–345.

—— (2007). Reversing the truth effect: Learning the interpretation of processing fluency in judgments of truth. *Journal of Experimental Psychology: Learning, Memory and Cognition*, *33*, 219–230.

Unkelbach, C., & Stahl, C. (2009). A multinomial modeling approach to dissociate different components of the truth effect. *Consciousness & Cognition*, *18*, 22–38.

Van den Bergh, O., Vrana, S., & Eelen, P. (1990). Letters from the heart: Affective categorization of letter combinations in typists and nontypists. *Journal of Experimental Psychology: Learning, Memory, and Cognition*, *16*, 1153–1161.

Wilson, M. (2002). Six views of embodied cognition. *Psychonomic Bulletin and Review*, *9 (4)*, 625–636.

Wilson, T. D., & Brekke, N. (1994). Mental contamination and mental correction: Unwanted influences on judgments and evaluations. *Psychological Bulletin*, *116*, 117–142.

Winkielman, P., & Cacioppo, J. T. (2001). Mind at ease puts a smile on the face: Psychophysiological evidence that processing facilitation leads to positive affect. *Journal of Personality and Social Psychology*, *81*, 989–1000.

Zajonc, R. B. (1968). Attitudinal effects of mere exposure. *Journal of Personality and Social Psychology Monographs*, *9 (2, Pt. 2)*, 1–2.

4 Once more with feeling!

Familiarity and positivity as integral consequences of previous exposure

Teresa Garcia-Marques,
Diane M. Mackie, Heather M. Claypool
and Leonel Garcia-Marques

Abstract

We argue that processing a previously-encountered stimulus is an experience that inextricably entwines feelings of familiarity and of positivity. Assuming that such experiences have important consequences for processing itself, we also argue that such feelings function to modulate or regulate processing. After defining what we mean by familiarity, we review evidence relevant to these claims from our own and others' research programs. These data suggest that not only do familiar stimuli seem more positive or preferable, but also that preference or positivity makes stimuli seem more familiar. The studies reviewed also indicate that when we process once more with feeling, this feeling prompts non-analytic, heuristic processing. We close with some speculation about the implications of our perspective. Since psychologists typically think of familiarity as about what we know, and positivity as about how we feel, one implication of our argument is that such dichotomous conceptualizations warrant reconsideration.

Imagine a world in which everything happens once and never again. A single day, a single sunset, a single serving of pie, a single kiss. The most far-reaching consequence of such a world would be that almost no learning could ever occur, and thus almost no knowledge could ever be acquired. In some basic sense, then, repetition is the stuff of which cognition is made. To write a chapter about the effects of prior exposure, therefore, would seem an impossible task, as it would need to deal with all of human cognition. Our goals in this chapter are, however, more modest. We intend to focus on the nature of the feelings that accompany repeated exposure to items or episodes, and on the effects those feelings have on cognitive processing.

In light of the data we have collected, we will argue that processing a previously-encountered stimulus is an experience that inextricably entwines feelings of familiarity and positivity. Familiarity is positive, and thus positivity seems familiar. We thus expect not only that the experience of re-exposure will make stimuli feel more positive or preferable, but that the experience of preference or positivity (even if arising from other sources) will also make stimuli seem more familiar.

After defining more closely what we mean by familiarity, we review evidence from our own and others' research programs that offer support for each of these claims. Assuming that such experiences will have important consequences for processing itself, we also argue that the feelings that arise when stimuli are repeated will function to modulate or regulate processing, and review evidence from our laboratories relevant to this claim. We close with some speculation about the implications and consequences of our perspective. Since psychologists typically think of familiarity as about what we know, and positivity as about how we feel, one implication of our argument is that we should perhaps reconsider such dichotomous conceptualizations.

What is familiarity?

It is well established that when people re-encounter a given item or episode, they often *feel*, even if they do not *know*, that they have come across the item or episode before. Thus repeated exposure is a source of familiarity feelings. It is also abundantly clear that items felt to be familiar are processed very differently from items that are not felt as familiar (e.g., Bruce, 1979; Jacoby, 1983; Shull, Hupp, & Haaf, 2002). But what is only starting to be clear now is the nature of the feeling that accompanies re-exposure as well as its specific role in the differential processing of repeated material.

Much of what we know about the feeling that accompanies the processing of a previously encountered stimulus comes from the investigation of the feeling of "fluency" (Whittlesea & Leboe, 2000). Processes that run quickly and smoothly feel fluent. So people feel perception to be fluent when they perceive the incoming stimulus easily (see Reber, Fazendeiro, & Winkielman, 2002). They feel retrieval to be fluent when information stored in memory comes quickly to consciousness (e.g., Jacoby, 1983). They feel decision making to be fluent when a decision seems to "pop out" directly in response to relevant goals (e.g., Reder & Ritter, 1992), and so forth. Reber, Wurtz, and Zimmerman (2004) showed that objective sources of fluency, such as speed, resource demands, and accuracy of mental processes, all of which may differ at different stages of general processing, promote a unified subjective experience of fluency. The feeling of fluency thus seems to index all the subprocesses that operate above and below the threshold of consciousness when people process stimuli fluently (Greifeneder, Bless, & Pham, 2011). The feeling of fluency can thus be thought of as a subjective cognitive experience whose diffuse quality makes it vulnerable to attribution and interpretation (Bornstein & D'Agostino, 1994).

The experience of fluency in processing can occur for many reasons (as is attested to in other chapters in this book; see also Alter & Oppenheimer, 2009). One of the experiences that, by necessity, incorporates the experience of fluency is re-exposure to a stimulus. A first encounter with a novel object triggers relatively effortful processing. Because people have no pre-existing mental representation, they must extract all the object's features and create a new representation of it. In all subsequent encounters, perceiving the object activates the now existing representation, and all its relevant features become accessible. Thus, the processing of a previously seen object is both faster and easier—more fluent (see Herzog & Hertwig, this volume; Greifeneder, Bless, & Scholl, Chapter 13, this volume). Such fluency can contribute to the feeling or sense of memory that something has been encountered previously (see Jacoby, 1991). But we do not think of familiarity as either this feeling of fluency or as an objective and conscious reference to memory. Instead, we see familiarity as a subjective sense that something has been encountered before and also argue that that "sense" is positive. Now, *once more*, the processor faces the stimulus, but this time *with a feeling*. It is that positive feeling of previous exposure that we call familiarity. In many cases, familiarity indicates true learning, knowledge, or cognitive competence. But it can also spring from minimal previous exposure and from fluency inductions that are not based in stimulus exposure. Our concern in this chapter is the feeling of familiarity that arises merely from previous exposure to stimuli. That is, we focus predominantly on cases in which previous exposure to the repeated item or episode are non-informative because they were brief or subliminal (e.g., Jacoby & Whitehouse, 1989) or carried task irrelevant information (e.g., Garcia-Marques & Mackie, 2007). Even in this case, we see familiarity as a feeling that can indicate more than just a sense that something has been encountered previously: familiarity is also an inherently positive experience that signals that a response is available. We further claim that familiarity is able to regulate processing.

Familiarity is positive

Of course we are not the first to contend that familiarity is positive. A long time ago, Titchener (1910) suggested that encountering a previously-presented stimulus was experienced with a warm glow. By now, the number of studies that can be cited in support is impressive.

We first offered support for our contention that familiarity feels positive by demonstrating that participants presented with a set of statements reported being happier if they had encountered them previously than if they had not (Garcia-Marques & Mackie, 2000). A conceptually-similar study developed by Monahan, Murphy, and Zajonc (2000) produced converging results. In their experiment participants reported being in a better mood if they had been subliminally exposed to five ideographs repeated five times than if they had been subliminally exposed to 25 uniquely different ideographs. In both these studies, then, repetition itself seemed to be experienced as a diffuse positive affective state. Further support for this assumption was offered by Harmon-Jones and Allen (2001) who found greater zygomatic (''smiling'') muscle-region activity for previously seen compared to novel photos and by Winkielman and Cacioppo (2001), who also showed that processing high-fluency stimuli (which repeated stimuli are) was associated with activation of the zygomaticus but had no effect on the corrugator (''frowning'') muscles. Other findings suggest the inherently positive affective nature of the familiarity signal that arises from the repeated stimulus. In one study from our lab, for example, repeated faces were judged to be happier than non-repeated faces (Claypool, Hugenberg, Housley, & Mackie, 2007). When considered together, this body of research clearly shows that the experience of processing familiar stimuli involves the characteristics of the experience of diffuse positive affect (see also Zárate, Sanders, & Garza, 2000).

The evidence that the experience of familiarity can trigger the same experiential quality as positive affect speaks directly to the long-running debate about the causes of the well-known and robust "mere exposure effect" (see Bornstein, 1989 for review; Zajonc, 1968). The mere-exposure effect occurs when previous exposure to a stimulus subsequently increases the *positivity, liking, interest value, attractiveness, appeal, pleasantness,* and *preference* of that stimulus. Zajonc (1968, 1980, 1984) advanced a possible explanation of the effect involving affective primacy: the hypothesis that the emotional valence of a stimulus is always accessed prior to and independently of any cognitive appraisal of the stimulus (see also Duckworth, Bargh, Garcia, & Chaiken, 2002; Murphy & Zajonc, 1993; Niedenthal, 1990). Such a mechanism would explain why people can discriminate previously-encountered from new stimuli affectively, even when they have very poor recognition of the same stimuli. This explanation was undermined, however, by the finding that people also made different judgments of repeated and novel stimuli on non-affective dimensions (brightness of color, for example) with equally poor recognition performance (Mandler, Nakamura, & Van Zandt, 1987).

A second and widely accepted account of the mere exposure effect is the misattribution hypothesis (Bornstein & D'Agostino, 1992). According to this view, previous exposure to a stimulus makes it more fluent and this fluency is experienced as a *non-affective* feeling of ease. This feeling of fluency can be attributed to *any* plausible characteristic of a stimulus, including liking. Like Mandler et al., (1987), then, Bornstein and D'Agostino attribute the mere exposure effect to non-specific activation, suggesting that the experience of perceptual fluency can and will be attributed to the most salient contextual features. Thus, for instance, if participants are asked to judge the brightness of a set of presented stimuli, previously-presented stimuli will be judged as brighter than new ones. But if participants are asked to judge the darkness of the stimuli, old stimuli will be judged to be darker (Mandler et al., 1987). When researchers ask how much perceivers like stimuli, the liking ratings of previously seen stimuli benefit from this non-specific activation just as any other judgment would.

Yet the data show clear limits on the "non-specificity" of whatever activation results from repeated exposure. Seamon, McKenna, and Binder (1998), Reber et al., (1998), and even Mandler's original studies (Mandler et al., 1987) demonstrate that whereas fluency reliably increases liking, it almost never increases disliking.[1] Our own research also argues against the non-specificity hypothesis (Claypool et al., 2007). In these studies, participants viewed familiar and novel faces, and then judged the faces as happy or angry. Whereas familiar faces were judged to be happier, they were also seen as *less* angry than their novel counterparts, a finding clearly inconsistent with the non-specific activation hypothesis.

Thus, the misattribution hypothesis would need to add to its theoretical assumptions one that directly relates fluency with the activation of a positive affective state.

Reber, Schwarz, and Winkielman (2004) do as much in proffering the *hedonic marking fluency hypothesis*, which states that fluency itself is "positively marked" and thus explains why people prefer easily processed (including familiar) stimuli. Their perspective, although somewhat similar to ours, is theoretically more similar to the feelings-as-information model (see Schwarz & Clore, 1996), suggesting as it does that positivity derives from the use of fluency as information. That is, processors infer their preferences from their feeling of fluency.

We don't see feelings of familiarity as informing processors about their preferences. In our view processors don't need to *infer* their preferences from their feeling of familiarity: the familiarity they are feeling *includes* their preferences. This is not at all to deny that from the processor's perspective, familiarity, fluency, and positivity are often both generally diffuse and without clearly identifiable causes. They are thus prone to misattributions (Bornstein & D'Agostino, 1994; Van den Bergh & Vrana, 1998; Winkielman, Halberstadt, Fazendeiro & Catty 2006; Winkielman, Schwarz, Fazendeiro, & Reber, 2003), just as many other feelings are (Clore, Gasper, & Garvin, 2001; Schachter & Singer, 1962). Our argument is not about whether or not familiarity is misattributed, but about what this feeling of familiarity is, and we see the evidence as consistent with it being inherently positive. Even Reber, Schwarz, & Winkielman (2004) conclude that it seems more likely that the affective reaction generated by processing familiar stimuli is itself responsible for increased liking. By assuming positivity to be inherent to familiarity we define positivity as one of familiarity's essential and integral features.

One challenge to our claim that familiarity feels positive might be found in research that suggests that the relation between familiarity and positive feeling is susceptible to learning and context effects. Although Unkelbach (2006) has demonstrated that learning can certainly influence whether familiarity is associated with positivity, the preponderance of research confirms the default relationship as one of close integrity (see also Phaf & Rotteveel, 2005). More recently, De Vries, Holland, Chenier, Starr, & Winkielman (2010) showed that the relation between judgments of familiarity and positivity can be moderated by concurrent mood states. In their studies, happiness seemed to eliminate not only the mere exposure effect but also the impact of repeated exposure on the positivity of EMG reactions. Although these data can be interpreted as challenging the idea that familiarity is inherently positive, other possibilities exist, as the authors themselves acknowledge. One possibility is that both the "memory" and the "positivity" aspects of familiarity need to be perceptible to have an impact. When positive affect is already high, the "warm glow" of familiarity may not be "felt." Presumably, there are also some contexts in which the "encountered it before" aspect of familiarity might be drowned out by other contextual signals. Such a view of familiarity has in fact been advanced by Whittlesea (1993; Whittlesea & Leboe, 2003), who has argued that only unexpected or inexplicable increments of familiarity (relative to a baseline) are felt, and that only felt familiarity affects subsequent judgment or processing. Finally, such results might also be explained by attributional processes; even if positivity is recognized, it may be attributed to the preexisting happy state and thus also fail to have its usual effects. Such possibilities suggest several empirical avenues that might be explored to further clarify the familiarity-positivity relation.

Positivity is familiar

Our claim is that re-encountering a stimulus is an experience that is inherently positive. If this is true, then not only can experiences of familiarity be expected to trigger positive feelings and judgments (as supported by the evidence just reviewed), but experiences of positivity can be expected to trigger feelings and judgments of familiarity. In other words, assuming as we do that positivity is intrinsic to the processing of repeated stimuli, the experience of positivity will also involve the experience of familiarity. Our labs and others have now produced considerable evidence that imbuing a stimulus with positivity increases the likelihood that that stimulus will also be judged as familiar.

In our initial studies examining this issue (Garcia-Marques, Mackie, Claypool, & Garcia-Marques, 2004), we first presented participants with a set of faces, some of which displayed happy and others neutral expressions. Later these faces were intermixed with a set of new faces (again some of which were smiling and some of which had neutral expressions). Participants judged whether each face was old (seen before) or new. Repeated faces were generally recognized (accurately) as old, and this did not vary based on the valence of the face. In contrast, novel faces were significantly more likely to be mistakenly judged as having been previously presented (i.e., as familiar) when they were smiling versus not. In a second study, novel and repeated words were preceded with subliminal primes that were either empty circles or circles containing happy faces. As in the study just described, repeated words were judged as old at equivalent rates across priming conditions. But new words subliminally primed with happy faces produced more false alarms than did neutrally-primed new words. Positivity seemed to also indicate familiarity.

In follow-up work (Housley, Claypool, Garcia-Marques, & Mackie, 2010), we showed that ingroup-designating pronouns ("we", "us"), which themselves are known to be perceived positively (Perdue, Dovidio, Gurtman, & Tyler, 1990), can trigger feelings of familiarity. In one experiment, participants first completed a filler task in which they named the capital cities of each US state. Later, they were shown several nonsense syllables ("SEH") and were told that some had been presented subliminally earlier during the capital-naming task. They were instructed to identify those that were old and those that were new. In actuality, none of the syllables had been previously presented. However, unbeknownst to the participant, immediately before each nonsense syllable was presented, it was subliminally primed with either an ingroup pronoun or a neutral (e.g., "it") pronoun. As expected, a greater number of the ingroup-primed syllables were identified as familiar, indicating that the association with positivity led to their being judged as familiar. A second study showed that nonsense syllables supraliminally primed with ingroup pronouns were rated as more familiar (than were neutrally-primed syllables) and that this effect was partially mediated by the positivity of those pronouns. Once again, making something feel positive also made it feel familiar.

Other studies have used other techniques to make some stimuli seem more positive than others, and have also consistently found that positive stimuli seem familiar. For example, in several correlational and experimental studies, Monin (2003) showed that faces perceived to be attractive were also judged to be more familiar. Phaf and Rotteveel (2005) made stimuli seem more positive or negative by making participants "feel" positive or negative while processing them. Participants were asked to contract their zygomaticus muscles (to induce positive affect), their corrugator muscles (to induce negative affect), or to manipulate a pen in their non-dominant hand (control condition) while making old/new judgments of neutral words. Participants who were "happy" while processing the words were most likely to falsely judge them as old.

Perhaps the most compelling evidence for the integral nature of familiarity and positivity comes from examining latencies to judgments about each of these concepts (Garcia-Marques, Mackie, Claypool, & Garcia-Marques, 2010). In an adaptation of the implicit association test, participants had to decide if words appearing in lowercase were positive or negative intermixed with deciding whether city names appearing in all capital letters had been previously presented or not. Results showed that when the concepts of familiarity and positivity shared the same response key, reaction times were faster than when familiarity was paired with negativity. Such results indicate a close association between familiarity and positivity. In a second experiment, participants had to decide which of two simultaneously-presented, side-by-side symbols was "old" and which was "new." The actual old symbol was subliminally preceded by a smiley face or a neutral circle across trials. Participants correctly responded that a symbol was old more quickly when it was primed by a happy face than when it was primed by a neutral circle. The activation of positivity facilitated judgments of familiarity and vice versa, exactly the result one would expect if familiarity is inherently positive.

Although the converging evidence for the finding that positivity triggers familiarity is compelling, no evidence pinpoints the precise mechanism that explains it. We have, however, provided some evidence that the effect depends crucially on positivity being assumed to be diagnostic of familiarity (as would be the case if familiarity and positivity were integral). In their classic work, Schwarz and Clore (1983) showed that individuals used affective states to guide judgments of life satisfaction, unless the real source of their mood was made salient. When people realized that their mood might reflect the weather, it no longer seemed a valid basis for judging life satisfaction (for a review of replications of these effects, see Clore, 1992; Schwarz, 2004). In the same way, we reasoned that whereas positivity might typically be diagnostic of familiarity (because they are inherently associated), making an alternative source of the positivity salient would direct perceivers away from making the plausible judgments of familiarity that they would typically make.

To provide evidence for this supposition, we (Claypool, Hall, Mackie, & Garcia-Marques, 2008) had participants read a positively- or neutrally-valenced story and answer questions about its content. Those in the source-salient condition were also asked how they felt at that moment, and we reasoned that both their mood and its true source (the valenced story) should be obvious for those required to answer this question. All participants were then falsely led to believe that during an earlier unrelated part of the experiment, they had been exposed to subliminally presented faces. We then showed them several faces and asked them to identify which were old and which were new (in reality, of course, all were novel). If the source of their mood had not been made salient, participants showed the typical effect: those who read the positive story labeled more faces as old than those who read the neutral story. When participants were led to think about the source of their good mood, this effect disappeared (Claypool et al., 2008). Just because perceivers typically or by default assume familiarity when they experience positivity does not mean, of course, that familiarity and positivity are inherent. But if they are inherent, perceivers should assume one from the other, unless given some reason not to, as our experiment demonstrates. Although not conclusive about the mechanism underlying the positivity-cues-familiarly effect, we argue once again that the most parsimonious explanation of all the findings reviewed here is that positivity is intrinsic to familiarity. This feature of familiarity is, in our view, what allows positivity generated by many other sources and in many other ways to nevertheless increase perceptions of familiarity.

Familiarity as a regulator of processing

We argue that the experience of re-encountering an already-processed stimulus encompasses feelings of both memory (in the sense of repetition) and positivity. Just as the feeling of having "learned" about the stimulus before includes positivity, we have also shown that positivity includes this feeling of repetition, that we "have a memory of" the stimulus. Assuming this close association led us to make one further set of predictions. If the feeling of familiarity signals that we are processing a stimulus about which learning has already occurred, we might sensibly predict that a functional cognitive system would use such a signal to regulate further information processing. Specifically, encountering a previously presented stimulus should favor reliance on already established knowledge structures, and thus privilege superficial, heuristic, or non-analytic modes of processing over the resource intensive processing typically needed to parse novel information. Further, if familiarity is truly imbued with positivity, as we have argued, then it could also affect processing in the same way, reducing analytic processing over all. In fact, of course, the literature reveals just such findings: induced in any number of ways, positive mood typically does reduce systematic and increase more superficial processing (Bless, Clore, Schwarz, Golisano, Rabe, & Wolk, 1996; Worth & Mackie, 1987). But what effect does familiarity have on processing?

We first tested our contention that familiarity reduces extensive processing in the persuasion domain, where paradigms developed to assess whether extensive or superficial processing occurs are so well established (Chaiken, 1980, 1987; Petty & Cacioppo, 1986). In our first demonstration (Garcia-Marques & Mackie, 2000), we simply exposed different participants to a message with either strong or weak content either once or four different times. Individuals exposed to the message only once were more persuaded when the message comprised strong arguments than when it had weak content, indicating that they had systematically processed the messages. In contrast, and as our model predicts, the individuals familiar with the message because they had seen it several times failed to show differential attitude change to messages with strong and weak content, suggesting non-analytic processing of content. A second study confirmed these results, while manipulating repetition in a more subtle way. Some participants faced with written strong or weak versions of a persuasive appeal had been exposed to an audio version of the same message earlier in the experiment as background noise, whereas others saw the messages for the first time. Once again, whereas those unfamiliar with the message found the strong message content more persuasive than the weak, individuals reading a familiar message showed no attitudinal differentiation between strong and weak versions of the persuasive message (see also Alter, Oppenheimer, Epley, & Eyre, 2007, Experiment 2).

Having established that message familiarity was associated with a more superficial, non-analytic mode of persuasive processing, we attempted in consequent experiments to establish the conditions under which and the processes by which this effect occurred. In two subsequent experiments (Claypool, Mackie, Garcia-Marques, McIntosh, & Udall, 2004), we manipulated the personal relevance of the persuasive message participants received, as well as the number of times participants were exposed to the appeal and the strength and weakness of the appeal's content. Regardless of message topic, operationalization of relevance, and number of repetitions, familiarity with message content decreased analytic processing of the messages under conditions of low relevance, and perceived familiarity with the message mediated this reduction. Only when personal relevance was increased did familiarity not reduce processing. Thus these experiments established that repetition reduced content processing, that perceived familiarity appeared to mediate the effect and that personal relevance appeared to moderate the effect.

To further investigate these underlying relations, we (Moons, Mackie, & Garcia-Marques, 2009) combined a typical persuasion paradigm with a process dissociation procedure that allowed us to look more closely at the relative influence on persuasion of familiarity signals produced by message repetition and argument quality signals produced by content processing. In three new experiments, we first manipulated personal relevance, making the issue of institutionalization of comprehensive exams as a graduation requirement personally relevant to half our participants and low in relevance to the rest. We then presented participants with 60 different strong, weak, and filler neutral arguments (20 of each) supporting comprehensive exams and asked them to indicate their agreement with each item. Participants had already seen half of the weak and half of the strong arguments earlier in the experimental session. Use of the process dissociation method revealed that repetition-induced familiarity automatically (without processing) increased the acceptance of strong and weak arguments regardless of motivation condition. When motivation was high, however, controlled processing also contributed to persuasion. In the case of strong arguments, the effects of familiarity and content processing both contributed to their greater acceptance. In the case of weak arguments, however, greater controlled processing dissipated the benefits of familiarity for agreement. These results thus revealed the processes underlying our repeatedly demonstrated effect of repetition on persuasion: familiarity is associated with reduced processing of and automatic persuasive benefits to repeated messages, benefits that are enhanced by motivation induced processing of strong arguments, but undermined by motivation induced processing of weak arguments.

Although the established use of strong and weak argument quality to assess processing depth makes the attitude domain a natural one in which to test the idea that familiarity reduces processing, it is certainly not the only and perhaps not even the most impactful domain in which such effects might occur. Social psychologists have long known, for example, that either resource intensive processing of individuating information or more resource independent group membership judgments can contribute to our overall impressions of individuals. By our reasoning that familiarity reduces processing, we would predict that the individual characteristics of targets made familiar in some way would contribute less to perceptions of them than would those same characteristics about unfamiliar targets. We (Garcia-Marques & Mackie, 2007) investigated just that idea in two studies in which participants read either incriminating or exculpatory individuating information about a defendant in a criminal case before making judgments of guilt. We expected in both cases that familiarity would trigger non-analytic processing, reducing the impact of individuating information and increasing the impact of category level information on perceptions of the suspect. Results bore out these predictions. In the first study, participants were subliminally exposed to the defendant's photo, another matched photo, or no photo at all before being presented with individuating evidence. Those familiar with the defendant's photo both processed and used the individuating information less. In a second study, some participants were subtly made familiar with the incriminating and exculpatory information itself, whereas others were not. In addition, the defendant was described either as a priest or as a skinhead, category memberships with clear evaluative implications in our participants' minds for guilt or innocence. Familiarity with the information reduced attention to its content and also tended to increase reliance on category information in guilt judgments. Thus we were able to provide two kinds of evidence supporting our hypothesis. First, making the target generally familiar reduced intensive processing of individuating behavior and increased reliance on category level judgments. Second, making the individuating information familiar reduced perceivers' processing of it, undermining its opportunity to contribute to impressions of the target.

Perhaps the most dramatic example of possible social consequences of familiarity's tendency to reduce processing comes from an application of our ideas to stereotyping. When it comes to perceiving members of groups, impressions can also be based on inferences about group membership characteristics, or more extensively processed individuating information. In this domain, the idea that familiarity reduces processing leads to a startlingly counter-intuitive idea: that familiar group members will be stereotyped *more* than unfamiliar ones. Smith, Miller, Maitner, Crump, Garcia-Marques, and Mackie (2006) showed in two experiments that repeated exposure to information about a target person reduced individuation and increased stereotyping of the target person based on social group memberships. Various manipulations were able to show that the effects was not due to mere exposure, nor to greater perceived social judgability (Yzerbyt, Dardenne, & Leyens, 1998), but rather reflected the use of feelings of familiarity as a regulator of processing mode, such that familiar targets apparently received less systematic or analytic processing. So although we typically expect that familiarity with another will increase detailed personal knowledge, familiarity alone can ironically undermine the collection of just such information, leaving us more vulnerable to stereotyping effects.

Conclusions

We have argued that the experience of re-encountering an already processed stimulus, the feeling we call familiarity, encompasses feelings of both memory (in the sense of repetition) and positivity. Just as the experience of having "learned" about the stimulus before includes positivity, we have also shown that positivity includes this feeling of repetition, that we "have a memory of" the stimulus. As we have seen, this association is so inherent that processors can sometimes be led astray, judging preference where there is only repetition, and repetition where there is only preference. And as we have also shown, perhaps because of their inherent association, both familiarity and positivity have the same regulatory effect on processing: both make superficial, heuristic, non-analytic processing more likely. Indeed we speculate that these interconnections reflect why familiarity involves both the experience of memory and a feeling of positivity: familiarity and positivity are signals that direct and regulate our interaction with the world. They tell us if we are dealing with the known or the unknown and, as an inherent aspect, whether that is good or bad and thus whether resources are to be invested or directed elsewhere.

Although we see the preponderance of the evidence as supporting these ideas, there are of course a number of important issues that demand more research attention. We have argued that familiarity in and of itself is positive, and that is why familiarity affects liking judgments. It might be argued that the impact of familiarity on positivity judgments, or even the apparent positivity of familiarity, is mediated by fluency of processing (see Klinger & Greenwald, 1994; Seamon, Brody, & Kauff, 1983). After all, manipulations that enhance the perceptual fluency of a particular stimulus (in ways other than by previous exposure) enhance liking for the stimulus (Manza, Zizak, & Reber, 1998; Reber, Schwarz, & Winkielman, 2004; Reber, Winkielman, & Schwarz, 1998; Rhodes, Halberstadt, & Brajkovich, 2001), leading some to suggest that fluency also is inherently positive (Winkielman & Cacioppo, 2001). If so, it could be that what we have argued to be the inherent positivity of familiarity (and thus its effect on downstream evaluative judgments) is in fact due to other processes. These possibilities appear in Figure 4.1 below. First, as reported above, exposure to a repeated stimulus triggers a match in memory and also an easy, fluent feeling. Data reviewed before suggests both of these (feelings of familiarity and feelings of fluency) may be inherently positive, and so the impact of a repeated stimulus on liking could be contributed to by both the inherent positivity of familiarity and the inherent positivity of fluency. This hypothesis is defined in Panel 1. The second possibility, pictured in Panel 2, is more parsimonious, theoretically important and challenging to our view. It assumes that the apparent influence of familiarity on liking is mediated by the positivity of fluency—only because repeated exposure triggers fluency (and its associated positivity) does repeated exposure increase liking. In this chapter we contrast this view with the competing hypothesis presented in Panel 3—that the apparent impact of fluency manipulations on liking may be mediated by a misattribution to familiarity (and its associated positivity). That is, manipulations of stimulus characteristics that increase perceptual fluency increase liking only because that fluency is mistaken for a match in memory and its associated positivity. This hypothesis is rendered viable by the fact that manipulations of fluency focus on enhancing accessibility and/or making perceptual details stronger or more distinctive and these are precisely the characteristics of memory traces that reflect true memories (Johnson, Foley, Suengas & Raye, 1988; Johnson Hashtroudi, Lindsay, 1993; Mather, Henkel & Johnson, 1997). This experience is so intrinsic to memory activation and so prevalent that, by default, any experience of ease that arises from processing specific features of the stimulus may be attributed to memory. It could be then that the demonstrated impact of fluency manipulations on liking judgments produce effects only because they simulate the characteristics of memory traces generated by repeated exposure; thus fluency effects on liking (or the apparent inherent positivity of fluency) could be mediated by familiarity. Because fluency and familiarity are both integral to processing of previously-encountered stimuli, however, it is very hard to empirically discriminate between the hypothesis that the effect of repeated exposure on liking is mediated by the positivity of fluent processing from the alternative hypothesis that the effect of fluency on liking is mediated by the positivity of familiarity.

Nevertheless these possibilities suggest many avenues for integration with previous research and development of future research. First, the third possibility just outlined links nicely with the work of Jacoby and colleagues (see, for example, Jacoby & Brooks, 1984; Jacoby & Dallas, 1981; Jacoby & Whitehouse,1989; Whittlesea, Jacoby, & Girard, 1990) showing that manipulations of perceptual fluency (stimulus features that ease processing) increase familiarity judgments. Further, this should not happen if we block any possible misattribution to familiarity, for example, by making the true source of the processing ease clear.

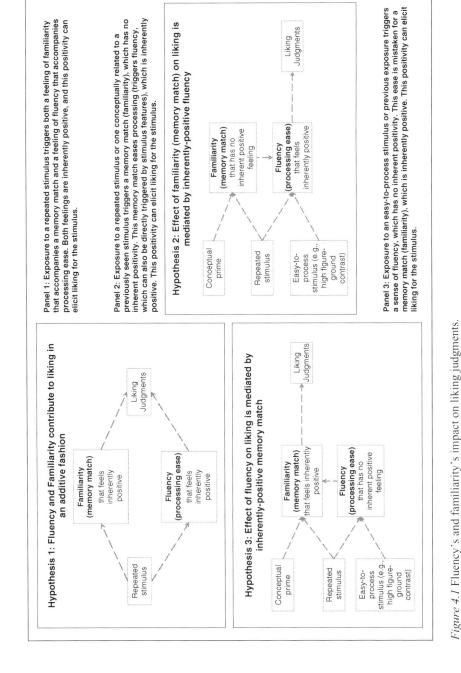

Figure 4.1 Fluency's and familiarity's impact on liking judgments.

Second, convincingly disentangling our second and third possibilities demands the creation of new paradigms. Manipulations of fluency that do not involve repeated exposure are well established in the literature. But tests of the second possibility require the development of similar manipulations for familiarity or memory match. One possibility is the use of conceptual fluency manipulations— stimuli that create a match in memory without physically mapping on to the memory trace. Conceptual fluency can be manipulated in different ways (see, for example, Fazendeiro, Winkielman, Luo & Lorah, 2005). One possibility is to promote repetition across language. Participant may be exposed to the same word repeatedly, and tested in a different language (e.g., "casa" followed by "house") or exposed to the same word repeatedly, but each time in a different language. Semantic priming effects have been shown to occur across languages (e.g. Smith, 1991), suggesting that memory match effects may be distinguished from perceptual fluency mechanisms. Another possibility is to repeatedly present stimuli but to manipulate how they are encoded on each exposure (the same physical stimulus differently encoded does not necessarily match a memory trace). Conceptual fluency manipulations have been achieved through cross-modal stimulus presentations (a photo of a kitten followed by the word kitten, for example). Results have suggested that those manipulations generate as much or more influence than do manipulations of perceptual fluency on liking (Whittlesea, 1993; see also Winkielman et al, 2003) and on recognition (Fazendeiro et al, 2005). Conceptual fluency manipulations were also shown to increase liking for arguments and products (see Day & Gentner, 2006, in Alter & Oppenheimer, 2009).

Third, both possibilities 2 and 3 are made viable by the apparent ease with which the positive feelings associated with either fluency or familiarity can be attributed or misattributed to other stimuli in the environment, a process which need not even be conscious (Oppenheimer, 2004, refers to a similar idea with the notion of *spontaneous discounting)*. Nevertheless, it seems to us that under certain circumstances processors might be sensitive to the presence of cues that make clear the source of a feeling (as suggested by Topolinski & Strack, 2010). Consistent with the idea that people can be sensitive to different sources of ease of processing, we have preliminary data that manipulations of perceptual features (typically referred to as perceptual fluency) can be experientially dissociated from manipulations of conceptual fluency (which implies memory activation). For example, enhanced recognition shown through a higher hit rate and a lower false alarm rate (mirror effect) typically found with familiar versus non-familiar stimuli (e.g. Joordens & Hockley, 2000), seems not to be replicated when percep-tual fluency alone is manipulated (Silva & Garcia-Marques, 2009). Such findings are consistent with previous research that seems to suggest that conceptual fluency is more tightly associated with its sources and thus its effects are not so easily confounded compared to perceptual fluency (which seems to be more easily confounded with conceptual fluency e.g., Shapiro, 1999; Whittlesea, 1993). Thus there are some reasons to believe that our cognitive system can, under certain circumstances, disentangle the different sources of both feelings, familiarity and fluency. Obviously empirically disentangling the hypotheses that relate the variables represented in Figure 4.1 remains an important research agenda.

In addition to further investigating the link between familiarity and positivity, it is equally important to consider alternative accounts for the reverse relation— for why positivity cues feelings of familiarity. As noted earlier, we have viewed the positivity-cues-familiarity effect as further evidence that familiarity and positivity are inherently intertwined. However, recent work suggests that a mnemonic-based account of this association may also be viable, at least when the positivity arises directly from the to-be-remembered information. Verde, Stone, Hatch, and Schnall (2010) demonstrated that positive items have more inter-item similarity than do neutral items, and this quality contributes to positive items being labeled as repeated or familiar. Their work certainly suggests a possible complementary mechanism that may contribute to the positivity-cues-familiarity link, and underscores the need for additional research to further pinpoint the exact relation between positivity and familiarity. Their work also suggests that regardless of this exact relation, there may in any given situation be multiple mechanisms that contribute to findings that show increased familiarity in the presence of positivity and increased positivity with the experience of familiarity.

Other research programs that have delved more deeply into the impact of lack of familiarity are also relevant to our theoretical concerns. Alter and colleagues (2007), for example, have assumed that a lack of fluency increases perceived difficulty of the task and lowers participants' confidence in their judgmental accuracy, which in turn triggers deeper processing. This approach shares some commonalities with the social judgeability approach (Yzerbyt et al, 1998), which similarly argues that a sense that one is able to judge well decreases processing intensity. Like ours, both approaches highlight the integral role "feelings" that arise from processing can have on future processing. In many of our studies, we have demonstrated an impact of repetition or familiarity that obtains even when perceived judgeability is held constant (Garcia-Marques & Mackie, 2007; Smith et al., 2006), but we have not addressed perceived difficulty or confidence in our studies to date. And, confidence is closely associated with familiarity and ease of processing (Briñol, Petty, & Tormala, 2006; Tormala et al., 2011). It may yet be true that multiple feelings—judgeability, confidence, perceived ease of the task, among others—arise from the feeling that we have dealt with the stimulus before, the feeling that we term familiarity. The cause of these multiple subjective experiences, how they relate to one another, and their common or unique consequences all await more research focus.

In conclusion, our approach assumes that when something happens "once more," it happens "with feeling"— with the positive feeling of familiarity. This link between repeated exposure and positive feelings is well established in the literature and it represents a golden opportunity to study the intertwining of cognition and affect. We claim that familiarity is intrinsically positive and in that sense, memory and affect, cognition and feelings, are inescapably connected. If true, it may be time for a fundamental shift in the way we typically conceive of both. Instead of simply seeing affect as only moderating cognition, or cognition as only modulating affect, we may start to look at the causes and consequences of affective experience that is integral to cognitive processes and processing. By trying to avoid the traditional distinction between heart and mind, we may better understand the real nature of each.

Note

1 This is not to say that familiarity will always result in positive judgments. It is possible that its positivity, in some cases, only corroborates in a positive way what is made accessible in our memory (see also Briñol, Petty, & Tormala, 2006), and, as we will discuss below, liking judgments can be recalibrated by correction processes or other more analytic processing strategies.

References

Alter, A. L., & Oppenheimer, D. M. (2009). Uniting the tribes of fluency to from a meta-cognitive nation. *Personality and Social Psychology Review, 13*, 219–235.

Alter A. L., Oppenheimer D. M., Epley N., & Eyre R. N. (2007). Overcoming intuition: Metacognitive difficulty activates analytic reasoning. *Journal of Experimental Psychology: General, 136*, 569–576.

Bless, H., Clore, G. L., Schwarz, N., Golisano, V., Rabe, C., & Wolk, M. (1996). Mood and the use of scripts: Does happy mood really lead to mindlessness? *Journal of Personality and Social Psychology, 71*, 665–679.

Bornstein, R. F. (1989). Exposure and affect: Overview and meta-analysis of research, 1968–1987. *Psychological Bulletin, 106*, 265–289.

Bornstein, R. F., & D'Agostino, P. R. (1992). Stimulus recognition and the mere exposure effect. *Journal of Personality and Social Psychology, 63*, 545–552.

—— (1994). The attribution and discounting of perceptual fluency: Preliminary tests of a perceptual fluency/attributional model of the mere exposure effect. *Social Cognition, 12*, 103–128.

Briñol, P., Petty, R. E., & Tormala, Z. L. (2006). The malleable meaning of subjective ease. *Psychological Science, 17*, 200–206.

Bruce V., (1979). Searching for politicians: An information-processing approach to face recognition. *Quarterly Journal of Experimental Psychology, 31*, 373–395.

Chaiken, S. (1980). Heuristic versus systematic information processing and the use of source versus message cues in persuasion. *Journal of Personality and Social. Psychology, 39*, 752–766.

—— (1987). The heuristic model of persuasion. In M.P. Zanna, JM Olson, & C.P. Herman (Eds.), *Social influence: The Ontario Symposium*. (Vol. 5, pp. 3–39). Hillsdale, NJ: Erlbaum.

Claypool, H. M., Hall, C. E., Mackie, D. M., & Garcia-Marques, T. (2008). Positive mood, attribution, and the illusion of familiarity. *Journal of Experimental Social Psychology, 44*, 721–728.

Claypool, H. M., Hugenberg, K., Housley, M. K., & Mackie, D. M. (2007). Familiar eyes are smiling: On the role of familiarity in the perception of facial affect. *European Journal of Social Psychology, 37*, 856–866.

Claypool, H. M., Mackie, D. M., Garcia-Marques, T., McIntosh, A., & Udall, A. (2004). The effects of personal relevance and repetition on persuasive processing. *Social Cognition, 22*, 310–335.

Clore, G. L. (1992). Cognitive phenomenology: Feelings and the construction of judgment. In L. L. Martin & A. Tesser (Eds.), *The construction of social judgments.* (pp. 133–163). Hillsdale, N.J.: Erlbaum.

Clore, G. L., Gasper, K., & Garvin, E. (2001). Affect as information. In J. P. Forgas (Ed.) *Handbook of Affect and Social Cognition.* (pp. 121–144). Mahwah, NJ: Erlbaum.

De Vries, M., Holland, R.W., Chenier, T., Starr, M.J., & Winkielman, P. (2010). Happiness cools the warm glow of familiarity: Psychophysiological evidence that mood modulates the familiarity-affect link. *Psychological Science, 21,* 321–328.

Duckworth, K. L., Bargh, J. A., Garcia, M., & Chaiken, S. (2002). The automatic evolution of novel stimuli. *Psychological Science, 13,* 513–519.

Fazendeiro, T., Winkielman, P., Luo, C., & Lorah, C. (2005). False recognition across meaning, language, and stimulus format: Conceptual relatedness and the feeling of familiarity. *Memory and Cognition, 33,* 249–260.

Garcia-Marques, T., & Mackie, D. M. (2000). The positive feeling of familiarity: Mood as an information processing regulation mechanism. In H. Bless and J. P. Forgas (Eds.) *The message within – the role of subjective experience in social cognition and behavior.* (pp. 240–261). USA: Psychology Press.

—— (2007). Familiarity impacts person perception. *European Journal of Social Psychology, 37,* 839–855.

Garcia-Marques, T., Mackie, D.M., Claypool, H., & Garcia-Marques, L. (2004). Positivity can cue familiarity. *Personality and Social Psychology Bulletin, 30,* 585–593.

—— (2010). Is it familiar or positive? Mutual facilitation of response latencies. *Social Cognition, 28,* 205–218.

Greifeneder, R., Bless, H., & Pham, M. T. (2011). When do people rely on affective and cognitive feelings in judgment? A review. *Personality and Social Psychology Review, 15,* 107–141.

Harmon-Jones, E., & Allen, J. B. (2001). The role of affect in the mere exposure effect: Evidence from psychophysiological and individual differences approaches. *Personality and Social Psychology Bulletin, 27,* 889–898.

Housley, M. K., Claypool, H. M., Garcia-Marques, T., & Mackie, D. M. (2010). "We" are familiar but "it" is not: Ingroup pronouns trigger feelings of familiarity. *Journal of Experimental Social Psychology, 46,* 114–119.

Jacoby, L.L. (1983). Perceptual enhancement: Persistent effects of an experience. *Journal of Experimental Psychology: Learning, Memory, and Cognition, 9,* 21–38.

—— (1991). A process dissociation framework: Separating automatic from intentional uses of memory. *Journal of Memory and Language, 30,* 513–541.

Jacoby, L. L., & Brooks, L. R. (1984). Nonanalytic cognition: Memory, perception and concept learning. In G. H. Bower (ed.) The psychology of learning and motivation: Advances in research and theory. (Vol. 18, pp. 1–47). New York: Academic Press.

Jacoby, L. L., & Dallas, M. (1981). On the relationship between autobiographical memory and perceptual learning. *Journal of Experimental Psychology: General, 3,* 306–340.

Jacoby, L. L., Kelley, C. M., & Dywan, J. (1989). Memory attributions. In H. L. Roediger and F. I. M. Craik (Eds.), *Varieties of memory and consciousness.* (pp. 391–422). Hillsdale, NJ: Erlbaum.

Jacoby, L. L., & Whitehouse, K. (1989). An illusion of memory: False recognition influenced by unconscious perception. *Journal of Experimental Psychology: General, 118,* 126–135.

Johnson, M. K., Foley, M. A., Suengas, A. G., & Raye, C. L. (1988). Phenomenal characteristics of memories for perceived and imagined autobiographical events. *Journal of Experimental Psychology: General, 117*, 371–376.

Johnson, M. K., Hashtroudi, S., & Lindsay, D. S. (1993). Source monitoring. *Psychological Bulletin, 114*, 3–28.

Joordens, S., & Hockley, W. E. (2000). Recollection and familiarity through the looking glass: When old does not mirror new. *Journal of Experimental Psychology: Learning, Memory, and Cognition, 26*, 1534–1555.

Mather, M., Henkel, L. A., & Johnson, M. K. (1997). Evaluating characteristics of false memories: Remember/know judgments and memory characteristics questionnaire compared. *Memory & Cognition, 25*, 826–837.

Klinger, M. R., & Greenwald, A. G. (1994). Preferences need no inferences?: The cognitive basis for unconscious emotional effects. In P.M. Niedenthal & S. Kitayama (Eds.), *The heart's eye: Emotional influences in perception and attention.* (pp. 67–85). Orlando, FL: Academic Press.

Mandler, G., Nakamura, Y., & Van Zandt, B. J. S. (1987). Nonspecific effects of exposure on stimuli that cannot be recognized. *Journal of Experimental Psychology: Learning, Memory, and Cognition, 13*, 646–648.

Manza, L., Zizak, D., & Reber, A. S. (1998). Artificial grammar learning and the mere exposure effect: Emotional preference tasks and the implicit learning process. In M. A. Stadler & P. A. Frensch (Eds.), *Handbook of implicit learning.* (pp. 201–222). Thousand Oaks, CA: Sage.

Monahan, J. L., Murphy, S. T., & Zajonc, R. B. (2000). Subliminal mere exposure: Specific, general, and diffuse effects. *Psychological Science, 11*, 462–466.

Monin, B. (2003). The warm glow heuristic: When liking leads to familiarity. *Journal of Personality and Social Psychology, 85*, 1035–1048.

Moons, W. G., Mackie, D. M., & Garcia-Marques, T. (2009). The impact of repetition-induced familiarity on agreement with weak and strong arguments. *Journal of Personality and Social Psychology, 96*, 32–44.

Murphy, S. T., & Zajonc, R. B. (1993). Affect, cognition, and awareness: Affective priming with optimal and suboptimal stimulus exposures. *Journal of Personality and Social Psychology, 64*, 723–739.

Niedenthal, P. M. (1990). Implicit perception of affective information. *Journal of Experimental Social Psychology, 26*, 505–527.

Oppenheimer, D. M. (2004). Spontaneous discounting of availability in frequency judgment tasks. *Psychological Science, 15*, 100–105.

Perdue, C. W., Dovidio, J. F., Gurtman, M. B., & Tyler, R. B. (1990). Us and them: Social categorization and the process of intergroup bias. *Journal of Personality and Social Psychology, 59*, 475–486.

Petty, R. E., & Cacioppo, J. T. (1986). *Communication and persuasion: Central and peripheral routes to attitude change.* New York: Springer-Verlag.

Phaf, R. H., & Rotteveel, M. (2005). Affective modulation of recognition bias. *Emotion, 5*, 309–318.

Reber, R., Fazendeiro, T.A., & Winkielman, P. (2002). Processing fluency as the source of experiences at the fringe of consciousness: Commentary on Mangan. URL: http://psyche.cs.monash.edu.au/v8/psyche-8-10-reber.html.

Reber, R., Schwarz, N., & Winkielman, P. (2004). Processing fluency and aesthetic pleasure: Is beauty in the perceiver's processing experience? *Personality and Social Psychology Review, 8*, 364–382.

Reber, R., Winkielman, P., & Schwarz, N. (1998). Effects of perceptual fluency on affective judgments. *Psychological Science*, *9*, 45–48.

Reber, R., Wurtz, P., & Zimmermann, T. D. (2004). Exploring "fringe" consciousness: The subjective experience of perceptual fluency and its objective bases. *Consciousness and Cognition*, *13*, 47–60.

Reder, L. M., & Ritter, F. E. (1992). What determines initial feeling of knowing? Familiarity with question terms, not the answer. *Journal of Experimental Psychology: Learning, Memory, and Cognition*, *18*, 435–451.

Rhodes, G., Halberstadt, J., & Brajkovich, G. (2001). Generalization of mere exposure effects in social stimuli. *Social Cognition*, *19*, 369–382.

Schachter, S., & Singer, J. E. (1962). Cognitive, social, and physiological determinants of emotional state. *Psychological Review*, *69*, 379–399.

Schwarz, N. (2004). Meta-cognitive experiences in consumer judgment and decision making. *Journal of Consumer Psychology*, *14*, 332–348.

Schwarz, N., & Clore, G. L. (1983). Mood, misattribution, and judgments of well-being: Informative and directive functions of affective states. *Journal of Personality and Social Psychology*, *45*, 513–523.

—— (1996). Feelings and phenomenal experience. In E. T. Higgins & A. W. Kruglanski (Eds.), *Social psychology: Handbook of basic principles.* (pp. 433–465). New York: Guilford.

Seamon, J.G., Brody, N., & Kauff, D.M. (1983). Affective discrimination of stimuli that are not recognized: Effects of shadowing, masking, and cerebral laterality. *Journal of Experimental Psychology: Learning, Memory, and Cognition*, *9*, 544–555.

Seamon, J.G., McKenna, P.A., & Binder, N. (1998). The mere exposure effect is differentially sensitive to different judgment tasks. *Consciousness and Cognition*, *7*, 85–102.

Shull, S. S., Hupp, J. M., & Haaf, R. A. (2002, May). The effect of familiarity on global local processing. Poster session presented at the annual meeting of the Midwestern Psychological Association, Chicago, IL.

Shapiro, S. (1999). When an ad's influence is beyond our conscious control: Perceptual and conceptual fluency effects caused by incidental exposure. *Journal of Consumer Research*, *26*, 16–36.

Silva, R., & Garcia-Marques, T. (2009). Mirror, mirror on the wall, tell me if what I feel is dissociated or not! Perceptual and conceptual fluency contributions to lexical decision and recognition memory tasks. Transfer of Knowledge Conference of the European Social Cognition Network 2. Warsaw, Poland.

Smith, M. C. (1991). On the recruitment of semantic information for word fragment completion: Evidence from bilingual priming. *Journal of Experimental Psychology: Learning, Memory and Cognition*, 17, 234–244.

Smith, E. R., Miller, D. A., Maitner, A. T., Crump, S. A., Garcia-Marques, T., & Mackie, D. M. (2006). Familiarity can increase stereotyping. *Journal of Experimental Social Psychology*, *42*, 471–478.

Titchener, E. B. (1910). The past decade in experimental psychology. *American Journal of Psychology*, *21*, 404–421.

Tormala, Z.L., Clarkson, J.J., & Henderson, M.D. (2011). Does fast or slow evaluation foster greater certainty? *Personality and Social Psychology Bulletin*, *37*, 422–434.

Topolinski, S., & Strack, F. (2010). False fame prevented: Avoiding fluency effects without judgmental correction. *Journal of Personality and Social Psychology*, *98*, 721–733.

Unkelbach, C. (2006). The learned interpretation of cognitive fluency. *Psychological Science*, *17*, 339–345.

Van den Bergh, O., & Vrana, S. R. (1998). Repetition and boredom in a perceptual fluency/attribution model. *Cognition and Emotion*, *12*, 533–553.

Verde, M. F., Stone, L. K., Hatch, H. S., & Schnall, S. (2010). Distinguishing between attributional and mnemonic sources of familiarity: The case of positive emotion bias. *Memory and Cognition*, *38*, 142–153.

Whittlesea, B. W. A. (1993). Illusions of familiarity. *Journal of Experimental Psychology: Learning, Memory, & Cognition*, *19*, 1235–1253.

Whittlesea, B. W. A., Jacoby, L. L., & Girard, K. A. (1990). Illusions of immediate memory: Evidence of an attributional basis for feelings of familiarity and perceptual quality. *Journal of Memory and Language*, *29*, 716–732.

Whittlesea, B.W.A., & Leboe, J.P. (2000). The heuristic basis of remembering and classification. *Journal of Experimental Psychology: General*, *129*, 84–106.

—— (2003). Two fluency heuristics (and how to tell them apart). T*he Journal of Memory and Language, 49*, 62–79.

Winkielman, P., & Cacioppo, J. T. (2001). Mind at ease puts a smile on the face: Psychophysiological evidence that processing facilitation elicits positive affect. *Journal of Personality and Social Psychology*, *81*, 989–1000.

Winkielman, P., Halberstadt, J., Fazendeiro, T., & Catty, S. (2006). Prototypes are attractive because they are easy on the mind. *Psychological Science*, *17*, 799–806.

Winkielman, P., Schwarz, N., Fazendeiro, T., & Reber, R. (2003). The hedonic marking of processing fluency: Implications for evaluative judgment. In J. Musch & K. C. Klauer (Eds.), *The psychology of evaluation: Affective processes in cognition and emotion.* (pp. 189–217). Mahwah, NJ: Erlbaum.

Worth, L. T., & Mackie, D. M. (1987). Cognitive mediation of positive mood in persuasion. *Social Cognition*, *5*, 76–94.

Yzerbyt, V. Y., Dardenne, B., & Leyens, J-Ph. (1998). Social judgeability concerns in impression formation. In V. Y. Yzerbyt, G. Lories, & B. Dardenne (Eds.), *Metacognition: Cognitive and social dimensions.* (pp. 126–156). Thousand Oaks, CA: Sage.

Zajonc, R.B. (1968). Attitudinal effects of mere exposure. *Journal of Personality and Social Psychology Monograph Supplement, 9 (2, Pt. 2)*, 1–27.

—— (1980). Feelings and thinking: Preferences need no inferences. *American Psychologist*, *35*, 151–175.

—— (1984). On the primacy of affect. *American Psychologist*, *39*, 124–129.

Zárate, M. A., Sanders, J. D., & Garza, A. (2000). Neurological disassociations of social perception processes. *Social Cognition*, *18*, 223–251.

5   Fluency in context

Discrepancy makes processing experiences informative

Jochim Hansen and Michaela Wänke

Abstract

This chapter summarizes studies that demonstrate that experiences of cognitive fluency inform social judgments and decisions particularly when the experiences are discrepant with the surrounding fluency context. Thereby, the context can be a prior expectation regarding the fluency of processing, or the actual situation in which cognitive processing happens. Evidence for the context principle is presented for both perceptual and memory-based processing fluency in diverse judgmental domains, such as attitudinal and moral judgments, truth estimations, familiarity judgments, and evaluations.

Signals are informative if they contrast with the background. In the context of a concreted city environment, for instance, a grey stop signal—although perceivable in principle—would not stand out as much as a red stop signal, which would have fatal consequences for car-drivers and pedestrians alike. The grey signal is pretty useless as informational cue because it lacks a strong contrast between background and foreground. Such a contrast, however, is necessary in order to allow individuals to extract the relevant information quickly and to apply it to judgments and behavior, such as to deciding whether to stop the car or not. As much as a perceptual pattern—such as a signal—is particularly informative when it stands out from the background, experiences of cognitive processing (that is, fluency) inform social judgments and decisions particularly when they contrast with the surrounding fluency context. In the following chapter, we summarize studies that support this general hypothesis. Thereby, we present evidence that the contrast principle holds for experiences of both perceptual and memory-based processing fluency in diverse judgmental domains, such as attitudinal and moral judgments, truth estimations, familiarity judgments, and evaluations.

That judgments and decisions in general are not absolute but are qualified by the surrounding context is indeed a very basic principle in psychology. In the domain of self-judgments, for instance, individuals often compare themselves with other people when they want to learn which qualities and traits they possess (e.g., Festinger, 1954). For example, individuals may perceive themselves as extraverted when other people, who are used as standard of comparison, behave rather introverted.[1] Research on life satisfaction and well-being also illustrates that the relative value of information matters more than the absolute value: Satisfaction judgments are often based on comparisons with a standard, such as past satisfaction (e.g., Strack, Schwarz, & Gschneidinger, 1985) or perceptions of other people's happiness (e.g., Hagerty, 2000), than on the objective quality of the situation.

In the perceptual domain, physical properties are frequently contrasted away from the surrounding (e.g., Helson, 1964). Moderately heavy weights appear heavier after lifting light weights than after lifting heavy weights. When cold hands are held in moderately warm water, the water appears hotter than when warm hands are held in the water. In all these examples, a discrepancy with the context has an effect on experiences and judgments. Even in experiencing humor and fun, the context is taken into account and is used as a piece of information that helps to interpret the information at hand (Wilson, Lisle, Kraft, & Wetzel, 1989). For instance, moderately funny movies are rated as less funny when people expect a funny movie and notice the discrepancy between this expectation and the actual humor in the movie (Geers & Lassiter, 1999).

What seems a prevalent principle in many areas of psychology does hold for fluency experiences of cognitive processing as well. That is, fluency experiences felt during information processing stand out and potentially inform judgments when they are discrepant with the surrounding context. The context, which is used as a standard of comparison, presents itself in one of two variants: It can be a prior *expectation* regarding the fluency of processing, and it can be the actual *situation* in which cognitive processing happens. When one expects that a task will be difficult but then it turns out to be very easy, or when a sentence can fluently be read in the context of other sentences that are rather difficult to read, these fluency experiences are especially likely to serve as a basis for judgments and decisions. As the research examples in this chapter show, people need not necessarily be aware of the influence of the context. Very subtle manipulations of the context can have large effects on the informational value of processing experiences. By contrasting fluency experiences with their context, they become potentially relevant for judgments, decisions, and behavior.

In the following, we discuss how the contrast principle affects the informative value of two types of fluency experiences, although it may apply for other types of fluency as well (see Alter & Oppenheimer, 2009, for a differentiation between different types of fluency). Both memory-based fluency (that is, the ease of retrieving or generating information) and perceptual fluency (that is, the ease of perceiving information) inform judgments at hand particularly when there is a discrepancy between the actual fluency and the surrounding contextual fluency.

Memory-based fluency in context

Individuals often base their judgments and decisions on the ease with which information is generated or retrieved from memory (for reviews see e.g., Schwarz, 1998; Schwarz, Bless, Wänke & Winkielman, 2003; Schwarz

& Vaughn, 2002; Wänke, Chapter 10, this volume). For instance, it has been demonstrated that the ease with which information about the self is retrieved has an influence on inferences about the self (Schwarz, Bless, Strack, Klumpp, Rittenauer-Schatka, & Simons, 1991). In one study participants were asked to retrieve either six or 12 instances of behaviors in which they had behaved very self-assertively (Schwarz et al., 1991). Retrieval of six instances was easy, whereas retrieval of 12 instances was difficult. After this manipulation, participants judged their own self-assertiveness. Although those participants who retrieved more behaviors had much more positive information about their self-assertiveness, they did not judge themselves as more assertive. In fact, the opposite was true. When only few instances of assertiveness were retrieved, participants rated themselves as more assertive than when many instances were retrieved. This was the case because it was easier to retrieve only six instances of assertive behaviors than 12. Participants thus used the ease as a basis for the inferences they draw about themselves. A comparable effect emerged when participants were asked to retrieve instances of unassertive behavior.

Besides self-assessments, this ease-of-retrieval effect has been shown in many domains. Ease of generating arguments in favor of or against a topic, for instance, has an effect on subsequent attitude judgments. When it is easy to retrieve arguments, which speak in favor of a topic, people favor the position more than when it is difficult (e.g., Greifeneder & Bless, 2007, 2008; Wänke, Bless, & Biller, 1996). When people believe that it is easy to retrieve positive product information, they prefer the respective brand to a competitor brand (Wänke, Bohner, & Jurkowitsch, 1997). When it is easy to retrieve own behaviors that increase health risks, people estimate the probability of suffering from the respective disease as higher (Raghubir & Menon, 1998, 2001; Rothman & Schwarz, 1998).

In all of these examples, ease is manipulated rather strongly by asking participants to generate either few or many pieces of information. In most cases, the number of requested pieces of information is much below (easy) and much above (difficult) the number that people can typically generate if no amount is specified. That is, level of ease in these experiments is usually manipulated as being discrepant with a default level—assuming that people generally expect a moderately difficult task in psychological experiments. Accordingly, it is very likely that participants experience some level of discrepancy between the actual ease and an expected standard. In order to test the hypothesis that a discrepancy between expected and actual ease of retrieval intensifies the use of retrieval ease in judgments, one has to vary not only the actual task requirement but the processing expectations as well. Ease (or difficulty) of retrieving information should inform judgments when the feeling occurs unexpectedly. The ease-of-retrieval effect should occur to a much lesser extent when the task requirement is as easy or difficult as expected.

It is important to note that such discrepancies may or may not involve explicit or conscious expectations, that is, the individual may not be aware of the standard in the retrieval situation. In fact, most expectations generally occur on a rather implicit level:

"Although we generate some expectancies consciously or explicitly (e.g., when we think about what someone may be like before meeting him or her), most expectancies are undoubtedly generated unconsciously or implicitly. For example, every step we take is based on the expectancy that the floor will not give way beneath us. The power of this expectancy is illustrated by the surprise (even shock) we experience when we suddenly lose our footing (as when we misjudge a step down). Yet, we obviously do not consciously generate the expectancy that our footing will be solid prior to each step we take."

(Olson, Roese, & Zanna, 1996, p. 212)

Similarly, we argue that it is the deviation from implicit expectations that makes fluency experiences particularly informative. Accordingly, it is not necessary that individuals actively generate such expectations or that they actively compare the fluency of different stimuli (e.g., thoughts) with each other. Rather, processing expectations can be regarded as processing "background" from which deviations stand out as "figures" and thus are possibly informative for diverse judgments, such as in the stop signal example. In other words, individuals are very sensitive to fluency changes. The processing background itself may vary across different situations and can therefore be manipulated.

Studies from our own lab and others' demonstrate the role of expectation of ease. In one study, an expectation of an easy or a difficult task was created prior to the retrieval of information (Hansen & Wänke, 2008, Experiment 3). Participants were told that that they will take part in a study on creativity. They were asked to solve five "creativity" tasks. With the first four tasks, processing expectations (that is, expectation of an easy versus difficult task) were manipulated. These tasks were designed and pre-tested to become increasingly easier or harder. So participants had the expectation that the following fifth task will be easy or difficult. The four tasks were the same in both conditions but only they were presented in reversed orders. The fifth task was the target task in which participants were asked to generate either two (easy) or eight (difficult) arguments, either in favor of or against the idea to allow political voting via the Internet. Then they rated their attitude towards Internet voting.

The results show that participants based their attitude judgments on the ease or difficulty of retrieval when these processing experiences were unexpected. Participants were more in favor of voting via the Internet when it was easy to generate pro arguments and difficult to generate con arguments. However, when the task requirement matched the prior expectations, participants did not use ease as basis for their judgments. Quite the contrary, they were more in favor of voting via the Internet when they generated more pro arguments although this was difficult. This finding supports the hypothesis that fluency informs judgments especially when it contrasts with the surrounding context, in this case with processing expectations. Additionally, a more direct measurement of how surprisingly easy (versus difficult) the processing fluency felt (that is, the difference between measures of actual and of expected ease) predicted the attitudes better than the actual ease of retrieval per se, which further supports the argument that discrepancy with an expectation augments the ease-of-retrieval effect.

A study by Wilcox and Song (2009) provides another illustration of the influence of discrepant memory-based fluency on judgments. In this study, the ease (versus difficulty) of a decision was manipulated, which can have a substantial impact on preferences (Novemsky, Dhar, Schwarz, & Simonson, 2007). In addition, ease was varied in a sequence of decisions, so that participants could use the level of ease of earlier decisions to form expectations for subsequent decisions. When the level of ease of subsequent decisions deviated from that of initial decisions, it created a discrepancy between actual and expected decision difficulty. Only in these cases preference judgments were based on decision difficulty (Wilcox & Song, 2009).

Another study went one step further and illustrated a comparable finding even when the context with which fluency experiences are contrasted was provided by a semantic prime and was not directly experienced as easy or difficult (Hansen & Wänke, 2008, Experiment 2). In that study participants worked on two separate tasks. In the first task, they were asked to evaluate to what degree 20 synonyms either of the word "easy" (e.g., *effortless*, *cushy*, *facile*) or of the word "difficult" (e.g., *awkward*, *complex*, *complicated*, *hard*) are similar to the word "easy" (or "difficult", respectively). This manipulation activated the concept "ease" versus "difficulty" and implicitly prepared participants for an easy versus difficult task. After this priming manipulation participants worked on a second, ostensibly unrelated task in which they generated either two (easy) or six (difficult) arguments against the implementation of international DNA databases. We then measured the attitude toward DNA databases. The hypothesis was that participants who worked on the difficult argument generation task would use the difficulty experience for their attitude judgments particularly if they had been primed with "ease." On the other hand, participants who worked on the easy argument generation task should use the experience particularly if they had been primed with "difficulty." And indeed, the findings showed that experienced ease (or difficulty) of retrieval informed attitude judgments only if the experience was discrepant with the primed context. This typical ease-of-retrieval effect did not occur when the prime was congruent to the actually experienced ease. Quite to the opposite, here participants who found *more* counter-arguments were more against the topic—although generation of arguments was difficult.

A further study on the influence of context-discrepant ease of retrieval on attitude judgments demonstrates that even the *experience* of ease or difficulty itself can be influenced by a context (Hansen & Wänke, 2008, Experiment 1). In this study, participants worked first on the same priming task as in the study reviewed previously. However, different from the former study, they were then asked to solve a moderately difficult argument generation task. That is, they were asked to generate four arguments either in favor of or against music in trams. So the actual task requirement was held objectively constant on a medium level of difficulty. Note that this setting is a mirror image of the design of standard ease-of-retrieval experiments. Whereas in previous studies actual task requirement was manipulated but the context was held constant, in this study the context was manipulated and the actual task requirement was held constant on a moderate level. The hypothesis was that participants who were primed with "ease" would experience the moderately difficult argument task as surprisingly difficult, and that participants who were primed with "difficulty" would experience the same task as surprisingly easy. This turned out to be the case. Additionally, these subjective fluency experiences were used as a basis for subsequent attitude judgments. Participants who were primed with "ease" found the argument generation task difficult. Therefore they were more in favor of music in streetcars if they had retrieved counter-arguments. They were more against the topic if it was difficult to retrieve pro arguments. This effect disappeared when "difficulty" was primed and the task was experienced as surprisingly easy.

Interestingly, the findings that fluency standards, which were primed in a semantic task, were used as fluency "background" in an entirely different domain (i.e., ease of argument generation) opens the possibility that fluency discrepancies can cross the borders of tasks and domains. Future research may address the question of domain specificity of fluency contexts: Can, for instance, the ease with which an individual retrieves memories during mind-wandering or the difficulty of climbing a steep hill serve as a fluency context for reading linguistically difficult or easy statements? If yes, the latter (i.e., reading of difficult statements) would be experienced as particularly difficult after mind-wandering but less so after mountain-wandering.

Perceptual fluency in context

Fluency is not only experienced on a memory-based level (that is, during retrieving and generating information as discussed above) but on a perceptual level as well. As with memory-based fluency, the informational value of perceptual fluency is affected by the context. The following section summarizes research on the influences of context-discrepant perceptual fluency on subjective truth, moral judgments, liking, and familiarity judgments.

Statements that can be fluently perceived are usually judged as more probably true than statements that are less fluent (Bacon, 1979; Begg, Anas, & Farinacci, 1992; Hasher, Goldstein, & Toppino, 1977; Reber & Schwarz, 1999; Unkelbach, 2007). In earlier demonstrations of this effect, fluency was manipulated by repeating the critical statements (Bacon, 1979; Begg et al., 1992; Hasher et al., 1977). Repeated exposure increases the perceived truth of statements compared to statements that have not been presented before (for a meta-analysis, see Dechêne, Stahl, Hansen, & Wänke, 2010). The purely perceptual figure-ground contrast in which the statements are presented influences truth judgments as well (Reber & Schwarz, 1999; Unkelbach, 2007). For instance, Reber and Schwarz (1999) showed their participants statements like "Orsorno is in Chile." They manipulated the visibility of the statements by the contrast of the color of the statements to an otherwise white background. Statements that had been shown in highly visible colors were rated as more probably true than statements in moderately visible colors.

In order to test whether an expectation of processing fluency moderates this effect, we conducted an experiment in which we presented thirteen consumer-related statements to our participants (Hansen, Dechêne, & Wänke, 2008). These statements were relatively ambiguous and at chance level in a pre-test in regard to their perceived truth (for example, "Nut bread is healthier than potato bread"). Participants were asked to rate whether the statement is true or false on a seven-point scale. As in Reber and Schwarz's study, the statements were written in different low- and high-contrast colors to manipulate the fluency. Crucially, the order of the statements was manipulated. Half of the participants started with statements of low fluency. They rated the truth of six statements with a low contrast, of six statements with a high contrast, and at the end one statement with again a low contrast. The other half rated first six highly visible statements, then six lowly visible statements, and at the end again a statement with a high fluency. Four of the statements served as target statements and were placed at the critical positions in the sets. For the last fluent (disfluent) statement in a series, high (low) fluency was as expected. For the first fluent (disfluent) statement in a series, low (high) fluency was surprising.

The hypothesis was that statements should be judged as more probably true when the perceptual fluency is high than when it is low particularly when this fluency is unexpected. And indeed, the truth effect could be replicated when the fluency was unexpected: Statements were rated as more probably true when the color contrast was high than when it was low. No effect, however, emerged when the (high and low) fluency had been expected. This finding indicates that perceptual fluency informs truth judgments particularly when it deviates from the context—such as ease of retrieval is used for an attitude judgment when it is discrepant with the context.

In an extension of these findings, Laham and colleagues (Laham, Alter, & Goodwin, 2009) provided participants with high contrast and low contrast descriptions of moral violations (for example, "a family eats its dead dog"). Again, expectations of fluency were manipulated by other preceding high contrast and low contrast descriptions. The results show that descriptions that had been processed surprisingly fluently were perceived as less negative and less morally wrong compared to surprisingly disfluent descriptions. No such difference occurred when level of fluency was as expected. Therefore, discrepancy with expectations influences the use of fluency even for moral judgments.

Not only expectations but also the surrounding context in general can provide a standard of comparison. When assessing the truth of a statement, it is noteworthy that observed truth advantages of fluent statements may theoretically manifest themselves in two ways (Dechêne et al., 2010). Firstly, the same item may be judged as more probably true when it is fluent than when it is less fluent. In demonstrations of truth advantages in which fluency is manipulated by repetition, for instance, repeated statements are judged as more probably true than the same statements at an earlier time (i.e., a within-items effect). However, in most studies on the truth effect, repeated (fluent) statements and new (less fluent) statements are presented together. Thus, secondly, at any time a repeated item can be contrasted with and rated as more probably true than a new item (i.e., a between-items effect).

If the context substantially contributes to truth advantages of fluently processed statements, then the between-items effect should be a more critical component of the observed truth advantage of repeated statements, and thus should be much stronger, than the within-item effect. Different evidence supports this assumption. First, as we have shown in a meta-analysis on the repetition-truth effect (Dechêne et al., 2010) between-items and within-items truth effects indeed differ. Although in average both the within-items effect and the between-items effect were significant with medium effect sizes, the between-items effect was significantly larger (Cohen's d =.49) than the within-items effect (Cohen's d =.39). Thus, a contrast between old and new stimuli boosts the effect of repetition truth. Additionally, much more between-items effects (n = 70) than with-items effects (n = 32) are reported in the literature, which may be a further indicator that the former are more robust effects and that a comparison with the fluency context informs truth judgments (Dechêne et al., 2010).

More directly, an experimental study corroborates this interpretation (Dechêne et al., 2009, Experiment 1). In this study participants judged the truth of several statements two times with a delay of one week in between the judgments. At the second truth judgment, the fluency context was manipulated. Some participants rated the truth of only familiar statements that they had encountered one week before. In this condition, no surrounding fluency context was provided. Other participants rated the truth of both familiar and new statements in an intermixed order. Here, the new statements provided a context that could be used to compare the fluency of the familiar items. As expected, the old, fluent statements were judged as more probably true especially when they were presented together with the new, less fluent items. A discrepancy between fluent and less fluent statements caused participants to base their truth judgment on their processing experiences. No truth advantage for the old items emerged when they were presented in a homogeneous list where all items were repeated and thus at a similar level of fluency.

A comparable effect was found for liking judgments (Dechêne et al., 2009, Experiment 2). Forty Kanji characters were randomly selected from a list of 120 characters and presented subliminally to our participants. Thereby, each character was repeated ten times. Afterwards participants rated the attractiveness of the stimuli. Some participants judged 20 old and 20 new characters. Other participants judged just the 40 old characters. Only when the stimuli were mixed with new stimuli, the typical mere-exposure effect (e.g., Bornstein, 1989; Bornstein & D'Agostino, 1994; Hansen & Wänke, 2009; Kunst-Wilson & Zajonc, 1980; Reber, Winkielman & Schwarz, 1998; Zajonc, 1968, 1980) could be replicated: Fluent characters were liked better. When only old stimuli were presented, no increase in attractiveness ratings—compared to ratings of a control group—could be observed. So, as for truth and moral judgments, fluency-mediated liking judgments depend on the context in which the fluency is perceived.

Judgments of familiarity are based on context-discrepant perceptual fluency as well (Whittlesea & Williams, 1998, 2000, 2001a, 2001b). Familiarity judgments result from a discrepancy between actual and expected fluency of processing a stimulus. This idea was tested in a series of experiments in which participants were presented with words as stimulus material. In a typical experiment (e.g., Whittlesea & Williams, 1998, Experiment 3), participants learned a list that consisted of natural words, regular non-words that looked like natural words (e.g., HENSION, MESSEL), and irregular non-words (e.g., STOFWUS, TLAMNIC). In a following recognition test, participants showed most false alarms for regular non-words. This finding can be interpreted as influence of the context of fluency: Regular non-words can be processed relatively fluently but they provide no meaning. So the actual perceptual fluency of reading the word is in conflict with a conceptual disfluency. This discrepancy makes the fluency experience particularly informative for the judgment at hand—in this case for recognition judgments.

In further studies (Whittlesea & Williams, 1998, Experiments 1 and 2), a discrepancy between fluency context and actual fluency was manipulated differently. Instead of regular non-words, pseudo-homonyms were presented (e.g., PHRAWG). These are words that sound like natural words when read aloud (e.g., FROG) but were unusually written. Participants were asked to read the words aloud, so that the phonological fluency was surprising given the written disfluency context. The surprising fluency informed memory judgments in these studies: Participants showed most false alarms for the pseudo-homonyms.

Although our framework is closely related to and strongly influenced by Whittlesea and Williams' discrepancy-attribution account (Whittlesea & Williams, 1998, 2000, 2001a, 2001b), we would like to point out several differences. Whereas Whittlesea and Williams assume that feelings of familiarity emerge directly from a discrepancy between expected and actual fluency, we argue that a discrepancy between actual fluency can be used as a basis for all different kinds of judgments (among them, of course, recognition judgments). In this sense, our account broadens the scope of the discrepancy account by showing that context-discrepant fluency informs not only feelings of familiarity, but many other social judgments as well, as has been shown in the studies reviewed above. Additionally, we refrain from narrowing contextual influences regarding fluency on only expectations. Instead, we conceptualize context as both (explicit and implicit) *expectations* and *situational* influences (as, for instance, fluency of other stimuli in a given set).

Why are discrepant fluency experiences informative?

The experiments reviewed above all show that the context, in which fluency occurs, has a strong influence on whether fluency is informative for social judgments. When fluency is discrepant with the context it is used as a basis for the judgment at hand. When fluency is congruent with the context, it is used to a lesser extent. One question that remains is *why* fluency has a stronger influence on judgments when there is a discrepancy with the context. Perhaps (low or high) fluency is not experienced at all when it occurs in the context of other stimuli or expectations of the same level of fluency. That is, it may be possible that the *experience* of fluency is contingent on at least some level of discrepancy. Without a discrepancy, participants may not know whether a task is easy or difficult, whether a stimulus is fluent or not. What speaks against this interpretation is that unambiguous fluency is experienced as fluent even if it is congruent with the context. This has been shown, for instance, when asking participants how difficult an objectively difficult (or easy) task had been, they can tell even if the level of difficulty was congruent with the context (Hansen & Wänke, 2008). Thus, this indicates that even context-congruent fluency is experienced, although it is not used as a basis for the judgments at hand (e.g., an attitude judgment). However, ratings of past task difficulty are reconstructed from memory. Consequently, it may be that the ease or difficulty is not experienced in congruent conditions, but can be "constructed" if asked for. All in all, it is an open question whether a lack of fluency experience is responsible for the non-usage of fluency in a congruent context or not.

Even if feelings of fluency occur, it could be that they are not well noticed in a congruent context. In contrast, when the fluency experiences are context-discrepant, they stand out more and cause attention and causal attributions (cf. Weiner, 1985; Wong & Weiner, 1981). This could be the reason for the effects reported in this chapter. Particularly context-discrepant fluency gains attention and therefore informs social judgments. In order to gain attention, fluency experiences must exceed a certain threshold to enter awareness. The larger the discrepancy between fluency of context and fluency of the target stimulus, the greater is the probability that individuals detect this discrepancy and use the fluency as cue for their judgments. Accordingly, a study by Hertwig, Herzog, Schooler, and Reimer (2008, Study 2) found that individuals could reliably discriminate differences in retrieval fluency when the retrieval latencies differed by more than 100 milliseconds. The larger the differences were, the better participants could discriminate and the larger fluency validity proved to be. However, although small fluency variations may not exceed the threshold of consciousness, they may sometimes nevertheless have an indirect influence on judgments via affect (e.g., Topolinski & Strack, 2009). The fact that even such indirect influences were not found in the congruence conditions of the studies cited in this chapter may indicate that fluency was not experienced in the first place.

One could argue, however, that perhaps even if context-congruent fluency occurs and exceeds the threshold of awareness, it is simply not used for social judgments because it is *attributed* to a different source. In other words, fluency may not be regarded as representative for the judgmental target when it did not deviate from the context fluency. We would like to argue, however, that the diagnosticity of fluency experiences because of their context-discrepancy is entirely different from a misattribution mechanism (i.e., representativeness considerations). Both processes may be at work largely independently and come to play at different subsequent steps in the judgmental process. First fluency experiences gain potential informational value particularly if they represent a change from a previous expectation or a discrepancy with the surrounding context. Even so, in a second step the experiences can be perceived as non-representative for the judgmental target and thus can be attributed to a different source. Whether individuals rely on the fluency when they form a judgment or not, depends on whether fluency is perceived to be representative for the target (see Greifeneder, Bless, & Pham, 2011).

However, although quite different in nature, both accounts may overlap in some experimental manipulations. In some misattribution studies on the ease-of-retrieval effect, for instance, participants were explicitly told that they would find the task easy (or difficult) because of a given reason, for example the pale letters on the answer sheet (Wänke, Schwarz, & Bless, 1995) or background music (Schwarz et al., 1991). In these cases, it cannot be distinguished whether fluency was not used for the judgment because it was indeed misattributed to the external source and thus not representative for the judgmental target (misattribution account) or because the misattribution instruction had created congruent context that rendered the fluency as uninformative (discrepancy account). Despite this confound in some studies, both accounts are based on quite different processes and are separable in principle, as the studies reviewed in this chapter show. In all these studies, no external sources for the fluency experiences were made salient or even available. For example, very implicit expectation and primed context manipulations were used in the ease-of-retrieval studies, or the heterogeneous list context in the truth and liking studies was not very obvious to our participants. Thus, misattributions of fluency experiences to an external source were unlikely.

Summary and implications

Fluency per se seems less likely to be responsible for the ease-of-retrieval effect, the truth effect, judgments of familiarity and liking than fluency in context. We have seen with several examples that subjective fluency experiences are especially informative for social judgments when they deviate from a baseline. Furthermore, the findings indicate that people monitor changes rather than states. Discrepancies are more informative than absolute levels of fluency. Fluency experiences are not less informative for social judgments in homogeneous contexts or in situations in which fluency occurs as expected. However, fluency gains informational value when there is a discrepancy from the surrounding or expectation context. So, absolute fluency has less informational value than relative fluency.

The research reviewed in this chapter shows this effect with different fluency manipulations: Ease of generating information, perceptual fluency, and repetition fluency all are particularly informative when they deviate from a standard. Moreover, the effect generalizes across different types of stimuli. Independent of whether self-generated arguments, ambiguous statements, or Kanji characters were used as stimuli in the studies, fluency effects emerged when the experiences of processing the stimuli were discrepant from a context. Diverse dependent variables, such as attitude judgments, truth judgments, familiarity and attractiveness ratings, contribute to the generalizability of the context-discrepant fluency effect.

The findings have important methodological implications for fluency research. First, they speak to whether a researcher should use a within- or between-participants design when s/he wants to investigate fluency effects. The findings reported in this chapter suggest that it is more likely to detect fluency effects in the first place when using within-participants designs, because here context-discrepancies are much more salient. So, researchers are well advised to use mixed-list or discrepant-expectation conditions when investigating fluency effects. Second, post-hoc "surprise"-measures may be incorporated in fluency studies as manipulation checks. Such checks could possibly help to identify individuals for whom fluency was not informative because of a congruent expectation (for instance, individuals who expected a stimulus to be disfluent and were thus not surprised by its actual disfluency).

Finally, one may ask the question why we found contrast effects throughout our studies and not assimilation effects. Actual fluency is usually contrasted away from the context. The reason for contrast effects may be that in all the reviewed studies (high or low) fluency pertains to separate representations (that is, to the context or to the actual stimulus) that are compared with each other. Of course, under certain circumstances, it is likely that the context and the stimulus are construed as part of the same mental representation. In such a case assimilation would be more likely. If the context and the stimulus are temporally or thematically related, for instance, they may be assimilated to each other. However, in the case of fluency, such a situation means that the stimulus fluency merges with the context fluency per definition and is thus not informative anymore. Accordingly, stimulus fluency may be unlikely to be used as basis for judgments and decisions in such cases.

Fluency experiences are flexible and context-dependent. The research reviewed in this chapter adds another piece of evidence to this fact. Not only is the interpretation of fluency experiences learnt and can be relearned (Unkelbach, 2007; Unkelbach & Greifeneder, Chapter 2 this volume), and are fluency experiences contextualized in the human body, which is needed to unfold their influences on judgments (Topolinski & Strack, 2009, Topolinski, Chapter 3 this volume). Fluency experiences are also influenced by and gain informational value in relation to their surrounding context.

Acknowledgment

Preparation of this chapter was supported by a grant from the Swiss National Science Foundation to Jochim Hansen (#PA00P1_124124). We thank Sascha Topolinski and the editors of this volume for helpful comments on an earlier version of this chapter.

Note

1 Under certain conditions, assimilation effects instead of contrast effects are found (e.g., Mussweiler, 2003). For experiences of cognitive fluency, however, contrast effects may be much more prevalent. We discuss this question in more detail below.

References

Alter, A. L., & Oppenheimer, D. M. (2009). Uniting the tribes of fluency to form a meta-cognitive nation. *Personality and Social Psychology Review, 13*, 219–235.

Bacon, F. T. (1979). Credibility of repeated statements: Memory for trivia. *Journal of Experimental Psychology: Human Learning and Memory, 5*, 241–252.

Begg, I. M., Anas, A., & Farinacci, S. (1992). Dissociation of processes in belief: Source recollection, statement familiarity, and the illusion of truth. *Journal of Experimental Psychology: General, 121*, 446–458.

Bornstein, R. F. (1989). Exposure and affect: Overview and meta-analysis of research, 1968–1987. *Psychological Bulletin, 106*, 265–289.

Bornstein, R. F., & D'Agostino, P. R. (1994). The attribution and discounting of perceptual fluency: Preliminary tests of a perceptual fluency/attributional model of the mere exposure effect. *Social Cognition, 12*, 103–128.

Dechêne, A., Stahl, C., Hansen, J., & Wänke, M. (2009). Mix me a list: Context moderates the truth effect and the mere exposure effect. *Journal of Experimental Social Psychology, 45*, 1117–1122.

—— (2010). The truth about the truth: A meta-analytic review of the truth effect. *Personality and Social Psychology Review, 14*, 238–257.

Festinger, L. (1954). A theory of social comparison processes. *Human Relations, 7*, 117–140.

Geers, A. L., & Lassiter, G. D. (1999). Affective expectations and information gain: Evidence for assimilation and contrast effects in affective experience. *Journal of Experimental Social Psychology, 35*, 394–413.

Greifeneder, R., & Bless, H. (2007). Relying on accessible content versus accessibility experiences: The case of processing capacity. *Social Cognition, 25*, 853–881.

—— (2008). Depression and reliance on ease-of-retrieval experiences. *European Journal of Social Psychology, 38*, 213–230.

Greifeneder, R., Bless, H., & Pham, M. T. (2011). When do people rely on affective and cognitive feelings in judgment? A review. *Personality and Social Psychology Review, 15*, 107–141.

Hagerty, M. R. (2000), Social comparisons of income in one's community: Evidence from national surveys of income and happiness. *Journal of Personality and Social Psychology, 78*, 764–771.

Hansen, J., Dechêne, A., & Wänke, M. (2008). Discrepant fluency increases subjective truth. *Journal of Experimental Social Psychology, 44*, 687–691.

Hansen, J., & Wänke, M. (2008). It's the difference that counts: Expectancy/experience discrepancy moderates the use of ease of retrieval in attitude judgments. *Social Cognition, 26*, 447–468.

—— (2009). Liking what's familiar: the importance of unconscious familiarity in the mere-exposure effect. *Social Cognition, 27*, 161–182.

Hasher, L., Goldstein, D., & Toppino, T. (1977). Frequency and the conference of referential validity. *Journal of Verbal Learning and Verbal Behavior, 16*, 107–112.

Helson, H. (1964). *Adaptation level theory: An experimental and systematic approach to behavior.* New York, NY: Harper & Row.

Hertwig, R., Herzog, S. M., Schooler, L. J., & Reimer, T. (2008). Fluency heuristic: A model of how the mind exploits a by-product of information retrieval. *Journal of Experimental Psychology: Learning, Memory, & Cognition, 34*, 1191–1206.

Kunst-Wilson, W. R., & Zajonc, R. B. (1980). Affective discrimination of stimuli that cannot be recognized. *Science, 207*, 557–558.

Laham, S. M., Alter, A. L., & Goodwin, G. (2009). Easy on the mind, easy on the wrong-doer: Discrepantly fluent violations are deemed less morally wrong. *Cognition, 112,* 462–466.

Lee, A. Y., & Labroo, A. A. (2004). Effects of conceptual and perceptual fluency on brand evaluation. *Journal of Marketing Research, 41,* 151–165.

Mussweiler, T. (2003). Comparison processes in social judgment: Mechanisms and consequences. *Psychological Review, 110,* 472–489.

Novemsky, N., Dhar, R., Schwarz, N., & Simonson, I. (2007). Preference fluency in choice. *Journal of Marketing Research, 44,* 347–356.

Olson, J. M., Roese, N. J., & Zanna, M. P. (1996). Expectancies. In E. T. Higgins & A. W. Kruglanski (Eds.), *Social psychology: Handbook of basic principles.* (pp. 211–238). New York, NY: Guilford press.

Raghubir, P., & Menon, G. (1998). AIDS and me, never the twain shall meet: The effects of information accessibility on judgments of risk and advertising effectiveness. *Journal of Consumer Research, 25,* 52–63.

—— (2001). Framing effects in risk perception of AIDS. *Marketing Letters, 12,* 145–155.

Reber, R., & Schwarz, N. (1999). Effects of perceptual fluency on judgments of truth. *Consciousness and Cognition, 8,* 338–342.

Reber, R., Winkielman, P., & Schwarz, N. (1998). Effects of perceptual fluency on affective judgments. *Psychological Science, 9,* 45–48.

Rothman, A. J., & Schwarz, N. (1998). Constructing perceptions of vulnerability: Personal relevance and the use of experiential information in health judgments. *Personality and Social Psychology Bulletin, 24,* 1053–1064.

Schwarz, N. (1998). Accessible content and accessibility experiences: The interplay of declarative and experiential information in judgment. *Personality and Social Psychology Review, 2,* 87–99.

Schwarz, N., Bless, H., Strack, F., Klumpp, G., Rittenauer-Schatka, H., & Simons, A. (1991). Ease of retrieval as information: Another look at the availability heuristic. *Journal of Personality and Social Psychology, 61,* 195–202.

Schwarz, N., Bless, H., Wänke, M., & Winkielman, P. (2003). Accessibility revisited. In G. V. Bodenhausen & A. J. Lambert (Eds.), *Foundations of social cognition: A Festschrift in honor of Robert S. Wyer, Jr.* (pp. 51–77). Mahwah, NJ: Lawrence Erlbaum Associates.

Schwarz, N., & Vaughn, L. A. (2002). The availability heuristic revisited: Ease of recall and content of recall as distinct sources of information. In T. Gilovich, D. Griffin, & D. Kahneman (Eds.), *Heuristics and biases: The psychology of intuitive judgment.* (pp. 103–119). New York, NY: Cambridge University Press.

Strack, F., Schwarz, N., & Gschneidinger, E. (1985). Happiness and reminiscing: The role of time perspective, mood, and mode of thinking. *Journal of Personality and Social Psychology, 49,* 1460–1469.

Topolinski, S., & Strack, F. (2009a). Motormouth: Mere exposure depends on stimulus-specific motor simulations. *Journal of Experimental Psychology: Learning, Memory, and Cognition, 35,* 423–433.

—— (2009b). Scanning the "fringe" of consciousness: What is felt and what is not felt in intuitions about semantic coherence. *Consciousness and Cognition, 18,* 608–618.

Unkelbach, C. (2007). Reversing the truth effect: Learning the interpretation of processing fluency in judgments of truth. *Journal of Experimental Psychology: Learning, Memory, and Cognition, 33,* 219–230.

Wänke, M., Bless, H., & Biller, B. (1996). Subjective experience versus content of information in the construction of attitude judgments. *Personality and Social Psychology Bulletin, 22*, 1150–1113.

Wänke, M., Bohner, G., & Jurkowitsch, A. (1997). There are many reasons to drive a BMW: Does imagined ease of argument generation influence attitudes? *Journal of Consumer Research, 24*, 170–177.

Wänke, M., Schwarz, N., & Bless, H. (1995). The availability heuristic revisited: Experienced ease of retrieval in mundane frequency estimates. *Acta Psychologica, 89*, 83–90.

Weiner, B. (1985). "Spontaneous" causal thinking. *Psychological Bulletin, 87*, 74–84.

Whittlesea, B. W. A. (2004). The perception of integrality: Remembering through the validation of expectation. *Journal of Experimental Psychology: Learning, Memory, and Cognition, 30*, 891–908.

Whittlesea, B. W. A., & Williams, L. D. (1998). Why do strangers fell familiar, but friends don't? A discrepancy-attribution account of feelings of familiarity. *Acta Psychologica, 98*, 141–165.

—— (2000). The source of feelings of familiarity: The discrepancy-attribution hypothesis. *Journal of Experimental Psychology: Learning, Memory, and Cognition, 26*, 547–565.

—— (2001a). The discrepancy-attribution hypothesis: I. The heuristic basis of feeling of familiarity. *Journal of Experimental Psychology: Learning, Memory, and Cognition, 27*, 3–13.

—— (2001b). The discrepancy-attribution hypothesis: II. Expectation, uncertainty, surprise, and feelings of familiarity. *Journal of Experimental Psychology: Learning, Memory, and Cognition, 27*, 14–33.

Wilcox, K., & Song, S. (2009). Preference fluency in sequential customization: The unexpected ease or difficulty of product feature decisions. In A. L. McGill & S. Shavitt (Eds.), *Advances in Consumer Research*, Vol. 36. (p. 653). Duluth, MN: Association for Consumer Research.

Wilson, T. D., Lisle, D. J., Kraft, D., & Wetzel, C. G. (1989). Preferences as expectation-driven inferences: Effects of affective expectations on affective experience. *Journal of Personality and Social Psychology, 56*, 519–530.

Wong, P. T. P. & Weiner, B. (1981). When people ask "why" questions, and the heuristics of attributional search. *Journal of Personality and Social Psychology, 40*, 650–663.

Zajonc, R. B. (1968). Attitudinal effects of mere exposure. *Journal of Personality and Social Psychology Monograph Supplement, 9*, 1–27.

—— (1980). Feeling and thinking: Preferences need no inferences. *American Psychologist, 35*, 151–175.

6   Disfluency sleeper effect

Disfluency today promotes fluency tomorrow

Daniel M. Oppenheimer and
Adam L. Alter

Abstract

According to a wealth of existing research, fluent stimuli are perceived to be truer, more likable, and more famous than disfluent stimuli. Participants in those studies made judgments immediately after they were exposed to the stimuli of interest, and until now researchers have not examined such judgments made from memory. The literature suggests that disfluency leads to deeper thinking and encoding, which ultimately facilitates retrieval. As such, information that is difficult to process today may be para- doxically easier to remember in the future. Since disfluency at encoding translates to fluency at retrieval, judgments of disfluent materials from memory may mimic judgments of fluent materials made immediately. This paper provides evidence for this disflu- ency sleeper effect, showing that delayed judgment reverses classic fluency findings.

Some cognitive processes are more challenging than others. Perceiving an object when it's far away, in the dark, or very small is harder than perceiving the object when it's nearby, well lit, or large. Remembering the details of a movie is tougher if you saw the movie a year ago than if you saw it yesterday. Understanding a sentence is more difficult when the sentence comes from a Shakespeare soliloquy than when it comes from a children's book.

The subjective feeling of ease (or difficulty) that accompanies these tasks is known as fluency (or disfluency) and it has been the subject of a great deal of recent research. All cognitive activity, from lower order processes such as perception to higher order processes such as deductive reasoning, can be placed along a continuum from fluent to disfluent (for a review, see Alter & Oppenheimer, 2009a).[1] For this reason, fluency is a ubiquitous metacognitive experience.

When a cognitive event feels fluent, we interpret the experience through the lens of what Norbert Schwarz (2004) labeled naïve theories. These naïve theories are context-specific, so they guide us to interpret fluency differently depending on the target judgment. For example, objects that are farther away are harder to see, which means that fluent objects seem nearer than disfluent objects (Alter &

Oppenheimer, 2008b). Similarly, events that happened recently are easier to remember, so people tend to assume that fluently recalled events happened more recently. Importantly, people learn to associate fluency with specific outcomes across many domains (Briñol, Petty, & Tormala, 2006; Unkelbach, 2006), which makes fluency a very useful cue for a wide array of judgments.

But judgments do not exist in a vacuum. People use judgments to plan behaviors and determine appropriate mental strategies. Somebody who expects a task to be trivially easy will approach it differently from somebody who expects the task to be challenging. As such, the fluency of a stimulus can be used not only as a direct cue about the nature of the stimulus, but also to determine the types of cognitive operations that people use when processing that stimulus. Recent research has examined the nature and implications of a number of these so-called *indirect fluency effects*.

One such finding is that disfluency prompts people to engage in deeper cognitive processing, which in turn facilitates encoding. This improved encoding leads to improved recall (Diemand-Yauman, Oppenheimer, & Vaughan, 2011). As a result, stimuli that are initially presented disfluently are encoded more deeply and subsequently recalled more easily. Perhaps paradoxically, then, information that is more difficult to process initially can be easier to retrieve later. This divergence in the level of fluency at presentation and recall could yield reversals of classic fluency effects when judgments are made from memory. The present manuscript explores this possibility.

In what follows, we begin by discussing some of the most classic and robust direct fluency effects (which we will later attempt to reverse by introducing a delay in the judgment process). We will then review the literature on indirect fluency effects with an emphasis on the impact of disfluency on memory, and more fully explicate the logic of these predictions. Finally, we will present a novel experiment which provides preliminary evidence for the *disfluency sleeper effect*—that classic fluency effects reverse when judgments are made from memory.

Direct effects of fluency

Perhaps the first observed effect of fluency on judgment was Zajonc's (1968) mere exposure effect. Zajonc showed that people prefer stimuli that they have seen before to otherwise similar but novel stimuli. Later research suggested that this effect arises in large part because people prefer fluent stimuli, and previously exposed stimuli are easier to retrieve from memory or to perceive than novel stimuli (Bornstein, 1989; Bornstein & D'Agostino, 1994).

The link between fluency and liking is not limited to mere exposure, and researchers have induced liking with a variety of fluency manipulations. For example, researchers have shown that people find images more aesthetically pleasing when those images are easy to perceive (e.g., because the foreground of the image contrasts highly with its background: Reber, Winkielman, & Schwarz, 1998). Similarly, objects or events that are difficult to imagine (Petrova &

Cialdini, 2005), difficult to choose (Iyengar & Lepper, 2000), or made to feel disfluent through facial feedback cues (brow furrowing: Stepper & Strack, 1993), are liked less than their relatively fluent counterparts (for a review, see Alter & Oppenheimer, 2009a).

As John Keats famously said in his poem Ode on a Grecian Urn, "Beauty is truth, truth beauty," so perhaps it should be no surprise that the same processes that lead us to find a stimulus beautiful should also lead us to believe that it is true. Indeed, ample evidence suggests that truth judgments are similarly influenced by fluency. For example, Reber and Schwarz (1999) asked participants to rate the truth value of phrases such as "Osorno is in Chile." Participants believed that the statements were more likely to be true when the figure/ground contrast was high, which facilitated perceptual fluency. Similarly when concepts are easier to remember, easier to process linguistically, or primed semantically, they are more likely to be judged true (for a review, see Alter & Oppenheimer, 2009a).

Just as metacognitive ease induces liking and perceptions of truthfulness, fluency also induces illusions of fame. For example, Jacoby, Woloshyn, and Kelley (1989) showed people a list of non-famous names under conditions of divided attention. Subsequently the familiarity and fluency created by prior exposure of those names led people to judge them to be famous. In another set of studies, proprioceptive disfluency induced by facial feedback (i.e., furrowing one's brow; Strack and Neumann, 2000) also influenced participants' judgments of fame.

Fame, truth, and liking are not the only judgments shaped by metacognitive ease; fluency has an impact on judgments of confidence, frequency, typicality, duration, intelligence, value, risk, blame, and distance—and this list is hardly exhaustive (for reviews, see Alter & Oppenheimer 2009a; Schwarz, 2004). As fluency increases, it exerts direct effects on our judgments across a wide array of topics.

Indirect effects of fluency

In the studies discussed above, fluency is used as a cue to inform judgment. That is, just as we might use the fact that a person has an advanced degree or reads philosophy in her spare time to help us determine her intelligence, we might also use our experience of fluency when we read a passage she has written to judge her intelligence (c.f., Oppenheimer, 2006). Fluency is just one more piece of information that directly influences judgment just like any other piece of information.

While the bulk of the literature on fluency has examined its direct impact on judgment, a growing body of work has begun to investigate a range of subtle, indirect paths through which fluency affects judgment (c.f., Oppenheimer, 2008). That is, fluency can change the manner in which we go about making judgments, causing people to search out more (or less) information, attend to different cues than they might otherwise (Shah & Oppenheimer, 2007), assimilate versus contrast information from primes (Greifeneder & Bless, 2010; see also Häfner, this volume, for further discussion), or use different strategies for solving problems (Alter, Oppenheimer, Epley, & Eyre, 2007). For example, researchers have examined how fluency influences which cognitive operations people recruit to process information (Alter & Oppenheimer, 2008b; Alter et al., 2007; Barry & Alter, 2010; Song & Schwarz, 2009; Wänke & Bless, 2000). Alter and his colleagues (2007) showed that people engaged in deeper, more systematic processing when information was presented disfluently. The researchers asked participants to complete the Cognitive Reflection Test (CRT; Frederick, 2005), a series of questions that inspire incorrect intuitive responses that can only be corrected with deliberate reconsideration. The CRT therefore measures how deeply a person is processing information. When the CRT was presented in a hard-to-read font, participants answered more questions correctly because they made fewer intuitively compelling errors. In other words, superficial features that made the test feel more difficult (the degraded font) led people to think more deeply about the material. Alter et al. (2007) also found that disfluency improved participants' syllogistic reasoning, deepened their processing of persuasive communication, and enhanced their processing of person perception cues.

Song and Schwarz (2008) provided convergent evidence when they asked participants about the animals Moses took aboard the ark. Participants were much more likely to catch that it was a trick question—Noah, not Moses, was the biblical protagonist of the ark story—if the question was presented disfluently. In this case, the question's disfluency didn't directly shape the judgment at hand (e.g., it's hard to process, so there must have been fewer animals), but rather changed the way in which people approached the judgment (e.g., it's hard to process, so I should be more careful in how I go about this task). In other words, fluency can act as a "cognitive control signal," helping people identify when they need to invest more cognitive effort to successfully answer a question.

Disfluency and learning

The fact that disfluency leads people to process information more deeply has some important implications. Most notably, it has long been known that people who process information more deeply are more successful at encoding that information (Craik & Tulving, 1975). In a classic set of studies, Craik and Tulving showed that when participants answered questions about superficial features of a word (e.g., whether the word was written in lower-case or capital letters) they encoded the information more shallowly than when they answered questions about the semantic content of the word (e.g., the definition of the word). The more deeply they had processed the words at encoding, the more successful they were at retrieving the words during a later recall task. Assuming that disfluency prompts systematic and deliberative processing (c.f., Alter et al., 2007), then information presented disfluently should be encoded more deeply. Consequently, people should be able to recall information with greater accuracy when they encode that information more deeply.

A recent series of studies validated this prediction (Diemand-Yauman et al., 2011). Diemand-Yauman and his colleagues gave participants 90 seconds to learn features of various alien creatures. Some of the participants saw the 21 items in easy to read Arial font, while other participants saw the items in harder to read grayscale *Bodoni MT* or *Comic Sans MS*. After a 15-minute distracter task, participants were given a cued-recall task. Participants in the fluent condition only correctly recalled 72.8 percent of the material, while those in the disfluent condition correctly recalled 86.5 percent. In other words, people had better memory for information presented in a disfluent manner.

To show the generalizability of the findings, Diemand-Yauman and his colleagues extended the effect to real world classroom environments. The researchers looked at high school English, history, physics, and chemistry classes, at both basic and advanced levels. In some classrooms, PowerPoint slides or supplementary readings were made disfluent through a font manipulation. For yoked control classrooms, in which the same topic was taught by the same teacher at the same level of difficulty, the information was presented in standard, easy to read fonts. Students exposed to the disfluent materials scored on average nearly half a standard deviation higher on course exams. (The exams in all classes were printed in normal, fluent font.) While there are untested moderators of this effect, the findings provide strong preliminary evidence that disfluency can, under the right circumstances, facilitate learning.

Disfluency sleeper effect

To this point we have suggested that information presented disfluently will be processed more deeply, which makes that information easier to retrieve in the long term. This finding also has counterintuitive paradoxical consequences, which we term the *fluency sleeper effect*. According to the effect, information presented *disfluently* will be processed more thoroughly initially, which could lead it to be encoded more deeply, which in turn causes it to be retrieved more fluently later. In other words information processed *disfluently* at original presentation might become relatively *fluent* after a delay. Meanwhile, information originally presented fluently may not be encoded as deeply, and may be more difficult to retrieve (and thus disfluent) after a delay.

If this logic holds, then the well-replicated effects of fluency on judgments of liking, truth, and fame should only occur if the judgments are made immediately after observing the stimulus (as is standard in paradigms for studying fluency). After a delay, these effects should disappear or even reverse. The present experiment aims to test that hypothesis.

Participants made judgments about the truth of trivia statements, the fame of celebrities, and how much they liked various line drawings. Some of the stimuli were presented in a fluent format and others were presented in an unclear format that promoted disfluent processing. Crucially, some participants made judgments immediately after seeing the stimuli, while others did so after a delay. To foreshadow the results, although fluency led to higher judgments of truth and liking when the judgments were made immediately (replicating existing results), the opposite pattern was found after a delay. This demonstrates the fluency sleeper effect: items that were initially processed as disfluent may be processed as fluent when judgments rely on information that must be retrieved from memory.

Method

Participants: One hundred and sixteen participants recruited through Amazon's Mechanical Turk platform took part in this study in exchange for monetary compensation. The sampling was restricted to US residents.

Stimuli: Three judgment domains were investigated: truth, liking, and fame judgments. For liking judgments, simple line drawings were downloaded from an online clipart database. To ensure that any results weren't specific to the particulars of a given image, three distinct pictures were used: a toaster, a horse, and an airplane. Disfluent versions of these images were created by rendering them in 75 percent grayscale (see Figure 6.1). For truth judgments, three statements describing the true location of an obscure city were created: Osorno is a city in Chile, Bollingen is a city in Switzerland, Lahti is a city in Finland. The cities were chosen such that typical Americans would not be sure of their locations. For fame judgments, three celebrities were selected: Michael Phelps, Meryl Streep, and Colin Powell. The celebrities were chosen such that the typical American would find them familiar. The statements (for truth judgments) or names (for fame judgments) were presented in either 12-point Times New Roman font for the fluent condition, or 11-point Monotype Corsiva Font for the disfluent condition (see Figure 6.1). Numerous experiments in the literature on fluency have shown that

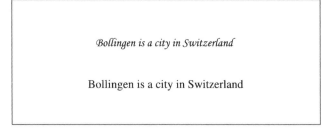

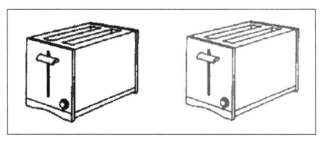

Figure 6.1 Examples of stimuli for the truth (top panel) and liking (bottom panel) questions. Disfluency was induced by using a more complex font (for truth stimuli) or rendering the image in 75% grayscale (for liking stimuli).

these manipulations reduce the fluency of text and images (see Alter & Oppenheimer, 2009a for a review).

Procedure: Participants were given the following instructions: "At different times in the survey, you will be shown an item with a black border around it. Please pay attention to this item because you will be asked to make a judgment about it later." After participants had read the instructions, a randomly selected fame, truth, or liking stimulus was presented within a black border in the center of the screen for three seconds.

For participants in the immediate judgment condition, participants were asked to make a judgment immediately following the three-second presentation interval. Participants were asked "how pretty is this picture?", "how likely is the statement to be true?", or "how famous is this person?" to assess liking, truth, and fame respectively. Ratings were made on a 1–9 scale, with lower numbers indicating lower values of liking, truth, and fame. Participants were then given a text box, and asked to report, to the best of their recollection, what the item within the black border had been. Participants then engaged in five minutes of unrelated distracter tasks in which they judged causal relationships between events.[2]

Participants in the delay condition engaged in the distracter tasks immediately following the three-second presentation interval. At the end of five minutes, they were asked to make a judgment about the item that "had appeared within the black border," after which they were prompted to recall what the item had been. The prompts and scales were the same as in the immediate condition. For a visual representation of the design, see Figure 6.2.

Participants completed two trials during the course of the experiment. After the completion of the first trial, all participants were then shown a second randomly selected stimulus with the constraint that it could not come from the same category of judgment (liking, truth, or fame) as the first stimulus. The procedure was repeated for this second stimulus; both delay and fluency were held constant such that a participant in the fluent-immediate condition for the first presentation would also be in the fluent immediate for the second presentation.

Results

Memory Coding: Answers to the recall question were coded so as to identify participants who had no recollection of the target stimulus. Answers where participants had no memory of the item (e.g., "I don't remember"), were so vague as to imply no memory (e.g., "something about a city"), or were completely wrong (e.g., "Harry Steel" for "Meryl Streep") were eliminated from further consideration (8.7 percent of the stimuli—8 fame, 10 truth, 2 liking). The unremembered items were split evenly between the fluent and disfluent conditions. Six of the unremembered items came from the immediate condition, suggesting that memory failures often arose among participants who weren't engaged in the task.

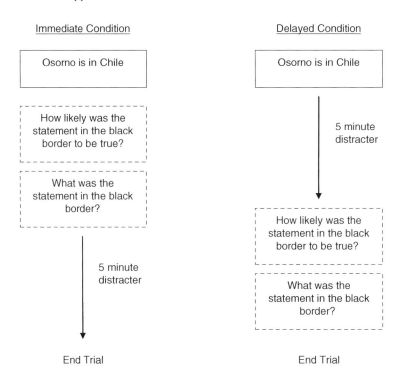

Figure 6.2 Schematic representation of the experimental design for Study 1. For frame
or liking judgements, the stimulus in the black box would be a line drawing
or celebrity name respectively. For the disfluent condition the font would be in
11 point Monotype Corsiva.

Primary Analysis: For fame judgments, all of the items were at ceiling across
all conditions. That is, people believed all three famous people were, indeed,
quite famous regardless of the font that the name was listed in. Because of this
there was no variance to be observed either within or across conditions. Thus, no
useful trends could be gleaned from this dependent measure and fame will not be
considered further in the results section.[3]

For liking and truth judgments, the trends were similar to one another (see
Figure 6.3) so they were analyzed together. While there were no main effects for
either fluency ($F(1,137) =.35$, $p >.1$) or timing ($F(1,137) = 1.2$, $p >.1$) a reliable
fluency by timing interaction was observed when controlling for stimulus[4]
($F(1, 137) = 5.4$, $p <.05$). In the immediate condition, fluent stimuli were given
higher ratings ($M = 5.0$, $SD = 1.6$) than disfluent stimuli ($M = 4.4$, $SD = 1.7$),
although this difference was not statistically significant. However, in the delayed
condition this trend reversed; fluent stimuli were given lower ratings ($M = 4.6$,
$SD = 2.1$) than disfluent stimuli ($M = 5.6$, $SD = 1.9$), although again, this difference was not statistically significant. There were no significant order effects
between first and second trials (all p's $>.1$)

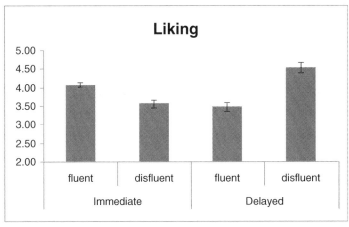

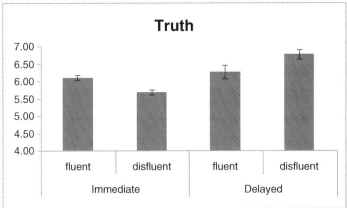

Figure 6.3 Ratings of liking (top panel) and truth (bottom panel) for fluent and disfluent stimuli when ratings are made immediately, or after a five minute delay. Ratings were on a 1-9 scale with lower numbers representing lower liking and truth values respectively. Error bars represent Standard Error, not confidence intervals.

Discussion

Dozens of previous studies have shown robustly that disfluency lowers judgments of truth, liking, and fame. However, the standard paradigms for studying fluency ask people to make judgments immediately following the fluency manipulation, ignoring how fluency might influence judgments made after a delay, (i.e. from memory). In this paper, we show that fluency effects reverse for delayed judgments. While fluency led to higher judgments of truth and liking during immediate judgment, the opposite pattern was observed after a five-minute delay.

This newly identified *disfluency sleeper effect* ostensibly shapes judgment through indirect relationships between fluency and the target judgment (c.f., Oppenheimer, 2008). Disfluency leads people to process information more deeply and systematically than they otherwise would (Alter et al., 2007). This leads them to encode the information more effectively, which leads them to remember it more easily (Diemand-Yauman et al., 2011). This ease of remembering is a form of fluency. Thus, disfluency at presentation leads to fluency at recall, and a reversal of classic fluency effects after a delay.

These results have important implications for fluency research. Most straightforward is the fact that timing is critical, and researchers might achieve very different outcomes when they ask questions following a delay. More generally, this effect demonstrates how powerfully indirect routes of fluency shape judgments. Fluency not only is used as a direct cue to inform judgment, but also changes the cognitive processes that we use to make those judgments. Disfluency leads us to attend to different information (Shah & Oppenheimer, 2007), think more systematically (Alter et al., 2007), think more abstractly (Alter & Oppenheimer, 2008b), contrast rather than assimilate primes (Greifeneder & Bless, 2010; Häfner, this volume) and more acutely perceive errors (Song & Schwarz, 2008). These indirect pathways can have opposing forces on judgment. For example, it may be that thinking harder about a text might lead people to think the author is less intelligent, but that thinking more abstractly about that same text (i.e., thinking about the broad, over-arching themes rather than the details) might increase one's evaluations of the author's intelligence. Depending on the specific properties of various texts, this could lead fluency to have nuanced, and seemingly contradictory affects. Fluency researchers need to be aware of these indirect effects lest they find their results skewed in unexpected ways.

These findings also have important practical implications, because they suggest that classic real world fluency effects might not persist when judgments are made following a delay. For example, fluency influences people's perceptions of value (Alter & Oppenheimer, 2006; 2008a), which has obvious implications for marketing and business. Fluency has been shown to impact risk judgments (Song and Schwarz, 2009) which is important for communicating medical risks. Fluency even affects the likelihood that people will disclose personal information online (Alter & Oppenheimer, 2009b), which has ramifications for privacy advocates. But the disfluency sleeper effect suggests that some of these effects could reverse given time delays. A marketer, risk communicator, or privacy advocate could easily design an intervention based on fluency, only to find it backfiring several months later when people are forced to rely on memory rather than processing the message in its original context.

Similarly, the disfluency sleeper effect has important implications for education and information retention. Diemand-Yauman and his colleagues (2011) showed that disfluency can improve retention in actual classroom settings. However, given that disfluency typically leads to lower liking, one might be concerned that a disfluency intervention in schools might lead students to dislike the material they are learning. While students may initially dislike disfluently presented material, the present findings suggest that after a delay, students might have a more positive evaluation of the material. In other words, disfluency might not only improve retention, but also might increase long-term interest and motivation to take advanced classes in the material. This is a possibility worthy of empirical scrutiny.

There are, of course, some caveats one must consider regarding these findings. Most notably, weaknesses in the stimuli for the fame judgments led to a ceiling effect making it impossible to determine whether the disfluency sleeper effect generalized to that domain. In general, while the present study identified the effect in two prominent domains (truth and liking), it would be worth examining to what extent the effect persists across a wider range of judgments. Similarly, while fluency has been instantiated in a number of ways (see Alter & Oppenheimer, 2009a), the present study only used perceptual fluency (font and figure/ground contrast) to operationalize the construct. One of the hallmarks of fluency is its consistency across different instantiations and it is important to validate the effect using fluency manipulations beyond the classic font manipulation.

Moreover, there is room to question the purported mechanism by which the disfluency sleeper effect operates. The effect ostensibly occurs because participants encode stimuli more deeply at initial presentation, which leads to easier retrieval at subsequent judgment. However, the present experiment did not measure retrieval fluency and thus cannot provide direct evidence of mediation.[5] Of course, to our knowledge, no other model of fluency effects has predicted this pattern of results, thus making the proposed mechanism at least plausible. Future research should investigate this question more thoroughly.

The present study delayed and distracted people for five minutes, but the question of what might happen over lengthier delays remains unanswered. One possibility is that very long delays would eliminate the effect; after a long enough delay, even with deep initial encoding, it becomes difficult to recall the stimuli. If it were possible to track down our participants and ask them to make judgments today (months after the study was run) odds are they wouldn't remember having been in the study at all, let alone the specifics of the stimuli. This suggests that there may be an inverted U-shaped curve representing the relationship between delay and the effects of disfluency. Immediate judgment leads people to dislike disfluent stimuli, short delays lead to increased liking, and longer delays may decline towards baseline. The specifics of this function remain an open empirical question.

Fluency is important because of its ubiquity and the breadth of judgments that it impacts. While fluency researchers have limited themselves to investigations of how fluency affects immediate judgment, the present study shows that there is still much to be learned about how fluency interacts with memory and delay. The possibility exists for exciting findings on this topic that have until this point remained dormant.

Notes

1 Throughout the chapter we will be using the terms fluency and disfluency to refer to this continuum—thus, when we say that fluency produces judgments that fall on one side of a continuum, it can be assumed that disfluency leads to judgments that fall on the opposite side of the same continuum.

2 This distracter served as the norming study for an unrelated paper (Khemlani et al., 2011). Participants were shown a series of causes (e.g., "Lance dropped his after meal cigarette" or "Natalie is clumsy") and were asked to evaluate on a 1–5 Likert scale how broad a range of effects were likely to be generated by that cause (where 1 meant "a few similar events" and 5 meant "many different events"). For more details on the distracter task, see Study 3 of Khemlani et al. (2011).

3 Mean = 8.2 (on a 1-9 scale), SE =.05.

4 While all of the different stimuli revealed the same trends across conditions, there was a strong main effect of item. For example, participants gave relatively high truth ratings to "Osorno is in Chile" (x = 6.8) but gave low ratings of liking to the image of the toaster (x = 3.2). The particular item of judgment was statistically controlled for (by including item as a covariate in the analyses) so as to reduce the variance introduced by this main effect. Because truth and liking judgments were elicited using different items, controlling for item had a secondary effect of controlling for domain of judgment as well.

5 A critic might note that unremembered items were split between fluent and disfluent conditions, and argue that disfluency did not bolster memory in this particular experiment. It is worth noting, however, that unremembered items were also roughly split between immediate and delayed conditions. Thus, using the logic above, one could argue that delay was not detrimental to memory. A more likely explanation is that a certain subset of the population was not taking the task seriously, and thus never encoded the stimuli to begin with (c.f., Oppenheimer, Meyvis, & Davidenko, 2009). In other words this evidence does not really speak to the issue of retrieval fluency.

References

Alter, A. L., & Oppenheimer, D. M. (2006). Predicting short-term stock fluctuations by using processing fluency. *Proceedings of the National Academy of Sciences, 103,* 9369–9372.

—— (2008a). Easy on the mind, easy on the wallet: The roles of familiarity and processing fluency in valuation judgments. *Psychonomic Bulletin and Review, 15,* 985–990.

—— (2008b). Effects of fluency on psychological distance and mental construal (or why New York is a large city, but *New York* is a civilized jungle). *Psychological Science, 19,* 161–167.

—— (2009a). Uniting the tribes of fluency to form a metacognitive nation. *Personality and Social Psychology Review, 13,* 219–235.

—— (2009b). Suppressing secrecy through metacognitive ease: Cognitive fluency encourages self-disclosure. *Psychological Science, 20,* 1414–1420.

Alter, A. L., Oppenheimer, D. M., Epley, N., & Eyre, R. N. (2007). Overcoming intuition: Metacognitive difficulty activates analytic reasoning. *Journal of Experimental Psychology: General, 136,* 569–576.

Barry, H. A., & Alter, A. L. (2010). The road to fantasy is paved with roadblocks. Unpublished manuscript, New York University.

Bornstein, R. F. (1989). Exposure and affect: Overview and meta-analysis of research, 1968–1987. *Psychological Bulletin, 106,* 265–289.

Bornstein, R. F., & D'Agostino, P. R. (1994). The attribution and discounting of perceptual fluency: Preliminary tests of a perceptual fluency/attributional model of the mere exposure effect. *Social Cognition, 12,* 103–128.

Briñol, P., Petty, R. E., & Tormala, Z. L. (2006). The malleable meaning of subjective ease. *Psychological Science, 17,* 200–206.

Craik, F., & Tulving, E. (1975). Depth of processing and the retention of words in episodic memory. *Journal of Experimental Psychology, 104,* 268–294.

Diemand-Yauman, C., Oppenheimer, D. M., & Vaughan, E. B. (2011). Fortune favors the **Bold** *(and the Italicized)*: Effects of disfluency on educational outcomes. *Cognition*, *118*, 111–115.

Frederick, S. (2005). Cognitive reflection and decision making. *Journal of Economic Perspectives*, *19*, 25–42.

Greifeneder, R., & Bless, H. (2010). The fate of activated information in impression formation: Fluency of concept activation moderates the emergence of assimilation versus contrast. *British Journal of Social Psychology*, *49*, 405–414.

Iyengar, S., & Lepper, M. (2000). When choice is demotivating: Can one desire too much of a good thing? *Journal of Personality and Social Psychology*, *76*, 995–1010.

Jacoby, L. L., Woloshyn, V., & Kelley, C. M. (1989). Becoming famous without being recognized: Unconscious influences of memory produced by dividing attention. *Journal of Experimental Psychology: General*, *118*, 115–125.

Khemlani, S. S., Sussman, A. B., & Oppenheimer, D. M. (2011). *Harry Potter* and the sorcerer's scope: Latent scope biases in explanatory reasoning. *Memory & Cognition*, *39*, 527–535.

Oppenheimer, D. M. (2006). Consequences of erudite vernacular utilized irrespective of necessity: Problems with using long words needlessly. *Applied Cognitive Psychology*, *20*, 139–156.

—— (2008). The secret life of fluency. *Trends in Cognitive Science*, *12*, 237–241.

Oppenheimer, D. M., Meyvis, T., Davidenko, N. (2009). Instructional manipulation checks: Detecting satisficing to increase statistical power. *Journal of Experimental Social Psychology*, *45*, 867–872.

Petrova, P. K., & Cialdini, R. B. (2005). Fluency of consumption imagery and the backfire effects of imagery appeals. *Journal of Consumer Research*, *32*, 442–452.

Reber, R., & Schwarz, N. (1999). Effects of perceptual fluency on judgments of truth. *Consciousness and Cognition*, *8*, 338–342.

Reber, R., Winkielman, P., & Schwarz, N. (1998). Effects of perceptual fluency on affective judgments. *Psychological Science*, *9*, 45–48.

Schwarz, N. (2004). Metacognitive experiences in consumer judgment and decision making. *Journal of Consumer Psychology*, *14*, 332–348.

Shah, A. K., & Oppenheimer, D. M. (2007). Easy does it: The role of fluency in cue weighting. *Judgement and Decision Making*, *2*, 371–379.

Song, H., & Schwarz, N. (2008). Fluency and the detection of misleading questions: Low processing fluency attenuates the Moses illusion. *Social Cognition*, *26*, 791–799.

—— (2009). If it's difficult to pronounce, it must be risky: Fluency, familiarity, and risk perception. *Psychological Science*, *20*, 135–138.

Stepper, S., & Strack, F. (1993). Proprioceptive determinants of emotional and nonemotional feelings. *Journal of Personality and Social Psychology*, *64*, 211–220.

Strack, F., & Neumann, R. (2000). Furrowing the brow may undermine perceived fame: The role of facial feedback in judgments of celebrity. *Personality and Social Psychology Bulletin*, *26*, 762–768.

Unkelbach, C. (2006). The learned interpretation of cognitive fluency. *Psychological Science*, *17*, 339–345.

Wänke, M., & Bless, H. (2000). The effects of subjective ease of retrieval on attitudinal judgments: The moderating role of processing motivation. In H. Bless & J. P. Forgas (Eds.), *The message within: The role of subjective experience in social cognition and behavior.* (pp. 143–161). New York: Psychology Press.

Zajonc, R. B. (1968). Attitudinal effects of mere exposure. *Journal of Personality and Social Psychology*, *9*, 1–27.

Part II
Fluency in social processing

7 Ease and persuasion

Multiple processes, meanings, and effects

Pablo Briñol, Zakary L. Tormala and Richard E. Petty

Abstract

This chapter describes the mechanisms through which the experience of processing ease, or fluency, can influence attitudes and persuasion. In particular, we argue that ease can impact attitude change not only by serving as a peripheral cue (e.g., being experienced as positive affect or as input to an availability heuristic), but also by affecting the thoughts people generate and the confidence with which those thoughts are held. Of importance, the conditions necessary for each of these processes to operate are specified in this review. Because the different mechanisms operate in different contexts, appreciation of the multiple roles for ease can shed new light on situations in which ease effects should be more or less likely to emerge, and more or less likely to persist.

This chapter describes the mechanisms by which the experience of processing ease, or fluency, can influence attitudes and persuasion, specifying the conditions under which several distinct processes are likely to operate. In particular, we argue that ease can impact attitude change not only by serving as a peripheral cue (e.g., being experienced as positive affect or as input to an availability heuristic), but also by affecting the thoughts people generate and the confidence with which those thoughts are held. We begin by providing a brief description of some of the persuasion paradigms in which ease has been studied. We focus on paradigms in which people persuade themselves through their own thoughts, either in response to persuasive messages from external sources or in response to instructions to produce their own messages. In each case, the ease with which those thoughts come to mind plays a critical role in persuasion. The next section describes work on ease of retrieval conducted in the domain of attitude change, focusing on the multiple processes by which ease of retrieval effects can operate and examining the moderating conditions for each of those processes. Finally, we provide an overview of persuasion research suggesting that ease can be associated with different meanings.

Persuasion as a function of thoughts

Classic and contemporary research on persuasion suggests that persuasive messages can influence people's attitudes through both thoughtful and non-thoughtful routes (e.g., Petty & Cacioppo, 1986). When persuasion is thoughtful, attitudes depend on the thoughts people generate in response to messages or message topics. The idea that persuasion depends on the extent to which individuals articulate and rehearse their own idiosyncratic thoughts to external messages was first outlined by Greenwald (1968) in what he called a *cognitive response theory* of attitude change (for a comprehensive review, see Petty, Ostrom, & Brock, 1981). This view essentially argues that people are persuaded (or resist persuasion) by virtue of their own thoughts rather than by learning the message per se, as had been argued by earlier learning theories (Hovland, Janis, & Kelley, 1953). Persuasive appeals that elicit thoughts that are primarily favorable toward a particular recommendation (e.g., "if that new laundry detergent makes my clothes smell fresh, I'll be more popular"), produce agreement whereas appeals that elicit unfavorable thoughts toward the recommendation do not (e.g., "I'm no better off just because that new laundry detergent comes in an attractive box"), regardless of whether the message content can be learned and recalled.

Although most work on persuasion focuses on messages that come from other people (e.g., advertisers), messages that people generate themselves can also be quite effective in producing attitude change. The persuasive effect of completely self-generated messages was shown in early research on role-playing. This literature shows that individuals who generate arguments (e.g., following instructions to convince a friend to quit smoking) are more persuaded than those who receive the same information passively (e.g., Janis & King, 1954). In this research, people were typically asked to generate messages on certain topics (e.g., the dangers of smoking), and their subsequent attitudes were compared with those in a control group who had either passively listened to the communication or who had received no message. Generally speaking, active generation of a message was shown to be a successful strategy for producing attitude change (Watts, 1967; Huesmann, Eron, Klein, Brice, & Fischer, 1983). Just as the act of generating a communication on a topic has been found to influence one's position on that topic, so too has the mere *anticipation* of performing such an act, by affecting the thoughts that people generate about the topic (e.g., Cialdini & Petty, 1979).

In addition to generating and anticipating messages, research has shown that people can persuade themselves when they try to remember past behaviors, imagine future behaviors, explain some behavior, or merely think about an event. For example, people who are asked to imagine hypothetical events come to believe that those events have a higher likelihood of occurring (e.g., Anderson, 1983; Anderson, Lepper, & Ross, 1983; Sherman, Cialdini, Schwartzman, & Reynolds, 1985). In another line of research, Tesser and colleagues showed that merely thinking about an attitude object, without any external information presented or requested, can lead to attitude change. For example, spontaneously thinking about a person who did something nice leads to more favorable evaluations of that person (compared to when distracted from thinking), whereas thinking about a person who was insulting leads to more negative evaluations (see Tesser, Martin, & Mendolia, 1995, for a review). Thus, when work on cognitive responses is considered along with the research just described on role-playing and mere thought, it suggests that virtually all attitude change stems from self-persuasion. That is, at least when people are thinking, attitude change is based on the extent to which people generate favorable rather than unfavorable thoughts, on their own or in response to a persuasive message.

Ease of thought generation

Traditional approaches to persuasion have focused on primary thoughts—that is, the thoughts individuals have about attitude objects—whether self-generated or in response to a message. Interestingly, though, recent research suggests that in addition to primary thoughts, people can have secondary thoughts that is, thoughts about their primary thoughts or *metacognitions* (Briñol & DeMarree, 2012; Petty, Briñol, Tormala, & Wegener, 2007). According to this metacognitive view, generating favorable or unfavorable thoughts in response to a persuasive message is an important factor in producing attitude change, but what people *think* about their thoughts is critically important as well (e.g., Petty, Briñol, & Tormala, 2002). Of particular relevance to the current chapter is the perceived ease with which people's thoughts come to mind.

One of the earliest demonstrations of the effect of ease of thought generation on judgment came from Schwarz, Bless, Strack, Klumpp, Rittenauer-Schatka, and Simons (1991) now classic *ease of retrieval* studies. Schwarz et al. asked participants to rate their own assertiveness after generating six versus twelve examples of their own assertive behavior. They found that people viewed themselves as more assertive after retrieving six rather than 12 examples. This result was initially surprising because a straightforward application of accessibility and self-persuasion principles would have suggested that people generating 12 instances of assertiveness would have judged themselves to be more assertive than those generating six instances. The fact that the opposite was observed suggested that something beyond the mere number and direction of thoughts generated must have played a role. Schwarz and colleagues concluded that people also considered the ease with which their thoughts could be retrieved or generated.

Since this initial demonstration, the ease of retrieval effect has been observed in numerous domains and across diverse topics and measures (see Schwarz, 1998, 2004, Sanna & Lunberg, 2012, for reviews). In an example from our own research that is particularly relevant to persuasion, Tormala, Petty, and Briñol (2002) asked undergraduates to generate either two or ten arguments in support of a new campus policy. Results indicated that generating two favorable thoughts led to more favorable attitudes than did generating ten favorable thoughts. Thus, thinking of fewer arguments was more persuasive than thinking of many, because of the ease of generating those arguments when just a few were requested.

When it was easier to think of favorable arguments, those arguments carried more weight. Thus, the subjective experience of ease can play an important role in self-persuasion. Next, we discuss why ease matters.

Multiple processes driving ease effects

How does ease influence persuasion? Perspectives have varied with respect to the mechanisms driving ease of retrieval effects. Understanding these mechanisms is critical for a number of reasons, however, not the least of which is that it has implications for the immediate and long-term consequences of persuasion stemming from ease. For example, the more (less) thoughtful the mechanism that is involved, the more (less) the persuasion it creates is expected to be durable, resistant, and impactful over time (Petty, Haugtvedt, & Smith, 1995). Consistent with the Elaboration Likelihood Model of persuasion (ELM; Petty & Cacioppo, 1986; Petty & Briñol, 2012), we suggest that the psychological processes mediating the effect of ease on attitude change can be organized into a finite set that operate at different points along an elaboration continuum. Under low thinking conditions, ease—like other variables—can influence attitudes by operating as a judgment cue or heuristic. This would typically produce an effect consistent with its valence which is generally positive (e.g., see Winkielman & Cacioppo, 2001). When the likelihood of thinking is relatively high, the same experience of ease can impact persuasion by affecting the direction of the thoughts that come to mind, or by serving as a piece of evidence (i.e., an argument) to be scrutinized. When elaboration is not constrained to be very low or high, ease can influence attitudes by affecting the amount of thinking that occurs. Thus, the ELM describes several processes of primary cognition through which variables such as ease can affect persuasion: by serving as a simple cue, by affecting either the amount or direction of thinking, and by functioning as an argument.

In addition to these four possibilities, we have recently proposed that any variable (including ease) can also impact whether or not people use their thoughts by influencing what people think about their thoughts. This idea is referred to as the *self-validation hypothesis* (Petty, Briñol, & Tormala, 2002). The key tenet is that generating or having thoughts is not sufficient for these thoughts to impact judgment. Rather, people must also have confidence in the thoughts. When people perceive their thoughts to be valid, they have confidence in them and rely on them in forming their judgments. When people have doubt about their thoughts or perceive them to be invalid, they do not use them as a basis for judgment. Thus, self-validation provides a fifth mechanism by which variables such as ease can influence attitudes—by affecting thought confidence. Unlike previous mechanisms of attitude change that focus on primary or first-order cognition, this new process emphasizes secondary or meta-cognition.

As an illustration of the integrative power of this conceptual framework, consider the effect of another subjective experience—one's incidental emotions—on evaluative judgments. Consistent with the ELM, prior research has shown that a person's emotions can influence attitudes through multiple processes (see Petty,

Fabrigar, & Wegener, 2003). First, when thinking is constrained to be low, emotions tend to serve as simple associative cues and produce evaluations consistent with their valence (e.g., happiness leads to more persuasion than sadness; Petty, Schumann, Richman, & Strathman, 1993). When the likelihood of thinking is not constrained to be high or low by other variables, emotions can affect the extent of thinking. For example, people may think about messages more when in a sad than happy state either because sadness signals a problem to be solved (Schwarz, Bless, & Bohner, 1991) or conveys a sense of uncertainty (Tiedens & Linton, 2001). When thinking is high, emotions can bias one's ongoing thoughts (Petty et al., 1993). For example, positive consequences seem more likely when people are in a happy rather than sad state (DeSteno, Petty, Wegener, & Rucker, 2000). Finally, the self-validation hypothesis suggests that emotions can also affect thought confidence (e.g., happy people have more confidence in their thoughts than do sad people). Consistent with this possibility, Briñol, Petty, and Barden (2007) found that when placed in a happy (versus sad) state following a persuasive message, participants relied more on their valenced thoughts as a basis for their attitudes (e.g., forming favorable attitudes when their thoughts were favorable).

We postulate that ease, like emotions, can influence persuasion through multiple mechanisms. First, when thinking is low, ease should act as a simple cue to persuasion by invoking positive affect or a simple heuristic. In fact, in the very first report of the ease of retrieval effect, the explanation was based on a heuristic account. Specifically, Schwarz, Bless, Strack, Klumpp, Rittenauer-Schatka, and Simons (1991; see also Schwarz, 1998) argued that the effect is driven by an availability heuristic (Tversky & Kahneman, 1974), whereby the easier it is to generate information in favor of something, the more supportive information people assume there must be. Conversely, having difficulty induces the perception that there is little support available. When it is difficult to generate a list of positive thoughts about a policy, for instance, people are assumed to infer that there must not be many positive things about it. When it is easy to generate positive thoughts, on the other hand, people are assumed to infer that there must be many positive things about the policy. These simple inferences could provide simple cues to guide persuasion when one's motivation or ability to think is relatively low (Rothman & Schwarz, 1998). Indeed, Kühnen (2010) recently provided evidence that ease can influence judgment by working as a simple cue (at least when ease is salient) when motivation and ability to think are low.

Also consistent with the notion that ease can operate through low thinking processes, ease has been known to provide a simple associative cue that produces judgments consistent with its valence. Specifically, ease has been shown to be associated with, and even actively produce, positive affect (Moons, Mackie, & Garcia-Marques, 2009; Winkielman & Cacioppo, 2001; Winkielman, Schwarz, Reber, & Fazendeiro, 2003). This feeling can become attached to or associated with a persuasive advocacy, and thus produce more favorable attitudes following that advocacy, perhaps via misattribution effects or classical conditioning.

In sum, under low thinking conditions, ease of retrieving or generating arguments can influence attitudes by operating as a cue implying that the arguments are frequent (Schwarz, Bless, Strack, Klumpp, Rittenauer-Schatka, and Simons, 1991), familiar (Garcia-Marques & Mackie, 2000), or true (Unkelbach, 2007). Which of these meanings drives persuasion likely depends on which is most salient in a particular context (e.g., a numerical context might prime frequency rather than familiarity). Of course, the meanings themselves also are malleable as a function of the context (e.g., ease can be interpreted as indicating truth or falsehood; Unkelbach, 2007). As we will describe later, we postulate that the inferences made from ease are more likely to be applied to external information (e.g., the persuasive message, the position advocated) under low thinking conditions, but to internal information (e.g., one's thoughts) under high thinking conditions.

In addition to this cue role that operates when thinking is low, when elaboration is not constrained to be high or low, ease can affect one's extent of information processing. Specifically, ease (compared to difficulty) appears to reduce processing activity (e.g., Alter, Oppenheimer, Epley, & Eyre, 2007). One potential reason is that when people feel confident due to ease of processing, they feel little need to seek out or consider additional information for their judgments. In contrast, when people lack confidence due to processing difficulty, they feel greater motivation to seek out and carefully scrutinize information that might provide more insight and a more valid judgment. Indeed, many forms of doubt stemming from sources other than difficulty have been found to increase information processing (see Petty & Briñol, 2009, for a review).

It is also clear that in the traditional ease of retrieval paradigm, the difficult condition involves more thinking than the easy condition. Indeed, in the difficult condition people are asked to generate a large number of thoughts, whereas in the easy condition people are asked to generate a lower number of thoughts. Recent research has shown that when people are asked to generate a large and difficult number of thoughts in this paradigm, they also spontaneously generate a number of unrequested thoughts—that is, thoughts in the opposite direction of those that are requested. Tormala, Falces, Briñol, and Petty (2007) found that the more difficult it is to retrieve or generate a given set of thoughts or arguments, the more likely it is that unrequested, or unwanted, thoughts also come to mind. Moreover, these unrequested thoughts are partly responsible for the ease of retrieval effect: when it is difficult to generate positive thoughts, for instance, more negative thoughts come to mind and those thoughts push attitudes in a negative direction (see also Wänke, this volume).

When people are motivated and able to think, ease can play other roles. For example, ease might bias thoughts in a positive manner, again assuming that ease is positively valenced. For example, if ease induces positive affect as suggested by Winkielman, Schwarz, Fazendeiro, and Reber (2003), then ease should increase the generation of favorable thoughts in response to persuasive messages and reduce the generation of counterarguments. In addition, when thinking is high, ease could be evaluated as evidence if it provides diagnostic information about the merits of an object. For example, processing ease could spark the perception that a product or device will be quick to learn, which could be interpreted as evidence supporting the claim that the device is simple and straightforward. Of course, if people believe that their judgments are somehow being biased or influenced by the ease or difficulty with which they can process information (e.g., very simple fonts might seem like a blatant attempt to make a product appear easy to use), and they do not want this to occur, people can adjust their judgments in a direction opposite to the expected bias (i.e., a correction effect; Wegener & Petty, 1997). In the domain of ease, discounting or correcting would leave people with the content of the thought (i.e., the primary cognition) as a basis for judgment (Strack & Hannover, 1996).

Finally, ease effects under high thinking conditions could stem from self-validation processes. Indeed, Tormala et al. (2002) found that self-validation can underlie ease effects in persuasion when people are motivated and able to think about an issue. In a series of studies, we found that when it was easy to generate positive thoughts about a policy (e.g., because two rather than ten were requested), participants were more confident in the validity of those specific thoughts. Furthermore, thought confidence mediated the effect of ease on attitudes following a persuasive message, but as we describe in the next section this only occurred under high elaboration conditions, when people had the motivation to reflect on their own thought processes.

As another example of ease affecting thought-confidence, consider work on embodiment suggesting that the feeling of ease can also stem from bodily experiences. For example, in a study applying self-validation to self-evaluation (Briñol & Petty, 2003, Experiment 4), participants were asked as part of an ostensible graphology study to think about and write about their best or worse qualities using their dominant or non-dominant hands. Then, participants rated the confidence they had in the thoughts they listed and they reported their self-esteem. Because writing with the non-dominant hand is difficult, whereas writing with the dominant hand is easy, it was expected (and found) that using the non-dominant hand decreased the confidence with which people held the thoughts they had listed. As a consequence, the effect of the best or worst qualities manipulation on state self-esteem was significantly greater when participants wrote their thoughts with their dominant rather than non-dominant hand. That is, writing positive thoughts about oneself with the dominant hand increased self-esteem relative to writing positive thoughts with the non-dominant hand, but writing negative thoughts with the dominant hand reduced self-esteem relative to writing with the non-dominant hand. Thus, people do not feel as badly about themselves even after listing negative self-relevant thoughts if they write those thoughts with difficultly.

In closing, we posit that under high thinking conditions, inferences about ease are more likely to be applied to one's thoughts, meaning self-validation processes are more likely to operate and there should be an interaction between ease and argument quality on attitudes. That is, regardless of whether ease operates through affect, familiarity, truth, or validity, it should interact with the direction of the thoughts under high thinking (such as when people have to actively generate their own thoughts). In other persuasion paradigms, however, in which thinking is constrained at a lower level, simple inferences of familiarity, truth, or affect stemming from ease are more likely to be applied to the arguments (not to the thoughts), producing a main effect on attitudes regardless of argument quality. For example, if people are not thinking carefully, weak and strong arguments alike might be seen as more familiar, likable, and true, leading to more persuasion. If people are thinking carefully, however, then the unfavorable thoughts to weak arguments would be seen as more familiar, likable, or true, leading to less persuasion. As noted, the particular inference that comes to mind can depend on a number of different factors. Furthermore, even if more than one inference (e.g., frequency and validity) is made based on ease in a particular situation, those inferences might operate differently at different levels of thinking (e.g., validity concerns are more likely to play a mediating role under high thinking conditions). Indeed, Tormala et al., (2002) showed in a self-persuasion paradigm that both frequency and validity inferences come to mind from ease but only the later mediated the impact of ease on attitudes. This result suggests that many inferences are possible based on ease, but the effect of those inferences on attitudes depends on the circumstances.

Specifying the process by which ease operates is important for persuasion because different mechanisms have implications for the durability and impactfulness of attitudes derived from subjective ease. More thoughtful processes of persuasion tend to be more consequential. Specifically, attitudes changed with high thought tend to be more persistent over time, resistant to change, and predictive of behavior than attitudes change by low thought processes (Petty, Haugtvedt, & Smith, 1995). This aspect is crucial because it shows that the same source variable (e.g., ease) can lead to the same outcome (more persuasion) by serving as a simple cue (for conditions of low elaboration) or by biasing the generation of positive thoughts (for conditions of high elaboration) or by validating those thoughts (for conditions in which people think about their thoughts). Although those effects might seem similar on the surface, the underlying mechanism that produces these effects for ease is different, leading to differences in the strength of the attitudes formed.

Multiple moderators of ease effects

In addition to proposing new processes driving the impact of ease on attitudes, persuasion research also points to unique moderators for each of these processes. Thus, thinking about the mechanisms for ease effects in persuasion also has implications for understanding the circumstances under which ease is more or less likely to matter. Next, we describe two of those moderating variables.

Elaboration

The first moderating factor relevant for understanding ease of retrieval effects in persuasion is elaboration, or extent of thinking. There have been differing perspectives and divergent findings with respect to whether ease effects on persuasion are more likely to emerge under low or high elaboration conditions. As noted earlier, the first explanation for ease effects assumed that they were heuristic in nature and, thus, most likely to operate when elaboration is low (see Schwarz, 1998). Some evidence has been produced that is consistent with this view (Grayson & Schwarz, 1999; Rothman & Schwarz, 1998; Ruder & Bless, 2003). Other research, however, has pointed to the exact opposite conclusion—that is, that ease effects are more likely to operate under high elaboration conditions, when people have the motivation and ability to attend to and interpret their own cognitive experience (Hirt, Kardes, & Markman, 2004; Tormala et al., 2002; Wänke & Bless, 2000).

This controversy may stem, at least in part, from different perspectives on the mechanism responsible for ease of retrieval effects. Researchers in this area originally assumed that ease of retrieval effects were mediated by availability inferences (see Schwarz, 1998). As explained earlier, difficulty in generating favorable arguments for a tax cut, for example, would be assumed to indicate in a simple cue-based fashion that few favorable arguments exist, implying that the tax cut is questionable. The experience of ease, on the other hand, would presumably suggest that many favorable arguments exist and, thus, that the tax cut is a good idea. Numerosity inferences like these are known to be especially likely under low elaboration conditions (e.g., Blankenship et al., 2008; Petty & Cacioppo, 1984). Thus, according to an availability account, ease of retrieval effects in persuasion should emerge mainly when elaboration is low.

As also noted earlier, however, other research (Tormala et al., 2002, 2007) suggests that ease effects can be mediated not only by perceptions of the number of arguments or thoughts available in memory, but also by feelings of confidence or validity associated with the particular arguments or thoughts retrieved. In particular, the easier it is to generate a list of arguments supporting a tax cut, the more confident one can be that those arguments are valid, or compelling (see also Wänke & Bless, 2000). Confidence has been implicated in ease of retrieval effects in other ways as well. Haddock, Rothman, Reber, and Schwarz (1999), for example, found that the easier it was for people to list arguments in support of their attitudes, the more certain they became of their attitudes. In any case, confidence or certainty adjustments of this nature have been found to be most likely and most influential on other outcomes when elaboration is high (Petty et al., 2002; Petty, Tormala, & Rucker, 2004; Tormala et al., 2002). Ultimately, our multiple roles perspective indicates that ease of retrieval likely plays a role in persuasion through distinct processes under different levels of elaboration likelihood.

Timing

Recent research has suggested that processing disfluency results in more detail-oriented, effortful strategies of problem solving (e.g., Alter et al., 2007). Song and Schwarz (2008) provided support for this idea using the Moses illusion (see Erickson & Mattson, 1981). In this illusion, when people are asked, "How many animals of each kind did Moses take on the ark?" most answer "two" even though the biblical protagonist actually was Noah, not Moses. When participants read the

Moses question in difficult-to-read (versus easy-to-read) font, however, they are more likely to take a careful approach and answer that Moses did not build the ark. This research suggests that compared to difficulty, ease might decrease processing of persuasive messages. We submit that this effect is likely moderated by the timing of the ease induction. In particular, ease (or fluency) might decrease message-processing when a sense of ease is induced before a message, because it increases feelings confidence, which is associated with decreased elaboration (e.g., Tiedens & Linton, 2001; Weary & Jacobson, 1997). As described already, though, our research on self-validation has shown that, by affecting thought confidence, ease of processing can also increase reliance on thoughts when the sense of ease accompanies message-processing (Tormala et al., 2002, 2007).

Bringing these two ideas together, it seems likely that ease can decrease thinking (e.g., by making people confident of their previous views) when induced before message-processing, or it can validate thinking (by making people confident in their thoughts about a message) when induced during or after message-processing. Future research should explore this question further by directly manipulating the timing of ease or fluency manipulations (for a review of other manipulations of timing, see Briñol & Petty, 2009). Also germane, future research should clarify the mental construct to which people apply their feeling of ease (e.g., attitudes vs. thoughts). If they apply ease to their initial attitude, they will likely feel more confident about that attitude and engage in reduced processing. If they apply ease to their thoughts, they should feel more confident about their thoughts and potentially change their attitudes to align them with those thoughts.

Multiple meanings of ease

As noted, people generally construe ease in retrieving thoughts as good by default. That is, all else equal, ease seems to have positive psychological value. For example, research has shown that processing fluency often translates into favorable judgments and feelings, including judgments of familiarity, truth, positive affect, liking, and beauty (e.g., Winkielman & Schwarz, 2001; Winkielman, et al., 2003). However, people need not perceive ease in such terms. Indeed, there could be natural variance in perceptions of ease and even room to manipulate those perceptions. If people's naïve theories regarding the meaning of ease vary (or could be varied), then different judgments could arise following the experience of ease.

In one study investigating this possibility, Briñol, Petty, and Tormala (2006) asked participants to generate either two or ten arguments in favor of a counterattitudinal proposal. In addition, Briñol et al. manipulated the perceived meaning of ease versus difficulty. Half of the participants were told that ease in generating thoughts generally reflected thoughts that were low in complexity and, accordingly, that intelligent people (who have more complex thoughts) typically experienced more difficulty generating thoughts than unintelligent people. The remaining participants received the opposite information implying that ease was an indicator of intelligence. Consistent with expectations, results indicated that the traditional ease-of-retrieval effect emerged only among participants who received the "ease is good" instructions. That is, among these participants, those listing two positive arguments (an easy task) reported more favorable attitudes than did participants listing ten positive arguments (a difficult task). Among participants receiving the "ease is bad" instructions, the opposite effect emerged; this group reported more favorable attitudes when listing ten rather than two positive arguments. The same pattern was observed when processing ease was manipulated in other ways as well. Thus, people's interpretation of the *meaning* of processing ease is critical in determining ease's downstream consequences (see also Unkelbach & Greifeneder, Chapter 2, this volume).

The studies by Briñol et al. (2006) resonate with other research revealing that a variety of metacognitive experiences can have flexible interpretations and effects. For instance, although people generally associate perceptual fluency with familiarity and perceptual difficulty with unfamiliarity or novelty (e.g., Jacoby, Kelley, Brown, & Jasechko, 1989; Monin, 2003), this association is malleable. People can be trained to associate fluency with unfamiliarity (and difficulty with familiarity), which reverses the traditional effect of fluency on familiarity judgments (Unkelbach, 2006; Labroo & Kim, 2009).

Other psychological constructs related to ease or fluency also have been shown to have divergent attitudinal effects depending on salient naïve theories. In one recent study, Tormala, Clarkson, and Henderson (2011) manipulated people's perceptions that they had evaluated an issue quickly or slowly. They found that perceiving fast evaluation generally boosted attitude certainty among participants who trusted their intuitive gut reactions, whereas it dampened certainty among those who believed thoughtful analyses were more optimal. Similarly, Tormala et al. found that perceiving fast (versus slow) evaluation increased attitude certainty when people evaluated familiar objects or were expressing their attitudes, but reduced attitude certainty when people evaluated unfamiliar objects or were forming their attitudes. Most germane to the current concerns, mediation analyses suggested that when people expressed their opinions or evaluated familiar objects (about which they presumably already had opinions), fast evaluation indicated greater ease of processing, which boosted certainty in the evaluation that came to mind.

Similar effects have been observed with respect to cognitive depletion, or mental fatigue. In one set of studies, Wan, Rucker, Tormala, and Clarkson (2010) showed that people typically associate cognitive depletion with having invested a great deal of effort thinking about a particular subject. Moreover, Wan et al. found that because thinking carefully about something—or believing that one has done so (Barden & Petty, 2008)—is associated with increased certainty, people who feel depleted while evaluating an object subsequently report greater attitude certainty with respect to that object. However, when people are induced to associate depletion with reduced information processing, this pattern is reversed such that participants who feel depleted report less attitude certainty than participants who do not. Thus, in many different but related domains, people's judgments regarding the meaning of their metacognitive experiences have been shown to be important determinants of attitudinal outcomes. What is more, people's judgments regarding the meaning of their metacognitive experiences are malleable, so people who are having similar metacognitive experiences can show very different judgments depending on their chronic or situational theories about these experiences (see also Job, Dweck, & Walton, 2010).

In sum, the meaning or valence of variables such as ease can vary across individuals and situations. If the meaning changes, the subsequent effects on attitudes also change (Briñol et al., 2006). This implies that the same variable might increase or decrease persuasion as a function of other variables such as naïve theories. For example, repetition of a judgment tends to increase the accessibility of the mental construct repeated, and therefore the ease with which it comes to mind. However, the meaning of that ease when it arises can vary as a function of a number of variables such as the construct repeated and even the number of repetitions. In other words, although repetition generally increases ease, that ease might have different meanings and effects depending on what is being repeated and how often.

In a series of recent studies, Briñol and Petty (2011) explored this possibility. In one experiment, participants were asked to list positive or negative thoughts about a proposal containing a mixture of strong and weak arguments, and to report their attitudes toward it. Next, participants were induced to repeatedly express either the thoughts they listed or the attitudes they reported. The key hypothesis was that repetition of a clear judgment (e.g., an attitude) would increase ease of retrieving the judgment and that ease would be interpreted as something good, producing an increase in attitude confidence. In contrast to attitudes, it was hypothesized that repeating one's thoughts might create a feeling of ease that was interpreted as something bad, undermining thought confidence. This is because thought repetition frequently is associated with rumination, which occurs when one is uncertain of one's thoughts. In essence, it was expected that repetition could increase or decrease certainty depending on whether thoughts or attitudes were being repeated, even though repetition increases ease, or fluency, in both cases. As predicted, the results indicated that repetition increased doubt when thoughts were repeated, whereas it increased confidence when attitudes were repeated. As a consequence of reducing thought-confidence, thought repetition decreased persuasion when the thoughts were positive but increased persuasion when thoughts were negative. These findings are consistent with previous research showing that repetition of mental content can be associated with either positive or negative consequences. For example, Holland, Verplanken, and van Knippenberg (2003) found that repeating one's attitude increased its accessibility and fostered greater attitude certainty (see also Petrocelli, Tormala, & Rucker, 2007). In contrast, Segerstrom, Stanton, Alden, and Shortridge (2003) showed that repeating thoughts that are perceived as uncontrollable (e.g., rumination) is associated with greater doubt and less well-being.

In addition to the specific construct rehearsed, it could be that the number of repetitions matters. For example, although more repetitions of a construct would increase ease relative to fewer repetitions of the same construct, the meaning of the ease that comes from excessive repetition might differ. That is, too many repetitions still increase ease but might trigger doubt if continuing repetition signals that something is wrong with the attitude or thought in question. The logic would be similar to what has been observed in the literature on mere exposure effects (e.g., Cacioppo & Petty, 1979; Zajonc, 1968; Bornstein, 1989), where initial repetition leads to positive reactions but further repetitions can lead to tedium and negative reactions (see also Herzog & Hertwig, Chapter 12, this volume).

Recent studies have uncovered precisely this type of curvilinear effect in the classic mere thought paradigm. Clarkson, Tormala, and Leone (2011) asked participants to think about an attitudinal issue for a brief, moderate, or extended period and then examined attitude polarization versus depolarization as a function of time. Clarkson et al. found that although attitude polarization increased when participants thought about an issue for a moderate as opposed to brief period of time, this effect was undone and even reversed at extended period of times such that attitudes actually depolarized when participants thought about the issue for too long. Moreover, this curvilinear effect of time on polarization was driven by perceived ease of thinking and thought confidence. The curvilinear effect of thought time on attitude polarization was initially attributed to the setting in of "reality constraints" as people thought too much about an attitude object (e.g., "this ice cream can't be that good!"; see Tesser, 1978). The self-validation hypothesis provides an alternative account. In particular, participants found it difficult to keep thinking new thoughts about an issue when the timeframe was too long, and this difficulty undermined their confidence in the thoughts they already had. Because thoughts were mostly attitude-consistent, reduced thought confidence led to attitude depolarization.

Summary and conclusions

The classic work on ease of retrieval, and much of the work we have discussed in this chapter, has relied on a paradigm in which the number of thoughts people generate is experimentally manipulated. In closing this review, it is important to note that there are many other sources of ease (and processing fluency more generally) that can be studied while holding the actual number of thoughts constant. For example, ease of processing is affected not only by exposure frequency (repetition and, thus, accessibility), but also by exposure duration, visual clarity, visual contrast, simplicity, symmetry, balance, prototypicality, priming, context congruity, and rhyme, among other variables (for a review see Alter & Oppenheimer, 2009). In one persuasion study exploring color contrast effects, Briñol et al. (2006) showed that people were more persuaded by strong arguments but less for weak arguments when the message appeared in a standard and easy-to-read format (black letters on a white background) rather than an unusual and difficult-to-read format (yellow letters on a pink background; see also Reber & Schwarz, 1999).

In closing, this review has described the ways ease, or processing fluency more generally, can affect attitude change and persuasion through different mechanisms in different circumstances. Although we have described the multiple roles ease can have in persuasion, self-validation processes (i.e., thought confidence) have been highlighted as a more recently discovered mechanism by which variables such as ease can impact attitudes and other judgments. Of importance, the conditions necessary for each of these processes to operate have been outlined. Some of these effects have been studied, whereas others demand future attention to learn more about the many roles ease can play in this domain. As described in this chapter, specifying these different roles is important because different mechanisms have implications for the durability and impactfulness of attitudes derived from subjective ease. That is, when ease produces attitudinal effects is a thoughtful way (e.g., biasing or validating thinking), the resulting attitudes are more likely to persist over time, resist change, and predict behavior than when ease produces effects in a relatively non-thoughtful way (e.g., serving as input to a heuristic). Moreover, because the different mechanisms operate in different contexts, appreciation of the multiple roles for ease can shed new light on situations in which ease effects should be more or less likely to emerge, and more or less likely to be consequential. Recent work has made great strides in understanding ease effects in attitude change, but there is substantial room to deepen our insights in this domain.

References

Alter, A. L., & Oppenheimer, D. M. (2009). Uniting the tribes of fluency to form a metacognitive nation. *Personality and Social Psychology Review, 13*, 219–235.

Alter, A. L., Oppenheimer, D. M., Epley, N., & Eyre, R. N. (2007). Overcoming intuition: Metacognitive difficulty activates analytic reasoning. *Journal of Experimental Psychology: General, 136*, 569–576.

Anderson, C. A. (1983). Imagination and expectation: The effect of imagining behavioral scripts on personal intentions. *Psychological Bulletin, 93*, 30–56.

Anderson, C. A., Lepper, M. R., & Ross, R. (1983). Perseverance of social theories: The role of explanation in the persistence of discredited information. *Journal of Personality and Social Psychology, 39*, 1037–1049.

Barden, J., & Petty, R. E. (2008). The mere perception of elaboration creates attitude certainty: Exploring the thoughtfulness heuristic. *Journal of Personality and Social Psychology, 95*, 489–509.

Blankenship, K. L., Wegener, D. T., Petty, R. E., Detweiler-Bedell, B., & Macy, C. L. (2008). Elaboration and consequences of anchored estimates: An attitudinal perspective on numerical anchoring. *Journal of Experimental Social Psychology, 44*, 1465–1476.

Bornstein, R. F. (1989). Exposure and affect: Overview and meta-analysis of research, 1968–1987. *Psychological Bulletin, 106*, 265–289.

Briñol, P., & DeMarree, K. G. (Eds.), (2012). *Social metacognition.* New York: Psychology Press.

Briñol, P., DeMarree, K. G., & Smith, K. (2010). The role of embodied change in perceiving and processing facial expressions of others. *Behavioral and Brain Sciences, 33*, 437–438.

Briñol, P., & Petty, R. E (2003). Overt head movements and persuasion: A self-validation analysis. *Journal of Personality and Social Psychology, 84*, 1123–1139.

—— (2009). Persuasion: Insights from the self-validation hypothesis. In M. P. Zanna (ed.) *Advances in experimental social psychology* (Vol. 41, pp. *69–118).* New York: Elsevier.

—— (2011). Thought repetition: The role of the object of repetition and the number of times. Unpublished manuscript.

—— (2012). The history of attitudes and persuasion research. In A. Kruglanski & W. Stroebe (Eds.), *Handbook of the history of social psychology.* (pp. 285–320) New York: Psychology Press.

Briñol, P., Petty, R. E., & Barden, J. (2007). Happiness versus sadness as a determinant of thought confidence in persuasion: A self-validation analysis. *Journal of Personality and Social Psychology*, *93*, 711–727.

Briñol, P., Petty, R. E., & Tormala, Z. L. (2006). The malleable meaning of subjective ease. *Psychological Science*, *17*, 200–206.

Briñol, P., Petty, R. E., & Wagner, B. C. (2012). Embodied validation: Our body can change and also validate our thoughts. In P. Briñol, & K. G. DeMarree (Eds.), *Social metacognition.* (pp. 219–240) New York: Psychology Press.

Cacioppo, J. T., & Petty, R. E. (1979). The effects of message repetition and position on cognitive responses, recall, and persuasion. *Journal of Personality and Social Psychology*, *37*, 97–109.

Cialdini, R. B., & Petty, R. E. (1981). Anticipatory opinion effects. In R. Petty, T. Ostrom, & T. Brock (Eds.), *Cognitive responses in persuasion* (pp. 217–235). Hillsdale, NJ: Erlbaum.

Clarkson, J. J., Tormala, Z. L., & Leone, C. (2011). A self-validation perspective on the mere thought effect. *Journal of Experimental Social Psychology*, *47*, 449–454.

DeSteno, D., Petty, R. E., Wegener, D. T., & Rucker, D. D. (2000). Beyond valence in the perception of likelihood: The role of emotion specificity. *Journal of Personality and Social Psychology*, *78*, 397–416.

Erickson, T. A., & Mattson, M. F. (1981). From words to meaning: A semantic illusion. *Journal of Verbal Learning and Verbal Behavior*, *20*, 540–552.

Garcia-Marques, T., & Mackie, D. (2000). The positive feeling of familiarity: Mood as an information processing regulation mechanism. In J. Forgas and H. Bless (Eds.), *The message within: The role of subjective experiences in social cognition and behavior.* Philadelphia: Psychology Press

Grayson, C. E., & Schwarz, N. (1999). Beliefs influence information processing strategies: Declarative and experiential information in risk assessment. *Social Cognition*, *17*, 1–18.

Greenwald, A. G. (1968). Cognitive learning, cognitive response to persuasion, and attitude change. In A. Greenwald, T. Brock, & T. Ostrom (Eds.), *Psychological foundations of attitudes.* New York: Academic Press.

Haddock, G., Rothman, A. J., Reber, R., & Schwarz, N. (1999). Forming judgments of attitude certainty, intensity, and importance: The role of subjective experiences. *Personality and Social Psychology Bulletin*, *25*, 771–782.

Hirt, E. R., Kardes, F. R., & Markman, K. D. (2004). Activating a mental simulation mind-set through generation of alternatives: Implications for debiasing in related and unrelated domains. *Journal of Experimental Social Psychology*, *40*, 374–383.

Holland, R., W., Verplanken, B., & van Knippenberg, A. (2003). From repetition to conviction: Attitude accessibility as a determinant of attitude certainty. *Journal of Experimental Social Psychology*, *39*, 594–601.

Hovland, C. I., Janis, I. L., & Kelley, H. H. (1953). *Communication and persuasion: Psychological studies of opinion change.* New Haven, CT: Yale University Press.

Huesmann, L. R., Eron, L. D., Klein, R., Brice, P., & Fischer, P. (1983). Mitigating the imitation of aggressive behaviors by changing children's attitudes about media violence. *Journal of Personality and Social Psychology, 44*, 899–910.

Jacoby, L. L., Kelley, C. M., Brown, J., & Jasechko, J. (1989). Becoming famous overnight: Limits on the ability to avoid unconscious influences of the past. *Journal of Personality and Social Psychology, 56*, 326–338.

Janis, I. L., & King, B. T. (1954). The influence of role-playing on opinion change. *Journal of Abnormal and Social Psychology, 49*, 211–218.

Job, V., Dweck, C. S., & Walton, G. M. (2010). Ego depletion – Is it all in your head?: Implicit theories about willpower affect self-regulation. *Psychological Science, 21*, 1686–1693.

Kühnen, U. (2010). Manipulation-checks as manipulation: Another look at the ease of retrieval heuristic. *Personality and Social Psychology Bulletin, 36*, 47–58.

Labroo, A. A., & Kim, S. (2009). The "instrumentality" heuristic: Why metacognitive difficulty is desirable during goal pursuit. *Psychological Science, 20*, 127–134.

Moons, W. G., Mackie, D. M., & Garcia-Marques, T. (2009). The impact of repetition-induced familiarity on agreement with weak and strong arguments. *Journal of Personality and Social Psychology, 96*, 32–44.

Monin, B. (2003). The warm glow heuristic: When liking leads to familiarity. *Journal of Personality and Social Psychology, 85*, 1035–1048.

Petrocelli, J. V., Tormala, Z. L., & Rucker, D. D. (2007). Unpacking attitude certainty: Attitude clarity and attitude correctness. *Journal of Personality and Social Psychology, 92*, 30–41.

Petty, R. E., & Briñol, P. (2012). The Elaboration Likelihood Model. In P. A. M. Van Lange, A. Kruglanski, & E. T. Higgins (Eds.), *Handbook of theories of social psychology.* (Vol.1, pp. 224–245) London: Sage.

Petty, R. E., & Briñol, P. (2009). Implicit ambivalence: A meta-cognitive approach. In R. E. Petty, R. H. Fazio, & P. Briñol (Eds.), *Attitudes: Insights from the new implicit measures* (pp. 119–161). New York: Psychology Press.

Petty, R. E., Briñol, P., & Tormala, Z. L. (2002). Thought confidence as a determinant of persuasion: The self-validation hypothesis. *Journal of Personality and Social Psychology, 82*, 722–741.

Petty, R. E., Briñol, P., Tormala, Z. L., & Wegener, D. T. (2007). The role of meta-cognition in social judgment. In E. T. Higgins & A. W. Kruglanski (Eds.), *Social psychology: A handbook of basic principles* (2nd ed., pp. 254–284). New York: Guilford Press.

Petty, R. E., & Cacioppo, J. T. (1984). The effects of involvement on response to argument quantity and quality: Central and peripheral routes to persuasion. *Journal of Personality and Social Psychology, 46*, 69–81.

—— (1986). *Communication and persuasion: Central and peripheral routes to attitude change*. New York: Springer-Verlag.

Petty, R. E., Fabrigar, L. R., & Wegener, D. T. (2003). Emotional factors in attitudes and persuasion. In R. J. Davidson, K. R. Scherer, & H. H. Goldsmith (Eds.), *Handbook of affective sciences* (pp. 752–772). Oxford: Oxford University Press.

Petty, R. E., Haugtvedt, C., & Smith, S. M. (1995). Elaboration as a determinant of attitude strength: Creating attitudes that are persistent, resistant, and predictive of behavior. In R. E. Petty & J. A. Krosnick (Eds.), *Attitude strength: Antecedents and consequences* (pp. 93–130). Mahwah, NJ: Erlbaum.

Petty, R. E., Ostrom, T. M., & Brock, T. C. (1981). *Cognitive responses in persuasion*. Hillsdale, NJ: Erlbaum.

Petty, R. E., Schumann, D. W., Richman, S. A., & Strathman, A. J. (1993). Positive mood and persuasion: Different roles for affect under high and low elaboration conditions. *Journal of Personality and Social Psychology*, *64*, 5–20.

Petty, R. E., Tormala, Z. L., & Rucker, D. D. (2004). Resisting persuasion by counterarguing: An attitude strength perspective. In J. T. Jost, M. R. Banaji, & D. A. Prentice (Eds.), *Perspectivism in social psychology: The yin and yang of scientific progress* (pp. 37–51). Washington, DC: American Psychological Association.

Petty, R. E., Wheeler, S. C., & Bizer, G. (2000). Matching effects in persuasion: An elaboration likelihood analysis. In G. Maio & J. Olson (Eds.), *Why we evaluate: Functions of attitudes* (pp. 133–162). Mahwah, NJ: Erlbaum.

Reber, R., & Schwarz, N. (1999). Effects of perceptual fluency on judgments of truth. *Consciousness and Cognition*, *8*, 338–342.

Rothman, A. J., & Schwarz, N. (1998). Constructing perceptions of vulnerability: Personal relevance and the use of experiential information in health judgments. *Personality and Social Psychology Bulletin*, *24*, 1053–1064.

Ruder, M., & Bless, H. (2003). Mood and the reliance on the ease of retrieval heuristic. *Journal of Personality and Social Psychology*, *85*, 20–32.

Sanna, L. J., & Lundberg, K. B. (2012). The experience of thinking: Metacognitive ease, fluency, and context. In P. Briñol, & K. G. DeMarree (Eds.), *Social metacognition*. (pp. 179–198) New York: Psychology Press.

Schwarz, N. (1998). Accessible content and accessibility experiences: The interplay of declarative and experiential information in judgment. *Personality and Social Psychology Review*, *2*, 87–99.

—— (2004). Meta-cognitive experiences in consumer judgment and decision making. *Journal of Consumer Psychology*, *14*, 332–348.

Schwarz, N., Bless, H., & Bohner, G. (1991). Mood and persuasion: Affective status influence the processing of persuasive communications. In M. Zanna (ed.) *Advances in experimental social psychology* (Vol. 24, pp. 161–197). San Diego, CA: Academic Press.

Schwarz, N., Bless, H., Strack, F., Klumpp, G., Rittenauer-Schatka, H., & Simons, A. (1991). Ease of retrieval as information: Another look at the availability heuristic. *Journal of Personality and Social Psychology, 61,* 195–202.

Segerstrom, S. C., Stanton, A. L., Alden, L. E., & Shortridge, B. E. (2003). A multidimensional structure for repetitive thought: What's on your mind, and how, and how much. *Journal of Personality and Social Psychology*, *85*, 909–921.

Sherman, S. J., Cialdini, R. B., Schwartzman, D. F., & Reynolds, K. D. (1985). Imagining can heighten or lower the perceived likelihood of contracting a disease: The mediating effect of ease of imagery. *Personality and Social Psychology Bulletin*, *16*, 405–418.

Song, H., & Schwarz, N. (2008). Fluency and the detection of distortions: Low processing fluency attenuates the Moses illusion. *Social Cognition*, *26*, 791–799.

Strack, F., & Hannover, B. (1996). Awareness of influence as a precondition for implementing correctional goals. In P. M. Gollwitzer & J. A. Bargh (Eds.), *The psychology of action: Linking cognition and motivation to behavior* (pp. 579–596). New York: Guilford.

Tesser, A. (1978). Self-generated attitude change. In L. Berkowitz (ed.) *Advances in experimental social psychology* (Vol. 11, pp. 289–338). New York: Academic Press.

Tesser, A., Martin, L., & Mendolia, M. (1995). The impact of thought on attitude extremity and attitude-behavior consistency. In R. E. Petty & J. A. Krosnick (Eds.), *Attitude strength: Antecedents and consequences* (pp. 73–92). Mahwah, NJ: Erlbaum Associates.

Tiedens, L. Z. & Linton, S. (2001). Judgment under emotional certainty and uncertainty: The effects of specific emotions on information processing. *Journal of Personality and Social Psychology, 81*, 973–988.

Tormala, Z. L, Clarkson, J. J., & Henderson, M. D. (2011). Does fast or slow evaluation foster greater certainty? *Personality and Social Psychology Bulletin, 37*, 422–434.

Tormala, Z. L., Falces, C., Briñol, P., & Petty, R. E. (2007). Ease of retrieval effects in social judgment: The role of unrequested cognitions. *Journal of Personality and Social Psychology, 93*, 143–157.

Tormala, Z. L., Petty, R. E., & Briñol, P. (2002). Ease of retrieval effects in persuasion: A self-validation analysis. *Personality and Social Psychology Bulletin, 28*, 1700–1712.

Tversky, A., & Kahneman, D. (1974). Judgment under uncertainty: Heuristics and biases. *Science, 185*, 1124–1130.

Unkelbach, C. (2006). The learned interpretation of cognitive fluency. *Psychological Science, 17*, 339–345.

—— (2007). Reversing the truth effect: Learning the interpretation of processing fluency in judgments of truth. *Journal of Experimental Psychology: Learning, Memory and Cognition, 33*, 219–230.

Wan, E. W., Rucker, D. D., Tormala, Z. L., & Clarkson, J. J. (2010). The effect of regulatory depletion on attitude certainty. *Journal of Marketing Research, 47*, 531–541.

Wänke, M., & Bless, H. (2000). The effects of subjective ease of retrieval on attitudinal judgments: The moderating role of processing motivation. In H. Bless & J. P. Forgas (Eds.), *The message within: The role of subjective experience in social cognition and behavior* (pp. 143–161). Philadelphia, PA: Taylor & Francis.

Watts, W. A. (1967). Relative persistence of opinion change induced by active compared to passive participation. *Journal of Personality and Social Psychology, 5*, 4–15.

Weary, G., & Jacobson, J. A. (1997). Causal uncertainty beliefs and diagnostic-information seeking. *Journal of Personality and Social Psychology, 73*, 839–848.

Wegener, D. T., & Petty, R. E. (1997). The flexible correction model: The role of naive theories of bias in bias correction. In M. P. Zanna (ed.) *Advances in experimental social psychology* (Vol. 29, pp. 141–208). Mahwah, NJ: Erlbaum.

Winkielman, P., & Cacioppo, J. T. (2001). Mind at ease puts a smile on the face: Psychophysiological evidence that processing facilitation elicits positive affect. *Journal of Personality and Social Psychology*, 81, 989–1000.

Winkielman, P., & Schwarz, N. (2001). How pleasant was your childhood? Beliefs about memory shape inferences from experienced difficulty of recall. *Psychological Science, 12*, 176–179.

Winkielman, P., Schwarz, N., Fazendeiro, T.A., & Reber, R. (2003). The hedonic marking of processing fluency: Implications for evaluative judgment. In J. Musch & K.C. Klauer (Eds.), *The psychology of evaluation: Affective processes in cognition and emotion* (pp. 189–217). Mahwah, NJ: Erlbaum.

Zajonc, R. B. (1968). Attitudinal effects of mere exposure. *Journal of Personality and Social Psychology, 9*, 1–27.

8 Assimilation or contrast?

How fluency channels comparison processing

Michael Häfner

Abstract

Based on the observation that most current social comparison models focus on information-based processes as predictors of comparative outcomes, this chapter asks if experiential processes might also have a meaningful and predictable influence on the direction of social comparisons. As immediate and readily available cues, it is argued, experiential cues might be a viable predictor, especially for spontaneous comparisons. It is further assumed that feelings of fluency as a potential experiential equivalent to psychological closeness or distance play a crucial role in determining the direction of spontaneous social comparisons. Three lines of research that support this argumentation are presented. In particular, evidence i) speaking to the general influence of fluency experiences on the direction of social comparisons, ii) showing the predictive strength of experiential processes in direct comparison with information-based influences, and, iii) pointing to underlying sensorimotor processes is presented.

Despite the fact that it is established psychological knowledge that people base their judgments not only on what they know about someone or something (i.e., content), but also on what they experience when processing information about the object of evaluation (see this volume), this knowledge has to date hardly been applied to one of the most central self-evaluative processes, namely to social comparison. Within this domain, cold processes based on declarative information dominate the literature: the bulk of social comparison research investigated the comparative nature of self-evaluations by studying how declarative self- and other-knowledge is compared and then transformed into relative judgments about the self. Given the fact that one of the classic studies on the influence of experiences on judgments was about the self (Schwarz, Bless, Strack, Klumpp, Rittenauer-Schatka, & Simons, 1991), the interesting question arises of whether the neglect of experiential processes implies that comparative judgments about the self are special in the sense that they are *not* based on or influenced by feelings. Does comparing to others really mean to rely on knowledge (i.e., information-based processing; Koriat, 2007), or do also experiences influence the direction of social comparisons (i.e., experience-based processing)?

In the remainder of this chapter, I will try to answer these questions by first briefly reviewing recent social comparison theories with a focus on their overarching themes, namely their focus on information-based processes and the role of perceived psychological distance in predicting the direction of social comparisons (i.e., assimilation or contrast). I will then propose feelings of fluency/disfluency as the experiential equivalent of perceived or construed psychological distance (Liberman, Stephan, & Trope, 2007) and argue that fluency experiences may directly shape the direction of social comparisons: whereas fluency experiences might signal psychological closeness and should therefore be associated with assimilation, disfluency experiences might signal psychological distance and hence be associated with self-evaluative contrast. Finally, I shall back up these propositions by three lines of research highlighting a) the general influence of fluency experiences on the direction of social comparisons; b) their predictive strength in a direct comparison with information-based influences; and, c) underlying sensorimotor processes.

The direction of social comparisons

By no means would it be possible or desirable to try and review the immense social comparison literature here. For the present purpose—namely building a case for the notion that experiences about (processing) comparison information may influence the direction of comparisons—elucidating common denominators of the various recent social comparison models seems to be more conducive.

Firstly, all (recent) social comparison models (e.g., Bless & Schwarz, 2010; Förster, Liberman, & Kuschel, 2008; Lockwood & Kunda, 1997; Mussweiler, 2003) share the basic and classic assumption that judgments about the self (i.e. the *target* of evaluation) cannot be derived in a social vacuum and are thus largely dependent upon the social *standards* surrounding the target (Festinger, 1954). Secondly, all models aim to predict the way in which the comparison of target and standard knowledge influences the relative direction of self-evaluations (see also Bless & Schwarz, 2010). In this quest, these models more or less implicitly share the crucial assumption that declarative information (i.e., accessible target and standard information) constitutes the basis of the comparison process: accessible information about a given standard has to be processed and has to be related to accessible knowledge about the self. Even though on a process level the following concrete transformations of accessible target and standard knowledge into self-evaluations vary dramatically over the various comparison models (from similarities/dissimilarities mindsets to global/local processing modes), virtually all of the models describe cold processes of information integration. Except for the inclusion-exclusion model (Schwarz & Bless, 1992; Bless & Schwarz, 2010) that identifies experiential influences on the social comparison process as "a promising avenue for future research," most models are quiet about other, potentially experiential influences.

In what follows, I shall first speculate about why this might be the case and then move on by introducing another common denominator of social comparison models, namely the perception of psychological closeness or distance, in order to show why (fluency) experiences might in fact have a valid and predictable influence on the direction of social comparisons.

Information- vs. experience-based processes

One of the reasons why social comparison theories focus on information-based processes, and largely ignore their experience-based brothers, might be rooted in Festinger's (1954) classic assumption. He suggested that in an effort to come to more accurate self-evaluations, people relate their own characteristics to those of other (preferably slightly outperforming) persons (see also, Buunk & Gibbons, 2000). In terms of modern dual systems theories, such behavior would most likely be described as intentional, reflective, information-based behavior (e.g., Koriat & Levy-Sadot, 1999; Strack & Deutsch, 2004): in order to achieve the goal of an accurate self-evaluation, people *actively* choose a standard of comparison (cf. Mussweiler & Rüter, 2003) and relate themselves to the standard (see also, Gilbert, Giesler, & Morris, 1995). As such, social comparisons *should* be mainly rooted in declarative knowledge that is transformed on the basis of motivated propositional reasoning processes. As it is precisely the contextual influences on these reasoning processes that are described in the social comparison models introduced earlier, it is no wonder, one might conclude, that these models focus on information-based processes. Be that as it may, the most important question for the present purpose is whether this implies that social comparisons are *per definition* intentional and thus rooted in declarative information, or if they cannot also take place without reflection, in a more spontaneous fashion, and, what are the underlying processes of these spontaneous comparisons.

Certainly, this question has been asked previously, and, more importantly, been answered (e.g., Gilbert et al., 1995; Mussweiler, Rüter, & Epstude, 2004): Gilbert and his colleagues show in an impressive set of studies that even though their participants knew that comparing to the available standard was non-diagnostic, they spontaneously compared and then "uncompared" themselves to this standard. Straightforwardly, intention therefore does not seem to be a necessary precursor of social comparisons.

Neither are cognitive resources a necessary precondition for social comparisons to "happen," as Mussweiler and his colleagues (2004) demonstrate in a no less impressive set of studies. In their research, participants were subliminally primed with a comparison standard such as, for instance, Michael Jordan or Bill Clinton, while they were contemplating about their athletic ability. Even though none of the participants were aware of the fact that they were primed with a comparison standard, the primes still affected their self-evaluations. Those primed with Bill Clinton came to a more favorable evaluation of their athletic ability (i.e., assimilation to a moderately athletic standard) than those primed with Michael

Jordan (i.e., contrast to an extremely able standard). Over and above working unintentionally, the latter finding implies that comparison information does not even have to be processed (or even selected) consciously in order to affect one's self-evaluations. Being exposed to comparison information seems to be enough to trigger some form of comparison process.

Taken together, the examples provided here unequivocally suggest that social comparisons can take place spontaneously, at minimal (if any) levels of cognitive effort and awareness. However, this research paints a less clear picture about the underlying processes. How can comparison information spontaneously affect self-evaluation? Are such spontaneous comparisons driven by the same—but then automated—processes as their intended equivalents? Or do other, possibly experiential, processes drive spontaneous comparisons? At least implicitly, the first possibility served as an explanation for the earlier findings in which spontaneous comparisons have been demonstrated. In particular, Mussweiler and his colleagues (2004) indirectly advocate the notion that spontaneous and intended comparisons do not really differ, as they do not introduce other explanations on the process level. Why should they, one may ask, as it seems perfectly reasonable to conceive of spontaneous comparisons as automated intended comparisons; because social comparisons are ubiquitous, people learn to quickly process comparison information in much the same way as they do reflectively (Mussweiler et al., 2004; Mussweiler & Epstude, 2009).

Recent research in cognitive psychology and current dual systems views, however, offers another perspective, namely that spontaneous, impulsive behavior is often grounded in experiences rather than in declarative knowledge (e.g., Koriat & Levy-Sadot, 1999; Koriat, Nussinson, Bless, & Shaked, 2008; Schwarz & Clore, 2007; Smith & Semin, 2004; Strack, 1992; Strack, & Deutsch, 2004). A massive amount of research has shown that these *experience-based processes* are quick, efficient and operate at minimal levels of conscious awareness: Experiences such as, for instance, the "feeling of knowing" of a stimulus emerge right on perception of a stimulus and are therefore readily usable for all sorts of judgments, long before other informational cues are accessible (Koriat, 2007). Hence, the interesting question arises if such experiential processes might also play a role in the determination of the direction of (spontaneous) social comparisons in a meaningful and predictable way (see also Häfner & Schubert, 2009). However, before answering this question, one first has to answer the question of *which* experience might at all be likely to do so in the case of social comparison processes.

Fluency as a signal of psychological closeness

Given the various different cognitive-motivational variables recent social comparison models focus on, it seems to be a difficult, if not impossible, endeavor to identify *one* experiential variable that possibly matches all these variables. However, a more abstract look at the different models reveals a common denominator: virtually all cognitive-motivational underpinnings that have been described as the predictors of assimilative versus contrastive social-comparative outcomes can be seen as one or another representation of psychological distance or closeness. On the one hand, feasible, similar others whom we tend to include into ourselves are usually close others. Unfeasible, dissimilar others whom we tend to exclude from the self are, on the other hand, usually standards that we perceive as psychologically distant (see also, Nussinson, Seibt, Häfner, & Strack, 2010; Liberman et al., 2007; Stephan, Liberman, & Trope, 2011). The initial question of which experience might be a candidate to validly predict the direction of spontaneous comparisons can thus be specified to the question of which experience might match the representation of psychological closeness and distance.

The important question thus is: How does psychological closeness *feel?* Rather good than bad; rather easy than difficult; rather familiar than unfamiliar, or, in other terms, rather fluent than disfluent! Those we know and are familiar with (i.e., come across frequently) are construed closer to us than people we do not know or come across less frequently (see, e.g., Festinger, 1951; Newcomb, 1961; Stephan et al., 2011; Zajonc, 1968). Stated differently, those we are at ease with (i.e., those who trigger a feeling of familiarity or fluency in us) are those we are closely related to, whereas those we are not at ease with (i.e., those who trigger a feeling of unfamiliarity or disfluency in us) are usually those we are more distanced to. Hence, feelings of fluency/disfluency seem to be a good experiential match of more cognitive-motivational construals of psychological distance.

The influence of fluency experiences on (spontaneous) social comparisons then seems straightforward: Fluency signals psychological closeness and should therefore lead to a stronger inclusion of a standard into the self, whereas disfluency should signal psychological distance and thus lead to the exclusion of a standard from the self (Häfner, 2009; Häfner & Schubert, 2009; Stephan et al., 2011; see also Förster et al., 2008). Ultimately, fluency experiences should thus be associated with self-evaluative assimilation. Conversely, disfluency should imply a greater distance of the standard to the self and should therefore lead to contrastive self-evaluations.

This line of reasoning can be nicely illustrated by or translated to classic comparison research. Lockwood and Kunda (1997), for instance, showed in their research that "student superstars" triggered very different self-evaluations in their fellow students depending on whether these fellow students were in the same or in another year. Those students who were direct fellows of the (unattainable) student superstars contrasted away whereas the first years assimilated in their self-evaluations and came closer to the superstars, even though they were in fact even farther away from the standards of comparison than their direct fellows. What Lockwood and Kunda explain in terms of perceived feasibility, can also be explained in terms of experienced fluency: it should feel much more difficult to be confronted with a superstar if one *should* be quite close but in fact is not, whereas it should feel easier if there is a long time to reach what the superstar already achieved. In a similar vein, one could argue that a description of a manually skilled person feels kind of more fluent (i.e., better fitting) if this person is male as compared to when it is female (Mussweiler & Bodenhausen, 2002), or that thinking about Einstein triggers more uneasiness than thinking about the abstract group of professors does (Dijksterhuis et al., 1998).

In conclusion, feelings of fluency seem to be associated with psychological closeness and assimilation, whereas feelings of disfluency seem to be associated with psychological distance and contrast. In what follows I shall present three lines of research that some colleagues of mine and I designed in order to put exactly this reasoning to an empirical test.

Experimental evidence

Based on the observation that most current social comparison models focus on the cognitive-motivational underpinnings of comparison processes, and therefore highlight the role of information-based processes, the present chapter asks the question if also experiential processes might have a meaningful and predictable influence on the direction of (spontaneous) social comparisons. As immediate and readily available cues, experiences might be a viable predictor of the direction of spontaneous comparisons. It is further assumed that fluency as a potential experiential equivalent of psychological closeness or distance plays a crucial role in determining the direction of spontaneous social comparisons. In what follows, I shall back up this line of argumentation with experimental findings: i) speaking to the general influence of fluency experiences on the direction of social comparisons; ii) showing the predictive strength of experiential processes in a direct comparison with information-based influences; and, iii) pointing to underlying sensorimotor processes.

The influence of fluency and familiarity on the direction of social comparisons

The aim of the first line of research that I will present now was quite simple and straightforward, namely demonstrating that fluency/familiarity experiences would influence the direction of spontaneous social comparisons in a meaningful and predictable way. Specifically, I wanted to test the assumption that fluency/ familiarity experiences would lead to self-evaluative assimilation whereas feelings of disfluency/unfamiliarity would be associated with self-evaluative contrast. Importantly, I am referring to spontaneous comparisons here, implying that people were not explicitly asked to engage in a (deliberate) social comparison. Rather, participants were incidentally presented with comparison information and also incidentally asked to provide a self-evaluation: participants were, in most of these experiments, asked to form a first impression of a person (i.e., the standard of comparison) briefly depicted on the screen. Before they were asked to share this impression by evaluating or describing the person at stake, participants were asked to indicate some personal information, among which they were asked to provide a self-evaluation on the crucial comparative dimension. In most of the studies we therefore asked participants to indicate how attractive they think they are. The idea behind this setup was that participants would process the standard of comparison without the explicit goal of comparing to the standard. Nevertheless, it is conceivable that they engaged in a spontaneous comparison when providing their self-evaluation (see e.g., Mussweiler et al., 2004).

To repeat, the important question guiding this first line of research was if such spontaneous self-evaluations would be influenced by fluency experiences associated with (the processing of) the standard of comparison. In a straightforward manner, conditions of fluency versus novelty were therefore compared in the first experiment (Häfner, 2009, Experiment 1B). For that matter, a classic mere exposure paradigm was used: in one of the conditions, female participants were subliminally primed with the beautiful female standard of comparison they were later presented with in a supraliminal fashion. The other half of participants was primed with a comparable standard, but not the one that both groups were later (in the so called impression formation task) presented with. As predicted, results were such that participants in the repeated exposure condition, who supposedly experienced a feeling of fluency or familiarity with the standard of comparison, saw themselves as more attractive than participants who lacked this experience, indicating that the former assimilated their self-evaluations toward the standard whereas the latter contrasted away.

Further corroborating this conclusion, a second experiment (Häfner, 2009, Experiment 2) found feelings of familiarity (that were assessed in a post-test) to moderate self-evaluations with regard to both attractive and unattractive standards of comparison. Importantly, results from this experiment show more unequivocally that familiarity triggers assimilation whereas a lack of familiarity triggers contrast: the higher the degree that participants indicated to be familiar with the unattractive standard (in a post-test), the *lower* perceptions of their own attractiveness they held (i.e., assimilation). This finding that familiarity can also lead to lower self-evaluations (i.e., assimilation toward a low standard) renders it virtually impossible that the positive affect possibly triggered by fluency experiences (Winkielman & Cacioppo, 2001) might account for the earlier results. Replicating the earlier finding, participants exposed to the familiar attractive standard indicated relatively higher self-evaluations than those who were unfamiliar with the standard. The same pattern of results was also found in another experiment in which we directly manipulated the (perceptual) fluency of attractive and unattractive standards rather than assessing it (Häfner & Schubert, 2009, Experiment 1).

Taken together, these results provide strong evidence for the notion that fluency experiences may shape the direction of spontaneous comparisons. Moreover, this influence does not seem to be driven by the affective quality of fluency experiences: when fluency is associated with a low standard, the positive experience nevertheless leads to a more negative self-evaluation. There thus seems to be a direct influence of fluency experiences on the direction of spontaneous comparisons, such that fluency is associated with assimilative comparisons whereas disfluency experiences seem to trigger contrastive comparisons. Hence, the answer to the first question that I initially posed is positive. Yes, fluency/

familiarity experiences do predict the direction of spontaneous social comparisons in a meaningful way.

Experience-based versus information-based processes in social comparison

Even though the first line of research could establish the notion that experience-based processes do play a role in spontaneous comparisons, two important issues cannot be clarified by these experiments. First, showing that experiences have an impact on comparative self-evaluations does not necessarily imply that this influence holds if there are other, information-based, influences at play. Second, the generality of the effects is not yet clear as in all of the above experiments fluency/familiarity experiences were directly bound to the standard by actually manipulating the perceptual fluency of the standard. Therefore, a second line of research was carried out in which we: i) directly pitted experience- and information-based processes against each other; and ii) induced experiences of fluency/familiarity independently of the standard (Häfner & Schubert, 2009).

The experimental setup was similar to the one used in the earlier experiments. However, in order to pit information- and experience-based processes against each other, we made use of two ostensibly independent experiments. Specifically, we introduced a first task that was designed to procedurally prime a search strategy for either similarities or dissimilarities (see Mussweiler, 2001). In this task, we asked participants to write down similarities or dissimilarities between a pair of pictures. Only thereafter did we provide participants with the "impression formation task" described above.

Importantly, we also used the first manipulation to induce a feeling of ease or difficulty. In particular, in one experiment (Häfner & Schubert, 2009, Experiment 2) we varied the factual similarities between the pictures by either presenting a pair of fairly similar (e.g., a rhino and a hippo) or fairly dissimilar (e.g., a rhino and a crocodile) pictures. Accordingly, generating similarities became either easy (for the similar pictures) or difficult (for the dissimilar pictures). In another experiment (Häfner & Schubert, 2009, Experiment 3), we aimed to achieve a comparable effect by asking people to either produce many (i.e., difficult) or only a couple of (i.e., simple) similarities/dissimilarities (see also, Schwarz et al., 1991). The logic applied to both studies is quite similar and was selected in order to enable us to test which of the two processes would dominate and thus give direction to the subsequent comparison. Would the primed search strategy determine the direction of the social comparison as it did in previous experiments (e.g., Mussweiler, 2001; Häfner, 2004), or would the experiences generated as a byproduct of the search strategy determine the direction of the spontaneous comparison process?

In line with our expectations, experiences of ease or difficulty were in both experiments the better predictors of comparative self-evaluations than the primed search strategy. Participants showed self-evaluative assimilation toward a social comparison standard when they experienced ease, independently of whether they were primed to look for similarities or dissimilarities. Conversely, when they experienced difficulty, self-evaluative contrast was the likely consequence, irrespective of whether participants were primed to search for similarities or differences.

Over and above the fact that these experiments clearly establish the importance of experiences on the direction of spontaneous comparisons, even in the presence of other, information-based cues, the present set of studies also speaks to the generality and subtlety of this influence: the experiences were induced by a task completely *independent* of the standard presentation. As such, these experiences were not diagnostic of the social distance to the standard; nevertheless, they spontaneously shaped the direction of the social comparison process. Taken together with the findings of the first line of research, it can thus already now be concluded that experiential processes do play an important role in shaping spontaneous social comparisons.

First evidence on the mediating role of experiences

As strong as we believe these findings are, they cannot fully establish the proposed mediating role of experiences. Even though we demonstrated that experiences in direct or indirect association with a standard of comparison do have an impact on the direction of spontaneous comparisons, we cannot be entirely sure that these experiences are a *necessary* precursor for spontaneous comparisons and that they *directly* influence the outcome of a comparison. In order to be able to show this mediating influence, we would have to show that being presented with potential standards of comparison spontaneously triggers an experience of fluency or disfluency, the amount of which mediates the self-evaluative outcome of the comparison. Unfortunately, however, this is not an easy endeavor as assessing these experiences by means of self-report might itself trigger experiences and thus may not offer as strong evidence as would be preferable (see also Kühnen, 2010).

Luckily, the literature on fluency and its underlying proprioceptive processes suggests another potential method of assessing fluency experiences in a non-obtrusive, online manner; namely by measuring spontaneous facial expressions (Topolinski, Likowski, Weyers, & Strack, 2009; Winkielman & Cacioppo, 2001). In particular, this research has shown that fluency experiences are associated with a smile, whereas disfluency experiences go along with a frown. Extended to the present logic, this implies that—given our line of argumentation is correct—psychologically distant standards should trigger a frown, whereas close standards should trigger a smile. The strength of the spontaneous facial expression should then predict the strength of assimilation versus contrast. Importantly, these spontaneous facial expressions can be assessed by means of electromyography without the participants being aware of what is being measured and without even having to be aware of the experience.

Following this reasoning, we conducted an experiment (Häfner & Schubert, 2011, Experiment 1) in which we presented male and female participants with different (moderately and highly attractive) standards of comparison and measured their spontaneous facial activity for the Musculus Corrugator supercilii (frowning) and the Musculus Zygomaticus major (smiling). In line with our expectations, we found the highly attractive female standards to trigger a frown in female participants (indicating disfluency or psychological distance). This frown faded away when the same participants were presented with moderately attractive standards (indicating a lack of disfluency or more psychological close-ness). Conversely, male participants showed spontaneous frowning activity when being presented with moderately attractive female standards whereas this frown vanished when they were presented with highly attractive women. Interestingly, we did not find the opposite pattern, or any effect, for the Zygomaticus.

These findings, as interesting as they are, still do not provide direct evidence for a mediating influence of experiences. Despite the fact that the present methodology served our purpose of assessing spontaneous fluency experiences in an unobtrusive way extremely well, these findings still do not fully establish the mediating effect of these experiences as we were testing the effects in a within-subjects design. Even though this design provides direct evidence for the notion that different levels of social distance are associated with different levels of spon-taneously experienced disfluency (as evidenced by increased Corrugator activ-ity), it was impossible to assess subsequent self-evaluations because participants were randomly presented with *all* different standards. As a between-subjects design is also not conducive in achieving the goal to show a direct mediation (because of unacceptably high interindividual differences in EMG activity), we carried out a second experiment in which we turned the logic around.

According to our previous findings, it can be concluded that frowning might trigger contrast whereas smiling (or doing nothing, at least not frowning) might trigger assimilation. In order to put this (admittedly indirect) reasoning to a test, we conducted an experiment in which we had participants smile unobtrusively (by moving up a sticker placed upon their cheek), or frown (by pulling two stickers placed close to their eyebrows as closely together as possible) while they were presented with comparison information (high and low standards were used in order to rule out the alternative explanation that it is affect that drives the effects, see above). In line with our expectations, we found assimilation toward the (high and low) standard of comparison for participants who "smiled" at the standard whereas participants who "frowned" showed self-evaluative contrast.

Over and above the fact that taken together these findings speak to the mediat-ing effect of fluency experiences on the direction of spontaneous social compari-sons, these findings raise the interesting question of how direct or indirect this effect is. Are fluency experiences *directly* shaping the direction of the comparison process, in much the same way as, for instance, mood may directly induce a global or local mode of information processing (Gasper & Clore, 2002)? Or, do fluency experiences serve as a cue that is (unconsciously) attributed to a standard, thereby *indirectly* shaping the direction of a comparison (Alter & Oppenheimer, 2009; Clore & Schnall, 2005; Häfner & Stapel, 2009; Whittlesea, 1993)? On the basis of the current data it is impossible to answer this question. My guess would, however, be that the influence is of direct nature: ultimately, social comparisons are in the service of regulating social distance, and should therefore work as quickly and as reliably as possible. Any additional processing step therefore seems to be a step too much.

Summary and conclusion

The present chapter set out to answer the question of whether experience-based processes have a meaningful and predictable influence on the direction of spontaneous social comparisons. Based on the observation that the processes underlying spontaneous comparisons were to date not entirely specified, I proposed that rather than being described as automated information-based processes, spontaneous social comparisons might be better described in terms of experience-based processes. In particular, I suggested that readily available feelings of fluency associated with comparison information might be seen as the experiential equivalent of perceived social distance (see also, Stephan et al., 2011) and as such predict spontaneous assimilation and contrast toward comparison information. Evidence from three different lines of research largely corroborating these assumptions was presented and discussed. First, it was demonstrated that fluency/familiarity experiences do in fact have an impact on the direction of social comparisons that, second, even holds in the presence of other, information-based cues. Third, and finally, I discussed some very recent evidence for the mediating role of these experiences in spontaneous social comparisons.

Taken together, I am therefore confident that there is much to the idea that spontaneous comparisons might qualitatively differ from more deliberate, intended comparisons. Just like for memory, other cues seem to be important when quickly trying to judge as opposed to thoroughly seeking for information (see also Koriat, 2007). As such, this idea does not only perfectly fit recent two systems perspectives on human behavior and judgment (e.g., Strack & Deutsch, 2004), recent theoretical developments on situated cognition (Smith & Semin, 2004) or embodiment (e.g., Barsalou, Niedenthal, Barbey, & Ruppert, 2003), but also more abstract and inclusive models of social comparison that are either explicitly (such as, for example, Bless & Schwarz, 2010) or implicitly open for such experiential influences (such as, for example, Förster et al., 2008). Last but not least, the present perspective does also find support in other recent findings showing experiential influences on the construction of social distance (Nussinson et al., 2010; Nussinson, Häfner, Seibt, Strack, & Trope, in press), and even social comparisons (Fayant, Muller, Nurra, Alexopoulos, & Palluel-Germain, 2011).

References

Alter, A. L., & Oppenheimer, D. M. (2009). Uniting the tribes of fluency to form a metacognitive nation. *Personality and Social Psychology Review*, *13*, 219–235.

Barsalou, L.W., Niedenthal, P.M., Barbey, A., & Ruppert, J. (2003). Social embodiment. In B. Ross (ed.) *The Psychology of Learning and Motivation*, Vol. 43 (pp. 43–92). San Diego: Academic Press.

Bless, H., & Schwarz, N. (2010). Mental construal and the emergence of assimilation and contrast effects: The inclusion/exclusion model. *Advances in Experimental Social Psychology*, *42*, 319–373.

Buunk, B. P., & Gibbons, F. X. (2000). Towards an enlightenment in social comparison theory: Moving beyond classic and renaissance approaches. In J. M. Suls & L. Wheeler (Eds.), *Handbook of social comparison: Theory and research* (pp. 487–499). Plenum: New York.

Clore, G. L., & Schnall, S. (2005). The influence of affect on attitude. In D. Albarracin & B. Johnson (Eds.), *Handbook of attitudes and attitude change: Basic principles* (pp. 437–490). Mahwah: Erlbaum.

Dijksterhuis, A., Spears, R., Postmes, T., Stapel, D.A., Koomen, W., van Knippenberg, A., & Scheepers, D. (1998). Seeing one thing and doing another: Contrast effects in automatic behavior. *Journal of Personality and Social Psychology*, *75*, 862–871.

Fayant, M.-P., Muller, D., Nurra, C., Alexopoulos, T., & Palluel-Germain, R. (2011). Moving forward is not only a metaphor: Approach and avoidance lead to self-evaluative assimilation and contrast. *Journal of Experimental Social Psychology*, *47*, 241–245.

Festinger, L. (1951). Architecture and group membership. *Journal of Social Issues*, *7*, 152–163.

—— (1954). A theory of social comparison processes. *Human Relations*, *7*, 117–140.

Förster, J., Liberman, N., & Kuschel, S. (2008). The effect of global versus local processing styles on assimilation versus contrast in social judgment. *Journal of Personality and Social Psychology*, *94*, 579–599.

Gasper, K., & Clore, G. L. (2002). Attending to the big picture: Mood and global versus local processing of visual information. *Psychological Science*, *13*, 33–39.

Gilbert, D. T., Giesler, R. B., & Morris, K. A. (1995). When comparisons arise. *Journal of Personality and Social Psychology*, *51*, 227–236.

Häfner, M. (2004). How dissimilar others may still resemble the self: Assimilation and contrast after social comparison. *Journal of Consumer Psychology*, 14, 187–196.

—— (2009). Knowing you, knowing me: Familiarity moderates comparison outcomes to idealized media images. *Social Cognition*, *27*, 496–508.

Häfner, M., & Schubert, T. (2009). Feel the difference! The influence of ease experiences on the direction of social comparison. *Journal of Experimental Social Psychology*, *45*, 291–294.

—— (2011). In the face of comparison information: On the proprioceptive underpinnings of spontaneous social comparisons. Manuscript submitted for publication.

Häfner, M., & Stapel, D. A. (2009). Familiarity can increase and decrease stereotyping: Heuristic processing versus enhanced usability. *Social Cognition*, *27*, 615–622.

Koriat, A. (2007). Metacognition and consciousness. In P. D. Zelazo, M. Moscovitch, & E. Thompson (Eds.), *The Cambridge handbook of consciousness* (pp. 289–325). Cambridge: Cambridge University Press.

Koriat, A., & Levy-Sadot, R. (1999). Processes underlying metacognitive judgments: Information-based and experience-based monitoring of one's own knowledge. In S. Chaiken & Y. Trope (Eds.), *Dual process theories in social psychology* (pp. 483–502). New York: Guilford Publications.

Koriat, A., Nussinson, R., Bless, H., & Shaked, N. (2008). Information-based and experience-based metacognitive judgments: Evidence from subjective confidence. In J. Dunlosky and R. A. Bjork (Eds.), *A handbook of memory and metamemory* (pp. 117–134). Mahwah, NJ: Erlbaum.

Kühnen, U. (2010). Manipulation-checks as manipulation: Another look at the ease of retrieval heuristic. *Personality and Social Psychology Bulletin, 36*, 47–58.

Liberman, N., Trope, Y., & Stephan, E. (2007). Psychological distance. In A. W. Kruglanski & E. T. Higgins (Eds.), *Social psychology: Handbook of basic principles.* New York: Guilford Press.

Lockwood, P., & Kunda, Z. (1997). Superstars and me: Predicting the impact of role models on the self. *Journal of Personality and Social Psychology, 73*, 91–103.

Mussweiler, T. (2001). "Seek and ye shall find:" Antecedents of assimilation and contrast in social comparison. *European Journal of Social Psychology, 31*, 499–509.

—— (2003). Comparison processes in social judgment: Mechanisms and consequences. *Psychological Review, 110*, 472–489.

Mussweiler, T., & Bodenhausen, G. V. (2002). I know you are but what am I? Self-evaluative consequences of judging ingroup and outgroup members. *Journal of Personality and Social Psychology, 82*, 19–32.

Mussweiler, T., & Epstude, K. (2009). Relatively fast! Efficiency advantages of comparative thinking. *Journal of Experimental Psychology: General, 138*, 1–21.

Mussweiler, T., & Rüter, K. (2003). What friends are for! The use of routine standards in social comparison. *Journal of Personality and Social Psychology, 85*, 467–481.

Mussweiler, T., Rüter, K., & Epstude, K. (2004). The man who wasn't there: Subliminal social standards influence self-evaluation. *Journal of Experimental Social Psychology, 40*, 689–696.

Newcomb, T. M. (1961). *The acquaintance process.* New York: Holt, Rinehart and Winston.

Nussinson, R., Seibt, B., Häfner, M., & Strack, F. (2010). Come a bit closer: Approach motor actions lead to feeling similar and behaviorally assimilating to others. *Social Cognition, 28*, 40–58.

Nussinson, R., Häfner, M., Seibt, B., Strack, F., & Trope, Y. (in press). Approach/ avoidance orientations affect self-construal, experienced closeness to close others, and identification with in-group. *Self and Identity.*

Schwarz, N. & Clore, G.L. (2007). Feelings and phenomenal experiences. In E. T. Higgins & A. Kruglanski (Eds.), *Social psychology: A handbook of basic principles.* 2nd ed. (pp. 385–407). New York: Guilford Press.

Schwarz, N., & Bless, H. (1992). Constructing reality and its alternatives: An inclusion/ exclusion model of assimilation and contrast effects in social judgment. In H. Martin & A. Tesser (Eds.), *The construction of social judgment* (pp. 217–245). Hillsdale, NJ: Erlbaum.

Schwarz, N., Bless, H., Strack, F., Klumpp, G., Rittenauer-Schatka, H., & Simons, A. (1991). Ease of retrieval as information: Another look at the availability heuristic. *Journal of Personality and Social Psychology, 61*, 195–202.

Smith, E. R., & Semin, G. R. (2004). Socially situated cognition: Cognition in its social context. *Advances in Experimental Social Psychology, 36*, 53–117.

Stephan, E., Liberman, N., & Trope, Y. (2011). The effects of time perspective and level of construal on social distance. *Journal of Experimental Social Psychology, 47*, 397–402.

Strack, F. (1992). The different routes to social judgments: Experiential versus informational strategies. In L. L. Martin & A. Tesser (Eds.), *The construction of social judgments* (pp. 249–257). Hillsdale, NJ: Lawrence Erlbaum Associates.

Strack, F., & Deutsch, R. (2004). Reflective and impulsive determinants of social behavior. *Personality and Social Psychology Review, 8*, 220–247.

Topolinski, S., Likowski, K. U., Weyers, P., & Strack, F. (2009). The face of fluency: Semantic coherence automatically elicits a specific pattern of facial muscle reactions. *Cognition and Emotion*, *23*, 260–271.

Whittlesea, B. W. A. (1993). Illusions of familiarity. *Journal of Experimental Psychology: Learning, Memory, and Cognition*, *19*, 1235–1253.

Winkielman, P., & Cacioppo, J. T. (2001). Mind at ease puts a smile on the face: Psychophysiological evidence that processing facilitation increases positive affect. *Journal of Personality and Social Psychology*, *81*, 989–1000.

Zajonc, R. B. (1968). Attitudinal effects of mere exposure. *Journal of Personality and Social Psychology Monograph Supplement*, *9*, 1–27.

9   When good blends go bad

How fluency can explain when we like and dislike ambiguity

Jamin Halberstadt and
Piotr Winkielman

Abstract

We argue that some of the appeal of faces (and their owners) comes from the ease with which they are processed: their cognitive fluency. Individuals that are good examples of their group are processed more fluently, which produces positive affect that can generalize to evaluations. Conversely, when a person's individual or group membership is ambiguous, the difficulty in resolving that ambiguity produces negative affect that can compete with or override an otherwise beautiful appearance. We apply this analysis to the apparent paradox of morphed faces, which are robustly attractive despite their ambiguous identity, by introducing the notion of context-dependent fluency. We show that the same morphed face can be a good example of one group but a poor example of another, and by changing the salience of potential social categories, we can change the ease with which the target is classified, and in turn how beautiful it appears. We also extend our analysis to blends of racial groups and illustrate implications for stereotype theory, including the novel prediction that good examples may be preferred to poor examples of stereotyped groups, even when those groups are negative.

A man looks at Mona Lisa's face. At first, he really likes it. Why? One source of his reaction is "what" he sees. He appreciates the gentle smile, the smooth complexion, the inquisitive eyes. But another source of affect is "how" he sees, how easy (fluent) are the mental operations in processing Mona Lisa's face. She triggers a warm feeling because she is so "easy on the eyes," so smooth and familiar, as if da Vinci captured the very essence of the human condition. But now something happens! The man realizes there is something "off" in the face he sees. Is this really Mona Lisa? There seems to be a bit of da Vinci's own face in the picture. Is this really a woman? The face seems partially male. And what about that mysterious smile? Or is it a smirk? The man is now confused. He does not know what to make of the picture, even though he's trying hard to decipher it perceptually and conceptually. Perhaps he does not like Mona Lisa after all!

This chapter deals with such complexities of facial attractiveness. We argue that some of the appeal of faces comes from the ease with which they are classified. Stimuli that are good examples of their type, like Mona Lisa is of human faces, are processed more easily, and the affect associated with this fluent processing generalizes to evaluations of the stimuli themselves. Conversely, when the identity or group membership of a target is ambiguous, the difficulty in resolving that ambiguity produces negative affect that can compete with or override an otherwise beautiful appearance.

The tension between beautiful content and effortful process is starkest in the case of facial blends, which are robustly attractive despite their "objective" ambiguity. We resolve this apparent paradox by introducing the notion of context-dependent fluency, in which ambiguous faces are disliked, but whether a face is ambiguous depends on the social category of which it is seen to be a member. We show that the same blended face can be a good example of one group but a poor example of another, and by changing the salience of potential social categories, we can change the ease with which the target is classified, and in turn how beautiful it appears. In what follows we apply this approach first to understanding the attractiveness of blends of individuals, then extend our analysis to blends of racial groups. Finally, we illustrate implications for stereotype theory, and show how a dynamic, context-specific theory of fluency makes surprising predictions when stereotype content and processing ease conflict.

Beauty-in-averageness

Galton (1878) first noted that photographically blending faces (in some cases, faces of criminals) increases their attractiveness. This phenomenon, replicated many times in the modern psychological literature, reflects the tendency for category exemplars to be more attractive as a function of their proximity to the category's central tendency (Langlois & Roggman, 1990). Halberstadt (2006) documented the generality of the "beauty-in-averageness" effect, reporting a correlation between judged typicality and (independently) judged attractiveness in a wide variety of natural and artificial categories, from random dot patterns ($r = .37$) to birds ($r = .50$) to wristwatches ($r = .65$). In nearly all cases, category exemplars were liked better as a function of their similarity to the category prototype.

Empirically, morphing appears to produce faces that are more "face-like," more similar to the perceiver's image of the typical face, than the images used to create them. Busey (1998), for example, found that morphs are located closer to the center of multi-dimensional face space than their parents (as well as the emergence of other features such as youth and adiposity). Convergently, Rhodes and Tremewan (1996) found that faces that were shifted toward the center of face space (by distorting them in the direction of a blend of all faces in the study) were more attractive than faces shifted away from the center (Halberstadt & Rhodes, 2003, reported the analogous effect using line drawings of birds). Rhodes et al. (2003) found that the center of face space itself can be shifted (via exposure to systematically distorted exemplars), with predictable effects on attractiveness. In all, these data suggest that blended faces are more similar to the perceivers' face prototype, which is itself a composite of the faces to which they have, over a lifetime, been exposed (cf. Potter & Corneille, 2008).

Just why prototypicality is attractive has been debated. In the case of faces, evolutionary psychologists have naturally invoked sexual selection, for example arguing that typicality is a proxy for various fitness-enhancing traits, such as heterozygosity or overall health (Symons, 1979; Thornhill & Gangestad, 1993). However, the demonstration of prototypicality effects in reproductively-irrelevant stimulus categories has led researchers to explore more general, proximate cognitive mechanisms.

Fluency as an explanation of the beauty in averageness effect

We have shown that classification fluency—the ease with which a stimulus can be classified as a member of its group—is an important part of the story (Winkielman, Halberstadt, Fazendeiro & Catty, 2006). In recent years, much research has been devoted to the idea that evaluative reactions to stimuli are partially caused by the ease with which they can be processed. There are several possible reasons for this association. One is that the experience of fluent processing might be pleasant in itself, because it signals low cognitive conflict and tells the organism about the success (or good trajectory) of recognition or categorization operations (Winkielman, Schwarz, Fazendeiro, & Reber, 2003). Fluency might also be positive because it is probabilistically associated with positive stimulus features (e.g., familiarity or safety), thereby functioning as a cue to stimulus evaluation (Gigerenzer, 2007).

Many studies have manipulated processing ease, using a variety of techniques. One is a simple priming manipulation, where an object is preceded by a perceptually congruent or incongruent stimulus. For example, in one study (Reber, Winkielman & Schwarz, 1998, Study 1), participants saw pictures of everyday objects, such as a desk or a plane, whose fluency was enhanced or reduced by prior subliminal presentation of matching or mismatching visual contours. The data showed that pictures preceded by matched contours were recognized faster, indicating greater fluency, and that these fluent pictures were liked more than disfluent pictures, preceded by mismatched contours. Other manipulations, such as varying viewing conditions (via contrast or clarity), stimulus duration, symmetry, comprehensibility of stimulus names or descriptions, predictability, and even rhymes, have yielded predictable changes in stimulus appeal (Reber, Schwarz & Winkielman, 2004; Winkielman et al., 2003). Furthermore, Winkielman and Cacioppo (2001) have shown that high fluency is associated with stronger activity over the zygomaticus muscle region (the "smiling" area, indicative of positive affect), but not with stronger activity of the corrugator region (the "frowning" muscles, indicative of negative affect).

Most important for our thesis, the *prototypicality* of an exemplar is a robust predictor of its fluency. In their classic study of category learning, Posner and Keele (1968) found that dot patterns were classified more slowly to the extent they were distorted from a prototype; the prototype itself was classified fastest, despite never having been presented in the study. Indeed, classification time has been often used as a measure of the distance of a stimulus from its central tendency (e.g., Dovidio, Evans, & Tyler, 1986; Rosch & Mervis, 1975; Smith, Shoben, & Rips, 1974).

The independent relations between typicality, fluency, and positive affect, raise the possibility that prototypes are liked because they are fluent. Winkielman et al. (2006) examined this idea in a series of three experiments. Participants first learned a category of random dot patterns (Experiment 1) or of common geometric patterns (Experiment 2) and then were presented with novel patterns varying across different levels of similarity to a prototype pattern. Participants classified these patterns into their respective categories as quickly as possible (a measure of fluency), and also rated the attractiveness of each. A close relationship between fluency, attractiveness, and the level of prototypicality was observed. Both fluency and attractiveness increased with prototypicality. Importantly, when fluency was statistically controlled, the relation between prototypicality and attractiveness dropped by half (though it remained significant). Finally, Experiment 3 showed that viewing prototypical, rather than non-prototypical patterns elicited significantly greater electromyographic activity, suggesting that viewing prototypes involves genuine affective reactions.

Importantly, these effects are not limited to low-level perceptual judgments but can occur even if the task is a high-level classification. For example, in a rich stimulus domain—abstract art—Halberstadt and Hooton (2008) found that typicality (i.e., how well a painting exemplified an artist's style) predicted its classification fluency (i.e., the time it took to associate a painting with its painter). Further, Halberstadt and Hooton found that the fluency of abstract paintings predicted their appeal: people preferred the paintings that were easiest to classify (which were, in turn, the best examples of the artist's work).

Can fluency explain the beauty-in-averageness effect in faces?

As described above, Winkielman et al. (2006) showed that dot patterns, as they approached the prototypes from which they were generated, were easier to classify, and consequently more beautiful. Similarly, perhaps faces, as they approach *their* prototypes (via morphing) get easier to classify and more beautiful. Can fluency explain the beauty-in-averageness effect in faces?

At first glance, the answer seems to be a surprising but resounding "no." Face blends are beautiful but indistinct, similar on all perceptual dimensions to the faces that constitute them, and therefore difficult to identify and discriminate from other faces. Such difficulty, according to fluency theory, should translate into *negative affect*, which should generalize to the faces themselves to make them *less* attractive. Nevertheless, we argue that an appreciation of the *category relativity* of both categorization and fluency can not only explain the appeal of such facial blends, but also provide a unified account of the relations among beauty, prototypicality, and classification.

A   B

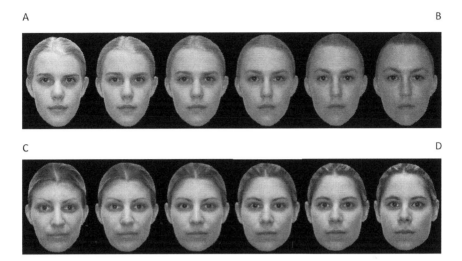

C   D

Figure 9.1 Examples of two morph continua. The four faces in the middle of each
continuum are blends of the "parents" at the endpoints. Faces typically get
increasingly attractive as they are increasingly blended.

This account begins with the critical assumption, easy to overlook, that both
prototypicality and fluency are products not of the stimulus, but of the cognitive
system. A stimulus is only typical with respect to a particular category, and the
same stimulus can be a good example of one category and a poor example of
another, or both a good and bad example of the same category in different
contexts (Barsalou, 1983). Changes in context activate different features of a
stimulus (e.g., a newspaper in the context of a library versus a house fire), as
evidenced by property verification times (Barsalou, 1982), and individuals themselves can shift their cognitive perspective to produce different—but reliable and
accurate—category structures from different points of view (Barsalou & Sewell,
1984). In the most dramatic example of category relativity, individuals can derive
reliable graded structures of entirely new ("ad hoc") categories in relation to
specific and momentary goals (Barsalou, 1982). In such cases, we propose that
the prototypicality of a stimulus, the ease with which it can be categorized, and
therefore the fluency-derived positive affect associated with it, can change
quickly in response to environmental input or idiosyncratic goals.

As an initial examination of this hypothesis with respect to faces, we examined
the fluency of the same morphed faces in two different contexts, one in which the
faces should be more fluent, and one in which they should be *less* fluent, as they
are increasingly blended. The critical stimuli were 26 Caucasian faces—two
"parents," which we called A and B, and 24 equally-spaced morphs between
them (i.e., 96 percent A/4 percent B, 92 percent A/8 percent B, etc.; see
Figure 9.1 for examples). In one condition, participants were shown A and B,

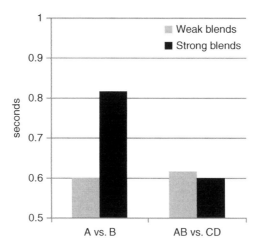

Figure 9.2 Classification time for weakly blended (at least 80% similar to one parent) and strongly blended morphs of A and B faces as a function of classification task (see text for details). Examples of AB and CD blends appear in Figure 9.1.

whom they were told represented members of two different groups. They were then shown the 26 A–B morphs and asked to judge whether each was an A group member or a B group member as quickly as possible. In a second condition, participants were again shown A and B but told they represented two members of the *same* group. They were then shown the 26 A–B morphs randomly inter-mixed with a different set of morphs—26 blends of two different faces, C and D—and asked to judge whether each was an A–B group member or a C–D group member as quickly as possible.

This paradigm provides an elegant test of the context-dependence of face fluency, because A–B morphs' classification fluency should be precisely reversed in the two experimental conditions. That is, when A and B are presented as members of different groups, blends of A and B should be relatively difficult to classify, because they are similar to both. However, when A and B are presented as members of the same group, blends should be relatively *easy* to classify because their similarity to both makes them highly prototypical A–B group members. In other words, an A–B blend is a poor exemplar of either A or B as individuals but a good exemplar of a group consisting of A and B members. Because good exemplars are fluent, blends should be classified slowly in the first case but quickly in the second. Indeed, as seen in Figure 9.2, more strongly blended faces (less than 80 percent similar to either parent) were easier to classify as A–B group members, but particularly difficult to classify as As and Bs, relative to weakly blended faces.

These data provide the first evidence that the fluency of facial composites is context-dependent (in this case on the perceiver's goal-derived category structure). If faces derive some of their attractiveness from their fluency, then this context dependence should have implications for the appeal of the A–B blends. In particular, their normally robust attractiveness should be reduced or reversed when they are classified in terms of their constituent faces, rather than in terms of a higher-order group containing both of them.

As a test of the attractiveness hypothesis, we solicited attractiveness judgments of the morphed faces described above, this time using the structure of the judgment task itself to situate the stimuli in different categorical contexts. Participants were again shown two faces and were told they represented members of two different groups, A and B, which was associated with different "family names." They were then presented with 26 A–B morphs of the faces (the A and B "parent" faces and 24 equally spaced blends between them) and then asked, in a control condition, to rate their attractiveness on a single sliding scale anchored at 1 ("very unattractive") and 9 ("very attractive"). In an experimental condition, participants were presented with *two* such scales, each labeled with a family name, and asked to make their rating on whichever scale was appropriate for a given face. Thus, in the experimental condition, but not the control condition, judgments require implicit classification of a composite face in terms of its group membership immediately prior to rating it, in order to use the correct scale. We expected that implicitly forcing participants to classify the ambiguous faces would create a feeling of disfluency, rendering blended faces relatively unattractive compared to the control condition.

Indeed, in the control condition, when faces were simply judged on a single attractiveness scale, morphs were rated higher than their parents, creating an "inverted U" relationship between morph level and attractiveness, a classic beauty-in-averageness effect. In the experimental condition, however, in which each judgment was preceded by classification, this quadratic relationship flattened out (see Figure 9.3, left panel), presumably because the difficulty associated with classifying the faces depressed their otherwise strong appeal. This account is supported by speeded classification data, generated by same participants, that confirmed that increasingly blended faces were increasingly difficult to categorize, and that categorization speed is associated with the extent to which the quadratic attractiveness function is flattened in the experimental condition.

It could be argued, however, that these data represent not a genuine fluency-driven change in the appeal of blended faces, but rather a change in standards against which the faces were judged. To verify that changes in the attractiveness of blends were driven by the difficulty of classifying them, we conducted a replication which required all participants to judge face morphs on family-specific scales, but which varied the cognitive difficulty involved in doing so by informing half of the participants of the family to which a stimulus belonged (and therefore which of the two scales should be used to rate it). Thus, the rating conditions were equated in terms of their use categories and multiple scales

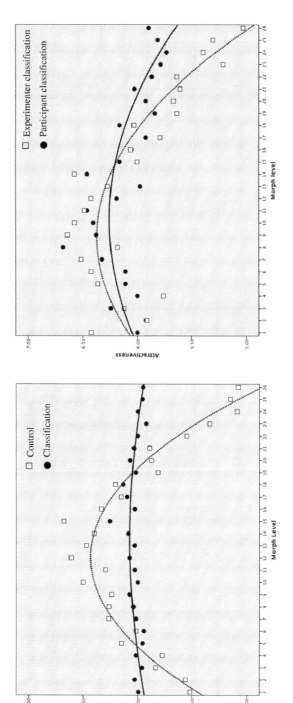

Figure 9.3 Attractiveness as a function of morph level (in 4% blend increments) and classification task (see text for details). In both studies, classification difficulty was associated with a decrease in the beauty-in-averageness effect.

(and in turn the standards for those scales); they varied only in whether the participants were required to classify the faces for themselves. As shown in the right side of Figure 9.3, the attractiveness of morphs relative to their parents (the beauty-in-averageness effect) was still reduced when judgments required implicit identification of the group to which the faces belonged, than when the family membership was provided, suggesting that the cognitive effort involved in classifying the faces played a role in their attractiveness.

In sum, these studies show that the relative attractiveness of blended faces depends critically on the effort required to classify them, which in turn depends on what they are being classified *as*. A face blend represents both a distortion of the faces that compose it, and at the same time a good example of the superordinate category (e.g., "faces") that includes it. Thus, by implicitly inducing participants to use the more specific categories, we dramatically altered the prototypicality of the blends, making them more difficult to process and consequently lowering (though not entirely reversing) their attractiveness. Most tellingly, blends were only less attractive when participants actively classified them: it was not enough for a blend merely to be an atypical category member; participants needed to experience the disfluency for themselves for typicality to have an effect on attractiveness.

Fluency and cross-race faces

Our model of context-dependent fluency can also be applied to "natural" morphs—bi- or multi-racial faces which, like laboratory blends, are notably attractive (Rhodes et al., 2005), as well as self-evidently difficult to classify. Indeed the inscrutability and mystique of cross-race faces has sometimes been cited as the source of their beauty (e.g., Beech, 2001), which if true would seem to falsify a fluency account of their attractiveness.

We believe the seemingly paradoxical, disfluent beauty of cross-race faces can be resolved by assuming that they are both typical and atypical of different categories under different conditions. That is, if cross-race faces are "faces" when judged for attractiveness, but race-specific exemplars when classified by race, fluency could explain their attractiveness in both cases. If so, then we should be able to reduce, or even reverse, the attractiveness of cross-race faces by encouraging race-specific processing prior to judgment. Barack Obama, for example, should be a fluent, and attractive, man, but a relatively disfluent and unattractive "Black man" (or "Caucasian man"), with category-relative fluency explaining his attractiveness in both cases.

To examine these ideas, we asked participants to rate the attractiveness of a series within-race and cross-race blends of Caucasian and Asian faces on a 1 to 7 scale (see Figure 9.4 for examples). We manipulated social category salience by asking some of the participants to classify the faces in terms of their race, as quickly and accurately as possible, immediately prior to rating them. Control participant made an unrelated prior judgment. As seen in Figure 9.5, cross-race blends were more attractive than within-race blends, as typically observed, but

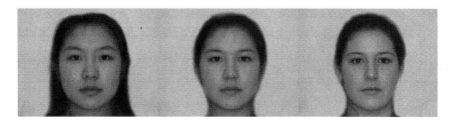

Figure 9.4 Examples of within-Asian, between Asian-Caucasian, and within-Caucasian morphs. All images are blends of two faces.

their advantage was significantly attenuated when participants first identified their race. An analysis of race classification times revealed that cross-races faces were also classified particularly slowly relative to within-race faces, consistent with the hypothesis that at least part of the difference in attractiveness is due to their ambiguity, and consequent disfluency, with respect to their group identity.

In a second study we measured *nonverbal* affective responses to cross-race faces, using facial electromyography (EMG) to record electrical activity from the zygomaticus (the "smiling") muscle regions. Facial EMG is a well validated nonverbal indicator of incipient emotional response, particularly appropriate for

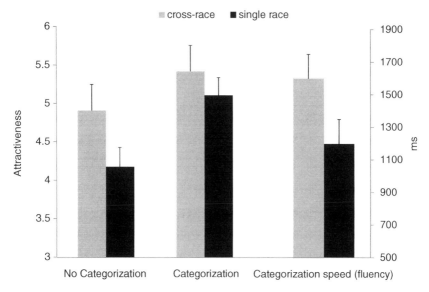

Figure 9.5 Attractiveness (left axis) and fluency (right axis) of within-race and between-race morphs as a function of experimental condition.

measuring the appeal of cross-race faces, which is fraught with self-presentational bias. Twelve participants were exposed to both within and between-race blends, which half of whom had previously classified by race. Analysis of baseline-adjusted zygomaticus activation revealed that participants smiled more to cross-race morphs in the control condition, but *less* to cross-race morphs (and more to within-race morphs) in the categorization condition.

Together, these studies show that racial classification reduces the appeal of cross-race faces. This is presumably due to the role cognitive fluency plays in the attractiveness of facial averages. With no need for racial classification, multi-race individuals are perceived fluently, which partly contributes to their appeal. When racial classification is required, however, the difficulty of performing such a task on multiracial individuals leads to a decline in their appeal, as reflected in participants' self-reports and their physiological responses.

Fluency and stereotyping

When the flexibility of perceivers' category use is taken into account, fluency provides a plausible account of why cross-race faces are generally attractive, and also predicts the conditions when they should be *un*attractive: when race categorization is required and/or salient. Interestingly, when considered more broadly, both positive *and* negative attitudes toward category blends (relative to unambiguous exemplars) appear at odds with intuitive stereotyping theory (formal theory being mostly silent on the issue), and illustrate the need for the incorporation of processing dynamics into any complete account of affect and social categorization.

Stereotypes are summary judgments of the perceived central tendency of a social group: category prototypes. As such they should form the basis of a graded group structure, such that individuals are better or worse examples of the group depending on their similarity to the stereotype (Cantor & Mischel, 1979). For example, Arnold Schwarzenegger is a prototypical "action hero" but a very atypical "politician;" Ronald Reagan is the opposite.

The question of how the affective component of stereotypes is generalized to group members as a function of their typicality has, oddly, received little attention (see Fiske, 1982, for an exception). Although many theories address the likelihood that a stereotype will be applied to a given individual (e.g., Devine, 1989; Fiske & Neuberg, 1990; Kunda & Spencer, 2003), these theories apparently assume that *if* the stereotype is applied, it is applied in full. Thus, if a perceiver hates politicians, then (all things being equal) she hates Ronald Reagan whenever he is seen as a politician (although a variety of individual and situational factors will influence whether he is indeed classified as such). Intuitively, however, the affect associated with a member of a stereotyped group should apply to group members in proportion to the member's fit to the stereotype: when both are being judged as politicians, Reagan should be judged more negatively than Schwarzenegger by people who hate politicians, and more positively by people who love them. When both are being judged as action heroes,

Schwarzenegger should be judged more positively than Reagan by people who love action heroes, and more negatively by those who hate them.

This intuitive analysis, however, assumes a linear relationship between category fit and affect generalization, and ignores the fact that the process of fitting an individual to a category itself generates affect that may influence the perceiver's overall evaluation. In the case of facial prototypes, we have seen how the effort involved in classification by race can influence their attractiveness. In the case of social prototypes, classification fluency could analogously produce a counterintuitive, nonlinear relation between typicality and liking, such that atypical members of negative groups, for example, are judged less favorably than prototypical members. In other words, for the perceiver who hates politicians, the very typical politician might be liked *more* than the atypical one, because the latter derives negative affect both from the overall category evaluation and from the disfluency created by classifying an atypical politician. If politicians are negative, Reagan, the consummate politician, may ironically be favored over Schwarzenegger, the less typical one.

To test this curious prediction we examined a fundamental and automatic dimension of person classification—gender—creating ten sets of faces that varied continuously in their "femaleness" by blending pairs of male and female faces to eight different degrees (examples appear in Figure 9.6). Participants judged the attractiveness of these faces in one of two conditions, modeled on the face perception tasks described above. In the critical, experimental condition, prior to judging each face, participants were asked to classify it as male or female; in a control condition, participants made an unrelated judgment (pressing a key when a target face appeared on the screen) prior to each rating.

An analysis of attractiveness as a function of morph level and prior classification, illustrated in Figure 9.7, revealed that faces were overall more attractive to the extent they were feminized (consistent with the literature on facial attractiveness; Perrett et al., 1998). More important, however, an interaction between morph level and classification condition showed that, as predicted, when (and only when) faces were classified by their gender, more ambiguous faces were less attractive than relatively unambiguous ones. The pattern is particularly interesting in light of the general preference for feminized faces: even though men were less attractive than women, more "manly" men were *more* attractive than less manly men!

This nonlinear pattern cannot be accommodated by a simple model of stereotype application in which a blend is judged positively as a function of its fit with a positive group. Instead, it suggests that the ambiguity of the stimulus has an additive, depressing effect on their appeal, and the fact that the effect is only evident when the faces are categorized suggests that it is the disfluency created by the process of classification that accounts for the negativity.

An aesthetic preference for women over men, however, is not the same as a group attitude. To examine the stereotypes more directly, we conducted a conceptual replication using a weakly negative target group: homosexual men. Not only did this domain allow us to examine attitudes toward the targets (rather than

Figure 9.6 Examples of gender blends used.

their attractiveness), but the fact that the stereotype of homosexual men includes feminized features allowed us to vary social category fit via manipulation of facial appearance. Analogous to the study on gender classification described above, we predicted that although participants would express more positive attitudes toward heterosexual men than toward homosexual men, they would, remarkably, like "more gay" men (i.e., men with feminized features) more than "less gay" men.

Stimuli were images of 30 Caucasian men, each morphed 50 percent with a "supermale" or "superfemale" image (averages of male and female faces whose gender-specific features have been enhanced, created by Rhodes, Hickford, & Jeffery, 2000) to produce a masculinized and feminized version of each individual. Participants estimated how much they would like the feminized or masculinized version (within subjects) of each of the 30 men, who were all described as either homosexual or heterosexual (between subjects). Participants also completed

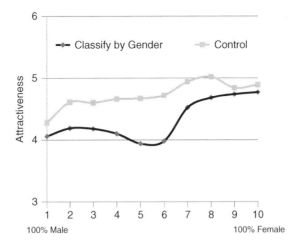

Figure 9.7 Attractiveness of morphed faces as a function of "femaleness" and classification condition.

Lamar and Kite's (1998) Components of Attitudes Toward Homosexuality scale, and were median-split in terms of their response to the item "Most gay men have identifiable feminine characteristics."

Analyses of liking judgments revealed that, although all participants preferred feminized over masculinized male images, the magnitude of the preference depended on whether the men were described as gay, and on participants' stereotypes about gay men's features. When the men were described as gay, participants who endorsed the stereotype that gay men have feminine features showed a greater preference for feminized men than participants who did not endorse the stereotype. The opposite was true when the men were described as heterosexual: participants who endorsed the stereotype showed a smaller preference for feminized men than participants who did not endorse the stereotype.

Importantly, participants did not differ in their *evaluation* of gay men as a group. For example, participants who thought gay men had feminine features did not think homosexuality was more or less "perverted" than participants who did not endorse this stereotype. Therefore, the data suggest that, as in the case of facial attractiveness, part of the evaluation of specific homosexual men was due to their similarity to the perceiver's stereotype of a homosexual man, regardless of whether the category itself was positive or negative. We propose that the affect associated with category fit is generated from fluent processing: Even when gay men are disliked as a group, "very gay" men (those who are good examples of the perceiver's category) will be easier to classify and paradoxically be evaluated more positively than "less gay" men.

It should be noted that confirmation of the mediating role of fluency still awaits confirmation from our ongoing research program, and that such confirmation may prove more complicated than it appears, depending on one's conception of fluency and its relation to positive affect. There are two general models of this relation: One assumes that fluency is a separate, temporally prior, and independent cause of positive affect. According to this "two step" model of fluency, some manipulation (e.g., blending) leads to a change in fluency, which participants subsequently explain by relating it to evaluative or other features of the stimulus (Jacoby, Kelley, & Dywan, 1989; Mandler, Nakamura, & Van Zandt, 1987). In this case, because fluency is clearly distinguishable from evaluative reactions, it can be statistically treated as such in causal and statistical models. However, a second general model (sometimes called "hedonic") assumes that fluency comes with an instant positive valence, either due to some intrinsic process (Winkielman et al., 2003) or to an automatic cue-learning history (Unkelbach & Greifeneder, Chapter 2, this volume). In this case—if positive affect is an integral and simultaneous component of fluency—statistical mediation becomes tricky, as by controlling for the mediator, one effectively controls for the DV itself. Future research may want to establish when fluency in attractiveness judgments functions more in line with the two-step or the intrinsic hedonic model, and what statistical models are most appropriate in which case.

Summary, implications, and conclusions

A recurring theme of this volume is that evaluations of the world are influenced not only by its content, but also by the ease with which that content is accessed and processed. In this chapter, we have shown how these two sources of affect combine to produce seemingly paradoxical effects on facial attractiveness and person perception. Using the principle of category-relative fluency, we showed how processing dynamics might play a role in the beauty-in-averageness effect, despite the apparent *ambiguity* of facial blends (i.e., the fact that they objectively resemble more than one group prototype). In fact, the ease with which a face can be classified and processed appears to depend on the category in which it is situated. In particular, blends, including bi-racial faces, can be subjectively seen as good examples of superordinate categories, such as "faces," making categorization fluent, which benefits attractiveness. However, they also can be subjectively seen as bad examples of the individuals or groups from which they were combined. So, making their componential structure salient decreases the blends' typicality, lowers the ease with which it can be categorized, and consequently hurts their aesthetic appeal. More generally, this research points out that 'objective' ambiguity (e.g., a stimulus created by averaging, morphing, blending, mixing, etc) matters less than how a stimulus is subjectively categorized. Superordinate categorization of a face (e.g., as a face, as a human, etc.) decreases its ambiguity by turning it into a good example of a higher-level category, while subordinate categorization (e.g., as a particular gender or member of a racial group) increases ambiguity by turning it into an, atypical, "bad" exemplar, with all the processing and preference costs this engenders.

Of course, some of these points have been made more or less explicitly before in the categorization literature. For example, classic approaches to categorization have long pointed out that the same two stimuli can be seen as belonging to just one or two separate categories. Further, the same stimulus can be perceived as typical or as atypical. What exactly happens depends on what dimensions are perceived as relevant, and whether the subjective representation of the relevant dimension is relatively fine-grained or relatively "coarse." These, in turn, depend on factors such as the relative range and frequency of stimuli in a category (Parducci, 1965), attention to the relevant dimension (Goldstone & Steyvers, 2001), and the current context and goals of the categorizer (Barsalou, 1982).

Analogously, work on intergroup relations has pointed out that individuals perceive others, and themselves, differently depending on the salience of their multiple social identities, and the level of social categorization (for a review, see Crisp & Hewstone, 2007). Thus, highlighting one group identity can make an individual seem typical, but highlighting another group identify can make the individual seem atypical. Similarly, highlighting superordinate categorization can make an individual seem like a "good" exemplar, but result in a loss of individual differentiation (Simon, Pantaleo, & Mummendey, 1995). Such superordinate categorization can be beneficial for the perception of common goals, common fate and reduction of prejudice, but come at the well-known cost of 'we-ness' (Gaertner & Dovidio, 2000). Critically, as our chapter highlights, all these categorization shifts have consequences not only for the content, but also the subjective ease of processing, and ease-related affect. For example, our framework predicts that stereotype-based judgments will be a function not only of what stereotype is applied, but also how *easily* it can be applied, leading to the counterintuitive hypothesis that very typical members of negative groups may be preferred to atypical ones.

Finally, it is interesting to note a certain paradox about recent work on fluency: Fluency became a "hot" topic of research because it highlighted that social judgments could be based on low-level, non-analytic, "content-free" aspects of stimulus processing—a point that resonated with Zajonc's (1980) famous claim that "preferences need no inferences." But more recently, the focus of fluency research has turned toward its interaction with higher-order processes—categorization, expectation, learning, metacognitive theories, etc (see other chapters in this volume). In our opinion this is a welcome development. After all, social perception represents a dynamic interplay of cognitive content and process, producing rich, nonlinear relations between objective stimulus features, subjective representations, experiences, and judgments that we have only begun to explore.

Acknowledgment

We gratefully acknowledge the generous and insightful comments from the book editors and from Klaus Fiedler.

References

Barsalou, L.W. (1982). Context-independent and context-dependent information in concepts. *Memory & Cognition, 10*, 82–93.

—— (1983). Ad hoc categories. *Memory & Cognition, 11*, 211–227.

—— (1993). Flexibility, structure, and linguistic vagary in concepts: Manifestations of a compositional system of perceptual symbols. In A.C. Collins, S.E. Gathercole, & M.A. Conway (Eds.), *Theories of memory* (pp. 29–101). London: Lawrence Erlbaum Associates.

Barsalou, L.W., & Sewell, D.R. 1984. Constructing representations of categories from different points of view. Emory Cognition Project Technical Report .#2, Emory University.

Beech, H. (2001). Eurasian Invasion. Time Magazine, 23 April 2001.

Busey, T. (1998). Physical and psychological representations of faces: Evidence from morphing. *Psychological Science, 9*, 476–482.

Cantor, N., & Mischel, M. (1979). Prototypes in person perception. *Advances in Experimental Social Psychology, 12*, 3–52.

Crisp, R. J., & Hewstone, M. (2007). Multiple social categorization. In M. P. Zanna (ed.) *Advances in experimental social psychology* (vol. 39, pp. 163–254). Orlando, FL: Academic Press

Devine, P. G. (1989). Stereotypes and prejudice: Their automatic and controlled components. *Journal of Personality and Social Psychology, 56*, 5–18.

Dovidio, J. F., Evans, N., & Tyler, R. B. (1986). Racial stereotypes: The contents of their cognitive representations. *Journal of Experimental Social Psychology, 22*, 22–37.

Fiske, S. T. (1982). Schema-triggered affect: Applications to social perception. In M. S. Clark & S. T. Fiske (Eds.), *Affect and cognition: The 17th Annual Carnegie Symposium on Cognition* (pp. 55–78). Hillsdale, NJ: Erlbaum.

Fiske, S. T., & Neuberg, S. L. (1990). A continuum of impression formation, from category-based to individuating processes: Influences of information and motivation on attention and interpretation. *Advances in Experimental Social Psychology, 23*, 1–74.

Galton, F. (1878). Composite portraits. *Journal of the Anthropological Institute of Great Britain & Ireland, 8*, 132–144.

Gaertner, S. L., & Dovidio, J. F. (2000). *Reducing intergroup bias: The Common Ingroup Identity Model*. Philadelphia, PA: Psychology Press.

Goldstone, R. L., & Steyvers, M. (2001). The sensitization and differentiation of dimensions during category learning. *Journal of Experimental Psychology: General, 130*, 116–139.

Gigerenzer, G. (2007). *Gut feelings: The intelligence of the unconscious*. New York: Viking Press.

Halberstadt, J. B. (2006). The generality and ultimate origins of the attractiveness of prototypes. *Personality & Social Psychology Review, 10*, 166–183.

Halberstadt, J., & Hooton, K. (2008). The affect disruption hypothesis: The effect of analytic thought on the fluency and appeal of art. *Cognition and Emotion, 22*, 964–976.

Halberstadt J., & Rhodes G. (2000). The attractiveness of nonface averages: Implications for an evolutionary explanation of the attractiveness of average faces. *Psychological Science, 4*, 285–289.

—— (2003). It's not just average faces that are attractive: Computer-manipulated averageness makes birds, fish, and automobiles attractive. *Psychonomic Bulletin and Review, 10*, 149–156.

Jacoby, L. L., Kelley C. M., & Dywan J. (1989). Memory attributions. In H. L. Roediger & F. I. M. Craik (Eds.), *Varieties of memory and consciousness: Essays in honour of Endel Tulving.* (pp. 391–422). Hillsdale, NJ: Erlbaum.

Kunda, Z., & Spencer, S. (2003). When do stereotypes come to mind and when do they color judgment? A goal-based theoretical framework for stereotype activation and application. *Psychological Bulletin, 129*, 522–544.

LaMar, L., and Kite, M. E. (1998). Sex differences in attitudes toward gay men and lesbians: A multi-dimensional perspective. *The Journal of Sex Research, 35*, 189–196.

Langlois, J. H., & Roggman, L.A. (1990). Attractive faces are only average. *Psychological Science, 1*, 115–121.

Mandler, G., Nakamura, Y., & Van Zandt, B. J. (1987). Nonspecific effects of exposure on stimuli that cannot be recognized. *Journal of Experimental Psychology: Learning, Memory, and Cognition, 13*, 646–648.

Parducci, A. (1965). Category judgments: A range-frequency model. *Psychological Review, 72*, 407–418.

Perrett, D. I., Lee, K. J., Penton-Voak, I., Rowland, D., Yoshikawa, S., Burt, D. M., Henzi, S. P., Castles, D. L., & Akamatsu, S. (1998). Effects of sexual dimorphism on facial attractiveness. *Nature, 394*, 884–887.

Potter, T., & Corneille, O. (2008). Locating attractiveness in the face space: Faces are more attractive when closer to their group prototype. *Psychonomic Bulletin & Review, 15*, 615–622.

Posner, M. I., & Keele, S. W. (1968). On the genesis of abstract ideas. *Journal of Experimental Psychology, 77*, 353–363.

Reber, R., Schwarz, N., & Winkielman, P. (2004). Processing fluency and aesthetic pleasure: Is beauty in the perceiver's processing experience? *Personality and Social Psychology Review, 8*, 364–382.

Reber, R., Winkielman, P., & Schwarz, N. (1998). Effects of perceptual fluency on affective judgments. *Psychological Science, 9*, 45–48.

Rhodes, G., Hickford, C., Jeffery, L. (2000). Sex-typicality and attractiveness: Are supermale and superfemale faces super-attractive? *British Journal of Psychology, 91*, 125–140.

Rhodes, G., Jeffery, L., Watson, T. L., Clifford, C. W. G., & Nakayama, K. (2003). Fitting the mind to the world: Face adaptation and attractiveness aftereffects. *Psychological Science, 14*, 558–566.

Rhodes, G., Lee, K., Palermo, R., Weiss, M., Yoshikawa, S., Clissa, P., Williams, T., Peters, M., Winkler, C., & Jeffery, L. (2005). Attractiveness of own-race, other-race, and mixed-race faces. *Perception, 34*, 319–340.

Rhodes, G., & Tremewan, T. (1996). Averageness, exaggeration, and facial attractiveness. *Psychological Science, 7*, 105–110.

Rosch, R., & Mervis, C. B. (1975) Family resemblances: Studies in the internal structure of categories. *Cognitive Psychology, 7*, 573–605.

Simon, B., Pantaleo, G., & Mummendey, A. (1995). Unique individual or interchangeable group member? The accentuation of intragroup differences versus similarities as an indicator of the individual self versus the collective self. *Journal of Personality and Social Psychology, 69*, 106–119.

Smith, E. E., Shoben, E. J., & Rips, L. J. (1974). Structure and process in semantic memory: A featural model for semantic decisions. *Psychological Review, 81*, 214–241.

Symons, D. (1979). *Evolution of human sexuality*. New York: Oxford University Press.

Thornhill, R., & Gangestad, S.W. (1993). Human facial beauty: Averageness, symmetry, and parasite resistance. *Human Nature, 4*, 237–269.

Winkielman, P., & Cacioppo, J. T. (2001). Mind at ease puts a smile on the face: Psychophysiological evidence that processing facilitation leads to positive affect. *Journal of Personality and Social Psychology, 81*, 989–1000.

Winkielman, P., Halberstadt, J., Fazendeiro, T., & Catty, S. (2006). Prototypes are attractive because they are easy on the mind. *Psychological Science, 17*, 799–806.

Winkielman, P., Schwarz, N., Fazendeiro, T., & Reber, R. (2003). The hedonic marking of processing fluency: Implications for evaluative judgment. In J. Musch & K. C. Klauer (Eds.), *The psychology of evaluation: Affective processes in cognition and emotion.* (pp. 189–217). Mahwah, NJ: Lawrence Erlbaum.

Zajonc, R. B. (1980). Feeling and thinking: Preferences need no inferences. *American Psychologist, 35*, 117–123.

10 Almost everything you always wanted to know about ease-of-retrieval effects

Michaela Wänke

Abstract

Many studies showed that when forming a judgment people tend to rely less on retrieved information when the retrieval felt difficult as compared to easy. This tendency has become known as the ease-of-retrieval effect. This chapter has two goals. First, it will give an overview of ease-of-retrieval effects, particularly in the realm of attitude judgments and persuasion. Second, it will review different experimental procedures and discuss methodological issues in ease of retrieval experiments with the objective to give some recommendations regarding best practice.

Background

As everyone knows, it is much easier to catch a fish from a pond with many fish than from a pond with only few fish. In reverse, it may seem justified to conclude that a pond contains many fish if catching one is easy. Indeed people seem to hold the meta-cognitive theory that a category must be large if they can easily think of exemplars. This is known as the availability heuristic, which was initially proposed for frequency and probability estimates: "A person is said to employ the availability heuristic whenever he estimates frequency or probability by the ease with which instances or associations could be brought to mind" (Tversky & Kahneman, 1973, p. 206). The classical research demonstrations were construed in such a way that retrieval of instances from one category felt easier than retrievals from another category for reasons unrelated to actual occurrence. When consequently the frequency estimates differed, this was seen as evidence for the use of ease of retrieval. For example, people overestimated the number of words beginning with the letter "k" compared to words that had "k" in third position, presumably because they had a retrieval strategy that helped them finding words beginning with "k" but they had no strategy for coming up with words that had "k" in third position (Tversky & Kahneman, 1973). Similarly, when people were presented with a list of 19 famous women and 20 non-famous men or a list of 19 famous men and 20 non-famous women and were later asked to judge whether the list contained more females or more males, they erroneously overestimated the frequency of the gender represented by the famous names (Tversky & Kahneman, 1973). Again, fame was assumed to have facilitated the recall of either male or female names and this experience of an easier recall presumably led to the overestimate.

The availability heuristic became highly influential and so did the notion that experienced ease in information processing influences judgments (as many chapters in this volume attest). These effects of experienced ease (fluency) are not restricted to the ease with which information can be recalled or generated (ease of retrieval) but encompasses other accessibility experiences such as the ease with which things can be imagined (ease of imagery) (Petrova & Cialdini, 2008) as well as experiences accompanying the processing of externally presented materials, such as the ease with which stimuli can be visually or auditorily perceived (perceptual ease), read or pronounced (linguistic ease), or the ease with which mental operations occur. Moreover the effects of ease on judgment are not limited to probability and frequency estimates but also affect judgments of truth, liking, risk, confidence, fame, typicality, and many more (for a review on types and effects of fluency see Alter & Oppenheimer, 2009). However, despite its immediate popularity, early research on the availability heuristic had rarely shown that it was indeed experienced ease that was driving the effects (for one exception see Gabrielcik & Fazio, 1984).

Coming back to the introductory example, one may also conclude that a pond has many fish if one catches many. Feeling or estimating ease is not necessary but simply looking at how many fish are in the net is sufficient. Unfortunately, in the classic studies, experienced ease and retrieved amount were indeed confounded. In the above-mentioned study for example, participants, who had been presented with famous women and non-famous men, did not merely estimate that there had been more women than men, but also *retrieved* more female than male exemplars. Hence the retrieval result and the retrieval experience held the same implications, and participants may have simply concluded that if they recalled more women than men there must have been more women than men. For this inference, the experience of ease would not be necessary. In a highly clever experiment, Schwarz, Bless, Strack, Klumpp, Rittenauer-Schatka & Simons (1991) disentangled experienced ease of retrieval from amount of retrieval. They asked their participants to recall either six or 12 incidents where they had behaved in a self-assertive way. As determined by a pretest, coming up with six examples felt easy whereas coming up with 12 examples felt difficult. Thus, in one condition, participants retrieved more examples but experienced difficulty, whereas in the other condition participants retrieved fewer examples but experienced ease. If retrieved amount was the crucial variable, those participants who had retrieved 12 instances of self-assertive behavior should have consequently reported higher self-assertiveness. This however, was not the case. In contrast, those participants who had retrieved only six instances of self-assertive behavior reported higher self-assertiveness than those who had retrieved 12 instances.

This by now classic experiment is notable for three reasons. First, it provided evidence that it is, as originally proposed, indeed the retrieval experience, rather than the number of retrieved information, that underlies frequency estimates (see also Wänke, Schwarz & Bless, 1995, for a replication of the classic letter study). Or in other words, the effects are driven by the ease of fishing rather than the number of fish caught. Second, the experiment showed that the impact of retrieval experiences affected judgments beyond frequency and probability judgments, in this case evaluative judgments. Since then, many other studies have shown that when retrieval of information feels easy, people are more likely to use the implications of that information for their judgment compared to when retrieval feels difficult. The first part of the present chapter will give an overview of some applications of ease of retrieval effects, particularly in the realm of attitude judgments and persuasion, followed by a discussion of the underlying processes. Finally, it should be noted that as innovative the experiment by Schwarz et al. (1991) was, it did not remove the confound between experience and amount or content of retrieval, it only reversed it. Still, the retrieved content differs between conditions. In the last part of the present chapter I will outline some procedures how to deal with the potential confound and address other methodological issues in ease-of-retrieval experiments.

Some examples for ease-of-retrieval effect

Various studies have shown that the ease with which previously presented material was recalled or that the ease with which reasons and arguments were self-generated affects many aspects of the resulting attitudes. In one study, research participants recalled brand features from a previously presented ad (Wänke & Bless, 2000). Based on pretesting, the presented features were either strong or weak depending on condition and recall was facilitated or made difficult. Both, pre-rated argument quality and subjective ease of recall had a significant effect on perceived argument compellingness and in turn on brand evaluation. As a result of both effects, easily retrieved *weak* arguments were considered as compelling as *strong* but difficult to retrieve arguments. These results suggest that if one does not have strong arguments one should at least make them easy to recall. Supporting this assumption, other research also found evidence for more favorable impact of brand attributes when they were easily recalled (Menon & Raghubir, 2003). Perhaps this is one side-effect of ad repetitions. With more repetitions advertised attributes or arguments will become more accessible in memory and thereby more convincing. That ease of recall makes an argument more convincing is perfectly in line with other fluency effects in persuasion. For example, arguments in radio advertising were more persuasive when presented in the form of familiar idiomatic phrases (e.g., "Don't put all your eggs in one basket") rather than in more literal—and less fluent—form ("Don't risk everything on a single venture") (Howard, 1997). Recent research also proposes that congruency between current mindsets on the one hand and message framing (Lee & Aaker, 2004) or linguistic forms (Semin, Higgins, Gil de Montes, Estourget, & Valencia, 2005) on the other hand elicits more fluent message processing, which in turn, heightens persuasion.

Recalling or processing presented attributes or arguments is one thing. Classical research on self-persuasion, however, suggests that self-generating arguments is a more effective persuasion strategy in so far as it produces longer lasting effects (e.g. Janis & King, 1954). Then again, as can be easily imagined by now, this also depends on the ease with which these arguments are generated. For instance, when asked to generate arguments for the use of public transport, people reported more favorable attitudes towards public transport when the retrieval of arguments felt easy compared to difficult. In turn, when asked to generate arguments *against* the use of public transport, they reported less favorable attitudes when the retrieval of arguments felt easy compared to difficult (Wänke, Bless & Biller, 1996; von Helversen. Gendolla, Winkielman, & Schmidt, 2008). Similar effects have been shown for various attitude objects (e.g. Briñol et al., 2006; Danziger, Moran & Raffaely, 2006; Haddock, 2002; Hansen & Wänke, 2008; Herzog, Hansen & Wänke, 2007; Ruder & Bless, 2003) and evidence suggests that these attitudes are rather stable (Weick & Guinote, 2008). Moreover, easy retrieval of attitude-supportive information also increases attitude strength (Haddock, Rothman, Reber & Schwarz, 1999) and confidence (Wänke et al., 1996; Tsai & McGill, 2011).

Clearly, these findings have important implications for applied domains. In marketing research, for example, consumers are often asked to list "likes" or "dislikes." The ease with which they are able to do this may well affect their subsequent overall judgment. Such a real world effect was reported for course evaluations at Duke University (Fox, 2006). Students evaluated their class on a form that only differed in one item between conditions. Students in one condition were asked to list two ways in which they felt the course could be improved whereas in the other condition they were asked to list ten ways. Interestingly, although, despite the instructions, the number of suggestions on how to improve the course did not differ between conditions, students subsequently reported higher satisfaction when they had been asked for ten improvement suggestions compared to only two. Presumably, they concluded that the course was fine if they had difficulty thinking of so many possible improvements (but see below for an alternative explanation).

Not surprisingly, eliciting such conclusions can make for successful persuasion strategies. Actually, it is not even necessary that persuasion targets engage in real retrieval; merely believing that retrieval would feel easy or difficult does the trick (Wänke, Bohner & Jurkowitsch, 1997). Ad recipients preferred BMW over Mercedes to a larger extent when the ad had suggested that one would be easily able to name one reason for preferring a BMW over a Mercedes compared to an ad that suggested they should be able to name ten reasons. Difficulties in generating reasons for preferring one alternative over another may not only thwart such a preference but may also lead to choice deferral or to choosing a compromise option (Novemsky, Dhar, Schwarz & Simonson, 2007).

While there is abundant evidence for ease-of-retrieval effects on the outcome of judgments, much less is known about effects on further information processing. Some evidence suggests that difficulty in retrieval may induce more systematic information processing (Wänke & Bless, 2000). In two studies, participants had to recall either strong or weak arguments before reporting their attitude. Dual process models would predict less differentiation between strong and weak arguments under low as compared to high involvement. Indeed, this classic pattern of results was replicated when recall was made easy. However, when recall was made difficult, strong arguments were more persuasive than weak arguments even when involvement was low (see also Alter et al., 2007 for similar effects of perceptual fluency).

Summary

Whenever individuals retrieve or generate information in order to construct a judgment, one may expect that the subjective experience accompanying the retrieval or generation process may affect the judgment. There is no reason to believe that ease-of-retrieval effects are constrained to specific domains. Accordingly, beyond effects on attitude formation and brand evaluation, similar effects have been shown in wide range of fields, for example stereotypes (Dijksterhuis, Macrae & Haddock, 1999; Weick & Guinote, 2008) and stereotype threat (Keller & Bless, 2005), judgments of perceived fairness (e.g. Müller., & Bless, 2010), risk (e.g. Grayson & Schwarz, 1999; Rothman & Schwarz, 1998; Vjastfjäll, Peters & Slovic, 2008), and predictions of future events and states (Kadous, Krische & Sedor, 2006; Keller & Bless, 2009; Spielmann, MacDonald & Wilson, 2009). In all these examples, judgments were more in line with the content of the retrieved information when the retrieval felt easy rather than difficult. The next paragraph will address why this is the case.

The when and why of ease-of-retrieval effects

For retrieval experiences to influence judgments a sequence of prerequisites have to be met (for a detailed discussion on moderators see Greifeneder, Bless, & Pham, 2011). In the first place—as trivial as it may sound—in order for ease-of-retrieval effects to emerge, people have to experience ease or difficulty. In experimental settings different manipulations have been employed (see methodological issues), most prominently the one introduced by Schwarz and colleagues (1991). However, while experiencing ease is a necessary condition for ease-of-retrieval effects to occur, it is not a sufficient one. Once ease or difficulty is experienced, its impact on the judgment depends on how it is attributed and which implications the attribution has for the judgment. Finally, situational or personality variables may determine to what extent people rely on their experience.

Experiencing ease

Sensitivity to inner feelings. Research has brought some evidence that ease-of-retrieval effects and, more generally, fluency effects depend on inter-individual differences. People who generally tend to rely on intuition as measured by the Rational-Experiential Scale (Pacini & Epstein, 1999) show larger effects (Danziger, Moran, & Raffaely, 2006; Keller & Bless, 2009) and so do people who are likely to focus on inner feelings or the self (Petrova, 2006) as measured by the Private Self-Consciousness scale (Feningstein, Scheier & Buss, 1975) or the Self-Construal scale (Singelis, 1994). While the former may also reflect greater willingness to rely on processing experiences (see below) the latter may indicate that people differ in the saliency of their experiences. Conditions that make inner feelings more salient, such as happy mood, also promote ease-of-retrieval effects (Ruder & Bless, 2003). At least sad mood seems to decrease the effects as Greifeneder and Bless (2008) showed when comparing depressed and non-depressed individuals.

Discrepancy promotes ease-of-retrieval effects. As elaborated elsewhere (Hansen & Wänke, Chapter 5, this volume), discrepancy between actual and expected processing effort makes the experience more noticeable and informative (Whittlesea & Williams, 2000, 2001a, 2001b). Accordingly, ease-of-retrieval effects can be expected to emerge more strongly when the experience is surprising. Hansen and Wänke (2008) presented tasks either in ascending or descending degree of difficulty before participants worked on the target task that consisted of generating either few or many arguments. Generating few supportive arguments led to more favorable attitudes than generating many pro arguments. However, this was only the case when the actual task difficulty mismatched what could be expected from the sequence. When the expectations due to the task sequence matched the task difficulty then the effects reversed. As with any signal, an experiential state is only informative if it diverges from a comparison state of the same type. Thus, deviant experiences are more likely to be used as information for a subsequent attitude judgment. If ease and difficulty correspond to a previous state or expectancy, they have less impact (see Hansen & Wänke, Chapter 5, this volume, for a more detailed discussion).

Attributions underlying ease-of-retrieval effects

Different processes may mediate the increased use of the retrieved information for the judgment at hand.

Frequency attributions. In line with the availability heuristic participants who in the study by Schwarz and colleagues (1991) recalled six self-assertive behaviors may have assumed from the experienced ease that they apparently quite often behave in a self-assertive manner, which in turn led them to think of themselves as relatively self-assertive. That ease-of-retrieval effects can indeed be mediated by frequency inferences was shown in a study by Greifeneder & Bless (2008). It is not unreasonable to assume that the meta-cognitive theory of easy retrieval indicating a large category may well underlie many ease-of-retrieval effects in the literature. Alternatively, other meta-cognitive theories may come into play and trigger (or undermine) the effects.

Attributions to information inherent qualities. When information was easily retrieved, retrievers had more confidence in its validity (Kelley & Lindsay, 1993; Tormala, Petty & Brinol, 2002), considered category exemplars as more typical (Oppenheimer & Frank, 2007), and brand attributes that were recalled easily as more compelling (Wänke & Bless, 2000). Given such inferences, it is not surprising that retrievers would be more willing to rely on this information for relevant judgments.

One may wonder, of course, why easy retrieval signals validity, makes arguments seem more convincing and exemplars more typical. Presumably, just as there is a learned association between ease and frequency, people may have learned other associations that serve as meta-cognitive lay-theories and guide the interpretation of the experience. What one knows for sure can be retrieved rather easily. When thinking about an issue the more important arguments usually come to mind before less important ones, and likewise typical category exemplars are more often mentioned and activated, and therefore more accessible than obscure ones (Silvera, Krull & Sassler, 2002). Based on these associations, people also seem to infer the reverse, namely that experienced ease signals validity, argument strength, typicality, and possibly other qualities.

In sum, ease may mean many things and some support using the retrieved information for the judgment at hand. That said, there are also attributions of ease that hamper basing judgments on retrieved information.

Attributions undermining ease-of-retrieval effects

What the mediating inferences in the previous section had in common was that they all pertain to some aspect of information that has implications for the judgment. The evaluative strength, validity, and representativeness of information are undoubtedly good criteria for whether to rely on the information for one's judgment or not. The accessibility experience may, however, also be attributed to causes irrelevant to the judgment at hand. Difficult retrieval may for example be seen as an indicator of poor memory (Winkielman, Schwarz & Belli, 1998), low expertise or interest on the side of the retriever (Biller, Bless & Schwarz, 1992; Schwarz & Schuman, 1997) as well as low significance of the remembered material or high temporal distance (e.g. Xu & Schwarz, 2005, and Schwarz, Cho & Xu, 2005, as cited from Schwarz, Song & Xu, 2009). If the experience is attributed in a way that makes it undiagnostic for the judgment at hand, it may not necessarily result in the previously described effects. One would, for example, not arrive at a negative brand evaluation following difficulties in retrieving favorable brand attributes when the reason for the difficult experience is attributed to one's low interest for the product category or a poorly executed advertising campaign.

Accordingly, many experiments have found that ease-of-retrieval effects decrease or vanish when an alternative attribution is provided. In some experimental settings the attribution is explicitly directed to an external source such as background music (e.g. Schwarz et al., 1991; Haddock et al., 1999) or the design of the questionnaire (Greifeneder & Bless, 2007; Ruder & Bless, 2003; Wänke et al., 1995). For example, in a replication of Tversky & Kahneman's (1973) classical experiment on frequency estimates of words beginning with a certain letter or having that letter in third position, participants were told that the generation of words beginning with a *t* would be facilitated by the pale letter *t* printed on their answer sheet (Wänke et al., 1995). This manipulation undermined the overestimate for words beginning with a *t*. It was assumed that when the experienced ease is attributed to the answer sheet it could not be interpreted as a signal for the high frequency of words beginning with the letter *t*.

In other studies, an alternative cause of attribution was offered less explicitly. Several studies had found that a question on how a politician had voted on some issues decreased reported interest in politics in a subsequent question (Bishop, Oldendick & Tuchfarber, 1984; Bishop, 1987). Presumably having difficulty in recalling the politician's voting led participants to conclude that their interest in politics was not as high as they may have thought. But this effect disappeared when the question about their interest was preceded by a question on the quality of the politician's public relations (Schwarz & Schuman, 1997). Apparently, the latter attribution rendered the retrieval experience inapplicable for judging one's interest in politics.

Finally, of course, naturally occurring characteristics of the situation or the material may also offer alternative accounts for the retrieval experience (Oppenheimer, 2004). Assumed expertise or perhaps lack of it may therefore explain why experienced difficulty is used less for judgments about others than for oneself (Caruso, 2008; Raghubir & Menon, 1998) or less for unfamiliar brands compared to familiar ones (Tybout, Sternthal, Malaviya, Bakamitsos, & Park, 2005). Likewise, when the recall concerns a rather distant past where one's memory is likely to fail, this alternative account may undermine ease-of-retrieval effects (Raghubir & Menon, 2005).

It is important to note, as many of the examples illustrate, that while a particular attribution may render the experience undiagnostic for one judgment, it may nevertheless have implications for another judgment. For example, depending on one's attribution, difficulty in retrieving favorable brand attributes may not lower the evaluation of the brand but instead the evaluation of the ad execution or one's self-assessed expertise in the product category.

Willingness to rely on feeling

Besides inter-individual differences on the Rational-Experiential Scale (Pacini & Epstein, 1999) (see above) other variables may affect the willingness to rely on feeling and thereby moderate ease of retrieval. For example, it has been suggested that powerful individuals tend to rely more on their feelings than powerless individuals (Guinote, 2010). Accordingly, power increases reliance on ease of retrieval (Weick & Guinote, 2008). Because power is associated with abstract thinking (Smith & Trope, 2006), one might also expect ease-of-retrieval effects to be more pronounced under conditions of abstract thinking. However, recent evidence suggests the opposite. Tsai & Thomas (2011) report ease-of-retrieval effects under conditions of concrete but not abstract thinking.

Given that relying on a feeling may seem like a mental shortcut to more systematic processing one may assume that ease of retrieval is used primarily when information processing is constrained. Indeed, there is evidence of diminished ease-of-retrieval effects when processing capacity (Greifeneder & Bless, 2007) or need for cognition (Florack & Zoabi, 2003) is high. In line with this perspective, ease-of-retrieval effects were also diminished when feelings of uncertainty had been induced (Müller et al., 2010). Note, that uncertainty would be expected to trigger more systematic and thoughtful processing. With regard to involvement, studies by Schwarz and colleagues (Rothman & Schwarz, 1998; Grayson & Schwarz, 1999) found that when participants were asked to recall risk-relevant behaviors, those who were likely to consider themselves barely at risk relied more on ease, whereas those who were more likely to consider themselves highly at risk were less likely to rely on ease. Unfortunately, however, involvement was not measured and the conclusion is only preliminary. Be that as it may, evidence that reliance on ease is a heuristic is contradictory. Other studies found stronger effects when need for cognition (Wänke & Bless, 2000), accuracy motivation (Tormala et al., 2002; Wänke & Bless, 2000), or involvement (Tormala et al., 2002) was high, or when need for structure was low (Hirt, Kardes & Markman, 2004). As of now, it is unclear what moderates the interplay between ease of retrieval and processing constraints.

Summary

The occurrence of ease-of-retrieval effects is common within many domains. Within these domains, they can pertain to different judgments depending on the theory the individual holds. They are more likely to emerge when the experience is unexpected and when people are attuned to rely on their inner feelings for judgments. Many retrieval experiences may have more than one possible cause. Attributions to any one of the possible causes might forestall inferences regarding another. What is worth mentioning at this point is that different attributions and interpretations of the experience may not only hold implications for different judgments, but may affect the same judgment in different ways. When difficulty in coming up with reasons for choosing a brand is interpreted as lack of strong reasons, confidence in brand choice will be low (see also Wänke et al., 1996). In contrast, difficulty could also be interpreted as putting much effort in the decision process (see also Labroo & Kim, 2009) and, consequently, confidence will be high (Tsai & McGill, in press).

This plasticity makes ease-of-retrieval effects hard to predict unless one can also predict how the experience is interpreted. It seems plausible that interpretations would be guided by the most salient causes in the situation and the most accessible lay-theories. The latter may also be activated by the question at hand. For example, when recalling favorable brand attributes in order to make a brand choice, ease of recall may be interpreted as an indicator of many attributes or very favorable attributes and lead to brand choice. When the attributes are recalled in order to judge the last time the commercial was seen, ease may be interpreted as an indicator for recency.

Methodological issues

Different procedures can be used to manipulate ease of retrieval. Following Schwarz and colleagues' study (1991), retrieving a high and a low number of information has become a standard manipulation in ease-of-retrieval studies. In the following, I will outline some issues to think about when using this procedure and describe some alternative manipulations.

Quality of retrieved information

Because a high number corresponds to experienced difficulty and a low number corresponds to experienced ease, but number and experience led to opposite predictions, Schwarz and colleagues could pitch both effects against each other. However, the procedure nevertheless entails a confound between experience and retrieved content. Participants who retrieve 12 instances, arguments, or exemplars also retrieve at least six instances, arguments, or exemplars, which differ in content from those retrieved by participants who only had to retrieve six in the first place. Further, the additionally retrieved instances, arguments, or exemplars may not only differ in content but also in various relevant qualities. Most accessible examples also tend to be more typical (Silvera et al., 2002), less ambivalent, and evaluatively more extreme. Perhaps the latter six instances of self-assertive behavior were actually less self-assertive than the earlier retrieved ones. Likewise, one can easily imagine that arguments generated with difficulty may tend to be weaker and less convincing. If so, lower persuasion would merely reflect the quality of generated arguments rather than the experience of retrieving them. There are several ways how to deal with this problem and control for alternative accounts.

One could simply ask participants to rate the retrieved information on relevant dimensions. Unfortunately, that is no solution. The self-ratings may of course also be affected by experienced ease. As elaborated above, an argument found only with difficulty is also perceived as less compelling (Wänke & Bless, 2000) and more easily processed stimuli tend to be rated as more typical (Oppenheimer & Frank, 2008). Thus, even if the self-ratings reveal a self-perceived lower quality of the retrieved information, this does not at all rule out an experiential account. In fact, it may also be conceived as a successful manipulation check.

External ratings may provide some way out (e.g. Schwarz et al., 1991, Experiment 2; Tsai & McGill, in press). A more elegant control is a yoked design in which the information retrieved by participants in the experiential conditions is presented to other participants (e.g. Kadous et al., 2006; Tsai & McGill, in press; Wänke et al., 1996; Weick & Guinote, 2008). For example, in one study (Wänke et al., 1996) participants retrieved either three or seven arguments why or why not to use public transport. Each participant's arguments were presented to a yoked participant, and all participants were asked for their attitudes toward public transport. This allowed to manipulate whether participants had retrieval experiences or not, while controlling for the content of the information. For those in the experiential condition, the typical ease effect emerged with less favorable attitudes after difficult retrieval of pro arguments and more favorable attitudes after difficult retrieval of contra arguments. If this had been due to difficult retrieval producing less compelling arguments, we should have observed parallel effects in the presentation-only conditions. In contrast, the results clearly showed more persuasion when many rather than few arguments were presented. What this rules out is that later retrieved arguments were weaker on an objective base. What it does not address, but what is entirely part of the theory, is that experienced difficulty may make arguments less convincing to the retrievers.

Another procedure to control for the possible influence of information content is a misattribution manipulation as described above. A misattribution manipulation adds a condition in which participants are (mis)informed about the source of their experience and thereby renders the experience undiagnostic for the judgment at hand. Whereas a misattribution manipulation denounces the validity of the experience, it does not affect the retrieved content. Thus, if a judgment were based merely on the objective content of the information, a misattribution of the experience would not affect it.

Unrequested retrievals

When exemplars of a particular category as opposed to another category have to be retrieved, it may be possible that during the search exemplars of the other category come to mind spontaneously. For example, when looking for supporting arguments, opposing arguments may inevitably come to mind as well. Intuitively one may expect this to be more likely later in the search process, when the stream of requested thoughts dries up and unrequested ones may intrude. If so, reduced persuasion after difficult retrieval may perhaps be a consequence of increased availability of counterarguments. Whereas some studies found evidence for the spontaneous retrieval of opposing arguments (Tormala, Falces, Brinol & Petty, 2007), others did not (Wänke et al., 1996). In any case, it may not be a bad idea to measure the retrieval of information that has opposite implications for the judgment. Yet, it should be pointed out that whether unrequested cognitions really mediate ease-of-retrieval effects or simply represent another dependent variable is an open question (see Fiedler, Schott & Meiser, 2011, for a detailed discussion about misinterpretations of mediation analyses). Given that misattribution manipulations undermine ease-of-retrieval effects, although they should not reduce unrequested cognitions, the evidence is more in favor of a genuine experiential effect rather than an artifact produced by unrequested retrievals.

Misattribution and discrepancy manipulations

The previous sections highlighted that a misattribution manipulation is an excellent procedure to rule out various alternative explanations. When inducing a misattribution manipulation, great care should be taken not to confound it with manipulating the discrepancy of the experience (see above or Hansen & Wänke,

Chapter 5, this volume). Consider, for example, a typical misattribution manipulation, where participants are explicitly told that they would find the task easy or difficult because of the music playing in the background or because the answer sheet might interfere with their thought generation (e.g., Menon & Raghubir, 2003; Ruder & Bless, 2003; Schwarz et al., 1991; Wänke et al., 1995). As a result of providing reasons for experienced ease or difficulty, ease effects are undermined. Unfortunately, we cannot distinguish whether ease was not used for the judgment because it was indeed misattributed to the external source (misattribution account) or because the misattribution instruction rendered the experience as expected and therefore undermined its informative value (discrepancy account). However, despite the confound in some experimental situations, the discrepancy account and the misattribution account are in principle independent from each other. The underlying processes come to play at different steps in the judgment process. As described above, in a first step, the experience has to emerge. This is where discrepancy from a previous state or expectancy may make the experience emerge or at least more noticeable. Misattribution applies to a later step, namely assessing the meaning of the emerged experience for the judgment. Given this sequence, a misattribution manipulation that is presented *after* the retrieval is experienced, and thus cannot affect the experience itself, is one way to avoid the confound. In such studies (e.g., Sanna & Schwarz, 2003; Winkielman & Schwarz, 2001) a discrepancy account can be dismissed as explanation for the undermining of ease effects. By the same token, discrepancy manipulations should not involve explicit expectations regarding the retrieval experience. Less blatant procedures, for example by priming a standard of comparison (Hansen & Wänke, 2008; see below), do not run the risk of providing a possible source of (mis)attribution and any effects should indeed be due to the induced level of discrepancy.

Missing the criterion

It sometimes happens that not all participants generate the requested amount and naturally there are more of these in the "difficult" condition. Recall the research example described above where students who were requested to provide ten suggestions for course improvement, on average only produced about two (Fox, 2006). How should one deal with such cases? On the one hand, perhaps one should leave them, as Fox did. After all, one could argue that the drop-outs merely reflect task difficulty. Participants aborted the task when it got too difficult. On the other hand, non-fulfillment of the requested amount offers an alternative explanation based entirely on the retrieval amount instead of the difficulty. Participants may regard the requested amount as a norm and draw inferences from their lower number. Coming back to the research example, students may have concluded that if having ten suggestions for improvement is normal they themselves must be quite content as they have only two. To rule out this alternative content-based explanation and really interpret the results as caused by the experience it is therefore crucial to have all participants complete the requested amount.[1] Thus, incomplete cases should be dropped.

To complicate matters, this entails not only unequal cell size but also systematically preselected samples. One way to control for the asymmetric "missings" is to let participants in the "easy" condition also generate the requested amount of the difficult condition after assessing the dependent variables. Then one could exclude participants who are unable to retrieve the high number equally from both conditions. This procedure—although cumbersome—ensures that the sample in both conditions does not systematically differ. Unfortunately, this is rarely done. In many studies, the number of those not having met the criterion is not reported. In the ideal world this might indeed indicate that all participants met the criterion. From a less trusting perspective, it might also indicate the inclusion of those participants who did not meet the criterion or an over-assignment to the "difficult" condition to make up for drop-outs.

Alternative manipulations

These methodological problems can be circumvented by other manipulations, although all have their advantages and disadvantages. To facilitate recall or generation, priming may be one option. Similarly, one could present cues facilitating recall or generation to a different degree. In one study (Wänke & Bless, 2000) participants were presented with an ad for a coffee maker and were later asked to recall favorable features of the coffee maker. Recall was made easy or difficult by presenting word-fragments that were either helpful or less helpful cues. For example, the feature "programmable timer" could be cued with "Pro_ _ _ _able Ti_ _ _" or with "_ r _ _ra _ma_le _ i _ _ r". Pictures or word-stems could also be used to trigger generation or recall. Alternatively, one could also ask participants to recall or generate material they had already produced at an earlier time. The repeated recall should be easier than the original episode.

While these procedures manipulate the actual retrieval process, interfering merely with the output process is another alternative. Typing their arguments in a font that was either high in contrast (black on white) led participants to more congruent judgments than typing an equal number of arguments in a font low in contrast (pink on yellow) (Briñol et al., 2006). Writing with the non-dominant hand (Petrova, 2006) also led to typical ease-of-retrieval effects. Fudging the keyboard or pen might also provide an opportunity to create the feeling of ease or difficulty in producing thoughts and there are certainly many other creative possibilities.

Another quite elegant manipulation that keeps amount constant but varies the accompanying experience involves bodily feedback. Numerous studies showed that furrowing one's brows during a task created a feeling of difficulty and consequently elicited fluency effects (e.g. Alter et al., 2007; Stepper & Strack, 1993). Arguably, this manipulation may, however, be vulnerable to demand effects. In a less obtrusive manipulation, Hansen and Wänke (2008) used semantic priming to create a standard that made the identical task feel either easy or difficult. Participants were asked to judge the similarity of 20 synonyms to either the word easy or to the word difficult. Following this they were asked to generate four arguments for or against playing music in streetcars. This had been pretested to be of medium difficulty. The priming induced participants to think intensively about either ease or difficulty and most likely brought situations and experiential states to mind that were accompanied by the respective feeling. This feeling served as an implicit standard so that the retrieval experience appeared significantly more difficult when ease was primed compared to difficulty. Alternatively a standard can be primed by a previous task. For example, participants in a study had to retrieve two arguments for or two arguments against voting by internet (Hansen & Wänke, 2008), a task that is relatively easy. The argument retrieval was preceded by three tasks of moderately low to moderately high difficulty. These three preceding tasks were presented either in order of increasing or decreasing difficulty. When difficulty was decreasing participants expected the target task to be easier than the preceding moderately easy one. Hence the retrieval of two arguments was about as easy as expected. In contrast, when the preceding tasks were increasingly more difficult, participants expected the target task to be more difficult than the preceding moderately difficult task. Therefore, retrieving two arguments seemed surprisingly easy. As a result, after retrieval of pro arguments participants reported more favourable attitudes in the latter as compared to the former condition. Vice versa, after the retrieval of two contra-arguments they reported less favourable attitudes when the retrieval was easier than expected compared to the condition of matching expectations.

Such manipulations that merely induce a standard emphasize once more the subjective nature of retrieval experiences. Ease or difficulty is not a task attribute but the feeling the task elicits within the individual. Neither is ease or difficulty identical with the objective effort mustered, but only with the subjective appraisal of this effort. This was nicely demonstrated in a study showing that although retrieval of few vs. many exemplars influenced not only subjective effort, but also objective effort as reflected by increases of systolic blood pressure, only subjective effort was related to judgment (von Helversen et al., 2008).

Summary

Operationalizing retrieval experience by amount of retrieval involves a number of experimental challenges and is open to alternative explanations. Unless there is a need to pitch implications of retrieved amount and retrieval experience against each other, manipulations that do not confound ease and amount of retrieval should be preferred. Having said so, many past studies that manipulated ease of retrieval by retrieved amount controlled for potential alternative accounts by using misattribution, external ratings, and yoked designs. It seems safe to say that in these studies the effects are not likely artifacts due to retrieved content. Altogether, such well-controlled studies and, moreover, experiments using different manipulations, attest to the validity of the phenomenon.

Concluding remarks

As this overview made clear, ease of retrieval (and more generally fluency as the rest of this volume demonstrates) is a thriving research topic. Over the past 20 years, research has accumulated a host of evidence, including some contradictory findings, which yet have to be resolved, and has generated new research questions and areas. Moreover, the ease-of-retrieval paradigm may well be used for applied purposes to change attitudes and behavior. This plethora of illustrations notwithstanding, the basic paradigm has perhaps not been disseminated sufficiently to a broader audience. For those familiar with the literature, still another demonstration that easily retrieved information has higher impact on the judgment than information retrieved with difficulty is hardly noteworthy and perhaps a waste of research. However, research in other areas often uses thought listings or recall of materials and focuses exclusively on the recalled amount. Opinion or market researchers, for example, count favorable and unfavorable beliefs in order to predict attitudes and behavior. In psychological—even in social psychological—research, number and valence of thoughts is often found as a dependent or mediating variable. It is easy to see how such research procedures could be improved by incorporating the implications of the ease-of-retrieval research. Thus, we should strive for making the dynamics of ease of retrieval a standard part of elementary method courses. Hopefully this chapter will contribute to this goal.

Note

1 For applied purposes, however, it may not really matter whether the effects are due to the retrieval experience or other inferences.

References

Alter, A., & Oppenheimer, D. (2009). Uniting the tribes of fluency to form a metacognitive nation. *Personality and Social Psychology Review*, *13*, 219–235.

Alter, A., Oppenheimer, D., Epley, R., & Eyre. R. (2007). Overcoming intuition: Metacognitive difficulty activates analytic reasoning. *Journal of Experimental Psychology: General*, *136*, 569–576.

Biller, B., Bless, H., & Schwarz, N. (1992, April). Die Leichtigkeit der Erinnerung als Information in der Urteilsbildung: Der Einfluß der Fragenreihenfolge [Ease of recall as information: The impact of question order]. Paper presented at Tagung experimentell arbeitender Psychologen, Osnabrück, FRG.

Bishop, G. F. (1987). Context effects on self-perceptions of interest in government and public affairs. In H. J. Hippler, N. Schwarz, & S. Sudman (Eds.), *Social information processing and survey methodology* (pp. 179–199). New York: Springer-Verlag.

Bishop, G.F., Oldendick, R. W., & Tuchfarber, A. (1984). What must my interest in politics be if I just told you "I don't know"?. *Public Opinion Quarterly, 48,* 510–519.

Briñol, P., Petty, R. E., & Tormala, Z. (2006) The malleable meaning of subjective ease. *Psychological. Science*, *17*, 200–206.

Caruso, E. M. (2008). Use of experienced retrieval ease in self and social judgments. *Journal of Experimental Social Psychology*, *44*, 148–155.

Danziger, S., Moran, S., & Raffaely, V. (2006). The influence of ease of retrieval on judgment as a function of attention to subjective experience. *Journal of Consumer Psychology*, *16*, 191–195.

Dijksterhuis, A., Macrae, C. N., & Haddock, G. (1999). When recollective experiences matter: Subjective ease of retrieval and stereotyping. *Personality and Social Psychology Bulletin*, *25*, 760–768.

Feningstein, A., Scheier, M.F., & Buss, A. H. (1975). Public and private self-consciousness: Assessment and theory. *Journal of Consulting and Clinical Psychology*, *43*, 522–527.

Fiedler, K., Schott, M., & Meiser, T. (2011). What mediation analysis can (not) do. *Journal of Experimental Social Psychology*, *47*, 1231–1236.

Florack, A., & Zoabi, H. (2003). Risikoverhalten bei Aktiengeschäften: Wenn Anleger nachdenklich werden [Risk behavior in share transactions: When investors think about reasons]. *Zeitschrift für Sozialpsychologie*, *34*, 65–78.

Fox, C. (2006). The availability heuristic in the classroom: How soliciting more criticism can boost your course ratings, *Judgement and Decision Making*, *1*, 86–90.

Gabrielcik, A., & Fazio, R. H. (1984). Priming and frequency estimation: A strict test of the availability heuristic. *Personality and Social Psychology Bulletin*, *10*, 85–89.

Grayson, C. E., & Schwarz, N. (1999). Beliefs influence information processing strategies: Declarative and experiential information in risk assessment. *Social Cognition*, *17*, 1–18.

Greifeneder, R., & Bless, H. (2007). Relying on accessible content versus accessibility experiences: The case of processing capacity. *Social Cognition*, *25*, 853–881.

—— (2008). Depression and reliance on ease-of-retrieval experiences. *European Journal of Social Psychology*, *38*, 213–230.

Greifeneder, R., Bless, H., & Pham, M. T. (2011). When do people rely on affective and cognitive feelings in judgment? A review. *Personality and Social Psychology Review*, *15*, 107–141.

Guinote, A. (2010). In touch with your feelings: power increases reliance on bodily information. *Social Cognition*, *28*, 110–121.

Haddock, G. (2002). It's easy to like or dislike Tony Blair: Accessibility experiences and the favourability of attitude judgments. *British Journal of Psychology*, *93*, 257–267.

Haddock, G., Rothman, A. J., Reber, R., & Schwarz, N. (1999). Forming judgments of attitude certainty, importance, and intensity: The role of subjective experiences. *Personality and Social Psychology Bulletin*, *25*, 771–782.

Hansen, J., & Wänke, M. (2008). It's the difference that counts: Expectancy/experience discrepancy moderates the use of ease-of- retrieval in attitude judgments. *Social Cognition*, *26*, 447–468.

Herzog, S. M., Hansen, J., & Wänke, M. (2007). Temporal distance and ease of retrieval. *Journal of Experimental Social Psychology*, *43*, 483–488.

Hirt, E. R., Kardes, F. R., & Markman, K. D. (2004). Activating a mental simulation mind-set through generation of alternatives: Implications for debiasing in related and unrelated domains. *Journal of Experimental Social Psychology*, *40*, 374–383.

Howard, D. J. (1997). Familiar phrases as peripheral persuasion cues. *Journal of Experimental Social Psychology*, *33*, 231–243.

Janis, I. L., & King, B. T. (1954), The influence of role-playing on opinion change. *Journal of Abnormal and Social Psychology*, *49*, 211–218.

Kadous, K., Krische, S. D., & Sedor, L. M. (2006). Using counter-explanation to limit analysts' forecast optimism. *The Accounting Review*, *81*, 377–397.

Keller, J., & Bless, H. (2009). Predicting future affective states: How ease-of-retrieval and faith in intuition moderate the impact of activated content. *European Journal of Social Psychology*, *39*, 467–476.

Keller, J., & Bless, H. (2005). When negative expectancies turn into negative performance: The role of ease of retrieval. *Journal of Experimental Social Psychology*, *41*, 535–541.

Kelley, C. M., & Lindsay, D. S. (1993). Remembering mistaken for knowing: Ease of retrieval as a basis for confidence in answers to general knowledge questions. *Journal of Memory and Language*, *32*, 1–24.

Labroo, A., & Kim, S. (2009). The 'instrumentality' heuristic: Why metacognitive difficulty is desirable during goal pursuit. *Psychological Science*, 20, 127–134.

Lee, A. Y., & Aaker, J. L. (2004). Bringing the frame into focus: The influence of regulatory fit on processing fluency and persuasion. *Journal of Personality and Social Psychology*, *86*, 205–218.

Menon, G., & Raghubir, P. (2003). Ease-of-retrieval as an automatic input in judgments: A mere-accessibility framework? *Journal of Consumer Research*, *30*, 230–243.

Müller, P., Greifeneder, R., Stahlberg, D., Van den Bos, K., & Bless, H. (2010). Shaping cooperation behavior: The role of accessibility experiences. *European Journal of Social Psychology*, *40*, 178–187.

Novemsky, N., Dhar, R., Schwarz, N., & Simonson, I. (2007). Preference fluency and consumer choice. *Journal of Marketing Research*, *44*, 347–356.

Oppenheimer, D. M. (2004). Spontaneous discounting of availability in frequency judgment tasks. *Psychological Science*, *15*, 100–105.

Oppenheimer, D. M., & Frank, M. C. (2008). A rose in any other font wouldn't smell as sweet: Fluency effects in categorization. *Cognition*, *106*, 1178–1194.

Pacini, R., & Epstein, S. (1999). The relation of rational and experiential information processing styles to personality, basic beliefs, and the ratio-bias phenomenon. *Journal of Personality and Social Psychology*, *76*, 972–987.

Petrova, P. K. (2006). Fluency effects: New domains and consequences for persuasion. Doctoral dissertation, Arizona State University.

Petrova, P. K., & Cialdini, R. B. (2005). Fluency of consumption imagery and the backfire effects of imagery appeals. *Journal of Consumer Research*, *32*, 442–452.

Raghubir, P., & Menon, G. (1998). AIDS and me, never the twain shall meet: The effects of information accessibility on judgments of risk and advertising effectiveness. *Journal of Consumer Research*, *25*, 52–63.

—— (2005). When and why is ease of retrieval informative? *Memory and Cognition*, *33*, 821–832.

Rothman, A. J., & Schwarz, N. (1998). Constructing perceptions of vulnerability: Personal relevance and the use of experiential information in health judgments. *Personality and Social Psychology Bulletin*, *24*, 1053–1064.

Ruder, M., & Bless, H. (2003). Mood and the reliance on the ease-of-retrieval heuristic. *Journal of Personality and Social Psychology*, *85*, 20–32.

Sanna, L. J., & Schwarz, N. (2003). Debiasing the hindsight bias: The role of accessibility experiences and (mis)attributions. *Journal of Experimental Social Psychology*, *39*, 287–295.

Schwarz, N., Bless, H., Strack, F., Klumpp, G., Rittenauer-Schatka, H., & Simons, A. (1991). Ease of retrieval as information: Another look at the availability heuristic. *Journal of Personality and Social Psychology*, *61*, 195–202.

Schwarz, N., & Schuman, H. (1997). Political knowledge, attribution, and inferred political interest: The operation of buffer items. *International Journal of Public Opinion Research*, *9*, 191–195.

Schwarz, N., Song, H., & Xu, J. (2009). When thinking is difficult: Metacognitive experiences as information. In M. Wänke (ed.) *Social psychology of consumer behavior* (pp. 201–223). New York, NY: Psychology Press.

Semin, G. R., Higgins, T., Gil de Montes, L., Estourget, Y., & Valencia, J. F. (2005). Linguistic signatures of regulatory focus: How abstraction fits promotion more than prevention. *Journal of Personality and Social Psychology*, *89*, 36–45.

Silvera, D., Krull, D., & Sassler, M. (2002). Typhoid Pollyanna: The effect of category valence on retrieval order of positive and negative category members. *European Journal of Cognitive Psychology*, *14*, 227–236.

Singelis, T. M. (1994). The measurement of independent and interdependent self-construals. *Personality and Social Psychology Bulletin*, 20, 580–591. doi:10.1177/0146167294205014

Smith, P. K., & Trope, Y. (2006). You focus on the forest when you are in charge of the trees: Power priming and abstract information processing. *Journal of Personality and Social Psychology*, *90*, 578–596.

Spielmann, S., MacDonald, G., & Wilson, A. (2009). On the rebound: Focusing on someone new helps anxiously attached individuals let go of ex-partners. *Personality and Social Psychology Bulletin*, *35*, 1382–1394.

Stepper, S., & Strack, F. (1993). Proprioceptive determinants of emotional and nonemotional feelings. *Journal of Personality and Social Psychology*, *64*, 211–220.

Tormala, Z., Falces, C., Briñol, P., & Petty, R. (2007). Ease of retrieval in social judgment: The role of unrequested cognition. *Journal of Personality and Social Psychology*, *93*, 143–157.

Tormala, Z. L., Petty, R. E., & Briñol, P. (2002). Ease-of-retrieval effects in persuasion: A self-validation analysis. *Personality and Social Psychology Bulletin*, *28*, 1700–1712.

Tsai, C.I., & McGill, A. L. (2011). No pain, no gain? How construal level and fluency affect consumer confidence. *Journal of Consumer Research*, 37, 807–821.

Tsai, C., & Thomas, M. (2011). When does feeling of fluency matter? How abstract and concrete thinking influence fluency effects, *Psychological Science*, *22*, 348–354.

Tversky, A., & Kahneman, D. (1973). Availability: A heuristic for judging frequency and probability. *Cognitive Psychology*, *5*, 207–232.

Tybout, A. M., Sternthal, B., Malaviya, P., Bakamitsos, G. A., & Park, S.-B. (2005). The influence of retrieval ease and content on judgments: The moderating effect of information accessibility. *Journal of Consumer Research*, *32*, 76–85.

Unkelbach, C. (2006). The learned interpretation of cognitive fluency. *Psychological Science, 17*, 339–345.

—— (2007). Reversing the truth effect: Learning the interpretation of processing fluency in judgments of truth. *Journal of Experimental Psychology: Learning, Memory, and Cognition*, *33*, 219–230.

Vjastfjäll, D., Peters, E., & Slovic, P. (2008). Affect, risk perception and future optimism after the tsunami disaster. *Judgment and Decision Making*, *3*, 64–72.

von Helversen, B., Gendolla, G., Winkielman, P., & Schmidt, R. (2008). Exploring the hardship of ease: Subjective and objective effort in the ease-of-processing paradigm. *Motivation & Emotion*, *32*, 1–10.

Wänke, M., & Bless, H. (2000). The effects of subjective ease of retrieval on attitudinal judgments: The moderating role of processing motivation. In H. Bless & J. P. Forgas (Eds.), *The message within: The role of subjective experience in social cognition and behavior* (pp. 143–161). Philadelphia, PA: Psychology Press.

Wänke, M., Bless, H., & Biller, B. (1996). Subjective experience versus content of information in the construction of attitude judgments. *Personality and Social Psychology Bulletin*, *22*, 1150–1113.

Wänke, M., Bohner, G., & Jurkowitsch, A. (1997). There are many reasons to drive a BMW: Does imagined ease of argument generation influence attitudes? *Journal of Consumer Research*, *24*, 170–177.

Wänke, M., Schwarz, N., & Bless, H. (1995). The availability heuristic revisited: Experienced ease of retrieval in mundane frequency estimates. *Acta Psychologica*, *89*, 83–90.

Weick, M., & Guinote, A. (2008). Power increases reliance on experiential knowledge: Evidence from ease-of-retrieval. *Journal of Personality and Social Psychology*, *94*, 956–970.

Whittlesea, B. W. A., & Williams, L. D. (2000). The source of feelings of familiarity: The discrepancy-attribution hypothesis. *Journal of Experimental Psychology: Learning, Memory, and Cognition*, *26*, 547–565.

—— (2001a). The discrepancy-attribution hypothesis: I. The heuristic basis of feeling of familiarity. *Journal of Experimental Psychology: Learning, Memory, and Cognition*, *27*, 3–13.

—— (2001b). The discrepancy-attribution hypothesis: II. Expectation, uncertainty, surprise, and feelings of familiarity. *Journal of Experimental Psychology: Learning, Memory, and Cognition*, *27*, 14–33.

Winkielman, P., & Schwarz, N. (2001). How pleasant was your childhood? Beliefs about memory shape inferences from experienced difficulty of recall. *Psychological Science*, *12*, 176–179.

Winkielman, P., Schwarz, N., & Belli, R. F. (1998). The role of ease of retrieval and attribution in memory judgments: Judging your memory as worse despite recalling more events. *Psychological Science*, *9*, 124–126.

Part III

Adaptive and strategic uses of fluency

11 Critical feeling

The strategic use of processing fluency

Rolf Reber

Abstract

This chapter introduces the notion of *critical feeling*, which denotes the evaluation of a judgment based on feeling and builds on the concept of critical thinking. Two basic approaches to critical feeling are introduced: (1) thinking about feelings; (2) refining one's feeling in order to optimize outcomes, for example through discrimination learning or selective exposure, and using feelings as information when monitoring the outcomes. The present analysis focuses on processing fluency, which is the ease with which contents are processed in the cognitive system. Research has shown that processing fluency influences various kinds of judgments, such as judgments of familiarity, affect, or truth, and recent work has connected fluency to virtue ethics in early Chinese thought, culturally shared taste, and synchronization of behavior, for example in military drill. I discuss this work and show how it can be applied to enhance feeling-based judgments and decisions.

Critical thinking has been a keystone of Western culture since the Enlightenment, and one goal of school and college education is the training of critical thinking skills. Critical thinking is the skill of evaluating arguments based on reason (e.g., Hughes & Lavery, 2004). Truth of a claim essentially boils down to two criteria. First, consistency: is the set of propositions on which an argument is based consistent? If there is any contradiction in the set of propositions, the argument as a whole cannot be true. Second, correspondence to reality: does a set of propositions correspond to facts in the outside world? If it corresponds or correlates only weakly with external facts, it is doubtful whether the argument as a whole is true. Critical thinking is about using the right procedures (in the sense of methods; techniques; ways of proceeding) based on reasoning to optimize judgments and decisions. Only rarely are feelings mentioned in the literature on critical thinking: David Hitchcock (1983, p. 8), for example, mentioned that people "have to rely on our instincts, on authority, on emotion, and so forth. This means that you should receive some practice in the rational assessment of such guides to belief." However, Hitchcock did not further elaborate on emotions or instincts, and discussed reliance on authority only briefly. We need a further concept to capture the optimization of desired outcomes based on feelings. This concept is critical feeling.

Critical feeling

I use the term *critical feeling* to denote the use of proper subjective experiences in order to optimize judgments and decision-making. Critical feeling and critical thinking are distinct in that the first is about finding the right procedures based on phenomenal experiences, whereas critical thinking is about finding the right procedures based on reasoning. In addition, critical thinking is often concerned with the factual truth of statements and is therefore related to beliefs whose truth can be evaluated, or about outcomes that can be measured, such as monetary value. Successful critical thinking means that one gets at true beliefs or at optimal financial outcomes. Critical feeling may be related to factual truth, as we shall discuss later. However, critical feeling is often related to beliefs whose factual truth is—if at all—difficult to evaluate, and to outcomes that are difficult to measure, such as pleasure, subjective satisfaction, taste, or virtue. In these cases, the criterion for successful critical feeling would be the felt state of pleasure, satisfaction, taste, or virtue.

Critical feeling may take two basic forms: first, critical thinking about feeling, which could be used to correct biases due to feelings; second, critical feeling could mean the strategic use of feelings to optimize outcomes. In this chapter, I shall focus on the strategic use of processing fluency (henceforth, fluency), the ease with which information is processed in the cognitive system (see Alter & Oppenheimer, 2009; Reber, Schwarz, & Winkielman, 2004).

The term critical feeling as a complement to critical thinking has been introduced by Paul Haack in an article on feeling in music education. He used the term just once, at the end, noting that students should learn about their reactions to music and scrutinize them, without imposing on students a certain experience as the right feeling; it "must be critical thinking about feeling" (Haack, 1990, p. 30).[1] This is the case when people are warned that a certain feeling may yield inaccurate conclusions and then correct their judgment. For example, when teachers are warned that bad handwriting may influence grading of essays, they correct their judgments and may no longer be influenced by the quality of handwriting (see Greifeneder, Alt, Bottenberg, Seele, Zelt, & Wagener 2010, for a study related to this topic, and Schwarz, Sanna, Skurnik, & Yoon, 2007, for problems with such correction mechanisms).

In addition to critical thinking about feeling, the term critical feeling may denote the strategic use of one's feelings in order to optimize outcomes. A first example is discrimination learning for refining one's experience. In this case, people do not think about the feeling, but they train the proper feeling by directing their perception to pre-existing differences in the stimulus materials. When an audience learns to classify styles in music, they learn to discriminate different kinds of music. What makes this kind of learning critical feeling is the fact that it is not aimed at analyzing the music and then come to a conclusion, but to listen and be able to classify the musical style from its experience. Experts in different domains—such as music, art, or wine-tasting—are able to experience the difference. In fact, the superiority of wine experts over novices to recognize wine-related odors did not depend on enhanced semantic memory or linguistic capabilities, but on superior perceptual skills (Parr, Heatherbell, & White, 2002).

A second example for the strategic use of one's feelings is the self-chosen exposure to situations that increase processing fluency. Easy information processing yields the feeling that processed information is familiar (e.g., Whittlesea, 1993), affectively positive (Reber, Winkielman, & Schwarz, 1998; Winkielman & Cacioppo, 2001) and true (e.g., Hansen, Dechêne, & Wänke, 2008; Reber & Schwarz, 1999). When using fluency strategically, people do think before they employ the feeling. In contrast to critical thinking about feeling, they do not reason about the feelings that result from self-chosen repeated exposure in order to correct inferences derived from those feelings; people just accept them. I shall in this chapter focus on processing fluency because it is easy to conceive how it can be used strategically. It awaits further research and theoretical analysis whether other feelings states, such as moods or emotions, could be put into service of critical feeling in the same way as fluency.

In the remainder of the chapter, I focus on providing an outline of the connection between critical feeling and fluency. Research on fluency and a formal analysis (Reber & Unkelbach, 2010) discussed below suggest the feasibility of an adaptive use of this feeling for optimizing outcomes, and we shall consider historical examples—Confucian thought and military drill—that illustrate the importance of this kind of enquiry. I shall discuss three instances of optimizing outcomes through strategic use of fluency. First, I sketch how members of a culture may expose themselves to cultural beliefs and practices in order to refine their actions until they "feel right." This practice goes back to Confucius (Reber & Slingerland, 2010). Second, I discuss how audiences may choose to expose themselves to art and music in order to develop what they think is refined taste. For that part, I rely on a famous study by Bourdieu (1984/1979) that has recently been connected to the fluency theory of aesthetic pleasure in order to explain the emergence of culturally shared tastes (Reber, 2012). Third, I outline how people who want to increase (or prevent) the adherence to a group can use critical feeling in that they seek out (or avoid) opportunities to move in synchrony with other group members. This section builds on an analysis of effects of military drill on liking (McNeill, 1995) in terms of shared fluency (Reber & Norenzayan, 2012). The conclusion and outlook section discusses three challenges: the use of critical feeling to unethical ends; the need to define critical feeling more clearly; and empirical findings that demonstrate the effectiveness of critical feeling.

Critical feeling through fluency means to know the consequences of fluency and to act accordingly. As mentioned earlier, thinking about feeling means knowing about biases due to a feeling and issuing corrective mechanisms if necessary; discrimination learning is based on pre-existing differences in the stimulus material that have to be distinguished through perception. In contrast to both thinking about feeling and discrimination learning, critical feeling through fluency means that people determine which information they wish to process fluently and consequently to be familiar with, to like, and intuitively to judge as true. They then expose themselves to this information and afterwards check their progress towards their goal of being familiar with this information by assessing how easily they can process it, or how familiar or how "right" it feels. Instead of an objective assessment, people use a "feelings-as-information"-heuristic (see Schwarz, 2012, for an overview) to monitor the progress toward the desired state.

Before I discuss research findings relevant to critical feeling through fluency, I summarize a formal analysis (Reber & Unkelbach, 2010) that reveals that, under certain assumptions, fluently processed statements might be more probably true than false. This analysis provides a formal foundation for why fluency as a feeling might be useful for judgments of truth and thus underpins the notion of critical feeling through fluency.

Why critical feeling might be useful

Repeated statements are judged as more probably true than statements never heard before (e.g., Hasher, Goldstein, & Toppino, 1977). This is even the case when a listener or reader does not recognize that the statement has been presented before (Brown & Nix, 1996). One hypothesis states that repeated exposure increases fluency that, in turn, increases the probability that a statement is judged as true (Begg, Anas, & Farinacci, 1992). Indeed, fluency manipulated by means other than repetition—for example, figure-ground contrast—increases judged truth of a statement in single-exposure paradigms (e.g., Reber & Schwarz, 1999; Unkelbach, 2007).

Is the fact that processing fluency due to repetition results in increased judgments of truth just a bias that misguides people into believing predominantly false statements? Or is the belief that fluent judgments are true adaptive in the sense that fluency serves as an ecological valid indicator of truth (see Herzog & Hertwig, Chapter 12, this volume)? Reber and Unkelbach (2010) examined this question. In our analysis, we considered only statements a person has encountered before and therefore was repeated, but not all those statements a person never encountered. This has to be kept in mind in the following analysis. We argued that true statements are repeated more often than wrong statements. Therefore, the probability that a statement can be processed fluently when it is true, p (fluent | true), is high. However, we were interested in the probability that a statement that is processed fluently is true, p (true | fluent). This amounts to a typical problem of Bayesian analysis (see Formula 1) where p (fluent | true), together with the base rate of true statements, p (true), and the conditional probability that a statement is fluent if not true, p (fluent | ¬true), determines the probability that a statement is true if it can be processed fluently, p (true | fluent). This is the probability we search for.

$$p(\text{true} \mid \text{fluent}) = \frac{p(\text{fluent} \mid \text{true}) * p(\text{true})}{p(\text{fluent} \mid \text{true}) * p(\text{true}) + p(\text{fluent} \mid \text{true}) * p(\neg\text{true})} \quad (1)$$

As we assumed that any repeated statement—whether true or not—becomes fluent to the same degree and therefore p (fluent | true) = p (fluent | ¬true), the formula can be simplified to (Formula 2):

$$p(\text{true} \mid \text{fluent}) = \frac{p(\text{true})}{p(\text{true}) + p(\neg\text{true})} \tag{2}$$

The detailed analysis and the assumptions behind it are reported in Reber and Unkelbach (2010). The important point here is that p (true | fluent) can be increased by increasing p (true). As p (true) + p (¬true) = 1 (which is a basic tenet of probability theory), an increase in p (true) results in a decrease in p (¬true). This means that a person can increase p (true) by increasing exposure to sources that he or she *a priori* believes are reliable.

Believing that sources are reliable does not mean that they indeed are reliable. Nevertheless, there is evidence that even pre-school children are quite good at distinguishing credible from incredible sources (Koenig, Clément, & Harris, 2004). Moreover, there is good reason to assume that statements one hears are more probably true than untrue: preliminary evidence that p (true) is high comes from research about the accuracy of encyclopedias, such as Wikipedia. One study examined the accuracy of both Wikipedia and a peer-reviewed website, the patient-oriented National Cancer Institute's Physician Data Query (PDQ) comprehensive cancer database (Rajagopalan, Khanna, Stott, Leiter, Showalter, Dicker, & Lawrence, 2010). The authors observed that inaccuracies were very rare on both sources (< 2 percent). These studies are of course not sufficient to make the point that p (true) is high in general, but they mark a starting point for the ecological study of the truth of statements one encounters. If further research confirms the general validity of these preliminary findings, the Bayesian analysis shows that people can rely on their feeling of ease in order to assess the factual truth of a statement. From this formal analysis, we can conclude that it would be useful to use fluency as a source for judgments of truth. Moreover, people can increase the probability of being exposed to true statements by strategically choosing those sources that have the reputation for being reliable. Of course, it remains an empirical question how reliable these sources are in reality.

This analysis pertains to truths that can be assessed by comparison to facts. However, Reber and Unkelbach (2010) argued that fluency affects judged truth in domains where the truth is difficult to determine. Therefore, the strategy of self-chosen exposure is not restricted to the factual domain. Scholars in anthropology (see Rappaport, 1999) distinguish two kinds of truth—let us call them factual truth and ritual truth. The latter cannot be evaluated by assessing statements according to rules of logic or by comparing them to states of the outside world. Ritual truth often comes by repetition and is related to such things as religious beliefs, moral norms, or subjective values. However, such beliefs about religion, values, and norms may be learned by the very same mechanisms as factual beliefs. Many such beliefs have been enculturated in childhood and obtain a status of subjective truth similar to factual truth. Factual truth and ritual truth differ insofar as the former, but not the latter, can be asserted by assessing a statement according to a rule of logic or by comparing a statement to an external fact. They do not necessarily differ, however, in their subjective experience. People often believe in the truth of their religious beliefs or their values in the same way as they believe in the fact that tigers are predators. Although religious beliefs are not cemented, many people keep them throughout their life. If adolescents or adults want to change their beliefs, they may choose to expose themselves to beliefs that they want to adopt. Gradually, the adopted belief is not only represented in their cognitive system, but it "feels right."[2] The person's hope is that he or she can become a good person by doing the right acts without effort—just by consulting what feels right. This hope goes back to Confucius, an early Chinese philosopher.

Inculcating beliefs

The basic idea of Confucian moral education is that individuals have to be trained in order to retrieve the right moral decision without mental effort (see Slingerland, 2003a). One may see Confucian thought as an ancient system that inculcates practices and beliefs through critical feeling. In contrast to modern Western ethics based on reasoning that build on explicit learning of moral concepts, Confucian thought is based on virtue ethics that builds on moral intuitions and moral skills (see Slingerland, 2010). A person who has learned the moral concepts of deontological or utilitarian ethics prominent in Western thought can use critical thinking skills in order to assess whether a decision is consistent with a norm (see Slingerland, 2010); feelings play no role in this assessment. In virtue ethics, in contrast, skill learning facilitates performance of the right actions. Critical feeling consists in choosing what cultural forms to learn and then to learn them until they can be performed fluently. The feeling of ease that comes with training is an indicator that one is on the right path. In more modern terms, and in terms of critical feeling as outlined above, after having chosen the values and beliefs one wants to adhere to, the adherent of Confucianism uses knowledge about effects of fluency strategically in order to optimize the outcomes, and uses felt fluency as information for progress in practice.

Confucianism is not interesting for historical reasons only. Early Chinese thought at the time of Confucius (551–479 BCE) has been plagued by a paradox that has not been solved satisfactorily ever since, but that modern psychological research may help resolve (Reber & Slingerland, 2011). The so-called paradox of wu-wei (Slingerland, 2003a, pp. 70ff.) is that the state of effortless action can only be attained through extended, effortful training in cultural forms (see Slingerland, 2003a, 2003b, 2010), and that one has to develop love for something one does not already love (Slingerland, 2003a, p. 13). This paradox can—from a cognitive point of view—be decomposed into two different paradoxes that are related to fluency (see Reber & Slingerland, 2011). First, effortless action can only be attained through investing effort, and ease can only be attained by going through difficulties; second, learning of the Confucian way seems only to be enjoyable if someone already loves it. From these two paradoxes, two questions arise that can be examined empirically. First, how can effort result in effortless action? Second, how can one force oneself to love something that one does not already love?[3] Reber and Slingerland (2011) discussed the psychological research pertinent to this old philosophical problem.

The first paradox—how effortless action arises from effort—is reflected in a paradox observed in skill acquisition. Learning outcomes are best on distributed schedule rather than on a blocked schedule, even though the latter needs less time (e.g., Simon & Bjork, 2001; 2002; see also Diemand-Yauman, Oppenheimer, & Vaughan, 2011). This means that when contents are so difficult that one has to invest effort, learning yields the best learning results—a finding that runs counter the folk intuition that the learning process should be made easy (Sweller & Chandler, 1994). Indeed, participants on the distributed schedule predicted that their performance will be worse than participants on a blocked schedule, which is the opposite of the later observed learning performance. In a classical study, Baddeley and Longman (1978) observed a related paradox inherent to skill learning when they examined the question of what kind of schedule is optimal to train postal workers on a newly introduced special typewriter. Performance was best for those who were on the distributed schedule: they needed fewer training hours than those on the blocked schedule to reach proficiency. Despite this positive result, postal workers trained on the distributed schedule were least satisfied with their training and wished to be transferred to a blocked training schedule in the future. In contrast, the postal workers in the blocked condition were the most satisfied even though they performed worst. In sum, people who expend effort later can perform a skill fluently, even though they do not like the learning and think that they will perform badly.

According to Confucius, people have to overcome morally insufficient natural or dominant responses in order to refine their behavior. By repeated training of cultural forms, which increases fluency, individuals acquire new habits that become dominant responses; they acquire a "second nature." Confucius realized that intensive, lifelong practice is needed in order to internalize cultural forms; but he did not seem to have the knowledge or an intuition about the distribution of practice and its consequences on liking the learning process.

The second paradox lies in the question "how one can force oneself to love something one does not already love?" (Slingerland, 2003a, p. 13). The fluency theory helps provide an answer to this apparent paradox (see Reber & Slingerland, 2011): Practice in Confucianism means that rituals, activities or readings are repeated. As fluency is affectively positive (Reber et al., 1998; Winkielman & Cacioppo, 2001), this training indeed may not only familiarize people with and instill the principles of a culture's virtues, but make these very principles—and the rituals and activities connected to them—more pleasurable. Please note that in the paragraphs before, I discussed liking the learning process, depending on the learning schedule. Liking the learning process is different from positive affect due to repeated exposure where people begin to like the contents they learn due to increased fluency, the process that underlies the emergence of pleasure with repeated practice. In fact, given the findings cited above (Baddeley & Longman, 1978), it would be interesting to examine whether a negative correlation could be found between liking the learning process and liking the learned contents. The question becomes whether difficult and effortful learning that people generally dislike yields more liking of the contents because distributed training may enhance positive effects of repetition (see Van den Bergh & Vrana, 1998). Although there surely are situations where people dislike both the learning process and the contents, finding negative correlations between liking the learning process and liking the contents would be counterintuitive from the viewpoint of the present theories of learning (e.g., Sweller & Chandler, 1994).

As we have seen, fluency not only increases positive affect but also the judged truth of propositions. Therefore, repetition of ethical principles not only increases the pleasure in these virtues, but also the experienced truth of the underlying principles. Truth goes further than just the propositional content of moral principles: Any activity performed in order to commit oneself to moral principles may itself become subjectively true due to the verbatim repetition of its acts, making any deviation from the sequence of acts included in the activity seeming to be wrong (see Boyer, 1992). However, critical feeling may also be used to prevent being unduly influenced by repeated exposure. Recent studies on repeated exposure become especially relevant here. In one study, Unkelbach, Fiedler, and Freytag (2007) presented their participants information about shares. Some shares were equally successful at the stock market, but information was repeated more often for shares of some companies than of others. A rational decision maker should be influenced by the success of a share but not by how often information about a share has been repeated. However, contradicting normative decision rules, Unkelbach et al. (2007) found that participants in their experiment were influenced by the frequency of exposure to information about a share. Shares that were repeated more often were both judged as more successful and were liked more. In another study, Weaver, Garcia, Schwarz, and Miller (2007) presented their participants an opinion three times, and participants had to judge how prevalent the opinion was. Crucially, the opinion came either from three different people or from one single source. Usually, people think that an opinion from three sources is more prevalent than an opinion from a single source. The authors observed, however, that people judged an opinion from a single source as being about as prevalent as an opinion from multiple sources. Critical feeling here means that a listener checks whether a repeated opinion comes from multiple sources or from a single source. This kind of critical thinking about feelings—which is one form of critical feeling, as seen earlier—complements critical thinking about the contents of a message.

The paradoxes and their solution are as topical nowadays as they were at Confucius's time. Given that people choose to expose themselves to what they like, as shown by research on selective exposure (Zillmann & Bryant, 1985), it is not surprising that they circumvent the effortful training necessary to overcome their dominant responses. Moreover, people do not seem to have an intuition that what has been learned with effort may be retrieved with ease. Critical feeling begins with the knowledge about the fact that difficulty at training often results in ease of executing a skill. Overcoming the tendency of hedonic adherence to dominant responses means that people know what they want to strive at. Once they know what thoughts and beliefs they want to adhere to, they use mere expose to the objects of belief as a strategy to inculcate these beliefs. They not only believe in the truths of the encountered statements, but when encountering statements that correspond to their beliefs, these statements "feel right." Essential to critical feeling, this feeling of rightness, along with the ease and positive affect when encountering the belief, provides a subjective criterion for the progress they have made in the practice of the right belief.

Inculcating taste

Shared exposure to rituals, readings, and music not only influence shared beliefs but results in shared preference for these forms—or shared tastes (see Reber, 2012). Again, as in the case of Confucian training of cultural practices, fluency through repetition may be used strategically in order to acquire the taste one wishes to develop. We start with the classical study on distinction by Pierre Bourdieu who made some relevant observations but explained them with processes related to social class. However, together with studies from cognitive and social psychology, these observations may be interpreted in terms of shared fluency and may provide some guidance about how to acquire a certain taste, that is, how to use critical feeling in the acquisition of taste.

In his study, Bourdieu (1984/1979) observed that members of the same class shared taste for music, fashion, or food, to name just a few. He concluded that members of a social class become acquainted with what the taste of their class has to be. Especially the upper classes are socialized to express a refined taste that stands out against popular (and therefore vulgar) taste. According to Bourdieu, members of the upper class do not necessarily enjoy music when listening to it, but feel satisfaction from playing well the game of society (Bourdieu, 1984, pp. 498ff.) in which one has to distinguish the refined from the vulgar, the fine arts from popular art, and so on. In psychological terms, members of the upper class may not feel aesthetic pleasure from listening to opera, but from pride due to having understood how to play the game of society.

Upwardly mobile members of the middle classes have often not been exposed to the music of the upper classes during their childhood. This lack of exposure leads to a taste that is different from the class they want to belong to. They therefore try to compensate their subjectively felt deficit by explicitly learning all they can about music and about what is the "right" musical taste. However, as Bourdieu (1984, pp. 74 and 328ff.) notes, members of the middle classes who want to mimic the taste of the upper classes are much less at ease when expressing their taste than the upper classes whose musical taste has been inculcated since early childhood. Moreover, acquiring musical knowledge does not seem to be necessary. Bigand and Poulin-Charronnat (2006) reviewed evidence that different aspects of music processing do not depend on expertise, which suggests they are independent of musical knowledge and therefore obviate knowledge acquisition. If learning all about music is the wrong way to acquire the tastes of the upper classes, what would be a more promising path to refined taste?

As for acquiring Confucian rituals, exposure to the music one wishes to appreciate seems to be the most promising way to acquire taste. Note that it is not necessary to listen repeatedly to the same piece of music. Listening to Fugue No. 1 in C-major by Bach, for example, increases not only familiarity with this particular piece, but contributes also to implicit learning of tonality and temporal characteristics of this musical style (see Tillmann, Bigand, & Bharucha, 2000). As implicit learning results in preference for grammatical stimuli (e.g., Gordon & Holyoak, 1983, for letter strings; Kuhn & Dienes, 2005, for tonal strings; Opacic, Stevens, & Tillmann, 2009, for sequences of classical dance movements), learning the principles of tonality presumably does not only change cognitive processing of music but also affective preference: regular musical elements are preferred to irregular ones.

This does not mean that acquiring knowledge about the music or art one wants to appreciate is useless in order to acquire the desired taste. Bullot and Reber (in press) developed a psycho-historical framework for artistic understanding that we linked to the fluency theory of aesthetic pleasure. In short, the fluency theory of aesthetic pleasure (Reber et al., 2004) cannot explain why people appreciate artworks that are perceptually disfluent, and these are—as mentioned before—the kind of artworks appreciated by the upper classes. Bullot and Reber (in press) analyzed several functions of disfluency in artworks that will not be discussed here. The decisive point is that knowing the context of art history and the intentions of an artist help understand why an artwork is hard to process. By understanding what the artist had in mind when creating the artwork, viewers can connect the features of the work with their knowledge so that the work can be processed more fluently at a conceptual level. The answer to the question whether knowledge plays a role for acquiring a certain taste lies in the fact that knowledge can enhance one's taste when this knowledge is relevant for understanding the artwork. Knowledge that does not contribute to this artistic understanding most presumably does not facilitate the processing of the artwork and therefore is expected to be useless from the standpoint of acquiring a pre-specified taste. Critical feeling includes selection of information to be acquired that is relevant to the experience of the artwork, and not to encyclopedic knowledge that might be irrelevant. Most often, exact dates of birth and death of artists are irrelevant, and in case one analyzes an artist's intentions along formal criteria (for example the work of Cezanne, see Bell, 1915), knowledge of an artist's social background, marital life, or political opinions does not contribute to the understanding of the work, and in turn does not contribute to conceptual fluency. In this case, knowing about the personal life of an artist may be useless at best, and a distraction from understanding the artwork properly at worst; at least when seen from the viewpoint of critical feeling.

In this and the last section, we have seen that both training in cultural forms and inculcating taste depend on repetition and thus increasing fluency. Critical feeling in these cases depends on exposing oneself to the propositions one wants to come to believe or to the objects one wants to come to like, and to use the feeling of fluency that results from repetition to monitor progress toward the desired goal. The next section examines another means to promote fluency and thus to foster positive affect: synchrony.

Synchronous movement and social cohesiveness

Military drill is still in use, despite the fact that close-order marching, which makes up much of military drill, would have been fatal since the invention of machine guns, and marching has no longer served to move troops since railroads and trucks came into use. Why do soldiers who readily realize these facts not object to this senseless sweating in the sun? Historian William McNeill (1995) examined this question and concluded that synchrony in drill and dance results in interpersonal liking. He acknowledged that there is not much evidence for this claim,[4] and that there is no psychological theory that could explain why muscular bonding yields positive affect.

The fluency theory explains positive effects of drill and dance by predicting that synchrony results in higher fluency that, in turn, is affectively more positive (see Reber & Norenzayan, 2012, for discussion). Wilson and Knoblich (2005) argued that motor coordination increases the predictability of another's actions, thus increasing the fluency with which another's actions can be processed. Early research documented effects of behavioral coordination on positive rapport (e.g., Bernieri, 1988; LaFrance & Broadbent, 1976). In line with these observations, Marsh, Richardson, and Schmidt (2009) examined a direct link between processing fluency and liking. Participants had to coordinate their actions—swinging a pendulum—in an easy or difficult coordination task. Participants in the easy coordination task later reported more liking for each other than participants in the difficult coordination task, which can be interpreted as a positive effect of interpersonal fluency (see Ackerman & Bargh, 2010) on affect. Wiltermuth and Heath (2009) found that synchronous activities of groups of three people resulted in greater trust, greater feelings of being in the same team, and more cooperation. Together, these studies suggest that processing fluency from synchrony increases mutual liking of those who participate in synchronous movement.

How can critical feeling be applied to synchronous action? If people want to have positive bonds with others, they might consider moving in synchrony with those they want to develop bonds with. In light of 20th-century history, such a recommendation seems odd. As McNeill (1995) remarks, the popularity of synchronous movement declined after World War II because Nazi propaganda relied heavily on synchronous movement, such as marches and parades that increased the rapport with the National Socialist Party. The same holds true for the other big totalitarian system of the 20th century, Stalinism. From that viewpoint, critical feeling should be used to prevent being "taken in" by any ideology or group one does not want to belong to. Indeed, if a person on rational grounds does not like to be member of a group, he or she should prevent sharing their activities, especially those including repeated exposure or aimed at synchrony between their group members, like marching, singing, or dancing.

However, bad experiences in the last century may have prevented good uses of synchronous movement. McNeill concluded that our "contemporary disregard of this aspect of human sociality is unwise and probably also unsustainable over the long haul" (McNeill, 1995, p. 157). Indeed, when people like to be part of a group, for example in aerobics training, folk dance, or as cheerleaders, they may seek out situations where they can move in synchrony that increases interpersonal fluency and therefore social cohesiveness (see Reber & Norenzayan, 2012). Critical feeling then includes strategic selection of situations where a person can move in synchrony with other members of a group one wants to belong to and the assessment of progress of integration into the group by gauging one's affect toward the group.

Conclusion and outlook

After the introduction of the term *critical feeling* and distinguishing it from the term *critical thinking*, I discussed several examples of how people can optimize outcomes by using feelings. Focusing on fluency, I have sketched how this feeling can be used strategically to acquire desired preferences and to develop adherence to beliefs. I was not able to cover all critical feeling related to fluency. For example, it awaits further elaboration how to use fluency critically in intuition (see Reber, Brun, & Mitterndorfer, 2008; Topolinski & Strack, 2009), aesthetic judgment (Reber et al., 2004; Topolinski, 2010), and evaluation of insights (see Topolinski & Reber, 2010).

The reader may have got the impression that my expectations of what critical feeling can do are too enthusiastic. Although I am convinced that critical feeling has large potential to enhance judgment and decision-making, there are at least three problems that have to be addressed in any account of critical feeling.

The first issue is ethical in nature. Like critical thinking, critical feeling can be used to both good and evil ends. For example, if politicians use repetition of slogans to get their political message through, one may question the morality behind such a campaign, especially if the campaign is intentionally built on an appeal to feelings instead of an appeal to arguments. Sometimes, critical feeling may be opposed to critical thinking. For example, critical thinking means to use arguments based on reason in a discussion. In contrast, using ridicule in order to intimidate an opponent in a discussion may be perfectly fine from the standpoint of critical feeling, but it is bad from a moral viewpoint.

The second problem is the definition of critical feeling. I have provided a preliminary definition by noting that critical feeling includes thinking about feelings, refining discrimination of one's perceptual abilities, and in particular using fluency strategically in order to optimize outcomes. Moreover, in discrimination learning and strategic use of fluency, the criterion for quality is often not an objective measurement, like in critical thinking, but a pre-defined feeling, such as subjective satisfaction with an outcome or ease of performing the right actions. However, it is desirable that the term critical feeling will be defined more clearly and will be delineated from terms such as emotional intelligence or mindfulness. Beyond differences to these earlier concepts, there are commonalities that need to be elaborated.

The third problem is empirical evidence. I have sketched how empirical findings on fluency, together with Bayesian statistics and sociological and historical analysis, can be combined into principles of critical feelings by deriving normative strategies for the use of feelings from personal desires and normative principles (e.g., moral norms) and descriptive data (e.g., how feelings work). For example, if people want to adhere to a certain religious group, and if they know that synchronous movement increases group cohesion, they may seek out situations where they have the opportunity to move in synchrony, such as singing or dancing, even if these activities are not of their primary interest. This is analogous to critical thinking where normative strategies for the use of reason are derived from of normative rules of logic and descriptive data on thought processes. However, having derived principles of critical feeling, it is an empirical question whether they are indeed effective. As for example the studies by Unkelbach et al. (2007) and Schwarz et al. (2007) have shown, not all correction strategies result in better judgments.

Moreover, there are instances when decisions based on spontaneous feelings are more satisfying than decisions based on analytical reasoning, for example in choosing a poster (Wilson, Lisle, Schooler, Hodges, Klaaren, & LaFleur, 1993) or choosing an apartment (Dijksterhuis, Bos, Nordgren, & van Baaren, 2006). However, there are other instances where weighing arguments performs at least as well as more spontaneous forms of decision-making (e.g., Newell, Wong, Cheung, & Rakow, 2009). It remains an empirical challenge to find out when reliance on feelings is advantageous and when it is not. Critical feeling, after all, may also mean that one has to know when it is best to judge or decide spontaneously, and when it is best to think twice.

Acknowledgment

I thank Hélène Reich Reber and Sabine Scholl for critical comments on an earlier version of this manuscript.

Note

1 A Google search (2010) for "critical feeling" yielded two alternative meanings for the term critical feeling: First, hope (or some other emotion) can be the critical feeling to overcome a loss. Critical feeling in this sense is synonymous to the one and decisive feeling that is needed to cope with a negative state. Second, one can have a critical feeling toward another person. Here, critical feeling denotes a deprecating feeling toward that person. Both alternative uses have nothing to do with the assessment-oriented evaluation of a feeling state that is the defining attribute of critical feeling in this chapter; they will not be discussed further.
2 Not all religious conversions are gradual (see James, 1985/1902, for examples). It would be interesting to observe how often sudden conversions experiences were preceded by exposure to the creed to be adopted.

3   Reber and Slingerland (2010) discussed a third paradox that the conscious intention to attain virtue actually undermines virtue; although certainly relevant to a discussion of critical feeling, this paradox is unrelated to fluency and will not be discussed here.
4   But see Faris (1976) for data that drill sergeants become surprisingly popular over time, suggesting that moving in synchrony yields liking.

References

Ackerman, J. M., & Bargh, J. A. (2010). Two to tango: Automatic social coordination and the role of felt effort. In B. Bruya (ed.) *Effortless attention: A new perspective in the cognitive science of attention and action*. Cambridge, MA: MIT Press.

Alter, A. L., & Oppenheimer, D. M. (2009). Uniting the tribes of fluency to form a meta-cognitive nation. *Personality and Social Psychology Review, 13*, 219–235.

Baddeley, A. D., & Longman, D. J. A. (1978). The influence of length and frequency of training session on the rate of learning to type. *Ergonomics, 21*, 627–635.

Begg, I. M., Anas, A., & Farinacci, S. (1992). Dissociation of processes in belief: Source recollection, statement familiarity, and the illusion of truth. *Journal of Experimental Psychology: General, 121*, 446–458.

Bell, C. (1915). *Art*. London: Chatto & Windus.

Bernieri, F. J. (1988). Coordinated movement and rapport in teacher-student interactions. *Journal of Nonverbal Behavior, 12*, 120–138.

Bigand, E., & Poulin-Charronnat, B. (2006). Are we "experienced listeners"? A review of the musical capacities that do not depend on formal musical training. *Cognition, 100*, 100–130.

Bourdieu, P. (1984). *Distinction: A social critique of the judgment of taste* (R. Nice, Trans.). Cambridge, MA: Harvard University Press. (Original work published 1979).

Boyer, P. (1992). *Tradition as truth and communication*. Cambridge: Cambridge University Press.

Brown, A. S., & Nix, L. A. (1996). Turning lies into truths: Referential validation of false-hoods. *Journal of Experimental Psychology: Learning, Memory, and Cognition, 22*, 1088–1100.

Bullot, N. J. & Reber, R. (in press). Artful mind meets art history: Toward a psycho-historical framework for the science of art appreciation. *Behavioral and Brain Sciences*.

Diemand-Yauman, C., Oppenheimer, D.M., & Vaughan, E.B. (2011). Fortune favors the bold (and the italicized): Effects of disfluency on retention. *Cognition, 118*, 114–118.

Dijksterhuis, A., Bos, M.W., Nordgren, L.F., & van Baaren, R.B. (2006). Complex choices better made unconsciously? *Science, 313*, 760–761.

Faris, J. H. (1976). The impact of basic combat training: the role of the drill sergeant. In N. Goldman & D. R. Segal (Eds.), *The social psychology of military service* (pp. 13–24). Newbury Park, CA: Sage.

Gordon, P. C., & Holyoak, K. J. (1983). Implicit learning and generalization of the "mere exposure" effect. *Journal of Personality and Social Psychology, 45*, 492–500.

Greifeneder, R., Alt. A., Bottenberg, K., Seele, T., Zelt, S., & Wagener, D. (2010). On writing legibly: Processing fluency systematically biases evaluations of handwritten material. *Social Psychological and Personality Science, 1*, 230–237.

Haack, P. (1990). Beyond objectivity: The feeling factor in listening. *Music Educators Journal, 77*, 28–32.

Hansen, J., Dechêne, A., & Wänke, M. (2008). Discrepant fluency increases subjective truth. *Journal of Experimental Social Psychology, 44*, 687–691.

Hasher, L., Goldstein, D., & Toppino, T. (1977). Frequency and the conference of referential validity. *Journal of Verbal Learning and Verbal Behavior, 16,* 107–112.

Hitchcock, D. (1983). *Critical thinking: A guide to evaluating information.* Toronto: Methuen.

Hughes, W., & Lavery, J. (2004). *Critical thinking: An introduction to the basic skills,* 4th edn. Peterborough, ON, Canada: Broadview Press.

James, W. (1985). *The varieties of religious experience.* New York: Penguin Classics (original work published 1902).

Koenig, M. A., Clément, F., & Harris, P. L. (2004). Trust in testimony: Children's use of true and false statements. *Psychological Science, 15,* 694–698.

Kuhn, G. & Dienes, Z. (2005). Implicit learning of non-local musical rules. *Journal of Experimental Psychology: Learning, Memory, & Cognition, 31,* 1417–1432.

LaFrance, M., & Broadbent, M. (1976). Group rapport: Posture sharing as a nonverbal indicator. *Group and Organization Studies, 1,* 328–333.

Marsh, K. L., Richardson, M. J., & Schmidt, R. C. (2009). Social connection through joint action and interpersonal coordination. *Topics in Cognitive Science, 1,* 320–339.

McNeill, W. H. (1995). *Keeping together in time: Dance and drill in human history.* Cambridge, MA: Harvard University Press.

Newell, B. R., Wong, K. Y., Cheung, C. H. J., & Rakow, T. (2009). Think, blink or sleep on it? The impact of modes of thought on complex decision making. *The Quarterly Journal of Experimental Psychology, 62,* 707–732.

Opacic, T., Stevens, C., & Tillmann, B. (2009). Unspoken knowledge: Implicit learning of structured human dance movement. *Journal of Experimental Psychology: Learning, Memory and Cognition, 35,* 1570–1577.

Parr, W. V., Heatherbell, D., & White, K. G. (2002). Demystifying wine expertise: Olfactory threshold, perceptual skill, and semantic memory in expert and novice wine judges. *Chemical Senses, 27,* 747–755.

Rajagopalan, M. S., Khanna, V., Stott, M., Leiter, Y., Showalter, T. N., Dicker, A., & Lawrence, Y. R. (2010). Accuracy of cancer information on the Internet: A comparison of a Wiki with a professionally maintained database. *Journal of Clinical Oncology, 28 (7s),* abstr 6058.

Rappaport, R. A. (1999). *Ritual and religion in the making of humanity.* Cambridge: Cambridge University Press.

Reber, R. (2012). Processing fluency, aesthetic pleasure, and culturally shared taste. In A. P. Shimamura & Palmer S. E. (Eds.), *Aesthetic science: Connecting minds, brains, and experience* (pp. 223–249). New York: Oxford University Press.

Reber, R., Brun, M., & Mitterndorfer, K. (2008). The use of heuristics in intuitive mathematical judgment. *Psychonomic Bulletin & Review, 15,* 1174–1178.

Reber, R., & Norenzayan, A. (2012). *The shared fluency theory of social cohesiveness.* Manuscript, available at SSRN: http://ssrn.com/abstract=1702407 or http://dx.doi.org/10.2139/ssrn.1702407.

Reber, R., & Schwarz, N. (1999). Effects of perceptual fluency on judgments of truth. *Consciousness and Cognition, 8,* 338–342.

Reber, R., Schwarz, N., & Winkielman, P. (2004). Processing fluency and aesthetic pleasure: Is beauty in the perceiver's processing experience? *Personality and Social Psychology Review, 8,* 364–382.

Reber, R., & Slingerland, E. G. (2011). Confucius meets cognition: New answers to old questions. *Religion, Brain, & Behavior, 1,* 135–145.

Reber, R., & Unkelbach, C. (2010). The epistemic status of processing fluency as source for judgments of truth. *Review of Philosophy and Psychology, 1,* 563–581.

Reber, R., Winkielman, P., & Schwarz, N. (1998). Effects of perceptual fluency on affective judgments. *Psychological Science*, *9*, 45–48.

Schwarz, N. (2012). Feelings-as-information theory. In P. Van Lange, A. Kruglanski, & E. T. Higgins (Eds.), *Handbook of theories of social psychology* (pp. 289–308). Thousand Oaks, CA: Sage.

Schwarz, N., Sanna, L. J., Skurnik, I., & Yoon, C. (2007). Metacognitive experiences and the intricacies of setting people straight: Implications for debiasing and public information campaigns. *Advances in Experimental Social Psychology*, *39*, 127–161.

Simon, D.A., & Bjork, R.A. (2001). Metacognition in motor learning. *Journal of Experimental Psychology: Learning, Memory and Cognition*, *27*, 907–912.

—— (2002). Models of performance in learning multi-segment movement tasks: Consequences for acquisition, retention and judgments of learning. *Journal of Experimental Psychology: Applied*, *8*, 222–232.

Slingerland, E. G. (2003a). *Effortless action. Wu-wei as conceptual metaphor and spiritual ideal in early China*. Oxford: Oxford University Press.

—— (2003b). *Confucius: Analects: With selections from traditional commentaries*. Indianapolis, Cambridge: Hackett Publishing Company.

—— (2010). Toward an empirically-responsible ethics: Cognitive science, virtue ethics, and effortless attention in early Chinese thought. In B. Bruya (ed.) *Effortless attention: A new perspective in the cognitive science of attention and action* (pp. 247–286). Cambridge, MA: MIT Press.

Sweller, J., & Chandler, P. (1994). Why some material is difficult to learn. *Cognition and Instruction*, *12*, 185–233.

Tillmann, B., Bharucha, J. J., & Bigand, E. (2000). Implicit learning of tonality: A self-organizing approach. *Psychological Review*, *107*, 885–913.

Topolinski, S. (2010). Moving the eye of the beholder: Motor components in vision determine aesthetic preference. *Psychological Science*, *21 (9)*, 1220–1224.

Topolinski, S., & Reber, R. (2010). Gaining insight into the "Aha"-experience. *Current Directions in Psychological Science*, 19, 402–405.

Topolinski, S., & Strack, F., (2009). The architecture of intuition: Fluency and affect determine intuitive judgments of semantic and visual coherence, and of grammaticality in artificial grammar learning. *Journal of Experimental Psychology: General*, *138 (1)*, 39–63.

Unkelbach, C. (2007). Reversing the truth effect: Learning the interpretation of processing fluency in judgments of truth. *Journal of Experimental Psychology: Learning, Memory and Cognition*, *33*, 219–230.

Unkelbach, C., Fiedler, K., & Freytag, P. (2007). Information repetition in evaluative judgments: Easy to monitor, hard to control. *Organizational Behavior & Human Decision Processes*, *103*, 37–52.

Van den Bergh, O. & Vrana, S. R. (1998). Repetition and boredom in a perceptual fluency/attributional model of affective judgments. *Cognition and Emotion*, *12*, 533–553.

Weaver, K., Garcia, S.M., Schwarz, N., & Miller, D. T. (2007). Inferring the popularity of an opinion from its familiarity: A repetitive voice can sound like a chorus. *Journal of Personality and Social Psychology*, *92*, 821–833.

Whittlesea, B. W. A. (1993). Illusions of familiarity. *Journal of Experimental Psychology: Learning, Memory, and Cognition*, *19*, 1235–1253.

Wilson, M., & Knoblich, G. (2005). The case for motor involvement in perceiving conspecifics. *Psychological Bulletin*, *131*, 460–473.

Wilson, T. D., Lisle, D. J., Schooler, J. W., Hodges, S. D., Klaaren, K. J., & LaFleur, S. J. (1993). Introspecting about reasons can reduce post-choice satisfaction. *Personality and Social Psychology Bulletin, 19*, 331–339.

Wiltermuth, S. S., & Heath, C. (2009). Synchrony and cooperation. *Psychological Science, 20*, 1–5.

Winkielman, P., & Cacioppo, J. T. (2001). Mind at ease puts a smile on the face: Psychophysiological evidence that processing facilitation leads to liking. *Journal of Personality and Social Psychology, 81*, 989–1000.

Zillmann, D., & Bryant, J. (1985). Affect, mood, and emotion as determinants of selective exposure. In D. Zillmann & J. Bryant (Eds.), *Selective exposure to communication* (pp. 157–190). Hillsdale, NJ: Lawrence Erlbaum.

12 The ecological validity of fluency

Stefan M. Herzog and Ralph Hertwig

Abstract

This chapter reviews the ecological validity of processing fluency; that is, the extent to which we can draw valid inferences about the external world by paying heed to our internal experience of fluency. As a proximal cue, fluency can help us navigate an uncertain world because it reflects the statistical structure of our environment. We can use the ecological connection between fluency and the world to inform our judgments and decisions. For example, retrieval fluency—the speed with which we retrieve objects from memory—reflects numerical quantities of importance, the truth of statements, the danger of objects and social information about what other people are doing. We hope to complement our descriptive understanding of how and when people use fluency with an understanding of where fluency is an ecologically valid cue and where it is not.

All things are difficult before they are easy.
　　　　　　Dr. Thomas Fuller, Gnomologia, 1732; British physician (1654–1734)

Our cognitive machinery has evolved in the service of enabling us to navigate an often dangerous and uncertain world. How successfully we deal with this world depends, among other factors, on the fit between the cognitive machinery and environmental structures (Brunswik, 1956; Simon, 1990). In this chapter, we ask the question of whether a seeming by-product of the operation of our cognitive machinery—the fluency of our own processing experiences (the extent to which a cognitive operation feels easy or hard, swift or slow)—tells us something valid about the world we live in. For example, can we infer that companies whose names we recognize fluently tend to be more profitable than companies we hesitate to recognize? Or are we entitled to believe in assertions more, the more fluently we are able to process them? In other words, to what extent does the internal experience of fluency permit us to make valid inferences about our external world? This question concerns the *ecological validity of fluency* or lack thereof.

When we first asked the question about the ecological validity of fluency (Hertwig, Herzog, Schooler, & Reimer, 2008; Schooler & Hertwig, 2005), we thought that we would have no difficulty in finding an unambiguous answer in the large body of research conducted on the subjective experience of fluency (for reviews see e.g., Alter & Oppenheimer, 2009; Oppenheimer, 2008; Reber, Schwarz, & Winkielman, 2004; Schwarz, 2004; Winkielman, Schwarz, Fazendeiro, & Reber, 2003; for broader reviews on feelings in judgment and decision-making see e.g., Bless & Forgas, 2000; Greifeneder, Bless, & Pham, 2011; Pham, 2004, 2007; Schwarz, 2002, 2011; Schwarz & Clore, 2007; Shah & Oppenheimer, 2008). Our expectation, however, was quickly frustrated. Although some of the reviews cited above do bring up the question of fluency's validity, none aimed to present a systematic review or answer to our question. We found short discussions about the validity of affective feelings and feelings in general (e.g., Pham, 2004; Schwarz, 2011), but no discussions about cognitive feelings or fluency in particular (see Reber & Unkelbach, 2010, for an exception). In order to fill this void, we conducted a literature search (see Appendix A).

This chapter reviews the results of our literature analysis and suggests why fluency is an ecologically valid cue in domains that have not yet been investigated. We will discuss to what extent retrieval fluency—the speed with which we retrieve objects from memory—is a valid cue for predicting numerical quantities of importance, for assessing the truth status of statements, for assessing danger and for predicting other people's behavior. But before we start with our review, there is one question begging for an answer: Why has the potentially precious information encapsulated in a seemingly subjective experience received such scant attention?

Perhaps, the issue of validity is just utterly trivial and uninteresting because researchers simply have taken it for granted that fluency empowers valid inferences about the world. The literature, however, does not suggest such a concurrence of opinions. Clearly, there are researchers who believe in the usefulness of feelings for judgments and decisions. For example, Oppenheimer (2008, p. 237) suggested, "knowledge of our ease of processing can lead to useful inferences about the external environment." At the same time, others, for instance, Topolinski and Strack (2010, p. 722), have highlighted that in some cases "fluency is not a valid cue and may have powerful biasing effects" or "may even cause irrational behavior with substantial economic consequences." For example, correctly and repeatedly telling people that a consumer claim is actually false can, paradoxically, cause them to misremember it as true because repeated exposure to the false claim increases its fluency (Skurnik, Yoon, Park, & Schwarz, 2005). Similarly, people believe more in statements that rhyme than in their non-rhyming counterparts because rhyming increases the statements' fluency, which, in turn, increases the statements' perceived truthfulness (McGlone & Tofighbakhsh, 2000). We are thus left with a somewhat dissonant message. Although some fluency researchers seem to believe that fluency can be a valid cue (see also Unkelbach & Greifeneder, Chapter 2, this volume), they and others caution us to pay heed to the potentially biasing effects of fluency.

Two perspectives on fluency: Ecological correspondence vs. susceptibility to manipulation

We suggest that this seeming tension between fluency's positive and negative evaluations can be reconciled by recognizing that fluency's validity depends simultaneously on the answers to two questions. The first is the question of *ecological correspondence*: Can fluency, in principle, accurately reflect environmental criteria (e.g., the success of companies) and thus potentially enable valid inferences about our world? We believe that the positive statements in the literature on fluency's validity pertain to this ecological question: Many fluency researchers seem to think that fluency can reflect properties of our environment. As mentioned before, there is little research available to corroborate this belief. This dearth of evidence, we suspect, stems from researchers mainly focusing on the second question, which we call the *susceptibility to manipulation question*: Can fluency-based judgments and decisions, in principle, be influenced by obviously irrelevant factors (e.g., such as rhyming) that sabotage the potential correspondence between fluency and external criteria? As the extensive literature on fluency effects shows, the answer is unambiguously positive (e.g., Alter & Oppenheimer, 2009; Oppenheimer, 2008; Schwarz, 2004). Obviously, warnings about fluency's potential biasing effects in the literature are informed by research on fluency's susceptibility to manipulation. Ecological correspondence and susceptibility to manipulation together imply that fluency will only lead to valid judgments and decisions to the extent that there is both an ecological correspondence between fluency and environmental criteria *and* an absence of sabotaging influences, which would otherwise dilute fluency's validity.

Although the distinction between these two key questions can resolve the tension between the positive and negative evaluations of fluency's claim to truth, there still seems to be a mismatch between what fluency researchers seem to believe and what they actually study: Although some researchers suggest that fluency can be a valid cue (e.g., Oppenheimer, 2008; Unkelbach, 2006), most of the empirical work demonstrates how fluency is influenced by irrelevant factors and thus that by relying on fluency people risk going astray. The resulting literature paints a rather bleak picture of the utility of fluency and leaves the reader with the impression that fluency is a potentially misleading cue and should be passed up.

The focus on fluency's susceptibility to manipulations and the resulting fluency illusions is reminiscent of the *heuristics and biases* research program's focus on the dark side of cognitive heuristics (Gilovich, Griffin, & Kahneman, 2002; Kahneman, Slovic, & Tversky, 1982). This program explicitly invoked the analogy between research in perception and research in judgment and decision making to motivate its guiding notion of *cognitive illusions* (e.g., Kahneman & Tversky, 1982): Just as visual illusions afford us insights into the working of our perceptual system that we will not gain under normal conditions, clever experimental paradigms can generate cognitive illusions that grant us insights into reasoning's opaque ways that we otherwise would not enjoy (but see Gigerenzer,

1996, for a critical discussion of cognitive illusions). However, cognitive illusions have been seductive far beyond their methodological utility. In Kahneman and Tversky's (1982, p. 124) words: "Although errors of judgments are but a method by which some cognitive processes are studied, the method has become a significant part of the message," and the use of heuristics became to be seen as leaving human reasoning prone to "severe and systematic errors" (Tversky & Kahneman, 1974, p. 1124).

When researchers construct paradigms whose very goal is to produce perceptual or cognitive illusions, they are—by design—collecting samples of situations that are not representative of what people normally experience. Although those studies can reveal some of our mind's operations, and undoubtedly can also provide an existence proof of perceptual or cognitive illusions, they do not afford us an unbiased assessment of how consequential such illusions are in our natural environment. And indeed, although researchers of human vision are masters in constructing ever more impressive perceptual illusions, they do not conclude from those illusions that our visual system is flawed or that we should not rely on it to navigate the world. On the contrary, vision researchers often marvel about the cleverness and elegance of our visual system and how well its in-built assumptions—which are revealed through visual illusions—match the informational structure of our environment. In fact, the very reason why we are fascinated by visual illusions is that we do not encounter them in our daily life—at least, for example, outside of 3D cinemas. In other words, just because "illusions" can be evoked in the lab, they need not wreak havoc outside of it (e.g., Funder, 1987; Krueger & Funder, 2004).

In stark contrast to vision researchers, scholars of human cognition have often concluded from famed demonstrations of cognitive illusions in the laboratory that those illusions indeed *are* a problem outside of the laboratory (e.g., Dawes, 2001; Piattelli-Palmarini, 1994). Although this conclusion could, of course, be true in principle, the appeal to findings from paradigms that, by their very design, were bound to produce cognitive illusions does not suffice. Such conclusions should be informed by studies using a *representative design*, that is, studies that randomly sample the stimuli from their respective environments (Brunswik, 1952; Dhami, Hertwig, & Hoffrage, 2004). Representative designs aim to preserve the natural properties of environments and thus allow us to assess the accuracy of judgments under representative circumstances. Furthermore, field studies can add external validity to the conclusions based on laboratory work (see, for example, Alter & Oppenheimer, 2006; Green & Jame, 2011).

We conjecture that what has been said about cognitive illusions can be generalized to research on fluency. Fluency researchers often—perhaps almost exclusively—decouple fluency and the criterion (e.g., the truth status of a statement) in their studies to show the "pure" contribution of fluency. To achieve this decoupling, fluency researchers use methods to manipulate fluency that have no ecological connection to the environmental criterion, thus creating "fluency illusions." For example, Reber and Schwarz (1999) orthogonally varied whether or not a statement was easy to read (i.e., color contrast of text) and whether a statement was true or not. They found that people believed more in statements that could be fluently read. Similar to the heuristics-and-biases program, the method became a significant part of the message; namely, fluency has come to be seen as an invalid cue that one should not rely on. But fluency's vulnerability, that is, findings indicating that people's judgment and decisions *can* be influenced by irrelevant sources of fluency, does not speak to the question of how ubiquitous and pernicious fluency illusions are beyond the confines of the experimental paradigms designed to demonstrate the very existence of those irrelevant influences. Consequently, we conjecture that the ecological question of whether and when fluency is an ecologically valid cue remains—after a vast number of investigations of fluency—by and large an open question. The myriad results stemming from the susceptibility paradigm simply fail to tell us much about fluency's ecological correspondence to environmental criteria.

This chapter reviews what we currently know about the ecological validity of fluency; namely, the extent to which we can predict the external world by relying on fluency. The details of our literature search can be found in Appendix A. In this review, we have only included studies that used a *representative design*, that is, a representative or random sample of stimuli from a reference class of objects (Brunswik, 1952; Dhami et al., 2004). The ecological validity of fluency pertains to inferences about environmental criteria (e.g., the success of companies or the truth of a statement) as opposed to inferences concerning one's own past experiences, such as whether or not one has previously encountered an object (e.g., Whittlesea & Leboe, 2000). In the latter case, fluency can be a valid cue for inferring prior exposure to an object because prior exposure enhances processing fluency (e.g., Jacoby & Dallas, 1981).

Although many different phenomena have been subsumed under the broad notion of fluency (Alter & Oppenheimer, 2009), most of what we know about the ecological validity of fluency comes from investigations of *retrieval fluency* (e.g., Hertwig et al., 2008; Schooler & Hertwig, 2005). Retrieval fluency refers to the time it takes a person to access and retrieve an item from memory. This time is empirically operationalized as *recognition speed*, that is, the time it takes a person to decide that she recognizes an object (Hertwig et al., 2008). Thus, the next part of this chapter is devoted to the ecological validity of retrieval fluency. We will discuss to what extent retrieval fluency is a valid cue for predicting numerical quantities of importance, for assessing the truth status of statements, for assessing danger, and for predicting other people's behavior. Before we turn to our review, one more clarification is in order. In the fluency literature, a distinction is made between objective fluency (e.g., in terms of objective retrieval speed) and fluency-based feelings (e.g., the subjective experience of familiarity), which depend on the discrepancy between processing expectations and objective fluency (e.g., Whittlesea, 2004). In this chapter we assume that objective fluency approximates the actual fluency experience well enough in the context of our ecological analysis. Future research should directly investigate the ecological validity of (reported) fluency experiences.

The ecological validity of retrieval fluency

Human memory is a notorious gambler. Each and every day it operates based on a wager about the world around us. Memory bets that one is more likely to need a piece of information again, the more often one has encountered it in the past (Anderson & Milson, 1989; Anderson & Schooler, 1991, 2000; Schooler & Anderson, 1997). The more often one encounters some piece of information, the higher is its activation strength in memory and the more likely will one be able to retrieve or recognize it and—should one retrieve it—the faster that retrieval will take place. Thus memory mirrors the frequency of past encounters with information and reveals these encounters in the probability of recognition and the amount of retrieval fluency. But why would memory do this?

If one reads the headline of a randomly drawn article from the *New York Times*, then the probability that it will contain a specific word (e.g., "Washington") is larger the more often this word previously had appeared in *New York Times* headlines (Anderson & Schooler, 1991). Similarly, if one receives a new email message, then the probability that this message was sent by a specific person will be larger the more often he or she has contacted us in the past (Anderson & Schooler, 1991; Pachur, Schooler, & Stevens, 2012). These two and many more examples illustrate a fundamental statistical property of our world: The odds of encountering a piece of information increases the more often one has encountered it in the past. Thus by mirroring environmental frequencies and successfully betting on this statistical property, our memory can make information more accessible that we are currently likely to need (e.g., Anderson & Schooler, 2000). Metaphorically speaking, human memory is like a public library that organizes its books according to their predicted popularity (see Anderson & Milson, 1989; Anderson & Schooler, 2000). Frequently checked out books, that is, popular books (e.g., the Dan Brown blockbusters), will be made available in special spaces near the entrance of the library to make it easy for members to find them. In contrast, less popular books (e.g., the books by Herta Müller, recipient of the 2009 Nobel Prize in literature), the ones rarely checked out in the past, will be relegated to the back of the library. Because of the environment being thus reflected in our memory, we can exploit our memory to make inferences about the environment. We can infer, for example, that the more fluently we retrieve an item from memory, the more often we must have encountered it in the past. Retrieval fluency, however, can do much more than that.

Predicting numerical quantities of importance

Given that in an environment, say, encompassing of the world's 20 most profitable companies, a criterion (e.g., a company's revenue) is correlated with how often we have encountered the names of these companies in the past (e.g., through newspapers and magazines), then retrieval fluency can act as a cue for that criterion (Hertwig et al., 2008; see also Schooler & Hertwig, 2005): The more fluently we retrieve an object (e.g., a company's name), the larger its

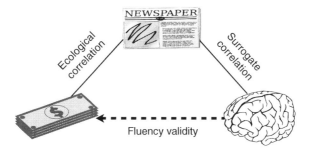

Figure 12.1 The ecological validity of retrieval fluency. An inaccessible or unknown
criterion (e.g., a company's sales volume) is reflected by a mediator
variable (e.g., the number of times the company is mentioned in the news),
and the mediator influences the fluency of retrieval. The mind, in turn, can use
retrieval fluency to infer the criterion (*fluency validity*). The degree to
which the criterion is reflected in the environment is called the *ecological
correlation*; the degree to which the environmental frequencies are reflected in
memory is termed the *surrogate correlation*. The figure is adapted from
Figure 1 in Goldstein and Gigerenzer (2002).

criterion value tends to be. That is, environmental frequencies (e.g., acquired
through newspapers and magazines) can act as a *mediator* that connects an
unknown criterion with our memory (Goldstein & Gigerenzer, 2002; Schooler &
Hertwig, 2005). In such cases, retrieval fluency can predict a variable that is not
itself a frequency, but could be anything from the population size of a city or the
revenue of a company to the income of athletes (Hertwig et al., 2008)—as long
as the criterion variable is reflected in environmental frequencies. The triangular
relationships between criterion, mediator and retrieval fluency is depicted in
Figure 12.1.

This ecological approach to retrieval fluency, of course, begs the question,
which environmental criteria can retrieval fluency predict? That is, which criteria
are reflected in mediators in the environment and which are not? The following
two perspectives shed light on this issue. First, from a *statistical perspective*
(Pachur, Todd, Gigerenzer, Schooler, & Goldstein, 2012), mediators in the environment (e.g., newspapers, people) reflect only those dimensions well, for which
people's proclivity to communicate about an object either substantially increases
or decreases as we move from objects with minimum values on the dimension to
objects with maximum values on the dimension. For example, assuming that
newsworthy things tend to happen in metropolitan areas, then it follows that
national newspapers will offer their readers more information about large cities
relative to hicksvilles. Consequently, mediators such as frequency of mentions in
newspapers strongly reflect a city's population size (e.g., Goldstein & Gigerenzer,
2002). In contrast, when objects with especially low *and* high values, respectively, pique our curiosity, then the mediators will not adequately reflect the

respective criteria dimensions. For example, not only very common animals, such as house cats, but also very rare and endangered animals, such as giant pandas, attract our attention (Richter & Späth, 2006). Similarly, the mediator will not reflect the true relation when people face two negatively correlated dimensions within one domain. For example, people frequently talk about very common yet relatively innocuous ailments, such as a cold or a migraine, but are also concerned with rare and frightening diseases, such as cholera or swine flu (Hertwig, Pachur, & Kurzenhäuser, 2005; Pachur & Hertwig, 2006).

Second, from a *topic perspective*, mediators in the environment (e.g., other people, the media, the entertainment industry) will expose us preferentially to objects that are "important" to those mediators. What is important to them? People and, by extension, the media talk and gossip about news that is, in one way or another, pertinent to human survival and reproduction, such as hazards, diseases, food, social status, attractiveness, competition, alliances, reputation and so on (e.g., Baumeister, Zhang, & Vohs, 2004; Davis & McLeod, 2003; Dunbar, 2004; Foster, 2004). Together with the statistical principle, we can predict that mediators—and thus retrieval fluency—will reflect those dimensions that both are important and do not correlate negatively with other important dimensions. Because, for example, in social environments, many important dimensions are positively correlated (resources, money, status, success, etc.), one can expect the mediators to reflect such social dimensions. Indeed, the income of athletes, the wealth of the richest people, the revenue of companies, and the success of tennis players are well reflected in the mediators (Hertwig et al., 2008; Scheibehenne & Bröder, 2007). In contrast, one can predict that the mediators will not reflect, for example, the incidence of disease rates (as discussed above) because people care about frequent, but also about rare, yet frightening diseases (e.g., Pachur & Hertwig, 2006). Furthermore, mediators will obviously not reflect obscure criteria that are of little interest to people (e.g., the distance between one European city and another arbitrarily chosen European city; Pohl, 2006).

What is the empirical evidence concerning the ecological validity of retrieval fluency? We searched for studies that reported on the validity of retrieval fluency among the references identified in our literature search (see Appendix A) and identified 25 domains with representative samples of objects (Brunswik, 1952; Dhami et al., 2004). In all these studies, retrieval fluency was operationalized as the time (in ms) that a participant took to judge whether or not she recognized a name (e.g., the music band Led Zeppelin). The retrieval *fluency validity* is defined as follows (Hertwig et al., 2008; Schooler & Hertwig, 2005): The resulting proportion of correct decisions if one always infers that the more fluently retrieved object has the larger criterion value (among all possible pairings of objects in the environment where both objects are recognized). Because decision-makers cannot discriminate differences in retrieval speed below 100 ms (Hertwig et al., 2008), we restricted the calculation of the fluency validity to pairs of objects for which difference in retrieval speed was equal to or larger than 100 ms (see Hertwig et al., 2008). We obtained the raw data and then calculated the fluency validities and other statistics for all domains (see Table 12.1).

Table 12.1 The Ecological Validity of Retrieval Fluency: Overview of Empirical Findings From 25 Domains

Domain	Reference class[a]	N	M	Rec. rate	Pairs	Val	d_R val	Val for quartiles of Δ fluency				% val > 50%	Source
								1st	2nd	3rd	4th		
POPULATION SIZE													
City population: Austria	14 largest Austrian cities[b]	66	14	0.51	18	0.63	0.69	0.54	0.62	0.63	0.72	0.71	Hilbig et al (2011)
City population: Austria	28 largest Austrian cities[c]	175[d]	28	0.28	22	0.65	0.82	0.59	0.68	0.61	0.73	0.77	Marewski & Schooler (2011, Studies 1-3)
City population: France	36 largest French cities[c]	175[d]	36	0.57	130	0.61	0.91	0.57	0.58	0.63	0.67	0.78	Marewski & Schooler (2011, Studies 1-3)
City population: Germany	30 largest German cities[c]	175[d]	30	0.97	192	0.65	1.50	0.61	0.63	0.66	0.70	0.92	Marewski & Schooler (2011, Studies 1-3)
City population: Italy	50 largest Italian cities[c]	175[d]	50	0.47	189	0.69	1.66	0.63	0.67	0.71	0.75	0.90	Marewski & Schooler (2011, Studies 1-3)
City population: Poland	14 largest Polish cities[b]	66	14	0.46	13	0.59	0.35	0.66	0.53	0.61	0.70	0.58	Hilbig et al (2011)
City population: Spain	38 largest Spanish cities[c]	175[d]	38	0.34	53	0.61	0.73	0.58	0.59	0.61	0.70	0.75	Marewski & Schooler (2011, Studies 1-3)
City population: Switzerland	14 largest Swiss cities[b]	68	14	0.64	27	0.73	1.35	0.64	0.70	0.78	0.87	0.88	Hilbig & Pohl (2009, Study 3)
City population: U.K.	30 largest U.K. cities[c]	175[d]	30	0.56	86	0.57	0.49	0.54	0.55	0.57	0.60	0.69	Marewski & Schooler (2011, Studies 1-3)
City population: U.S.	118 largest U.S. cities	120[e]	118	0.52	147	0.67	2.07	0.60	0.63	0.69	0.74	0.93	Hertwig et al. (2008, Study 1)

City population: U.S.	261 largest U.S. cities	68	261	0.30	1,152	0.64	2.51	0.59	0.64	0.66	0.68	0.97	Hilbig et al (2010)
City population: U.S.	28 largest U.S. cities[c]	175[d]	28	0.77	133	0.64	1.27	0.59	0.62	0.66	0.69	0.89	Marewski & Schooler (2011, Studies 1-3)
City population: Worldwide	61 largest cities worldwide	29	61	0.63	518	0.54	0.47	0.51	0.52	0.53	0.56	0.72	Hilbig (2010)

ECONOMIC SUCCESS

Athletes' income	50 richest athletes	40	50	0.24	51	0.61	0.72	0.55	0.62	0.63	0.60	0.75	Hertwig et al (2008, Study 1)
Billionaire's fortune	100 wealthiest people	40	100	0.09	44	0.62	0.70	0.62	0.67	0.63	0.67	0.76	Hertwig et al (2008, Study 1)
Companies' market capitalization	Market capitalization of 80 companies	21	80	0.52	612	0.64	4.38	0.57	0.62	0.67	0.71	1.00	Marewski & Schooler (2011, Study 5)
Companies' revenue	100 German companies with highest revenue	40	100[f]	0.46	842	0.58	1.29	0.56	0.58	0.60	0.59	0.95	Hertwig et al (2008, Study 1)
Country's GDP	GDP of 162 countries	20	162	0.90	7,122	0.64	1.87	0.56	0.61	0.67	0.70	1.00	Marewski & Schooler (2011, Study 4)
Music artists' cumulative record sales	106 most successful artists in the U.S.	40	106[f]	0.69	1,684	0.57	1.32	0.55	0.57	0.58	0.60	0.98	Hertwig et al (2008, Study 1)

(continued)

Table 12.1 (continued)

Domain	Reference class[a]	N	M	Rec. rate	Pairs	Val	d_R val	Val for quartiles of Δfluency				% val > 50%	Source
								1st	2nd	3rd	4th		
FAMILIARITY & POPULARITY													
Familiarity: Companies	84 companies from the S&P 100 Index	22	84	0.84	1,884	0.68	2.93	0.60	0.66	0.72	0.76	1.00	Herzog et al (2011)
Familiarity: infectious diseases	54 infectious diseases' name recognition	20	54	0.46	222	0.78	3.77	0.64	0.76	0.83	0.90	1.00	Marewski & Schooler (2011, Study 6)
Familiarity: Politicians	189 German politicians' name recognition	19	189	0.36	1,757	0.76	5.13	0.67	0.74	0.80	0.85	1.00	Marewski & Schooler (2011, Study 7)
Popularity of sports	25 most popular sports in Germany	80	25	1.00	227	0.53	0.29	0.51	0.53	0.52	0.56	0.60	Pachur et al (2012)
DISEASE INCIDENCE													
Incidence: Cancer	Incidence of 24 types of cancers in Germany	40	24	0.69	112	0.56	0.86	0.57	0.52	0.59	0.58	0.83	Hertwig et al (2005, Study 2)
Incidence: Infectious diseases	Incidence of 24 types of infectious diseases in Germany	100[g]	24	0.58	74	0.38	-1.33	0.47	0.38	0.34	0.33	0.07	Hertwig et al (2005, Study 2); Pachur & Hertwig (2006, Study 2)

SUMMARY ACROSS ALL DOMAINS

1st quartile	40	28	0.46	53	0.58	0.70	0.55	0.57	0.60	0.60	0.75
M_R	76	53	0.54	239	0.62	1.18	0.58	0.61	0.64	0.68	0.85
3rd quartile	175	100	0.69	612	0.65	1.87	0.61	0.66	0.67	0.73	0.97

Note. N refers to the total number of participants in the dataset and M to the number of objects in the domain. The following columns show averaged values across participants (using a 20%-trimmed mean, M_R; Wilcox & Keselman, 2003; see also Note 1): *Rec. rate* refers to the recognition rate (proportion of objects recognized), *pairs* to the number of simulated fluency pairs, *val* to the fluency validity, *val for quartiles of Δfluency* to the fluency validity for the first, second, third and fourth quartile of absolute differences in retrieval speed (within participants), respectively. *d_R val* refers to a robust one-sample Cohen's *d* effect size (cf. Algina et al., 2005) of the fluency validities (compared against 50%) and *% val > 50%* refers to the proportion of participants for which fluency validity was larger than 50%. Because people cannot detect differences in retrieval fluency below 100 ms (Hertwig et al, 2008, Study 2), all statistics were calculated only for object pairs with a difference of 100 ms or more. The retrieval fluency validity is defined as follows (Hertwig et al, 2008; Schooler & Hertwig, 2005): the proportion of correct decisions one would make if one would always infer that the more fluently retrieved object has the larger criterion value (among all possible pairings of objects in the reference class where both objects are recognized by a participant).

a See the referenced articles for detailed descriptions of the domains and reference classes.

b In the original study, the largest city was excluded from the reference class.

c In the original study, the capital city was excluded from the reference class and only one-word city names of similar word length (i.e., 5–8 letters) were used.

d We collapsed the respective datasets across Studies 1, 2 and 3 from Marewski & Schooler (2011).

e Participants were presented with a random third of the 118 cities.

f Unlike in the original analysis, we did not exclude objects with overly long names (see Hertwig et al, 2008, footnote 5, p. 1194).

g We collapsed the datasets from Hertwig et al (2005, Study 2) and Pachur and Hertwig (2006, Study 2).

All obtained fluency validities were above chance level (range [0.53, 0.78])—with the sole exception of the infectious diseases domain, where validity was only 38 percent; this low validity is consistent with the observation that the number of times infectious diseases are mentioned in the media is a poor predictor of the diseases' actual incidence (Pachur & Hertwig, 2006). Averaged across all 25 domains, the fluency validity was 62 percent (interquartile range or IQR: [.58, .65]).[1] Thus retrieval fluency enables people to draw inferences that clearly surpass chance level.[2] Robust Cohen's *d* effect sizes (cf. Algina, Keselman, & Penfield, 2005), comparing the fluency validities against chance level, averaged 1.18 across domains (IQR [0.70, 1.87]), thus indicating large effect sizes (see Cohen, 1988). Furthermore, fluency was a valid cue for the large majority of participants: Averaged across domains, 85 percent (IQR [0.75, 0.97]) of participants enjoyed validities above chance level.

Roughly half of the domains (13 out of 25) pertain to inferences about population size. To see whether our conclusions about fluency's validity are unduly influenced by this "drosophila" type of domain, we grouped the domains into four classes based on the type of criterion that was to be inferred (see Table 12.1): population size (13 datasets), economic success (e.g., people; six datasets), familiarity and popularity (e.g., politicians; four datasets), and disease incidence (two datasets). Three results emerged. First, retrieval fluency is also a valid cue in domains other than population size inferences ($M_R = 61\%$, IQR [0.57, 0.65]). Second, fluency seems equally potent in inferring economic success ($M_R = 61\%$, IQR [0.59, 0.63]) and population size ($M_R = 63\%$, IQR [0.61, 0.65]). Third, fluency also enables inferences about familiarity and popularity (Mdn = 72%, IQR [0.65, 0.77]), which is not surprising given that familiarity and popularity are nearly synonymous with being frequently talked, written, and heard about. Given that we only have two domains about disease incidences (with fluency validities of 38 percent and 56 percent, respectively), it is difficult to draw any conclusions about this domain. Research on risk perception, however, suggests that media coverage of, for instance, incidents of infectious diseases is not necessarily a good proxy for actual incidence rates (e.g., Hertwig et al., 2005).

Even though an average fluency validity of 62 percent may not seem terribly impressive, it would be misleading to compare it to the utopian benchmark of making 100 percent correct inferences. Even strategies that can process large amounts of information and do so in a computationally expensive way (e.g., Bayesian networks) do not achieve perfect accuracy in real-world environments and often do not perform much better than simple heuristics (e.g., take-the-best; Martignon & Hoffrage, 2002). Thus rather than comparing fluency validities to perfect accuracy, one should compare them to the accuracy of inferences that are based on information *other* than retrieval fluency, that is, on cues drawn from our semantic knowledge (e.g., whether a city has an airport or not). For instance, when one calculates the accuracy of participants' actual decisions in three domains investigated in Hertwig et al. (2008, Study 3) and focuses on only those decisions in which participants concluded that the *less* fluently recognized object was larger (i.e., participants obviously relied on information other than retrieval fluency) one finds the following: Participants' inferences were actually *less* accurate than those that they would have made had they always relied on retrieval fluency (6, 7, and 11 percentage points lower accuracy, respectively; Hertwig et al., 2008, p. 1204). This result suggests that retrieval fluency can lead to inferences at least as accurate as those from knowledge-based strategies that "think harder" about the problem by using cue knowledge.

Another convenient property of retrieval fluency is that it is more likely to be correct when it becomes easier to use. Specifically, the larger the differences in, say, two company names' retrieval fluency, the more easily the retrieval fluency can be distinguished and the more likely the resulting inference will be correct. This is because larger differences in retrieval fluency translate into larger differences in the environmental frequencies and—given an ecological correlation between the criterion and the mediators in the environment—also into larger differences on the criterion (Hertwig et al., 2008). Figure 12.2 shows for the five domains investigated in Hertwig et al. (2008, Study 1) how the fluency validity increases as the difference in retrieval fluency increases. For example, whereas indistinguishable differences in retrieval fluency (i.e., below 100 ms) imply a validity of 54 percent when inferring which of two US cities is larger, validity rises to 71 percent for differences larger than 700 ms. This result also emerges in the other domains. Table 12.1 shows the fluency validity in each domain separately for quartiles of absolute differences in retrieval speed (i.e., for the first, second, third and fourth quartile of absolute differences within each participant). In all but one domain (infectious diseases), the fluency validity increased from

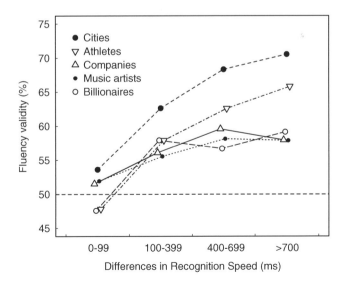

Figure 12.2 The validity of retrieval fluency as a function of increasing differences in retrieval fluency between the two objects (adapted from Hertwig et al.'s, 2008, Figure 2).

the smallest fourth of fluency differences ($M_R = 58\%$, IQR [0.55, 0.61]) to the largest differences ($M_R = 68\%$, IQR [0.60, 0.73]). This implies that inferences based on differences in retrieval fluency are most valid when they are most likely to be correctly assessed—that is, when the differences are large (Hertwig et al., 2008).

How and when do people use retrieval fluency in making quantitative inferences about the world? Clearly, people do not invariably rely on retrieval fluency for their judgments and decisions. Whether and how people use subjective experiences depends on the validity and the direction of the fluency cue, both of which people can extract from experience (i.e., Brunswikian cue learning; Unkelbach, 2006; Unkelbach & Greifeneder, Chapter 2, this volume) and their naïve theories about the mental processes that they apply to the task (e.g., people discount the informational value of their subjective experiences when they attribute them to a non-diagnostic source; Schwarz, 2004). Although there is extensive research on how and when people use cognitive and affective feelings (e.g., Greifeneder et al., 2011; Oppenheimer, 2008; Schwarz, 2004), there are only a few process models in the literature of how they take advantage of their sense of fluency. Schooler and Hertwig (2005; see also Hertwig et al., 2008; Marewski & Schooler, 2011; Volz, Schooler, & von Cramon, 2010) proposed the *fluency heuristic* that infers that the faster of two recognized object scores higher on a criterion, given that the retrieval difference is larger than 100 ms. This fluency heuristic is most useful when people merely recognize two objects, and thus cannot apply knowledge-based strategies; in those cases, using retrieval fluency leads to decisions that are clearly better than chance and people's decisions are well described by the fluency heuristic (Marewski & Schooler, 2011). In contrast, when further knowledge about the objects is available, people seem to use knowledge-based strategies, which tend to be more accurate than the fluency heuristic for such cases (Marewski & Schooler, 2011; see also Hilbig, Erdfelder, & Pohl, 2011).

As of now, we have analyzed the ecological validity of retrieval fluency when inferring numerical quantities of importance in the world. Next, we turn to a different kind of a criterion: the truth (or lack thereof) of a statement.

Is this really true? Inferring the likely truth of statements

"In Malaya, if a man goes to jail for being drunk, his wife goes too." Is this statement true or false? A simple rhetorical tool to increase the perceived truthfulness of such a statement is: repeat it (e.g., Arkes, Boehm, & Xu, 1991; Bacon, 1979; Begg, Anas, & Farinacci, 1992; Brown & Nix, 1996; Hasher, Goldstein, & Toppino, 1977; Hertwig, Gigerenzer, & Hoffrage, 1997; for a meta-analysis see Dechêne, Stahl, Hansen, & Wänke, 2010). As the character Bernard Marx in Aldous Huxley's (1932) *Brave new world* conjectured, "Sixty-two thousand four hundred repetitions make one truth!"

There are two complementary explanations for the effect that repetition increases the perceived truth of statements. First, people may conclude that repeated statements must be true *because* they recall having seen or heard them before (Brown & Nix, 1996; i.e., a form of convergent validity; Arkes et al., 1991). Second, people may unwittingly put more faith in repeated statements because repetition increases processing fluency (Feustel, Shiffrin, & Salasoo, 1983), which in turn increases the perception of truth (Begg et al., 1992). People may judge fluently processed statements as true because they have learned that the experience of fluency "correlates positively with the truth of a statement" (Unkelbach, 2007, p. 219).

But is it reasonable to assume that fluency is a cue to a statement's truth value? Some have argued that "there is no logical reason for repetition to affect rated truth" (Begg et al., 1992, p. 447). In fact, Ludwig Wittgenstein ridiculed the tendency to buy into the veridicality of a statement based on its mere repetition, comparing it to purchasing two copies of the same newspaper to double-check whether the information in the first copy is correct (Kenny, 2006; see Unkelbach, Fiedler, & Freytag, 2007, for an empirical demonstration of this phenomenon). To make matters worse, a statement's processing fluency can be influenced by factors that are totally unrelated to how often one has encountered it in the past. For example, people are more inclined to believe statements the more legible they are (Hansen, Dechêne, & Wänke, 2008; Reber & Schwarz, 1999) or when they rhyme (McGlone & Tofighbakhsh, 2000).

However, there are also arguments as to why there may be an exploitable association between repetition and truth (and thus also between fluency and truth). Russell (1940), Wittgenstein's teacher and colleague at Cambridge, for instance, noted that it is often difficult, if not even impossible, to obtain direct evidence regarding the truth of statements. Based on this premise, Russell argued that it may be reasonable to believe more strongly in a statement as a function of how many other people endorse it. Assuming that one is more likely to encounter a statement the more it is endorsed by people, one could then infer that the more often one encounters a statement, the more people believe it to be true; hence one may infer that the more likely it is to be true. Consistent with this chain of inferences, true factual statements tend to be processed faster (i.e., more fluently) than wrong factual statements (Shtulman & Valcarcel, 2012; Unkelbach & Stahl, 2009). This then implies that, holding everything else constant, true factual statements tend to be repeated more often than wrong factual statements.

Furthermore, a Bayesian analysis (Reber & Unkelbach, 2010) shows that evaluating fluent statements as true ones will result in beliefs that are more likely to be true than mere chance (50 percent) if one is *a priori* more likely to experience true than false statements in the world. The intuition behind the Bayesian argument is as follows (see Reber & Unkelbach, 2010, for a detailed discussion): Arguably, repeatedly encountered statements become more fluent regardless of whether they are actually true, that is, $p(\text{fluent} \mid \text{true}) = p(\text{fluent} \mid \neg\text{true})$. If this premise holds, the posterior probability that a statement is true given that it is fluently processed reduces to the prior probability of the statement being true in the first place (and its complement, the prior probability that the statement is *not* true).

$$p(\text{true} \mid \text{fluent}) = \frac{p(\text{true})}{p(\text{true}) + p(\neg\text{true})} \tag{1}$$

Equation 1 implies that the probability of a statement being true given that it is processed fluently is larger than 50 percent whenever the probability that a randomly encountered statement is true is higher than 50 percent. But why should this prior probability of a statement being true be larger than 50 percent?

To the extent that conversation is a cooperative venture, speakers aim to communicate relevant information (Sperber & Wilson, 1986) and this, among other things, implies that they say what they think is true (see Grice's, 1975, *maxim of quality*). If we can reasonably assume that most other speakers are cooperative in a certain domain, then we can also assume that statements we hear will more likely to be true than not. This in turn implies that the prior probability that a statement is true will be higher than 50 percent and thus fluency will be indicative of truth. Of course, there are domains (e.g., marketing, political campaigns) in which communication tends to be adversarial and competitive rather than cooperative and here fluency is not likely to be a valid cue to the truth status of statements.

Predicting numerical quantities and assessing the truth of statements are important tasks, but they pale in comparison to the importance of the criterion that we will discuss in the next section.

Is it going to kill me? Assessing danger

When organisms encounter an unknown living creature or a novel food, the question arises: Is this new thing dangerous? Is it going to kill me? This question is so important, so evolutionarily old and needs to be "answered" so swiftly that living creatures are likely to have some in-built mechanisms that spit out the answer (LeDoux, 1996). One strategy is to turn the inference—"Is it dangerous?"—into a hard-wired or learned preference—"Do I like it? Do I dislike it?" If organisms avoid dangerous things because they do not like them (or are even afraid of them), then they are more likely to survive and reproduce—also because preferences can inform behavior much faster than inferences (e.g., LeDoux, 1996; Zajonc, 1998).

As we do not know whether a new, unfamiliar object or living being is potentially dangerous, *neophobia*—disliking the new—is an evolutionarily prudent strategy: Start with dislike—be cautious!—and only start liking something to the extent it has proven itself to be innocuous (e.g., Hill, 1978; Kalat & Rozin, 1973). Bornstein (1989, p. 282) argued that:

> Only after repeated exposures coupled with a consistent absence of negative reinforcement associated with the stimulus can one reliably conclude that the object is nonthreatening. A long-term memory of a stimulus with an absence of negative associations is a much more reliable index of (lack of) dangerousness than is a short-term memory trace.

The mirror image of the biological predisposition for caution when encountering novel and potentially harmful objects is the complementary preference for familiar objects (Hill, 1978; Zajonc, 1968, 1998, 2001)[3]—its rationale can be summarized with the slogan: "[A]fter all, these objects have not killed you yet!" (Smith, 2000, p. 119). The phenomenon that humans' and animals' preference for objects increases through repeated exposure is known as the *mere exposure effect* (Zajonc, 1968; Hill, 1978; for reviews see Bornstein, 1989; Zajonc, 2001) and can be seen as a form of classical conditioning where the absence of aversive events—when encountering an object—constitutes the unconditioned stimulus (Zajonc, 2001).

Next we propose a Bayesian analysis that illustrates why repeated exposure is a valid cue for danger (or lack thereof) in the reference class of objects that have not attacked or harmed us yet (see Appendix B for a more detailed treatment). We start with two sets of assumptions. First, every object has a constant probability θ of attacking or harming us in each episode; with the complimentary probability $1 - \theta$, we are "merely exposed" to the object without any experienced harm (or death). Second, we are maximally unsure about the value of this probability θ prior to the first encounter with the object. That is, any value from 0 percent to 100 percent is equally likely a priori (i.e., uniform prior distribution). Given those two assumptions, a Bayesian mean posterior estimate of θ after n harmless episodes is: $p(\text{"hit"} \mid n) = 1/(n + 2)$. Figure 12.3 shows how this "danger

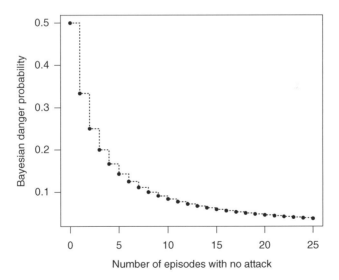

Figure 12.3 Bayesian analysis illustrating why repeated exposure is a valid cue for danger (or lack thereof) in the reference class of objects that have not attacked or harmed us yet. The figure plots the Bayesian mean posterior estimate of the probability θ with which an object attacks or harms us in any episode as a function of the number of harmless episodes so far—assuming an uniform prior distribution over θ: $p(\text{"hit"} \mid n) = 1/(n + 2)$. See main text and Appendix B for details.

probability" θ decreases as the number of harmless episodes increases: After 0, 1, 2, 3, 4 or 5 episodes, p("hit" | n) takes values of 50%, 33%, 25%, 20%, 17% and 14%, respectively. Because the decrease slows down as n increases, 10 harmless episodes can make us confident that in all likelihood the object is harmless; $p($"hit" $| n = 10) = 8\%$. Although purely speculative, this marginal decrease in assessed dangerousness coincides with the observation that the mere exposure effect typically levels off after ten to 20 presentations (Bornstein, 1989), which translates into danger probabilities of 8 percent to 5 percent in our analysis.

Because the repeated exposure to an object increases its retrieval fluency (e.g., Anderson & Schooler, 2000; Jacoby & Dallas, 1981), keeping everything else constant, high retrieval fluency signals safety. An inbuilt preference for fluent objects is thus adaptive because—according to our analysis—more fluently recognized objects tend to be less dangerous than less fluently retrieved objects. (We assume here that any negative reinforcement due to a harmful episode with an object, for example, an attack or food poisoning, can override the danger assessment based on retrieval fluency; that is, fluency's validity is conditional on not yet being attacked or harmed by an object; see also Bornstein's, 1989, quote above.)

Monkey see, monkey do? Retrieval fluency, imitation, and other people's behavior

Retrieval fluency not only predicts numerical quantities, truth and danger, but also signals social information: It is a cue to popularity because the more popular something is (e.g., a brand name, a movie, or a financial service) the more often one encounters it in everyday life (e.g., in conversations, on the streets, in newspapers, or in advertisements) and thus the higher its retrieval fluency. As a consequence, whenever a person chooses the more fluent out of two options (e.g., two brands of wine), she is likely to choose what most other people would choose—at least above chance level (see Todd & Heuvelink, 2007, for a related argument for recognition). Retrieval fluency can thus be used as a cue in social heuristics (Hertwig & Herzog, 2009), such as the *imitate-the-majority heuristic* (Boyd & Richerson, 2005; Hertwig, Hoffrage, & the ABC Research Group, 2012).

When people are unsure about what to do, they often look to what other people are doing (e.g., Bikhchandani, Hirshleifer, & Welch, 1998; Boyd & Richerson, 1985, 2005; Festinger, 1954). But why would they be interested in other people's behavior and imitate it? Let us distinguish two broad classes of domains, namely, matters of fact (e.g., which of two projects will be more successful?) and matters of taste (e.g., which of two songs is "better"?).

When it comes to *matters of fact*, imitation can improve our decisions to the extent that one can profit from the "wisdom of the crowds" (Surowiecki, 2004). For example, when we are unsure about how fast we are allowed to drive in a foreign country, we might adjust our speed so that we drive as fast (or even a bit slower) than most other drivers. Imitation is generally a good strategy whenever environments are stable (i.e., the "correct answers" do not change rapidly), individual learning is costly, and when there are original learners in the population (i.e., not everybody is copying everybody else; Bikhchandani et al., 1998; Boyd & Richerson, 1985, 2005). Under those conditions, decisions based on retrieval fluency are likely to be good because retrieval fluency tracks the wisdom of crowds.

In contrast, when it comes to *matters of taste*, there are—by definition—no agreed upon objective criteria. In many domains, whatever happens to be popular (i.e., what most people are thinking or doing) can, but does not need to, reflect objective "goodness" of the thing in question; rather, popularity *defines* a socially validated reality. For example, although a band may be (objectively) better than another in terms of technical skills, listeners may still widely disagree as to which one plays the better music. Consider the following experimental study as an illustration (Salganik, Dodds, & Watts, 2006). In an artificial music market, consumers were able to download novel songs for free and could see how often other consumers had downloaded them previously. Not surprisingly, consumers' choices were influenced by the observed behavior of other consumers. As a consequence, some songs gained momentum and increased in popularity (i.e., downloads) partly by the mere fact that they—for whatever arbitrary reason— happened to be preferred in the early stages of the evolution of the market. Salganik et al. (2006) implemented several instances of such a market. Although those "parallel universes" were identical with respect to their starting conditions, the resulting popularity rankings of the songs turned out to be markedly different because different songs initially gained popularity for partly arbitrary reasons. Consequently, popularity was only weakly predicted by the inherent "quality" of the songs, as measured by the popularity ranking from a control condition where no social information was available and participants' choices thus only reflected their taste and the songs' characteristics. In sum, imitation behavior made some songs popular and others not.

When popularity socially defines—rather than just merely reflects—criteria, cues that track popularity—such as retrieval fluency—are valid cues by definition. Their validity only depends on how well they track popularity. Yet, popularity always needs to be defined relative to a reference class of people. It could, for example, pertain to the musical taste of all citizens of a nation (e.g., reflected in nationwide music charts) or of one's social class (Bourdieu, 1979/1984). Because we share with our proximate reference groups the exposure to similar objects (e.g., artifacts, events, activities, cultural products like music; Bourdieu, 1979/1984; Reber & Norenzayan, 2010), retrieval fluency will also reflect what is popular within our reference groups—in addition to what is popular in more general terms (see also Reber, Chapter 11, this volume).

When it comes to matters of taste, there are at least three reasons why going with the more fluent—and thus in all likelihood more popular—option can be advantageous. First, doing what most people do can bring coordination gains (e.g., Schelling, 1980; Todd & Heuvelink, 2007). For example, if people visit bars whose names they fluently retrieve from memory (e.g., because they have repeatedly heard other people gushing about it), then they will end up going to the same places and can enjoy the atmosphere of a busily crowded bar.

Second, doing what most people do can bring *social gains*. Humans want to belong to other people (Baumeister & Leary, 1995) and strive to be similar—but not too similar—to people from significant reference groups (Brewer, 1991; Leonardelli, Pickett, & Brewer, 2010). Whenever we want to blend in with others (e.g., with respect to food, drinks, clothing, music, or literature), choosing the more fluent of two options (e.g., two brands of beer) will help reach this goal. Indeed, when consumers feel too dissimilar from other people, they prefer popular products to unpopular products (He, Cong, Liu, & Zhou, 2010); choosing more fluent consumer products could thus be a strategy to blend in again. Furthermore, because shared exposure to the same objects increases social cohesiveness (Reber & Norenzayan, 2010), choosing popular options should thus increase social cohesion.

There is still another, third way, in which choosing the more fluent and thus more popular option can be advantageous. In many domains, people differ in their tastes, are cognizant of their preferences and therefore can implement them. For example, some people prefer and order French red wines, whereas others prefer and order Californian red wines. Some people enjoy and watch action movies, whereas others enjoy and watch documentaries about wildlife. In other domains, however, people differ in their tastes, but because they lack the relevant first-hand experiences, they may not yet know—at the time of initial choice—which option they are going to enjoy more. Take, for instance, a tourist who plans to visit the Canary Islands. But which one? After having visited, say, Tenerife and Fuerteventura the traveler could probably say whether she is more a Tenerife or a Fuerteventura "type," but she does not know it ahead of time. Thus, unless the tourist has some insightful private information about her likely preferences, her choice task amounts to inferring which type she is.

From a Bayesian perspective, as soon as one type of preference is more prevalent in the population than the other and thus represents the majority preference (e.g., most people prefer Tenerife over Fuerteventura), an agent is a priori more likely to have this preference than not—unless there is strong "private evidence" to the contrary (e.g., the tourist has already visited both islands and prefers Fuerteventura over Tenerife). This is because the posterior probability that the agent has this majority preference equals the base rate of this preference in the population in the absence of private, diagnostic evidence. And even if the agent should have some private, diagnostic evidence, the posterior probability will—through the logic of Bayes theorem (integration of private evidence with base rates)—be at least partly determined by the base rate. Because fluency tracks the popularity of options, as we have argued above, choosing the more fluent option (e.g., Tenerife) amounts to choosing the option that is more likely one's preferred option—unless one knows otherwise. Fluency is thus a helpful cue in novel domains where one lacks clear preferences and relevant experience.

Conclusion

Although we know a lot about how and when fluency influences our judgments and decisions (see e.g., Oppenheimer, 2008; Schwarz, 2004), we are only starting to understand when it is an ecologically valid cue for the world that we live in. As we have reviewed in this chapter, fluency can help us navigate an uncertain world because it reflects the statistical structure of our environment and thus connects our minds to the world. We can then use this ecological connection between fluency and the world to inform our judgments and decisions. For example, retrieval fluency—the speed with which we retrieve objects from memory—reflects numerical quantities of importance, the truth of statements, the danger of objects and social information about what other people are doing. But there is certainly more to be learned. We hope we have been able to persuade other fluency researchers to open the next chapter in the investigation of fluency: the descriptive and normative chapter delineating those environmental and social conditions that turn fluency into an ecologically valid cue and those that rob it of its validity.

Acknowledgment

Stefan M. Herzog, Max Planck Institute for Human Development, Berlin; Ralph Hertwig, Max Planck Institute for Human Development, Berlin.

We thank Rolf Reber and Christian Unkelbach for helpful comments, Benjamin Hilbig, Julian Marewski, Thorsten Pachur and Lael Schooler for providing us with their raw data, Laura Wiles for editing the manuscript, and the Swiss National Science Foundation for a grant to the first and to the second author (100014-129572/1).

Notes

1 Because of skewness and thick tails in the data, we used robust statistics (e.g., Erceg-Hurn & Mirosevich, 2008) to summarize the data within a domain, as well as across domains. We used the 20%-trimmed mean as a robust measure of central tendency (abbreviated as "M_R"); it is a better estimator of the population mean than the sample mean when the data are not normally distributed (Wilcox & Keselman, 2003).

2 We have conceptualized retrieval fluency as the speed with which a word is recognized (Hertwig et al., 2008; Schooler & Hertwig, 2005). Others, however, adopted a broader conception of retrieval fluency that, next to quantitative differences in recognition speed, also uses the distinction between a "recognized" and a "not recognized" judgment as a qualitative difference in retrieval fluency (e.g., Newell & Fernandez, 2006; but see Schooler & Hertwig, 2005). The ecological validity of recognition is defined as the proportion of correct decisions that a person would make if she always inferred that the recognized object has the larger criterion value than the unrecognized object among all possible pairings of objects in the environment where one object is recognized and the other is not (see Goldstein & Gigerenzer's, 2002, *recognition validity*). Ecological validity of retrieval fluency and recognition both thrive on the same environmental frequencies mediating between the criterion and memory (see Figure 12.1). Therefore, studies showing that reliance on recognition results in relatively accurate inferences in a domain by extension also indicate that retrieval fluency would be a valid cue in those domains (for overviews on the ecological validity of recognition, see Gigerenzer & Goldstein, 2011; Herzog & Hertwig, 2011; Pachur, Todd, et al., 2012). The recognition validity, however, will inevitably be larger than the respective fluency validity within the same domain because recognized and unrecognized objects differ, on average, more

in their activation strengths (and thus environmental frequencies) than two recognized objects (see Hertwig et al., 2008, p. 1203). The validity of such a more inclusive conception of retrieval fluency (including the qualitative difference between recognized and not recognized) would thus lie between that of retrieval fluency proper and that of recognition.

3 The preference for familiar stimuli seems to contradict the notion that humans and animals often show a behavioral preference for novelty (e.g., a rat's preference for a new, unfamiliar compartment; e.g., Bardo, Bowling, Robinet, Rowlett, Lacy, & Mattingly, 1993). This seeming contradiction can be resolved, however, by noting that evaluative and behavioral preferences are not the same. Zajonc (1968, p. 21) argued that "orienting toward a novel stimulus in preference to a familiar one may indicate that it is less liked rather than it is better liked. Ordinarily, when confronted with a novel stimulus the animal's orienting response enables it to discover if the novel stimulus constitutes a source of danger. It need not explore familiar stimuli in this respect."

References

Algina, J., Keselman, H. J., & Penfield, R. D. (2005). An alternative to Cohen's standardized mean difference effect size: A robust parameter and confidence interval in the two independent groups case. *Psychological Methods*, *10*, 317–328.

Alter, A. L., & Oppenheimer, D. M. (2006). Predicting short-term stock fluctuations by using processing fluency. *Proceedings of the National Academy of Sciences of the United States of America*, *103*, 9369–9372.

—— (2009). Uniting the tribes of fluency to form a metacognitive nation. *Personality and Social Psychology Review*, *13*, 219–235.

Anderson, J. R., & Milson, R. (1989). Human memory: An adaptive perspective. *Psychological Review*, *96*, 703–719.

Anderson, J. R., & Schooler, L. J. (1991). Reflections of the environment in memory. *Psychological Science*, *2*, 396–408.

—— (2000). The adaptive nature of memory. In F. I. M. Craik & E. Tulving (Eds.), *The Oxford handbook of memory* (pp. 557–570). Oxford: Oxford University Press.

Arkes, H. R., Boehm, L. E., & Xu, G. (1991). Determinants of judged validity. *Journal of Experimental Social Psychology*, *27*, 576–605.

Bacon, F. T. (1979). Credibility of repeated statements: Memory for trivia. *Journal of Experimental Psychology: Human Learning and Memory*, *5*, 241–252.

Bardo, M. T., Bowling, S. L., Robinet, P. M., Rowlett, J. K., Lacy, M., & Mattingly, B. A. (1993). Role of dopamine D1 and D2 receptors in novelty-maintained place preference. *Experimental and Clinical Psychopharmacology*, *1*, 101–109.

Baumeister, R. F., & Leary, M. R. (1995). The need to belong: Desire for interpersonal attachments as a fundamental human motivation. *Psychological Bulletin*, *117*, 497–529.

Baumeister, R. F., Zhang, L., & Vohs, K. D. (2004). Gossip as cultural learning. *Review of General Psychology*, *8*, 111–121.

Begg, I. M., Anas, A., & Farinacci, S. (1992). Dissociation of processes in belief: Source recollection, statement familiarity, and the illusion of truth. *Journal of Experimental Psychology: General*, *121*, 446–458.

Bikhchandani, S., Hirshleifer, D., & Welch, I. (1998). Learning from the behavior of others: Conformity, fads, and informational cascades. *Journal of Economic Perspectives*, *12*, 151–170.

Bless, H., & Forgas, J. P. (Eds.), (2000). *The message within: The role of subjective experience in social cognition and behavior.* Philadelphia: Psychology Press.

Bornstein, R. F. (1989). Exposure and affect: Overview and meta-analysis of research, 1968–1987. *Psychological Bulletin, 106,* 265–289.

Bourdieu, P. (1979/1984). *Distinction: A social critique of the judgment of taste* (R. Nice, Trans.). Cambridge, MA: Harvard University Press.

Boyd, R., & Richerson, P. J. (1985). *Culture and the evolutionary process.* Chicago: University of Chicago Press.

—— (2005). *The origin and evolution of cultures.* Oxford: Oxford University Press.

Brewer, M. B. (1991). The social self: On being the same and different at the same time. *Personality and Social Psychology Bulletin, 17,* 475–482.

Brown, A. S., & Nix, L. A. (1996). Turning lies into truths: Referential validation of falsehoods. *Journal of Experimental Psychology: Learning, Memory, and Cognition, 22,* 1088–1100.

Brunswik, E. (1952). The conceptual framework of psychology. In *International encyclopedia of unified science* (Vol. 1, No. 10, pp. 656–760). Chicago: University of Chicago Press.

—— (1956). *Perception and the representative design of psychological experiments.* Berkeley: University of California Press.

Cohen, J. (1988). *Statistical power analysis for the behavioral sciences* (2nd ed.). Hillsdale, NJ: Erlbaum.

Davis, H., & McLeod, S. L. (2003). Why humans value sensational news: An evolutionary perspective. *Evolution and Human Behavior, 24,* 208–216.

Dawes, R. M. (2001). *Everyday irrationality: How pseudo-scientists, lunatics, and the rest of us systematically fail to think rationally.* Boulder, CO: Westview Press.

Dechêne, A., Stahl, C., Hansen, J., & Wänke, M. (2010). The truth about the truth: A meta-analytic review of the truth effect. *Personality and Social Psychology Review, 14,* 238–257.

Dhami, M. K., Hertwig, R., & Hoffrage, U. (2004). The role of representative design in an ecological approach to cognition. *Psychological Bulletin, 130,* 959–988.

Dunbar, R. I. M. (2004). Gossip in evolutionary perspective. *Review of General Psychology, 8,* 100–110.

Erceg-Hurn, D. M., & Mirosevich, V. M. (2008). Modern robust statistical methods: An easy way to maximize the accuracy and power of your research. *American Psychologist, 63,* 591–601.

Festinger, L. (1954). A theory of social comparison processes. *Human Relations, 7,* 117–140.

Feustel, T. C., Shiffrin, R. M., & Salasoo, A. (1983). Episodic and lexical contributions to the repetition effect in word identification. *Journal of Experimental Psychology: General, 112,* 309–346.

Foster, E. K. (2004). Research on gossip: Taxonomy, methods, and future directions. *Review of General Psychology, 8,* 78–99.

Funder, D. C. (1987). Errors and mistakes: Evaluating the accuracy of social judgment. *Psychological Bulletin, 101,* 75–90.

Gaissmaier, W. (2007). *The mnemonic decision maker: How search in memory shapes decision making.* Doctoral dissertation, Freie Universität Berlin, Berlin, Germany.

Gigerenzer, G. (1996). On narrow norms and vague heuristics: A reply to Kahneman and Tversky (1996). *Psychological Review, 103,* 592–596.

Gigerenzer, G., & Goldstein, D. G. (2011). The recognition heuristic: A decade of research. *Judgment and Decision Making, 6,* 100–121.

Gilovich, T., Griffin, D., & Kahneman, D. (Eds.), (2002). *Heuristics and biases: The psychology of intuitive judgment*. New York: Cambridge University Press.

Goldstein, D. G., & Gigerenzer, G. (2002). Models of ecological rationality: The recognition heuristic. *Psychological Review, 109*, 75–90.

Green, T., & Jame, R. (2011). *Company name fluency, investor recognition, and firm value*. Unpublished manuscript.

Greifeneder, R., Bless, H., & Pham, M. T. (2011). When do people rely on affective and cognitive feelings in judgment? A review. *Personality and Social Psychology Review, 15*, 107–141.

Grice, H. P. (1975). Logic and conversation. In P. Cole & J. L. Morgan (Eds.), *Syntax and semantics: Speech acts* (Vol. 3, pp. 41–58). New York: Academic Press.

Hansen, J., Dechêne, A., & Wänke, M. (2008). Discrepant fluency increases subjective truth. *Journal of Experimental Social Psychology, 44*, 687–691.

Hasher, L., Goldstein, D., & Toppino, T. (1977). Frequency and the conference of referential validity. *Journal of Verbal Learning and Verbal Behavior, 16*, 107–112.

He, L., Cong, F., Liu, Y., & Zhou, X. (2010). The pursuit of optimal distinctiveness and consumer preferences. *Scandinavian Journal of Psychology, 51*, 411–417.

Hertwig, R., Gigerenzer, G., & Hoffrage, U. (1997). The reiteration effect in hindsight bias. *Psychological Review, 104*, 194–202.

Hertwig, R., & Herzog, S. M. (2009). Fast and frugal heuristics: Tools of social rationality. *Social Cognition, 27*, 661–698.

Hertwig, R., Herzog, S. M., Schooler, L. J., & Reimer, T. (2008). Fluency heuristic: A model of how the mind exploits a by-product of information retrieval. *Journal of Experimental Psychology: Learning, Memory, and Cognition, 34*, 1191–1206.

Hertwig, R., Hoffrage, U., & the ABC Research Group (2012). *Simple heuristics in a social world*. New York: Oxford University Press.

Hertwig, R., Pachur, T., & Kurzenhäuser, S. (2005). Judgments of risk frequencies: Tests of possible cognitive mechanisms. *Journal of Experimental Psychology: Learning, Memory, and Cognition, 31*, 621–642.

Herzog, S. M., & Hertwig, R. (2011). The wisdom of ignorant crowds: Predicting sport outcomes by mere recognition. *Judgment and Decision Making, 6*, 58–72.

Herzog, S. M., Hertwig, R., & Steinmann, F. (2011). *Can experts mimic laypeople's "ignorance"?* Manuscript in preparation.

Hilbig, B. E. (2010). Reconsidering "evidence" for fast-and-frugal heuristics. *Psychonomic Bulletin & Review, 17*, 923–930.

Hilbig, B. E., Erdfelder, E., & Pohl, R. F. (2010). [Recognition probabilities and speeds for the 261 most populous U.S. cities]. Unpublished raw data.

—— (2011). Fluent, fast, and frugal? A formal model evaluation of the interplay between memory, fluency, and comparative judgments. *Journal of Experimental Psychology: Learning, Memory, and Cognition, 37*, 827–839.

Hilbig, B. E., & Pohl, R. F. (2009). Ignorance- versus evidence-based decision making: A decision time analysis of the recognition heuristic. *Journal of Experimental Psychology: Learning, Memory, and Cognition, 35*, 1296–1305.

Hill, W. F. (1978). Effects of mere exposure on preferences in nonhuman mammals. *Psychological Bulletin, 85*, 1177–1198.

Huxley, A. (1932). *Brave new world*. London: Chatto & Windus.

Jacoby, L. L., & Dallas, M. (1981). On the relationship between autobiographical memory and perceptual learning. *Journal of Experimental Psychology: General, 110*, 306–340.

Kahneman, D., & Tversky, A. (1982). On the study of statistical intuitions. *Cognition, 11*, 123–141.

Kahneman, D., Slovic, P., & Tversky, A. (Eds.), (1982). *Judgment under uncertainty: Heuristics and biases*. New York: Cambridge University Press.

Kalat, J. W., & Rozin. P. (1973). "Learned safety" as a mechanism in long-delay taste-aversion learning in rats. *Journal of Comparative and Physiological Psychology*, *83*, 198–207.

Kenny, A. (2006). *Wittgenstein*. Oxford: Blackwell.

Keynes, J. M. (1921). *A treatise on probability*. London: Macmillan.

Krueger, J. I., & Funder, D. C. (2004). Towards a balanced social psychology: Causes, consequences, and cures for the problem-seeking approach to social behavior and cognition. *Behavioral and Brain Sciences*, *27*, 313–376.

Kruschke, J. K. (2011). *Doing Bayesian data analysis: A tutorial with R and BUGS*. Burlington, MA: Academic Press.

LeDoux, J. E. (1996). *The emotional brain*. New York: Simon & Schuster.

Leonardelli, G. J., Pickett, C. L., & Brewer, M. B. (2010). Optimal distinctiveness theory: A framework for social identity, social cognition and intergroup relations. In M. Zanna & J. Olson (Eds.), *Advances in Experimental Social Psychology* (Vol. 43, pp. 63–113). New York: Elsevier.

Marewski, J. N., & Schooler, L. J. (2011). Cognitive niches: An ecological model of strategy selection. *Psychological Review*, *118*, 393–437.

Martignon, L., & Hoffrage, U. (2002). Fast, frugal, and fit: Simple heuristics for paired comparison. *Theory and Decision*, *52*, 29–71.

McGlone, M. S., & Tofighbakhsh, J. (2000). Birds of a feather flock conjointly (?): Rhyme as reason in aphorisms. *Psychological Science*, *11*, 424–428.

Oppenheimer, D. M. (2008). The secret life of fluency. *Trends in Cognitive Sciences*, *12*, 237–241.

Newell, B. R., & Fernandez, D. (2006). On the binary quality of recognition and the inconsequentiality of further knowledge: Two critical tests of the recognition heuristic. *Journal of Behavioral Decision Making*, *19*, 333–346.

Pachur, T., & Hertwig, R. (2006). On the psychology of the recognition heuristic: Retrieval primacy as a key determinant of its use. *Journal of Experimental Psychology: Learning, Memory, and Cognition*, *32*, 983–1002.

Pachur, T., Rieskamp, J., & Hertwig, R. (2012). *Judging social statistics: How exhaustive does sampling need to be?* Manuscript submitted for publication.

Pachur, T., Schooler, L. J., & Stevens, J. R. (2012). When will we meet again? Regularities in the dynamics of social contact reflected in memory and decision making. In R. Hertwig, U. Hoffrage, & the ABC Research Group (Eds.), *Simple heuristics in a social world* (pp. 199–224). New York: Oxford University Press.

Pachur, T., Todd, P. M., Gigerenzer, G., Schooler, L. J., & Goldstein, D. G. (2012). When is the recognition heuristic an adaptive tool? In P. Todd, G. Gigerenzer, & the ABC Research Group (Eds.), *Ecological rationality: Intelligence in the world* (pp. 113–143). New York: Oxford University Press.

Pham, M. T. (2004). The logic of feeling. *Journal of Consumer Psychology*, *14*, 360–369.

—— (2007). Emotion and rationality: A critical review and interpretation of empirical evidence. *Review of General Psychology*, *11*, 155–178.

Piattelli-Palmarini, M. (1994) *Inevitable illusions: How mistakes of reason rule our minds*. New York: John Wiley & Sons.

Pohl, R. F. (2006). Empirical tests of the recognition heuristic. *Journal of Behavioral Decision Making, 19*, 251–271.

Reber, R., & Norenzayan, A. (2010). *The shared fluency theory of social cohesiveness*. Unpublished manuscript.

Reber, R., & Schwarz, N. (1999). Effects of perceptual fluency on judgments of truth. *Consciousness and Cognition*, *8*, 338–342.

Reber, R., Schwarz, N., & Winkielman, P. (2004). Processing fluency and aesthetic pleasure: Is beauty in the perceiver's processing experience? *Personality and Social Psychology Review*, *8*, 364–382.

Reber, R., & Unkelbach, C. (2010). The epistemic status of processing fluency as source for judgments of truth. *Review of Philosophy and Psychology*, *1*, 563–581.

Richter, T., & Späth, P. (2006). Recognition is used as one cue among others in judgment and decision making. *Journal of Experimental Psychology: Learning, Memory, and Cognition*, *32*, 150–162.

Russell, B. (1940). *An inquiry into meaning and truth*. New York: Norton.

Salganik, M. J., Dodds, P. S., & Watts, D. J. (2006). Experimental study of inequality and unpredictability in an artificial cultural market. *Science*, *311*, 854–856.

Scheibehenne, B., & Bröder, A. (2007). Predicting Wimbledon 2005 tennis results by mere player name recognition? *International Journal of Forecasting*, *23*, 415–426.

Schelling, T. C. (1980). *The strategy of conflict*. Cambridge, MA: Harvard University Press.

Schooler, L. J., & Anderson, J. R. (1997). The role of process in the rational analysis of memory. *Cognitive Psychology*, *32*, 219–250.

Schooler, L. J., & Hertwig, R. (2005). How forgetting aids heuristic inference. *Psychological Review*, *112*, 610–628.

Schwarz, N. (2002). Situated cognition and the wisdom of feelings: Cognitive tuning. In L. F. Feldman Barrett & P. Salovey (Eds.), *The wisdom in feelings* (pp. 144–166). New York: Guilford.

—— (2004). Meta-cognitive experiences in consumer judgment and decision making. *Journal of Consumer Psychology*, *14*, 332–348.

—— (2011). Feelings-as-information theory. In P. Van Lange, A. Kruglanski, & E. T. Higgins (Eds.), *Handbook of theories of social psychology* (Vol. 1, pp. 289–308). Los Angeles, CA: Sage.

Schwarz, N., & Clore, G. L. (2007). Feelings and phenomenal experiences. In A. Kruglanski & E. T. Higgins (Eds.), *Social psychology: A handbook of basic principles* (2nd ed., pp. 385–407). New York: Guilford Press.

Shah, A. K., & Oppenheimer, D. M. (2008). Heuristics made easy: An effort-reduction framework. *Psychological Bulletin*, *134*, 207–222.

Shtulman, A., & Valcarcel, J. (2012). Scientific knowledge suppresses but does not supplant earlier intuitions. *Cognition*, *124*, 209–215.

Simon, H. A. (1990). Invariants of human behavior. *Annual Review of Psychology*, *41*, 1–20.

Skurnik, I., Yoon, C., Park, D. C., & Schwarz, N. (2005). How warnings about false claims become recommendations. *Journal of Consumer Research*, *31*, 713–724.

Smith, E. R. (2000). Subjective experience of familiarity: Functional basis in connectionist memory. In H. Bless & J. P. Forgas (Eds.), *The message within: The role of subjective experience in social cognition and behavior* (pp. 109–124). Philadelphia: Psychology Press.

Sperber, D., & Wilson, D. (1986). *Relevance: Communication and cognition*. Oxford: Blackwell.

Surowiecki, J. (2004). *The wisdom of crowds*. New York: Doubleday.

Todd, P., & Heuvelink, A. (2007). Shaping social environments with simple recognition heuristics. In P. Carruthers, S. Laurence, & S. Stich (Eds.), *The innate mind: Culture and cognition* (pp. 165–181). Oxford: Oxford University Press.

Topolinski, S., & Strack, F. (2010). False fame prevented: Avoiding fluency effects without judgmental correction. *Journal of Personality and Social Psychology*, *98*, 721–733.

Tversky, A., & Kahneman, D. (1974). Judgment under uncertainty: Heuristics and biases. *Science*, *185*, 1124–1131.

Unkelbach, C. (2006). The learned interpretation of cognitive fluency. *Psychological Science*, *17*, 339–345.

—— (2007). Reversing the truth effect: Learning the interpretation of processing fluency in judgments of truth. *Journal of Experimental Psychology: Learning, Memory, and Cognition*, *33*, 219–230.

Unkelbach, C., Fiedler, K., & Freytag, P. (2007). Information repetition in evaluative judgments: Easy to monitor, hard to control. *Organizational Behavior and Human Decision Processes*, *103*, 37–52.

Unkelbach, C., & Stahl, C. (2009). A multinomial modeling approach to dissociate different components of the truth effect. *Consciousness & Cognition*, *18*, 22–38.

Volz, K. G., Schooler, L. J., & von Cramon, D. Y. (2010). It just felt right: The neural correlates of the fluency heuristic. *Consciousness and Cognition*, *19*, 829–837.

Whittlesea, B. W. A. (2004). The perception of integrality: Remembering through the validation of expectation. *Journal of Experimental Psychology: Learning, Memory, and Cognition*, *30*, 891–908.

Whittlesea, B. W. A., & Leboe, J. P. (2000). The heuristic basis of remembering and classification: Fluency, generation, and resemblance. *Journal of Experimental Psychology: General*, *129*, 84–106.

Wilcox, R. R., & Keselman, H. J. (2003). Modern robust data analysis methods: Measures of central tendency. *Psychological Methods*, *8*, 254–274.

Winkielman, P., Schwarz, N., Fazendeiro, T. A., & Reber, R. (2003). The hedonic marking of processing fluency: Implications for evaluative judgment. In J. Musch & K. C. Klauer (Eds.), *The psychology of evaluation: Affective processes in cognition and emotion* (pp. 189–217). Mahwah, NJ: Erlbaum.

Zajonc, R. B. (1968). Attitudinal effects of mere exposure. *Journal of Personality and Social Psychology Monograph Supplement*, *9*, 1–27.

—— (1998). Emotions. In D. T. Gilbert, S. T. Fiske, & G. Lindzey (Eds.), *The handbook of social psychology* (pp. 591–632). Boston, MA: McGraw-Hill.

—— (2001). Mere exposure: A gateway to the subliminal. *Current Directions in Psychological Science*, *10*, 224–228.

Appendix A

Our literature search was conducted as follows. We constructed search terms by combining "fluency," "ease," "meta-cognitive experience," "meta-cognitive experiences," "experience," or "experiences" with "validity" or "accuracy" to form strings (e.g., "fluency validity" or "accuracy of meta-cognitive experiences") and then searched PsycInfo and GoogleScholar on November 4, 2010. On PsycInfo, we found a total of 40 hits, but most articles concerned reading and mathematical skills. Our searches turned up more hits on GoogleScholar, but suffered from a very low specificity. In our experience, the most informative search query was ["fluency validity" OR "fluency * validity" OR "validity of fluency"], which yielded 82 hits on GoogleScholar.

We further performed a citation pearl search by inspecting the cited and citing references of the following papers: Alter and Oppenheimer (2006, 2009), Hertwig et al. (2008), Oppenheimer (2008), Reber and Unkelbach (2010), Schooler and Hertwig (2005), Unkelbach (2006, 2009), and Unkelbach and Stahl (2009). We also contacted several key researchers and asked them to name, in their view, potentially relevant articles concerned with the ecological validity of fluency.

We identified the following references as relevant: Alter and Oppenheimer (2006), Green and Jame (2011), Hertwig et al. (2005, 2008), Hilbig (2010), Hilbig, Erdfelder, and Pohl (2011), Hilbig and Pohl (2009), Marewski and Schooler (2011), Pachur and Hertwig (2006), Schooler and Hertwig (2005), Unkelbach and Stahl (2009); as well as unpublished data from Herzog, Hertwig, and Steinmann (2011), Hilbig, Erdfelder, and Pohl (2010), and Pachur, Rieskamp, and Hertwig (2012). The raw data from Newell and Fernandez (2006, Study 2) were not available in a form amenable to re-analysis. Gaissmaier (2007, Chapter 3) discusses how retrieval fluency can inform the cue search order of knowledge-based strategies; we will not discuss this approach in this chapter.

Appendix B

In what follows, we develop the Bayesian answer to the question: What is the probability that an object will attack me in the next episode given that it has not yet attacked me in n (e.g., 5) previous episodes?

We start with two sets of assumptions. First, every object has a constant probability θ of attacking or harming us in each episode; with the complementary probability $1 - \theta$, we are "merely exposed" to the object without any experienced harm (or death). Second, we are maximally unsure about the value of this probability θ prior to the first encounter with the object. That is, any value from 0 percent to 100 percent is equally likely *a priori* (i.e., uniform prior distribution).

The Bayesian mean posterior probability of getting a "hit" (i.e., an attack) in the next trial after observing m "hits" (i.e., attacks) in n previous trials (i.e., episodes) and assuming a uniform prior distribution is (see, e.g., Kruschke, 2011, p. 84): $p(\text{"hit"} \mid n, m) = (m + 1)/(n + 2)$. In our analysis, there are by definition no hits (i.e., no attacks, that is, $m = 0$) and thus the formula simplifies to $p(\text{"hit"} \mid n, m = 0) = 1/(n + 2)$. The Bayesian mean posterior estimate of the probability that an object will attack me in the next episode given that it has not yet attacked me in n episodes is thus: $p(\text{"hit"} \mid n) = 1/(n + 2)$. One can, of course, assume other prior distributions. For instance, more "pessimistic" priors put more weight on *high* values of θ a priori, and will squeeze the curve in Figure 12.3 upwards; more "optimistic" priors put more weight on *low* values of θ a priori and will squeeze the curve downwards.

Our analysis can be seen as the reversal of Laplace's *rule of succession* (Keynes, 1921, pp. 367–383) and could thus be called the *rule of non-succession*. Let us briefly illustrate the rule of succession. We assume an event x (e.g., the rising of the sun in the morning) that has been successively observed n times (e.g., for 1,000 mornings). Prior to the first observation, one was completely uncertain about the value of the probability that this event x will happen (i.e., we assume an uniform prior). Then, the Bayesian mean posterior probability of the hypothesis H that x will happen in the observation period $n + 1$ is $p(H \mid n) = (n + 1)/(n + 2)$. For the example above, this probability is thus $(1,000 + 1)/(1,000 + 2) = 99.9\%$. Whereas in our Bayesian mere-exposure analysis the number of "hits" m equals zero (by definition), in the rule of succession m equals the number of trials n (by definition). When plotting $p(H \mid n)$ as a function of n, one will obtain a mirror curve of the one shown in Figure 12.3 (i.e., imagine mirroring the curve at a horizontal line at .5); as the number of successive observations increase, so does $p(H \mid n)$.

13 About swift defaults and sophisticated safety nets

A process perspective on fluency's validity in judgment

Rainer Greifeneder, Herbert Bless and Sabine G. Scholl

Abstract

Western societies usually cherish rational thought but distrust their feelings as sound basis of information. Contrary to this perception of feelings as being maladaptive, this contribution argues that fluency experiences generally allow for valid judgments and decision. For this argument, we focus on the processes underlying the use of fluency in judgment, in particular the two process steps of attribution and interpretation. We argue that these two process steps operate on swift defaults but are backed-up with sophisticated safety nets. Together, defaults and safety-nets allow for both efficient judgment formation and generally valid judgments. We conclude that it is time to have more faith in fluency as information when forming judgments.

Western societies cherish rational thought and recommend reaching important judgments and decisions via conscious deliberation of content information. Reliance on feelings, in contrast, is often considered erroneous and fallible (e.g., Elster, 1999). Undoubtedly, if politicians or CEOs justified decisions by referring to "how it feels," they would be perceived as spooky at best, if not downright irresponsible. This reputation of feelings as irrational is noteworthy because individuals frequently rely on fluency experiences in judgment (see Greifeneder, Bless, & Pham, 2011, for a recent review of empirical evidence). Would such frequent reliance have evolved, if reliance on fluency was generally misleading? Contrary to such a pessimistic perspective, we argue that fluency experiences may promote valid judgments. For this argument, we presuppose that fluency is generally an ecologically valid source of information (see also Herzog & Hertwig, Chapter 12, this volume). Going beyond such *source validity*, we adopt a process perspective and examine to what extent two of the critical process steps in fluency-based judgments—attribution and interpretation (see Unkelbach & Greifeneder, Chapter 2, this volume)—may promote or hamper *judgment validity*. We suggest that these two process steps operate on swift defaults which are, however, backed-up with sophisticated safety nets. We believe that a more refined understanding of judgment validity is critical given that individuals rely on fluency when forming important judgments and decisions, such as whether to display trust or cooperative behavior (Greifeneder, Müller, Stahlberg, Van den Bos, & Bless, 2011a, 2011b; Müller, Greifeneder, Stahlberg, Van den Bos, & Bless, 2010).

The present chapter is organized as follows. First, we reflect on why feelings are often perceived as misleading, despite good reasons to assume that fluency has source validity. In a second and third step, we then examine the potential effects that two critical process steps may have on judgment validity, namely attribution—which links fluency to a source—and interpretation—which assigns meaning with respect to a criterion.[1]

Why feelings are perceived as misleading

Without doubt, feelings in general, and fluency experiences in particular, may lead astray—just as conscious rational thought, or content-based heuristic thinking may be misleading (Tversky & Kahneman, 1974). For feelings, many of these misleading instances are particularly salient, because they are often characterized by strong intensity—consider the folk wisdom that "hatred or love are blind." Such instances stand out, such as black sheep in a large herd of white ones. This standing out, however, is not informative about how often such instances occur, so that we may fall prey to a sampling error when judging feelings as misleading based on salient instances.

Curiously, the perception of feelings as troublemakers is fostered by those who investigate the impact of feelings, because these researchers often report on seemingly misleading influences of feelings in judgment. Consider what we will refer to as Tversky and Kahneman's (1973, Experiment 3) *letter experiment*. Participants were asked, for instance, whether there are more English words that begin with the letter "r" than words with the letter "r" in the third position. The researchers found that words beginning with "r" were judged to be more numerous, even though the opposite is true in the English language. This systematic error was explained by reliance on fluency experiences in judgment. Participants presumably formed frequency judgments based on the experience of ease or difficulty associated with the recall of content from memory—after all, if it feels easy to retrieve words that start with the consonant "r," there are probably many. However, because recall fluency is not necessarily indicative of category frequency, the letter experiment exemplifies a situation in which fluency constitutes a misleading source of information.

Similarly, in what we will refer to as the *fame experiment*, participants were asked to read aloud a list of non-famous names such as "Sebastian Weisdorf" (Jacoby, Kelley, Brown, & Jasechko, 1989). One day later, participants formed fame judgments about previously presented (and therefore old) non-famous names and new non-famous names. The old names were rated as more famous than the new names, seemingly because the old names (including Sebastian Weisdorf) felt more familiar than the new ones. Again, feelings of familiarity (fluency) seem to have produced erroneous judgments.

At face value, such scientific evidence suggests that feelings are troublemakers. It should be kept in mind, however, that experiments of this kind are intentionally constructed so that reliance on fluency experiences will lead astray. This is because, from a scientific perspective, seemingly wrong judgments are often particularly diagnostic (see Greifeneder, 2007). Researchers therefore take great effort in designing experiments in which the use of fluency is unjustified, because this is one way to show that feelings were relied upon in the first place (for a similar argument in other domains, e.g., Gilovich, Griffin, & Kahneman, 2002; Kahneman & Tversky, 1996; Kruglanski & Ajzen, 1983). This, however, does not render such illogical uses *representative* for the totality of instances in which feelings are used in judgment, and hence not diagnostic about judgment validity (Greifeneder et al., 2011).

Together, the tendency of erroneous feeling-based judgments to stand out and researchers' preference for investigating seemingly illogical uses of feelings in judgment may have contributed to the dodgy light that feelings are often perceived in. The following is to argue that such a perspective does not do justice to the validity of feelings in judgment. In what follows, we will focus on fluency experiences specifically. The majority of our conjectures, however, will likely hold for a broader class of feelings, too.

Our discussion centers around two critical process components in fluency-based judgments—attribution and interpretation (see Unkelbach & Greifeneder, Chapter 2, this volume)—and their effects on judgment validity. A precondition for this argument is that fluency allows—at least theoretically—for valid judgments when used appropriately. This precondition of source validity is shortly discussed next.

Source validity

We start our argument by assuming that there is reason to have faith in the ecological validity of fluency as an information cue. In addition to the empirical evidence reviewed by Herzog and Hertwig (Chapter 12, this volume), several conceptual arguments may be advanced in support of this argument.

First, fluency has been suggested to be a result of constant monitoring of cognitive activity and to continuously code the "how" of our cognition (Whittlesea & Williams, 2000). This coding not only encompasses that something was processed, but also the architectural properties of the underlying associative network. For instance, the strength and closeness of associations likely influence the ease or difficulty with which some piece of information can be recalled from memory. By being dependent on this learnt network structure, fluency experiences do not reflect single events in a vacuum, but single events against the background of a larger whole, the individual's learning history. This larger whole renders fluency experiences particularly valuable information carriers.

Second, because we are usually not aware of the architectural properties of our associative network system, fluency experiences may tell us more than we can consciously know. This is not only true for architectural properties, but also for content that remains below the threshold of consciousness. Consider, for instance, tip-of-the-tongue states, in which participants feel that they know a certain piece of information, yet are currently unable to access it (Schwartz, 2002; see also feeling of knowing, Koriat, 1993; Nelson, Gerler, & Narens, 1984). Similarly, with feelings of familiarity, individuals feel to have encountered an object or a person before (i.e., are familiar with it), but are not able to specify this encounter (e.g., Whittlesea, 1993). Fluency experiences may thus reflect information that is not consciously accessible.

To the extent that integrating a lot of information that is accessible both consciously and subconsciously promotes reliability, fluency experiences should allow for relatively accurate judgments. This statistical argument is reflected in the characterization of fluency experiences as "meta-summaries" (Koriat & Levy-Sadot, 1999), which holds that fluency experiences integrate multiple pieces of information into a single whole. Compared to single pieces of accessible content information, fluency experiences are therefore relatively efficient information carriers (see also Greifeneder & Bless, 2007). That such meta-summaries may be quite accurate predictors has been shown, for instance, in the realm of feelings of knowing. Hart (1965) asked participants to answer general knowledge questions such as "How many sides are there in a hexagon?" For non-recalled answers, participants made feeling of knowing predictions, which were then compared to recognition performance. As expected, feelings of knowing predicted recognition reliably above chance, thus attesting to the idea that fluency experiences may allow for valid judgments.

In sum, fluency experiences may be expected to be a reasonably valid source of information because they code current events against the background of a large information basis and because they code multiple pieces of information into a single whole. Arguably, these considerations may increase faith in the source validity of fluency experiences, but do not allow to qualify how valid judgments based on fluency experiences are. To answer this question about *judgment validity*, it is important to focus on the judgmental processes that underlie the *use* of (ecologically valid) fluency experiences in judgment. What follows is to address this question, separately for attribution and interpretation.

Attribution: what causes fluency?

For a feeling to influence judgment, it needs to be attributed. In the course of the attribution process, it is determined what presumably caused fluency, and what fluency may therefore be informative about (see Unkelbach & Greifeneder, Chapter 2, this volume). In what follows, we first describe general aspects of this attribution process, which we label as "swift defaults," because they operate on efficient but fallible rules. In a second step, we focus on more specific aspects of the attribution process, which we label as "sophisticated safety nets," because they likely ensure that attribution is not a constant source of error.

Swift defaults

Whittlesea, Jacoby, and Girard (1990) conceptualized the attribution process as automatic. The attribution process is further said to be controlled by whatever is salient and applicable at the time of attribution, that is, what happens in temporal contiguity to the experienced feeling. This tendency has been referred to as immediacy principle (Clore et al., 2001) or aboutness principle (Higgins, 1996). As a result, fluency experiences are generally perceived as immediate reactions to whatever is currently in the focus of attention—"Why else would I be experiencing fluency just now?"

While ascribing causality by contiguity allows for swift and effortless attribution, it widely opens the door for biases. Tversky and Kahneman (1973), for example, took advantage of the attribution inference based on temporal contiguity. In their letter experiment, participants presumably judged the frequency of words with the letter "r" in the first compared to the third position based on the fluency with which instances of the respective category come to mind. This likely occurred because participants did not attribute experienced fluency to its true cause—that memory cues words by their first and not by their third letter—but spontaneously misattributed experienced recall fluency to an apparent cause— that some word categories are more frequent than others. Participants seem to haven fallen prey to temporal contiguity, which supposedly suggested that perceived recall fluency is telling about ecological frequency, because it was experienced *when* frequency was judged.

Similarly, in the fame experiment, Jacoby, Kelley, Brown and Jasechko, (1989) exploited the attribution by contiguity mechanism. The finding that participants judged old non-famous names (e.g., Sebastian Weisdorf) as more famous than new non-famous names likely occurred because perceived fluency associated with old non-famous names was not attributed to its true cause—recall fluency caused by prior exposure—but misattributed to an apparent cause—recall fluency caused by fame—simply because the fluency experience and the fame assessment coincided. Both of these examples illustrate that the attribution inference is parsimonious but fallible.

Unfortunately, misattributions based on contiguity are not confined to the laboratory. Consider the case of unintentional plagiarism, which has been linked to misattributed fluency experiences (Jacoby, Kelley, & Dywan, 1989). Plagiarism may occur unintentionally presumably because the previous exposure to a sentence influences the fluency with which the sentence presents itself later, thus rendering the sentence compelling when authors put their "own" thoughts into words. In this case, fluency from prior exposure is not attributed to its true cause—prior exposure—, but misattributed to an apparent cause—compellingness— simply because fluency is felt when compellingness is considered. As another non-laboratory example consider that individuals have been shown to overestimate the prevalence of extreme causes of death, such as flood, homicide, or tornado (Lichtenstein, Slovic, Fischhoff, Layman, & Combs, 1978). This overestimation presumably occurs due to biased media-coverage, which heightens the accessibility of certain lethal events and thereby distorts accessibility-based judgments of actual frequency (Combs & Slovic, 1979).

Such findings illustrate that attribution based on contiguity may lead astray when joint occurrence is not indicative of causality. This may have far-reaching consequences. For instance, in the realm of education, it has been shown that essays are evaluated more positively when written in legible compared to less legible handwriting (Greifeneder, Zelt, Seele, Bottenberg, & Alt, 2012; James, 1929). Presumably, this legibility bias occurred because fluency is not attributed to its true source—differences in legibility—, but misattributed to an apparent cause—the work's quality (Greifeneder et al., 2010). Again, this misattribution likely arises because fluency is experienced *when* the work's quality is assessed (temporal contiguity), and does not reflect a causal relationship between handwriting legibility and work quality.

Sophisticated safety nets

Naïve theories of causation. Since attribution depends largely on temporal contiguity, it has been referred to as fluency's Achilles' heel (Greifeneder et al., 2010). Fortunately, however, contiguity is not the sole criterion for attribution, which is probably more accurately assessed when appropriate naïve theories about causation are available. For instance, when individuals are explicitly told that handwriting legibility causes differences in perceived fluency, handwriting legibility is no longer used to evaluate the work's quality (Greifeneder et al., 2010). Apparently perceived fluency is then correctly attributed to differences in legibility, and no longer misattributed to the work's quality. This suggests that once individuals know about fluency's true source, temporal contiguity is less powerful. More generally, naïve theories of causation seem to qualify contiguity.

As a second example consider findings by Jacoby and Whitehouse (1989). The authors observed that processing fluency may be enhanced when a test word is preceded by a masked prime. When this priming occurred unobtrusively, participants experienced an illusion of familiarity presumably because they did not correctly attribute fluency to priming. However, when the primes were presented for longer durations, participants were less likely to display an illusion of familiarity, seemingly because they correctly attributed fluency to the priming procedure. Note that this example is different from the handwriting example in that participants were not told about fluency's true source, but identified the true source themselves.

As a third example consider an experiment in which participants also spontaneously identified the true source of fluency. Oppenheimer (2004) reported that retrieval fluency is generally a good proxy for judging the frequency of names in a population, because familiar names are generally more prevalent. However, when evaluating celebrity names such as "Bush," for which fluency is less or not indicative of prevalence, participants' frequency judgments were not influenced by retrieval fluency. Presumably this is because participants were aware of the fact that intensive media coverage is the reason for why celebrity names felt so fluent, and therefore ceased to use recall fluency as an indicator of name frequency. This example illustrates that appropriate naïve theories of causation may be available to individuals as part of their "world knowledge" and need not necessarily be provided as part of experimental procedures.

Together these findings suggest that although the contiguity principle renders the attribution mechanism fallible, it is not the sole criterion determining attribution. All things considered, however, incorrect attribution may still be the largest source of error when it comes to the validity of fluency in judgment. This is because the automaticity and speed that the contiguity-based immediacy (or aboutness) principle grants comes with a price: whenever contiguity is not indicative of causality, the contiguity rule likely points to an incorrect source of fluency. Nevertheless, misattribution in the "wild" may be less likely than one would expect based on evidence accrued in the laboratory. This is because in experimental settings researchers try to disentangle the cause of the feeling from the judgment situation, for instance by manipulating fluency orthogonally to the judgment task (e.g., Reber & Schwarz, 1999). In contrast, in natural settings, dissociations between cause of feeling and judgment situation may be less likely (see Bless, Keller, & Igou, 2009).

Correlations between causes. In addition to naïve theories of causation there is a second safety net, which is statistical in nature. Specifically, fluency may promote valid judgments even if it is attributed to a wrong cause because true and wrong causes often covary. Consider again the letter experiment conducted by Tversky and Kahneman (1973), in which participants incorrectly attributed fluency resulting from architectural properties of memory to word category frequency. For the consonants chosen by Tversky and Kahneman (1973)—for instance, the letter "r"—there are more words in the English language where this letter occurs in the third compared to the first position. For these letters, fluency resulting from architectural properties of memory organization is negatively correlated to word frequency. Critically, however, there are only eight consonants in the English language for which this is true, whereas for 14 consonants there are more words that have the respective consonant in the first compared to third position (as spelt out in the original contribution, Tversky & Kahneman, 1973). For this majority of cases, fluency resulting from architectural properties of memory organization is positively correlated to frequency. Hence, in this majority of cases, relying on fluency when judging frequency will result in valid judgments even though fluency was misattributed. More generally, when wrong and correct attribution targets covary, misattribution may result in valid judgments.

Interpretation: What does fluency mean?

Once fluency is attributed, individuals need to draw inferences from fluency with respect to a criterion. Should we infer from fluent recall that something is frequent or infrequent, true or wrong, good or bad? This step is generally referred to as interpretation (see Unkelbach & Greifeneder, Chapter 2, this volume). Again, we differentiate "swift defaults" and "sophisticated safety nets."

Swift defaults

Context dependency. In the fame experiment, participants inferred fame from fluency (Jacoby, Kelley, Brown et al., 1989). But how come that these individuals interpreted fluency as fame, and not as frequency, like participants in the letter experiment did (Tversky & Kahneman, 1973)? Again, contiguity seems to be an important player, in that fluency gains meaning within the (temporal) context it is experienced. Consider a set-up of Schwarz and Schuman (1997), who created conditions of recall difficulty by asking US participants if they remembered anything special their representative had done for the district. Subsequently, participants were asked to evaluate either their representative's effort to keep them informed (public relations), or how closely they themselves followed politics (political interest). Now think of yourself: when asked about the representative's public relations behavior, the recall disfluency previously experienced in relation to the representative's voting behavior likely suggests that *public relations* are bad—after all, when you experience difficulties in recalling the representative's voting behavior, her/his public relations would seem ineffective. But when asked about your own interest in politics, the experienced disfluency likely signals *disinterest*—after all, when you have difficulties recalling such voting behavior, are you really serious about politics? This example illustrates that what we infer from fluency is often dependent on the context in which fluency is experienced.

Naïve theories of meaning. The context seems to trigger the judgmental domain that fluency is informative about (e.g., frequency, truth, valence, etc.), but is likely silent in which direction on each judgmental continuum fluency points. How do we know whether fluency signals, for instance, that a name is famous or insignificant? Schwarz (2004a) proposed that individuals hold naïve theories about what fluency means in a specific context. These naïve theories of meaning are supposed to link fluency experiences and judgmental inferences. Presumably it is such a naïve theory of meaning that let participants in the fame experiment know that fluency means fame and not insignificance.

Often, naïve theories of meaning reflect learned contingencies in the environment (for the critical role of learning, see Unkelbach, 2006, 2007). For instance, individuals may have observed that when they are interested in something (such as in politics, see above example, Schwarz & Schuman, 1997), it is easy to recall details about this topic. Likewise, when they are not interested, individuals may have experienced that recall of pertaining information is difficult. In both cases, a certain level of interest is associated with certain recall experiences. Now suppose that you have problems recalling a specific piece of information (e.g., your representative's voting behavior). If you want to draw conclusions about your interest in the associated larger topic (e.g., politics), one possibility is to reverse the interest-fluency logic into a fluency-to-interest inference. For instance, you may infer from recall difficulty (e.g., "I can't think of anything the representative did") that you are not interested in politics (e.g., "I never really cared").

The politics example illustrates that meaning may result from basic psychological inference principles. These inferences principles are relatively swift but rough and may therefore pose several threats to judgment validity. First, a high level of contextual dependency opens the door for unsystematic influences of many kinds. Second, the described inference process reverses the logical order of antecedent and consequent, in that something about the antecedent (e.g., political interest) is inferred from the consequent (e.g., recall fluency). This inference is only correct when the contingency is biunique—that is, true in both directions (see Bless & Schwarz, 1999, for an extended discussion). If the relationship is not bi-unique, inferring the antecedent from the consequent may result in error. Third, when cause and consequence covary sequentially over extended periods of time, individuals may not be able to observe contingencies and therefore may hold wrong naïve theories. One such example has been reported by Benjamin, Bjork, and Schwartz (1998, Experiment 1). Participants were asked to answer general knowledge questions and to estimate the likelihood of being able to retrieve the respective answers in a later free recall test. Results show that participants were more likely to retrieve answers the longer they had initially taken to answer the general knowledge questions. Future recall performance was thus positively correlated with initial recall latencies, presumably because initial elaboration increases the likelihood of later recall (e.g., Craik & Lockhart, 1972). Participants' initial estimations, however, were different. Specifically, participants judged future retrieval to be *less* likely the longer initial retrieval latencies were, thus committing a prediction error with potentially serious consequences for the allocation of learning times. It would seem that this prediction error occurred because participants held a wrong naïve theory of meaning about what fluency in recall means. The existence of such a wrong naïve theory may be due to a dearth of clearly observable contingencies in the environment (for related evidence, see Nelson & Leonesio, 1988).

Sophisticated safety nets

That interpretation operates on swift defaults may result in erroneous judgments. Which safety nets are in place? First, there is reason to assume that associatively represented contingencies may not be correlational but more akin to partial regression coefficients, as has been argued for in the realm of associatively represented heuristics (Smith & DeCoster, 2000; Uleman, 1999). One may therefore speculate that individuals rely on reversed inferences particularly when these have proven reliable in the past.

Second, because the meaning of fluency is often derived from learned contingencies, it reflects what individuals have learned about themselves and their ecology over long periods of time. To the extent that many observations allow for more reliable inference rules, relatively accurate interpretations may be expected. In this respect, it is noteworthy that naïve theories of meaning are not highly subjective and idiosyncratic, but socially shared. This is because the variation in the environment is similar across individuals so that inferred theories of meaning are similar, too. In line with this reasoning, Schwarz (2004b) observed a remarkably high consensus in participants' agreement on naïve theories. Interestingly, this also suggests that naïve theories of meaning are generally stable within individuals.

In sum, interpretation is influenced by contextual variables and naïve theories of meaning. Both carry some threat to validity, as the underlying rules are often efficient but not perfectly accurate. Specifying this threat in absolute terms is difficult; however, a relative comparison to conscious integration of accessible content information is plausible. This argument is based on the notion that judgments formed on the basis of declarative knowledge are also inferential, and depend on acquired naïve theories of meaning. For instance, an alternative explanation to Tversky and Kahneman's (1973) letter experiment is that participants actually recalled more words having the letter "r" in the first compared to third position. When forming a frequency judgment based on this recalled content, participants may have come to the conclusion that words with the letter "r" in the first position are more numerous, because "when I can recall many words, the category is probably numerous." Such a naïve theory of meaning may be correct, but may also be wrong—as in the letter experiment, where the recall of more words with the letter "r" in the first position is not indicative of true category frequency in the environment. As this example illustrates, judgments based on content information may also require naïve theories of meaning that have been learned throughout ontogenesis. To the extent that naïve theories used for drawing inferences based on content information versus fluency experiences are similarly valid, one would expect that content-based versus fluency-based judgments should result in judgments of similar validity.

The role of expertise

The present chapter's main focus is on the impact that attribution and interpretation may have on the validity of fluency-based judgments. We have suggested that the validity of reliance on fluency experiences in judgment depends in many respects on learned contingencies that are reflected in naïve theories of causation—which qualify the contiguity principle in attribution—and naïve theories of meaning—which guide interpretation. Because both often depend on prior learning, one may argue that fluency will be a more accurate indicator in judgment the more learning has occurred, that is, the more refined the associative network structure is. Fluency experiences should therefore allow for more valid judgments the more expertise a person has acquired in a specific domain. And in their domain of expertise, experts compared to novices may be expected to draw more accurate conclusions from fluency. To our knowledge, no evidence directly addressing this conclusion is available, despite interesting implications.

Note that the validity with which experts compared to novices form judgments based on fluency needs to be treated separately from the frequency with which they do so. With respect to frequency, prior research has shown that experts compared to novices rely less (and not more) on fluency (e.g., Janssen, Müller, & Greifeneder, 2011; Ofir, 2000; Tybout, Sternthal, Malaviya, Bakamitsos, & Park, 2005). Perhaps this is (a) because experts have not only more refined fluency experiences, but also more refined factual knowledge, and (b) because experts perceive their factual knowledge as relatively more telling based on the societal norm that sound judgments should reflect conscious rational thought. The specific reasons for this difference are, however, not yet fully understood and further research is needed to more closely understand the role expertise is playing in the validity of, and reliance on, fluency in judgment. Until then, it is interesting to note the apparent discrepancy between more accurate fluency-based judgments for experts compared to novices, but less frequent reliance on fluency as information. Perhaps what is needed is that experts (are allowed to) have more faith in their fluency experiences.

Conclusion

In this chapter, we have discussed several threats to the validity of fluency-based judgments, which result from underlying mechanisms that are speedy and efficient, but rough and sometimes fallible. However, in most cases, the weaknesses of these mechanisms seem to be at least partially counteracted by other mechanisms, such as when the fallibility of the contiguity principle in attribution is qualified by naïve theories of causation. By and large, fluency may therefore allow for reasonably valid judgments. This should be seen in light of the fact that the validity of alternative judgment pathways, such as conscious integration of accessible content information, may be lowered by factors that usually not affect fluency-based judgments. For instance, it has been suggested that the integration and weighing of single pieces of content information is error-prone (e.g., Wänke, 1996). Moreover, content-based judgment formation has been argued to be seriously constrained by limitations of consciousness (e.g., Dijksterhuis & Nordgren, 2006; Miller, 1956). Both of these aspects do not apply to fluency-based judgments. Consequently, one may venture the speculative conclusion that all things considered, fluency-based judgments are not less valid than content-based judgments, but perhaps even more. This conclusion is in line with the claim that fluency-based and content-based judgments are generally aligned, as illustrated in the letter experiment (Tversky & Kahneman, 1973). We therefore suggest that it is time to have more faith in fluency-experiences, and to embrace the enrichment a "feeling" perspective can bring to models of human functioning, both within and beyond the realm of psychology.

Acknowledgment

We gratefully acknowledge the support of a post-doctoral grant from the Deutsche Forschungsgemeinschaft and a post-doctoral grant from the Baden-Württemberg Stiftung, both awarded to the first author.

Note

1 Note that attribution and interpretation often work in tandem and may be "amalgamated" within one step (for a discussion see Unkelbach & Greifeneder, Chapter 2, this volume).

While it is conceptually important to separate the two process steps, many examples in the literature are ambiguous with respect to whether a specific pattern of results is due to differences in attribution ("caused by") or interpretation ("indicative of"). We have approached this ambiguity by selecting examples according to whether the attribution or interpretation process was likely dominant. We acknowledge, however, that some of the cited evidence could also be categorized differently. To resolve this ambiguity in future research, it will be important to conceptualize whether fluency can be attributed to specific causes (e.g., prior exposure)—which strongly constrain interpretation and thus result in an amalgamation of attribution and interpretation— or only to more general causes (e.g., recall)—which open the door for a larger set of possible inferences.

References

Benjamin, A. S., Bjork, R. A., & Schwartz, B. L. (1998). The mismeasure of memory: When retrieval fluency is misleading as a metamnemonic index. *Journal of Experimental Psychology: General, 127,* 55–68.

Bless, H., Keller, J., & Igou, E. R. (2009). Metacognition. In F. Strack & J. Förster (Eds.), *Social cognition: The basis of human interaction* (pp. 157–177). New York: Psychology Press.

Bless, H., & Schwarz, N. (1999). Sufficient and necessary conditions in dual-mode models: The case of mood and information processing. In S. Chaiken & Y. Trope (Eds.), *Dual-process theories in social psychology* (pp. 423–440). New York: Guilford Press.

Clore, G. L., Wyer, R. S., Dienes, B. P. A., Gasper, K., Gohm, C., & Isbell, L. (2001). Affective feelings as feedback: Some cognitive consequences. In L. L. Martin & G. L. Clore (Eds.), *Theories of mood and cognition: A user's guidebook* (pp. 27–62). Mahwah, NJ: Lawrence Erlbaum Associates.

Combs, B., & Slovic, P. (1979). Newspaper coverage of causes of death. *Journalism Quarterly, 56,* 837–843.

Craik, F. I., & Lockhart, R. S. (1972). Levels of processing: A framework for memory research. *Journal of Verbal Learning and Verbal Behavior, 11,* 671–684.

Dijksterhuis, A., & Nordgren, L. F. (2006). A theory of unconscious thought. *Perspectives on Psychological Science, 1,* 95–109.

Elster, J. (1999). *Alchemies of the mind: Rationality and the emotions.* Cambridge: Cambridge University Press.

Gilovich, T., Griffin, D., & Kahneman, D. (2002). *Heuristics and biases: The psychology of intuitive judgment.* New York: Cambridge University Press.

Greifeneder, R. (2007). *Reliance on accessibility experiences in judgment and decision making.* Lengerich: Pabst Science Publishers.

Greifeneder, R., Alt, A., Bottenberg, K., Seele, T., Zelt, S., & Wagener, D. (2010). On writing legibly: Processing fluency systematically biases evaluations of handwritten material. *Social Psychological and Personality Science, 1,* 230–237.

Greifeneder, R., & Bless, H. (2007). Relying on accessible content versus accessibility experiences: The case of processing capacity. *Social Cognition, 25,* 853–881.

Greifeneder, R., Bless, H., & Pham, M. T. (2011). When do people rely on affective and cognitive feelings in judgment? A review. *Personality and Social Psychology Review, 15,* 107–141.

Greifeneder, R., Müller, P., Stahlberg, D., Van den Bos, K., & Bless, H. (2011). Beyond procedure's content: Cognitive subjective experiences in procedural justice judgments. *Experimental Psychology, 58,* 341–352. doi:10.1027/1618-3169/a000101

Greifeneder, R., Müller, P., Stahlberg, D., Van den Bos, K., & Bless, H. (2011). Guiding Trustful Behavior: The Role of Accessible Content and Accessibility Experiences. *Journal of Behavioral Decision Making, 24,* 498–514. doi:10.1002/bdm.705

Greifeneder, R., Zelt, S., Seele, T., Bottenberg, K., & Alt, A. (2012). Towards a better understanding of the legibility bias in performance assessments: The case of gender-based inferences. *British Journal of Educational Psychology, 82,* 361–374. doi:10.1111/j.2044-8279.2011.02029.x

Hart, J. T. (1965). Memory and the feeling-of-knowing experience. *Journal of Educational Psychology, 56,* 208–216.

Higgins, E. T. (1996). Knowledge activation: Accessibility, applicability, and salience. In E. T. Higgins & A. W. Kruglanski (Eds.), *Social psychology: Handbook of basic principles* (pp. 133–168). New York: Guilford Press.

Jacoby, L. L., Kelley, C. M., Brown, J., & Jasechko, J. (1989). Becoming famous overnight: Limits of the ability to avoid unconscious influences of the past. *Journal of Personality and Social Psychology, 56,* 326–338.

Jacoby, L. L., Kelley, C. M., & Dywan, J. (1989). Memory attributions. In H. L. Roediger, III & F. I. M. Craik (Eds.), *Varieties of memory and consciousness: Essays in honour of Endel Tulving* (pp. 391–422). Hillsdale, NJ, England: Lawrence Erlbaum Associates, Inc.

Jacoby, L. L., & Whitehouse, K. (1989). An illusion of memory: False recognition influenced by unconscious perception. *Journal of Experimental Psychology: General, 118,* 126–135.

James, H. W. (1929). The effect of handwriting upon grading. *The English Journal, 16,* 180–185.

Janssen, J., Müller, P., & Greifeneder, R. (2011). Cognitive processes in procedural justice judgments. The role of ease-of-retrieval, uncertainty, and experience. *Journal of Organizational Behavior, 32,* 726–750. doi:10.1002/job.700

Kahneman, D., & Tversky, A. (1996). On the reality of cognitive illusions. *Psychological Review, 103,* 582–591.

Koriat, A. (1993). How do we know that we know? The accessibility model of the feeling of knowing. *Psychological Review, 100,* 609–639.

Koriat, A., & Levy-Sadot, R. (1999). Processes underlying metacognitive judgments: Information-based and experience-based monitoring of one's own knowledge. In S. Chaiken & Y. Trope (Eds.), *Dual-process theories in social psychology.* (pp. 483–502). New York: Guilford Press.

Kruglanski, A. W., & Ajzen, I. (1983). Bias and error in human judgment. *European Journal of Social Psychology, 13,* 1–44.

Lichtenstein, S., Slovic, P., Fischhoff, B., Layman, M., & Combs, B. (1978). Judged frequency of lethal events. *Journal of Experimental Psychology: Human Learning and Memory, 4,* 551–578.

Miller, G. A. (1956). The magical number seven, plus or minus two: some limits on our capacity for processing information. *Psychological Review, 63,* 81–97.

Müller, P., Greifeneder, R., Stahlberg, D., Van den Bos, K., & Bless, H. (2010). Shaping cooperation behavior: The role of accessibility experiences. *European Journal of Social Psychology, 40,* 178–187.

Nelson, T. O., Gerler, D., & Narens, L. (1984). Accuracy of feeling-of-knowing judgments for predicting perceptual identification and relearning. *Journal of Experimental Psychology: General, 113,* 282–300.

Nelson, T. O., & Leonesio, R. J. (1988). Allocation of self-paced study time and the "labor-in-vain effect." *Journal of Experimental Psychology: Learning, Memory, and Cognition, 14*, 676–686.

Ofir, C. (2000). Ease of recall vs recalled evidence in judgment: Experts vs laymen. *Organizational Behavior and Human Decision Processes, 81*, 28–42.

Oppenheimer, D. M. (2004). Spontaneous discounting of availability in frequency judgment tasks. *Psychological Science, 15*, 100–105. doi:10.1111/j.0963-7214.2004.01502005.x

Reber, R. & Schwarz, N. (1999). Effects of perceptual fluency on judgments of truth. *Consciousness and Cognition: An International Journal, 8*, 338–342.

Schwartz, B. L. (2002). *Tip-of-the-tongue states: Phenomenology, mechanism, and lexical retrieval.* Mahwah, NJ: Lawrence Erlbaum Associates.

Schwarz, N. (2004a). Metacognitive experiences in consumer judgment and decision making. *Journal of Consumer Psychology, 14*, 332–348.

—— (2004b). Metacognitive experiences: Response to commentaries. *Journal of Consumer Psychology, 14*, 370–373.

Schwarz, N., & Schuman, H. (1997). Political knowledge, attribution, and inferred interest in politics: The operation of buffer items. *International Journal of Public Opinion Research, 9*, 191–195.

Smith, E. R., & DeCoster, J. (2000). Dual-process models in social and cognitive psychology: Conceptual integration and links to underlying memory systems. *Personality and Social Psychology Review, 4*, 108–131.

Tversky, A., & Kahneman, D. (1973). Availability: A heuristic for judging frequency and probability. *Cognitive Psychology, 5*, 207–232.

—— (1974). Judgment under uncertainty: Heuristics and biases. *Science, 185*, 1124–1131.

Tybout, A. M., Sternthal, B., Malaviya, P., Bakamitsos, G. A., & Park, S.-B. (2005). Information accessibility as a moderator of judgments: The role of content versus retrieval ease. *Journal of Consumer Research, 32*, 76–85.

Uleman, J. S. (1999). Spontaneous versus intentional inferences in impression formation. In S. Chaiken & Y. Trope (Eds.), *Dual process theories in social psychology* (pp. 141–160). New York, NY: Guilford Press.

Unkelbach, C. (2006). The learned interpretation of cognitive fluency. *Psychological Science, 17*, 339–345.

—— (2007). Reversing the truth effect: Learning the interpretation of processing fluency in judgments of truth. *Journal of Experimental Psychology: Learning, Memory and Cognition, 33*, 219–230.

Wänke, M. (1996). Comparative judgments as a function of the direction of comparison versus word order. *Public Opinion Quarterly, 60*, 400–409.

Whittlesea, B. W. A. (1993). Illusions of familiarity. *Journal of Experimental Psychology: Learning, Memory, and Cognition, 19*, 1235–1253.

Whittlesea, B. W. A., Jacoby, L. L., & Girard, K. (1990). Illusions of immediate memory: Evidence of an attributional basis for feelings of familiarity and perceptual quality. *Journal of Memory and Language, 29*, 716–732.

Whittlesea, B. W. A., & Williams, L. D. (2000). The source of feelings of familiarity: The discrepancy-attribution hypothesis. *Journal of Experimental Psychology: Learning, Memory and Cognition, 26*, 547–565.

14 Fluency and behavior regulation

Adaptive and maladaptive consequences of a good feeling

Klaus Fiedler

Abstract

Although the term "fluency" is used in different ways, with reference to various operational definitions, research converges in emphasizing not only the positive hedonic value of fluency but also the useful adaptive function of the fluency cue for decision making and behavior regulation. However, this positive image may be misleading and maladaptive. With reference to three criteria of successful adaptive regulation, persistence, facilitation through priming, and optimal decision strategies, the present chapter demonstrates that high fluency can under many conditions induce an illusion of learning and success, undermine the signaling function of priming, and interfere with optimal decision making. The message to be conveyed for future research is that measures of adaptive success should be included in appropriate research designs, rather than stressing the hedonic value of fluency as an end in itself and presupposing its adaptive value for behavior regulation and decision-making.

The fluency phenomenon: an intriguing research topic

The concept of fluency has become a prominent theme during the last two decades of research and theorizing on cognition, meta-cognition, and adaptive behavior. Although the term "fluency" is used in various ways, there is wide agreement among researchers in cognitive (Whittlesea, 1993) and social psychology (Reber & Schwarz, 2006), in decision research (Marewski & Schooler, 2011) and even in neuro-science (Volz, Schooler & von Cramon, 2010) that fluency can be generally understood as the experienced ease of performing perceptual, conceptual, or motor tasks. At the operational level, this general cognitive feeling (Unkelbach, 2006, 2007) can reflect many causes: ease of retrieving experiences from autobiographical memory (Schwarz, Bless, Strack, Klumpp, Rittenauer-Schatka & Simons, 1991), absence of blocking (Topolinski & Strack, 2010), facilitation through identity priming (Kurilla & Westerman, 2008), or subjective feelings of knowing or recognition due to prior exposure (Florer & Allen, 2000; Hertwig, Herzog, Schooler & Reimer, 2008). Other fluency treatments include enhanced color contrast, high readability of text, repeated exposure, familiarity of context, subtle primes that facilitate problem solving, absence of memory load, and convenient presentation formats (see also Unkelbach & Greifeneder, Chapter 2, this volume). In the absence of any explicit attempt to distinguish different types of fluency, I will use the construct inclusively, considering any of the aforementioned manipulations as appropriate means of inducing fluency.

The hedonic and adaptive value of fluency

While the means of inducing fluency and the specific research topics are manifold, there is wide consensus that fluency has a positive image, both hedonically and adaptively. Hedonically, the warm glow of fluency feels pleasant and safe (Corneille, Monin & Pleyers, 2005; de Vries, Holland, Chenier, Starr & Winkielman, 2010; Belke, Leder, Strobach & Carbon, 2010; Winkielman & Cacioppo, 2001). With regard to the organism's adaptation to an uncertain environment, moreover, it has been argued that "retrieval fluency can be a proxy for real-world quantities" (Hertwig et al., 2008; see also Herzog & Hertwig, Chapter 12, this volume) and that it affords an adaptive decision heuristic that exploits the correspondence between cognition and the environment (de Vries et al., 2010; Hertwig et al., 2008; Volz et al., 2010). Moreover, the positive image of fluency receives further support from research showing its function as a catalyst and a lubricant of positive affective states (Freitas, Azizian, Travers & Berry, 2005), creative problem-solving (Milgram & Arad, 1981), attitude change (Wänke & Bless, 2000), advertising (Labroo & Lee, 2006), motivation to learn (Van Zandt & Himelstein, 1961), and risk assessment (Winkielman, Schwarz, Fazendeiro & Reber, 2003).

Such beneficial consequences are by no means meant to be restricted to the most intense feelings of fluency experienced in a few stellar moments of life. Even ordinary and very subtle instances of fluency that stem from repetition priming, quick perception of an environmental stimulus, easy pronunciation of an utterance, or ease of retrieving singular items from memory are supposed to trigger confidence and adaptive responding.

To be sure, pluralistic research has not totally overlooked the possibility that experienced fluency may also instigate premature responding (e.g., Alter & Oppenheimer, 2009), cognitive fallacies (Song & Schwarz, 2008), illusions of familiarity (Rhodes & Castel, 2008; Whittlesea, 1993), wrong recognition decisions (Huber, Clark, Curran & Winkielman, 2008; Jacoby, Kelley, Brown & Jasechko, 1989), or undue risk-seeking (Song & Schwarz, 2008). However, such unwanted fluency effects receive little attention in social psychology and decision research (but see Greifeneder, Bless, & Scholl, Chapter 13, this volume). They would be typically framed as unavoidable side-effects of the predominantly pleasant and functional influence of the self-confidence, self-efficacy, and cooperation induced by the feeling of fluency. Thus, if a basketball player has a flow experience (Csikszentmihalyi, 1990), so that his "hot hand" enables him to score many points even in very difficult situations, a few failing attempts resulting from over-confidence will be tolerated as an inevitable side-effect of an otherwise highly functional state of motivation.

Even in those areas of cognitive psychology and meta-cognition, in which the costs and illusory side-effects of fluency have been acknowledged (Bjork, 1994, 1999; Koriat & Bjork, 2005; Koriat & Ma'ayan, 2005), there is no clearly spelled out theoretical framework within which the effects and aftereffects of fluency can be interpreted. An adaptive function of the fluency cue is silently taken for granted and sometimes related to evolutionary selection (Reber & Schwarz, 2006). Based on the diagnostic value of retrieval fluency for preference choices, the fluency heuristic has been praised as "one tool in the mind's repertoire of strategies that artfully probes memory for encapsulated frequency information that can veridically reflect statistical regularities in the world" (Hertwig et al., 2008, p. 1191). Yet, hardly anybody has ever tried to explicate the functional context within which the heuristic's adaptive value can be tested.

Quest for a functional analysis

Thus, the problem I am tackling here is not so much the bias towards an unduly positive image of fluency. The chief problem is rather that research has been largely content with "sexy findings" and local illustrations of the hedonic and diagnostic value of fluency. Measures of adaptive success beyond the local task are not included in the study designs. Empirical findings mainly revolve around immediate concomitants of fluency: the consumer preferences for fluently experienced products (Novemsky, Dhar, Schwarz & Simonson, 2007), the approach reactions toward familiar objects (Zajonc, 2001), or the self-efficacy or self-assertiveness gained from easiness experience (Schwarz et al., 1991). Although these phenomena accord with the predominant cover story of fluency as a generalized proxy for "go" rather than "stop", they do not allow for a critical test of its adaptive functions.

In the center of this simplifying cover story are three most prominent classes of findings: the exposure effect (Bornstein, 1989; Zajonc, 1968), the truth effect (Dechêne, Stahl, Hansen & Wänke, 2010; Reber & Schwarz, 1999), and the fluency heuristic (Hertwig et al., 2008). While the exposure effect says that fluency mediates the enhanced liking and attraction of repeatedly presented stimuli, the truth effect refers to the enhanced belief in the truth of familiar propositions and communications. Both phenomena represent fluency effects conceived as research ends in and of themselves. The fluency heuristic refers to the adaptive rationality of a fast and frugal binary decision rule. In binary choice situations, choosing the one option that can be more easily retrieved from memory will often be correct, identifying the actually better option. In this paradigm, the emphasis is on the objective validity of a decision heuristic rather than only the subjective experience of liking or truth. Across all three paradigms, however, researchers have rarely ever tried to assess and explain the functional value of exposure effects, truth effects, or heuristic strategies with reference to clearly defined adaptive goals, or long-term assessment of motivation, achievement, and utilities (but see Reber & Unkelbach, 2010, for an exception).

Scope of the present chapter

In the present article, I make an attempt to outline such a functional analysis with reference to specific, well-established paradigms. From this perspective, it will soon be apparent that the adaptive value of the fluency cue is highly questionable. In several task contexts, it can indeed be profoundly maladaptive, impair achievement, undermine motivation, and inhibit learning and regulation processes.

What is the purpose of such an alternative look on a flourishing and fascinating research topic? Why is it important to engage in deeper reflection on both the benefits and the costs of feeling states? I believe tackling these issues is worthwhile for several reasons. First, starting to locate fluency within a functional framework can reveal new insights and so far overlooked implications. Second, a systematic analysis of both adaptive and maladaptive functions can inspire new experiments and designs for future research. And last but not least, a critical analysis of the fluency phenomenon will highlight the need to build functional theories beyond the uncritical presupposition that heuristics and feelings must serve some adaptive or even evolutionary function. The framework I am offering suggests ways of transcending such presuppositions and going beyond such local issues as hedonic experience and its brain correlates. To gain a deeper understanding of fluency in adaptive regulation, it is rather essential to embed meta-cognitive feelings in distinct problem environments.

Outlines of a functional analysis of fluency in specific paradigms

Three criteria of successful adaptive regulation will be discussed in this major section: persistence; facilitation through priming; and optimal decision strategies. The first subsection will deal with persistence on effort-demanding tasks. Granting that within a wide range of such tasks, achievement is a monotonically increasing function of persistence, it follows that successful adaptive regulation amounts to fostering persistence and continued effort expenditure. Not surprisingly, feelings of fluency can be counterproductive in these situations, signaling that progress is sufficient and further effort expenditure is unnecessary. Three paradigms will serve to illustrate this consideration: the generation effect paradigm in memory research, the illusion of learning phenomenon, and effort justification in research on cognitive dissonance theory. In the second subsection devoted to the adaptive facilitation through priming, we will again see that fluency does not support priming effects, which profit instead from degraded and difficult presentation formats experienced as disfluent. Once more, what appears to indicate a benevolent situation might actually inhibit an adaptive cognitive function. This issue will be discussed with reference to evaluative priming and research on affect and cognition. In the third subsection, the adaptive value of decision strategies will be discussed with reference to two prominent research topics, the impact of fluency from regulatory fit (Higgins, 2005) on optimal response strategies and the ecological validity of the fluency heuristic advocated by Hertwig et al. (2008; see also Herzog & Hertwig, Chapter 12, this volume).

Fluency and persistence on effort-demanding tasks

The generation advantage in learning and memory

An intriguing paradigm to start the discussion of persistence regulation can be found in the so-called generation effect (Dosher & Russo, 1976; Hirshman & Bjork, 1988; Slamecka & Graf, 1978). Originating in the levels-of-processing approach to understanding efficient learning, this paradigm is based on the comparison between two types of stimulus encoding, involving self-generated and experimenter-provided stimuli. In a typical experiment (e.g., Fiedler, Nickel, Asbeck & Pagel, 2003), participants would be presented with a list of words, of which one half is presented completely and only has to be read, whereas the other half appears in degraded format (scrambled letters; word-stem completion) so that the participants themselves have to generate the words' meaning. The canonical finding is a substantial memory advantage of self-generated over completely provided stimuli (for a review, see Mulligan & Lozito, 2004). This finding has multiple implications for efficient learning in such applied domains as education (learning by discovery), eyewitness testimony (memory illusions through mental simulation), or egocentric attributions.

It is easy to see that the encoding tasks used for the generation condition are more disfluent, effortful, interrupted, hard, and delayed than the convenient formats used for experimenter-provided stimulus presentation. Reading a clearly written word is smoother than struggling to find a word in an anagram task; listening to connected speech is easier than understanding degraded acoustic input. Indeed, most treatments that have been used to manipulate fluency can also be found in the generation-effect literature, converging in the general conclusion that self-generated, hard to encode stimuli have a strong and persistent learning advantage over externally provided, easy to encode stimuli.

Thus, in contrast to its image of an ecologically valid indicator of unproblematic situations, the fluency cue may actually be deceptive and dysfunctional. Disfluent encoding conditions turn out to be more predictive of learning progress than fluent conditions (Miele, Finn & Molden, 2011). Support for this conclusion comes from many findings gathered during the last four decades of memory research: on the generation effect proper (Mulligan & Lozito, 2004), the recall advantage of inconsistent and hard-to-process information in person memory (Hastie & Kumar, 1979; Stangor & McMillan, 1992), the superiority of deeper levels of processing (Craik & Tulving, 1975), and the production effect (MacLeod, Gopie, Hourihan, Neary & Ozubko, 2010).

To be sure, the presentation of self-generated versus experimenter-provided stimuli does not represent a pure manipulation of fluency. It confounds several aspects (just as almost every fluency manipulation). Self-generated stimulus episodes are not only experienced as hard and resisting smooth processing; they are also tied to idiosyncratic memory traces or associated with creative, productive mindsets. For a more specific test of the assumption that the quantitative degree of generation effort facilitates learning, rather than the qualitative nature of the generation task, Fiedler, Lachnit, Fay, and Krug (1992) let participants generate target words in three graded conditions, which all involved generation but at different degrees of difficulty. For example, they had to generate the target word "wheels" from text frames that varied in the number and richness of cues:

The car has four: _____
The car has: _____
Car: _____

As expected, the subsequent recall performance increased from the easiest to the hardest presentation condition, thus corroborating the functionality of disfluency.

One might object that the generation advantage may come along with serious depletion effects, because effortful processing is capacity-demanding and may thus exploit precious resources. However, although capacity constraints may set some upper limit for resource-intensive, effortful processing, exceeding this limit may be less likely than expected. The pertinent literature suggests that, across a wide range of task conditions, non-fluent generation experience will actually help the individual to mobilize and to optimally allocate mental resources. The phenomenon of "covered displaced rehearsal" (Grosofsky, Payne & Campbell, 1994), for instance, refers to the flexible utilization of mental resources in a mixed task context, in which easy read items alternate with hard generate items. On such a task, the unexploited resources from easy trials are flexibly used to support the demanding encoding processes for the neighboring difficult trials, reflecting a nice case of adaptive regulation.

With reference to Muraven and Baumeister's (2000) muscle metaphor for ego-depletion effects, one might indeed concede that extended generative exercising can put the mind in a depleted state (analogous to stiffness after physical exertion). However, just as the long-term effect of physical exercising is to strengthen the muscle (and protect it from stiffness when in a good condition) and to keep the entire body healthy and fit, there is little evidence to suggest that extended generative activity turns into dysfunctional fatigue or motivation loss. Over a wide range of effort levels and task settings, resistance experience and struggling with difficulties will benefit good learning (Bjork, 1994), whereas fluency feelings prevent the learner from sufficiently deep processing and encoding effort expenditure (see Alter, Oppenheimer, Epley & Eyre, 2007).

Illusion of learning

Indeed, the seminal research by Bjork, Koriat, and colleagues (Bjork, 1994, 1999; Koriat & Bjork, 2005; Koriat & Ma'ayan, 2005) highlights the danger that experienced ease and fluency produce illusions of learning that undermine persistent studying and achievement motivation. This research program is exceptional as it goes beyond the local hedonic experience and immediate cueing function of fluency and actually focuses on the more long-lasting consequences for learning and achievement. Across a wide variety of mental and motor tasks— ranging from paired-associate learning to academic learning and motor exercise in sports—the empirical evidence from this paradigm converges in demonstrating that efficient learning originates in uneasy, disfluent, inconvenient task conditions (see Bjork, 1994). The feeling of fluency in a student exposed to an easy to read, richly illustrated textbook may cause an over-confident illusion of learning and understanding, which prevents him or her from recognizing persistent deficits and knowledge gaps and often leads to the premature truncation of incomplete learning processes. Likewise, the feeling of ease and flow that results from a smooth training unit in sports (e.g., a tennis ball machine calling for predictable sequences of forehand and backhand strokes) causes less learning progress than inconvenient and disfluent training units (e.g., involving ball machines programmed to produce random sequences).

The bottom line of this intriguing body of evidence is that, in the context of learning of specific intellectual and motor tasks, the dysfunctional and seductive role of the fluency cue is to induce an illusion of high achievement, which may undermine continued learning and useful over-learning. Little evidence can be found in this literature for the notion that fluency encourages self-confident and goal-oriented learning mediated by an ongoing approach tendency or "go" signal. What the available evidence highlights, instead, is that good learning arises from hard work rather than flow experiences. Even when this is not the whole story and when future research will reveal some refined mixture of hard and easy feelings to be optimal for learning, the illusion of learning effect highlights the need to study adaptive functions empirically, rather than simply presupposing the adaptive importance of the fluency cue.

Dissonance and under-justification

Quite remote from research on memory and meta-cognition, Festinger's (1957) famous work on dissonance theory is replete with further evidence for the functional superiority of disfluency over fluency. A number of impressive demonstrations have been obtained in the so-called effort-justification paradigm. If an individual has to struggle for a goal, to wait a long time, to pay a higher price, or to succeed against many competitors, the subjective experience is all but fluent or easy. However, the resulting motivation and performance are greatly enhanced by the experience of unease, effort expenditure, investment, and goal-blocking. In dissonance-theoretical terms, the high effort invested in goal attainment has to be justified by an increasingly positive attitude toward the goal he or she has been struggling for. This dissonance-reducing process will typically result in strong and enduring commitment toward the task at hand, along with a distinct enhancement of performance. For example, Axsom and Cooper (1985) demonstrated that the effectiveness of an overweight therapy program could be enhanced by engaging the patients in a difficult and enduring visual discrimination task, which was experienced as effortful, unpleasant, and time-consuming. Although this extra effort was not intrinsically related to the goal of the therapy (reducing weight), enhanced effort expenditure was the key to effective short-term and long-term learning (as evident in a follow-up after six months).

Perhaps even more impressive than these effort-justification experiments with human participants are the animal experiments portrayed in Lawrence and Festinger's (1962) book on dissonance-like processes in animal learning. Applying the idea of effort justification to the partial-reinforcement effect in conditioning, Lawrence and Festinger argued that performance increases and learned responses are more enduring and resistant to extinction when animals have to work hard for reward, to overcome many obstacles in a maze, or to tolerate many unreinforced trials. These sources of frustration, goal-blocking, and delay of reinforcement qualify as powerful disfluency treatments. Yet, they are well-known to be catalysts of efficient animal learning, in experimental research as in dressage.

It is tempting to speculate about the limits of the partial reinforcement effect and the wisdom that efficient animal training has to be straining and unpleasant. What these anecdotal and experimental demonstrations tell us, certainly, is not that goal blocking and delay per se should be maximized. After all, if a reinforcement schedule decreases from 70 percent to 30 percent to 0 percent reinforcement, there is of course a point where no learning will take place any longer. What these studies indeed suggest is that some optimal switch between reward and frustration creates the highest level of motivation, learning, and persistence. The joint experience of scarce and therefore particularly enjoyable reward, along with frequent failure experiences and high levels of effort expenditure, seems to be optimal for performance. Analogous to these considerations on animal learning, a few researchers have shown that differential fluency changes or contrast experiences can have stronger effects on human participants than the zero-order state of fluency per se (Hansen & Wänke, 2008; Whittlesea & Leboe, 2003).

Response facilitation through adaptive priming effects

In cognitive psychology, social cognition, abnormal psychology, and several applied domains, researchers have been so busy in studying priming effects and the underlying cognitive processes that they have almost lost sight of the adaptive functions of priming. After all, "priming" means to prepare an organism for fast and accurate responding to uncertain but potentially quite significant events in the environment. The ability to utilize preceding prime stimuli to increase the predictability of subsequent target stimuli is among the most basic modules of adaptive behavior. Well-adapted organisms profit from situational primes that signal dangers, chances, and affordances; they use semantic primes for efficient language comprehension and fast reading; procedural priming facilitates the carry-over of mental operations and problem-solving procedures between tasks; and categorical priming facilitates fast and efficient inductive inferences.

Unlike the motivational persistence criterion, which is desirable most of the time—except for abnormal cases of obsession or inability to exit sunk-cost situations—the adaptive value of priming depends on the very behavior it facilitates. Priming can foster correct or incorrect responses, prosocial or antisocial tendencies. However, granting that task performance is generally above chance, with dominant responses being mostly correct, the overall function of priming should be to support responses that tend to be valid and beneficial.

A strong and consistent finding obtained across various priming paradigms is that, all other things being equal, response facilitation through priming is maximized under encoding conditions that can be assumed to be experienced as disfluent (De Houwer, Hermans & Spruyt, 2001; Fiedler, 2003; Gawronski, Deutsch & Seidel, 2005). That is, priming effects tend to be strong and robust when primes are presented subliminally, for a brief fraction of a second, in degraded format, when primes go unrecognized, and when the individual is distracted from, rather than attending to, the prime. In contrast, priming effects tend to be reduced, eliminated, or even reversed when primes are presented long enough to be fully perceived, in convenient and comprehensible format, and when individuals can easily recognize and memorize the prime and its relation to the target. Thus, hard-to-encode primes seem to be utilized more readily to prepare for environmental targets than easy-to-decode primes—quite contrary to the commonly accepted adaptive formula that fluency triggers "go" or "use" whereas disfluency signals "stop" or "discard."

Providing a comprehensive explanation of this seemingly paradoxical advantage of hard over easy primes would exceed the scope of this chapter (for more evidence, see Fiedler, Blümke & Unkelbach, 2011). Although the various accounts that have been offered differ in terms of rhetoric and theoretical background, there seems to be general agreement that easily recognized and identified primes tend to be discounted and functionally separated, rather than assimilated to and integrated with the target (Estes & Jones, 2009; Huber et al., 2008).

Fluency in evaluative-priming

Let us illustrate this phenomenon with reference to the evaluative-priming paradigm, in which evaluatively positive and negative primes are supposed to signal benevolent or malevolent situations, respectively. In a typical experiment (cf. Fazio, Jackson, Dunton & Williams, 1995; Hermans, Spruyt & Eelen, 2003; Klauer & Musch, 2003), every trial in a sequential design involves a positive or negative prime stimulus immediately followed by a positive or negative target. Participants are instructed to evaluate targets, as quickly and accurately as possible, as either positive or negative. A distinct facilitation effect is usually manifested in faster (and sometimes more accurate) responses to targets preceded by primes of the same valence. Thus, in accordance with the adaptive meta-theory of priming, evaluative primes seem to help the organism to anticipate and prepare for evaluatively congruent target stimuli.

However, although the congruity effect in evaluative priming is commonly considered a regular and robust finding (Fazio, 2001), it largely disappears when primes are easily processed and recognized. One straightforward way to demonstrate this phenomenon is by manipulating presentation time. Short SOAs (of 300 ms or less) have been shown to yield stronger priming effects than longer SOAs (cf. Hermans et al., 2003).

There are other ways to operationalize disfluency in a priming experiment. Using somewhat longer time frames (SOA = 450 ms), Alexopoulos, Fiedler and Freytag (2012) used reduced color contrast and a delayed fading-in procedure to present positive and negative prime words in disfluent format. Again, the facilitation in the evaluation of congruent target words was confined to trials involving degraded primes and disappeared for other trials involving easier encoding (e.g., higher color contrast).

Chan, Ybarra, and Schwarz (2006) varied the familiarity of the stimulus words and found that only unfamiliar words (as defined by their word-frequency count) produced the regular priming effect, which vanished however in the familiar-word condition. Assuming that fluency is sensitive to word frequency, this finding provides further evidence for a disfluency advantage in priming.

For the sake of convergent validation, let us consider one more experiment using still another manipulation of disfluency. Fiedler and Schenck (2001) and later Fiedler, Schenck, Watling, and Menges (2005) measured the time needed to identify a slowly appearing trait word (e.g., "aggressive") that either matched or mismatched a behavior primed a few seconds before in a picture or in a film-clip (e.g., showing a person attacking another (match), a person feeding another (non-match)). Before the trait identification task, participants were asked to verify whether a verb (e.g., "attack" or "embrace") fit the content of the picture or film or not. When the verb probe did not fit the primed behavior, the prime's facilitation effect on the trait identification task was stronger than in the fit condition, although faster verification latencies showed that fit increased fluency.

The Zeigarnik effect paradigm as a precursor

How can we explain this peculiar dependence of priming on disfluency? In the absence of an ultimate answer to this question, the old notion of a Zeigarnik (1927) effect offers a plausible hint. As long as the solution to a task is blocked or incomplete, the individual continues to allocate mental and motivational resources to the task. As soon as a job is complete or solved successfully, however, resources can be re-allocated to other jobs and the completed task ceases to influence the individual's behavior. By analogy, a fluently processed prime may suggest an easily solvable situation in which the prime can be dismissed and resources can be allocated elsewhere (cf. Fiedler et al., 2011; Wicklund & Braun, 1987).

Exploiting response strategies and ecological structures for optimal decision making

Fluency from regulatory fit

So far, we have been almost exclusively concerned with fluency manipulations that rely on encoding difficulty and effort expenditure. Another operational approach to the study of fluency builds on the degree of fit between task features and participants' preferred cognitive or motivational state. Most prominent examples can be found in the regulatory-fit framework advanced by Higgins and colleagues (Freitas & Higgins, 2002; Higgins, 2005). Basic to this approach is the distinction between two motivational tendencies, promotion focus (the motive to win or succeed) and prevention focus (the motive not to loose or fail). A regulatory fit exists when a person with a promotion focus (conceived as a personality trait or state) is working on a task that calls for a promotion focus, or when a prevention focus person is facing a prevention-focus task. A growing body of evidence shows that such fitting situations are experienced as smooth and satisfying, whereas task settings that do not fit the individual's disposition are accompanied by a feeling of unease and discomfort (Higgins, 2005)

Similar findings were obtained for other variants of fit experience. For instance, people with a preference for intuitive rather than deliberative processing styles have been found to feel better during decision tasks that involve more intuitive than deliberative mental operations (Betsch & Kunz, 2008). However, despite all this evidence for the preference and enjoyment of fitting situations, there is a conspicuous paucity of evidence on the impact of fit on performance proper. Based on theoretical reasons alone, one can derive that fitting task situations may often cause regulation failure and maladaptive decision strategies.

To illustrate this challenging point, let us consider the face recognition performance in a domain in which a motivational response bias is well established, namely, in eyewitnesses identification decisions. Performance on this task has been often found to suffer from liberal response biases (Wells, Malpass, Lindsay, Fisher, Turtle & Fulero, 2000). Witnesses tend to be too quick to identify a suspect when the lineup does not include the actual perpetrator. Such a bias toward positive decisions, which yields many hits but also many false alarms, is responsible for a high rate of innocents being falsely convicted in court decisions (Wells et al., 2000). Figure 14.1 illustrates this point. The horizontal axis represents the memory strength with which the witness believes to recognize the perpetrator, and the corresponding tendency to make a positive decision.. Let us assume that memory strength is generally higher when the line-up actually includes the perpetrator (right distribution) than when only an innocent suspect is included (left distribution). The solid vertical line exemplifies the typical liberal criterion that characterizes eyewitness responses. The demand characteristics of the lineup task clearly induce a promotion focus so that a relatively weak level of memory strength is sufficient to make an identification decision. As a consequence, a relative high hit rate of 85 percent (i.e., the area proportion under the solid curve that is right of the criterion) comes along with a considerable

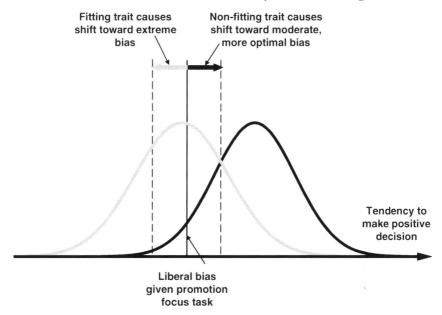

Fitting trait causes shift toward extreme bias

Non-fitting trait causes shift toward moderate, more optimal bias

Tendency to make positive decision

Liberal bias given promotion focus task

Figure 14.1 Graphical illustration of the impact of regulatory fit versus non-fit on response biases in an eyewitness-identification task

false-alarm rate of 40 percent (i.e., the area proportion under the grey curve that is right of the criterion.

Now consider what happens when the promotion focus of the task setting fits the motivational structure of a witness with a strong trait-like promotion focus, thus producing fluency by fit. When such a witness with a strong dispositional promotion focus approaches the line-up task, the criterion will become even more liberal, as shown in the left-ward shift in the bottom part of Figure 14.1. As a consequence, the hit rate will further increase slightly, but the false-alarm rate will increase strongly. In other words, the more extreme criterion resulting from a fit of two response biases—reflecting the person and the task—will strengthen the overall bias and reduce overall performance.

As a matter of rule, a signal-detection analysis implies optimal performance for intermediate decision criterion at the intersection of the two distribution curves. Such a criterion will maximize the difference between hits and false alarms. To the extent that the criterion shifts to a more extreme position than this ideal point, performance will decrease. Following Molden and Higgins' (2008) suggestion to interpret promotion and prevention focus as liberal and conservative strategies, respectively, it follows logically that any fit that further amplifies the already existing non-optimal response bias in either direction will reduce the overall performance.

Thus, for probabilistic decision tasks that match the assumptions of the signal detection model, a non-fit advantage can be derived on theoretical grounds.

Within this task domain, adaptive regulation means to compensate one bias by a strategy shift in the opposite direction rather than to amplify a bias by another, fitting bias.[1] It may still be the case that fitting task settings feel fine and are experienced as fluent. An eye-witness with a promotion-focus personality trait will probably feel better during a lineup than a prevention focus personality. However, such a witness may be particularly overconfident and prone to false identification. Just as the illusion of learning, the enhanced feeling of fluency that results from fitting motivational biases may be a deceptive meta-cognitive cue. Under the conditions depicted here, it seems more likely that fluency is predictive of regulation failure than of smooth performance and successful adaptive problem solving.

How smart is the fluency heuristic?

In a highly recognized recent article, Hertwig et al. (2008, p. 1192) delineated the fluency heuristic, which states: "If two objects, a and b, are recognized, and one of two objects is more fluently retrieved, then infer that this object has the higher value with respect to the criterion." Applying this simple decision rule is supposed to provide correct judgments and decisions under uncertainty, based on ecological analyses and computer simulations that suggest that the actual ecological validity of such a simple measure of fluency is quite impressive. Supplementing the recognition heuristic (Goldstein & Gigerenzer, 2002), which can be conceived as an all-or-none heuristic that distinguishes between zero and non-zero fluency, the fluency heuristic is deemed to exploit the ecological validity of ease of retrieval fluency as a cue to actual occurrence rates in the environment.

Indeed, Hertwig and colleagues found fluency to be significantly related to COSMAS measures of the frequency with which cities, companies, music artists, athletes, and billionaires were mentioned in the media (see also Herzog & Hertwig, Chapter 12, this volume). To explain the ecological validity of the fluency cue, the authors postulate a common cause model, assuming that both the criterion (media coverage) and the cognitive heuristic (fluency of retrieval) reflect the same latent cause (actual size or prominence of the target stimuli).

In this binary-choice paradigm, a natural criterion for adaptive behavior is the rate of accurate choices under uncertainty, when the correct answer is neither known nor predictable from other cues. Unlike the persistence criterion that maximizes effort expenditure or the ability of priming to enable fast and automatic responding, the adaptive value of the fluency heuristic is said to be restricted to those situations in which fluency (e.g., the ease of retrieval of cities) is an ecologically valid cue of the judgment criterion (e.g., population size).[2] Such a restriction, to be sure, renders the heuristic's validity tautological, because it excludes from the domain those situations in which the heuristic is not valid. A more interesting empirical question that suggests itself is whether judges and decision-makers are able to identify those task settings in which the heuristic is valid and not to apply it when the fluency cue does not bear an ecological correlation to the criterion (e.g., Oppenheimer, 2004).

This is however a highly demanding meta-cognitive discrimination task. A famous study that highlights the error proneness of retrieval fluency (or availability) was published by Combs and Slovic (1979). These authors demonstrated that when comparing risks, or causes of death, people may overestimate fluent causes that are over-represented in the media (e.g., murder) but underestimate less fluent causes (e.g., suicide) that appear less frequently in the media. In other words, the fluency cue may inform either correct or incorrect decisions depending on whether it is valid or invalid in a certain domain. Determining the adaptive value of the fluency heuristic therefore calls for an effective cognitive procedure for scaling domain-specific validity.

So how can this be accomplished? How can the validity of the fluency heuristic in a certain domain be determined? Proponents of representative sampling approaches (Cooksey, 1996; Dhami, Hertwig & Hoffrage, 2004) would typically calculate validity relative to an entire reference set. For instance, to calculate the fluency validity for risks judgments, one would have to consider the entire set of all pairs of risks, or causes of death, that were assessed by Combs and Slovic (1979). Across this unrestricted set, including also many trivial ones (lightning vs. cancer), it seems clear that fluency (i.e., ease of retrieval of lightning or cancer cases) will correlate strongly with actual prevalence orders. However, this way of estimating validity confounds fluency with lots of other sources of validity. Thus, for many easy comparisons, one may never resort to fluency because one knows the correct alternative anyway, or one may use other cues but fluency. For example, as a psychologist who occasionally reads statistical yearbooks, I know that the mortality of cancer is more prevalent than of lightning. Or I may follow an expert or informant, who knows an answer, rather than trusting in my differential feeling of fluency. In other words, an appropriate reference set for evaluating fluency validity may not be the entire set of all possible paired comparisons but the subset of pairs for which direct knowledge or other cues are not available. According to this rationale, which amounts to asking for the incremental validity of the fluency heuristic beyond the validity of other cues, the validity may turn out to be quite modest.[3]

Again, the purpose here is neither to present a comprehensive review of the fluency heuristic nor to provide new empirical evidence on its validity. The purpose was only to clarify that determining the adaptive value of the fluency heuristic is more problematic than expected at first sight. Calling the heuristic per se smart or ecologically valid would be a category mistake. What renders the use of the heuristic adaptive (or maladaptive) is the ability (or inability) to figure out those domains in which the heuristic is valid.

Conclusions

In this chapter, I have presented the outlines of a functional analysis of fluency in several paradigms that call for three different criteria of adaptive regulation: persistence on learning tasks, facilitation of fast responding in priming paradigms, and optimal response strategies in decision making as a function of regulatory fit and reliance on the fluency heuristic. Within this functional framework, it can be assumed, for instance, that a well-adapted animal persistently strives for food, is sensitive to primes that signal predators, develops behavioral strategies that fit the structure of territory, and relies on clever choice heuristics. Likewise, a successful student works hard (persistence), is socially sensitive (e.g., nonverbal priming), and exploits ecological baserates (e.g., probability matching strategies) and cultural wisdom (e.g., majority heuristic). With regard to all these criteria, we have seen that feelings of fluency need not be valid indicators of adaptive success and benevolence. In many task contexts, they may rather function as deceptive and misleading cues that prevent organisms from tailoring their behavior to the demands of the current task.

With regard to persistence and motivation strength, the typical function of fluency is to truncate effort expenditure. Although this may be adaptive in specific situations (e.g., when successful goal attainment calls for rest or re-allocation of resources), effort truncation is likely to be dysfunctional in many achievement settings. Regarding priming facilitation, too, we have seen that priming effects tend to be strongest when primes are experienced as disfluent rather than fluent. Again, there may be exceptions to the rule, and strength of priming need not always benefit adaptive responding. However, granting that in the long run primes tend to be diagnostic, fluency can be expected to reduce this adaptive advantage. The impact of fluency on the third criterion, optimizing decision strategies, can be expected to be maladaptive either when fluency from fit prevents one from adopting an optimal intermediate decision criterion or when the fluency heuristic is employed in situations in which the fluency cue is not an ecologically valid proxy of reality.

The goal of the present chapter was definitely not just to discredit the positive image of the fluency cue. My attempts to outline a framework for the functional analysis of fluency research should rather be understood as a tentative suggestion of how adaptive notions can be tackled conceptually and empirically, raising them from rhetoric devices to testable hypotheses. There can be no doubt that, at a very general, non-committal level fluency sometimes serves adaptive functions in some domains. For example, meta-cognitive variation in fluency is required to regulate between continued effort expenditure on an old task versus re-allocation of resources to a new task. Or, with regard to maximal productivity and motivation, the fluency experience must regulate the optimal variation of effort and rest or recreation phases. However, with regard to all these regulatory processes, experiments that simply demonstrate the positivity or warm glow of fluency, the possibility or priming, the preference for regulatory fit, or the validity of the fluency cue in some situations tell us little about the adaptive success of fluency-based regulation. Whether and in what specific situations fluency actually serves what adaptive function is an open empirical question or, to quote Oppenheimer (2008, p. 237), "the role of fluency is more nuanced than previously believed..."

Therefore, the real motivation underlying this chapter is to highlight the need to include functionalist analyses in research designs. The three criteria I have introduced here are actually meant as possible demonstrations of how adaptive value can be measured or manipulated. Rather than simply presupposing that priming serves an obvious adaptive function, researchers should try to somehow measure adaptive gains resulting from priming. Otherwise, the adaptive value assigned to priming remains an empty assumption. Similarly, studies on regulatory fit should not stop with the phenomenological demonstration that fit feels good, but it should continue to analyze the consequences of this feeling within a clearly spelled out functional framework (such as signal-detection analysis). The benefits of the fluency heuristic, too, should be tested rigorously using experimental designs that allow for cogent tests of the incremental validity in task contexts that specify the costs and benefits of incorrect and correct decisions.

I believe that engaging in serious attempts along these lines will not be frustrating and disturb our favorite phenomena and research paradigms. I rather believe that making functionalist analyses an integral part of research designs can actually enrich the study of fluency and inspire new findings, even though these findings may turn out to be more complex than commonly assumed in current mainstream research.

Acknowledgment

The research underlying the present paper was supported by a Koselleck grant from the Deutsche Forschungsgemeinschaft (FI 294 / 23-01).

Notes

1 The compensatory nature of regulatory processes is also clearly spelled out in Bischof's (1975) cybernetic model, which specifies the conditions under which organisms either seek for familiarity and security or for novelty and curiosity. As a matter of rule, sensation-seeking motives and preferences for unfamiliar stimuli should not be expected to increase in situations that are already novel and uncertain. Rather such motives are most likely in secure and familiar settings.

2 Note that the ecological validity criterion (applied to the fluency heuristic) calls for the appropriate utilization of an ecological contingency between attributes of individual stimuli (fluency) and aspects of environmental reality (actual prevalence). Strategies, in contrast, would typically abstract from the individuating predictors and base decisions on the baserates and payoffs of the predicted aspects (cf. Kareev, Fiedler, & Avrahami, 2009).

3 In the false-fame effect (Jacoby, Kelley, Brown & Jasechko, 1989), for an illustrious example, fluently recognized persons are systematically mistaken for famous persons.

References

Alexopoulos, T., Fiedler, K., & Freytag, P. (2012). The impact of open and closed mind-sets on evaluative priming. *Cognition & Emotion.*

Alter, A., & Oppenheimer, D. (2009). Suppressing secrecy through metacognitive ease: Cognitive fluency encourages self-disclosure. *Psychological Science, 20,* 1414–1420.

Alter, A. L., Oppenheimer, D. M., Epley, N., & Eyre, R.N. (2007). Overcoming intuition: Metacognitive difficulty activates analytic reasoning. *Journal of Experimental Psychology: General, 136,* 569–576.

Axsom, D., & Cooper, J. (1985). Cognitive dissonance and psychotherapy: The role of effort justification in inducing weight loss. *Journal of Experimental Social Psychology*, *21*, 149–160.

Belke, B., Leder, H., Strobach, T., & Carbon, C. (2010). Cognitive fluency: High-level processing dynamics in art appreciation. *Psychology of Aesthetics, Creativity, and the Arts*, *4*, 214–222.

Betsch, C., & Kunz, J. J. (2008). Individual strategy preferences and decisional fit. *Journal of Behavioral Decision Making*, *21*, 532–555.

Bischof, N. (1975). A systems approach toward the functional connections of attachment and fear. *Child Development*, *46*, 801–817.

Bjork, R. A. (1994). Memory and metamemory considerations in the training of human beings. In J. Metcalfe, A. P. Shimamura, J. Metcalfe, & A. P. Shimamura (Eds.), *Metacognition: Knowing about knowing* (pp. 185–205). Cambridge, MA: MIT Press.

——— (1999). Assessing our own competence: Heuristics and illusions. In D. Gopher, A. Koriat, D. Gopher, & A. Koriat (Eds.), *Attention and performance XVII: Cognitive regulation of performance: Interaction of theory and application* (pp. 435–459). Cambridge, MA: MIT Press.

Bornstein, R. F. (1989). Exposure and affect: Overview and meta-analysis of research, 1967–1987. *Psychological Bulletin*, *106*, 265–289.

Chan, E., Ybarra, O., & Schwarz, N. (2006). Reversing the affective congruency effect: The role of target word frequency of occurrence. *Journal of Experimental Social Psychology*, *42*, 365–372.

Combs, B., & Slovic, P. (1979). Newspaper coverage of causes of death. *Public Opinion Quarterly*, *56*, 837–843.

Cooksey, R. (1996). The methodology of social judgement theory. *Thinking & Reasoning*, *2*, 141–173.

Corneille, O., Monin, B., & Pleyers, G. (2005). Is positivity a cue or a response option? Warm glow vs evaluative matching in the familiarity for attractive and not-so-attractive face. *Journal of Experimental Social Psychology*, *41*, 431–437.

Craik, F. I. M., & Tulving, E. (1975). Depth of processing and the retention of words in episodic memory. *Journal of Experimental Psychology: General*, *104*, 268–294.

Csikszentmihalyi, M. (1990). *Flow: The psychology of optimal experience.* New York: Harper & Row.

Dechêne, A., Stahl, C., Hansen, J., & Wänke, M. (2010). The truth about the truth: A meta-analytic review of the truth effect. *Personality and Social Psychology Review*, *14*, 238–257.

De Houwer, J., Hermans, D., & Spruyt, A. (2001). Affective priming of pronunciation responses: Effects of target degradation. *Journal of Experimental Social Psychology*, *37*, 85–91.

de Vries, M., Holland, R., Chenier, T., Starr, M., & Winkielman, P. (2010). Happiness cools the warm glow of familiarity: Psychophysiological evidence that mood modulates the familiarity-affect link. *Psychological Science*, *21*, 321–328.

Dhami, M., Hertwig, R., & Hoffrage, U. (2004). The role of representative design in an ecological approach to cognition. *Psychological Bulletin*, *130*, 959–988.

Dosher, B. A., & Russo, J. (1976). Memory for internally generated stimuli. *Journal of Experimental Psychology: Human Learning and Memory*, *2*, 633–640.

Estes, Z., & Jones, L.L. (2009). Integrative priming occurs rapidly and uncontrollably during lexical processing. *Journal of Experimental Psychology: General*, *138*, 112–130.

Fazio, R. H. (2001). On the automatic activation of associated evaluations: An overview. *Cognition and Emotion, 15*, 115–141.

Fazio, R.H., Jackson, J.R., Dunton, B.C., & Williams, C.J. (1995). Variability in automatic activation as an unobtrusive measure of racial attitudes: A bona fide pipeline? *Journal of Personality and Social Psychology, 69*, 1013–1027.

Festinger, L. (1957). *A theory of cognitive dissonance.* Stanford: Stanford University Press.

Fiedler, K. (2003). The hidden vicissitudes of the priming paradigm in evaluative judgment research. In: J. Musch & K.C. Klauer (Eds.), *The psychology of evaluation: Affective processes in cognition and emotion* (pp. 109–137). Mahwah, NJ: Lawrence Erlbaum.

Fiedler, K., Blümke, M., & Unkelbach, C. (2011). On the adaptive flexibility of evaluative priming. *Memory & Cognition, 39*, 557–572.

Fiedler, K., Lachnit, H., Fay, D., & Krug, C. (1992). Mobilization of cognitive resources and the generation effect. *The Quarterly Journal of Experimental Psychology A: Human Experimental Psychology, 45A*, 149–171.

Fiedler, K., Nickel, S., Asbeck, J., & Pagel, U. (2003). Mood and the generation effect. *Cognition and Emotion, 17*, 585–608.

Fiedler, K., & Schenck, W. (2001). Spontaneous inferences from pictorially presented behaviors. Personality and Social Psychology Bulletin, 27, 1533–1546.

Fiedler, K., Schenck, W., Watling, M., & Menges, J. (2005). Priming trait inferences through pictures and moving pictures: The impact of open and closed mindsets. *Journal of Personality and Social Psychology, 88*, 229–244.

Florer, F. L., & Allen, G. (2000). Feelings of knowing in the Ranschburg effect. *The American Journal of Psychology, 113*, 179–198.

Freitas, A. L., Azizian, A., Travers, S., & Berry, S. A. (2005). The evaluative connotation of processing fluency: Inherently positive or moderated by motivational context?. *Journal of Experimental Social Psychology, 41*, 636–644.

Freitas, A. L., & Higgins, E. T. (2002). Enjoying goal-directed action: The role of regulatory fit. *Psychological Science, 13*, 1–6.

Gawronski, B., Deutsch, R., & Seidel, O. (2005). Contextual influences on implicit evaluation: A test of additive versus contrastive effects of evaluative context stimuli in affective priming. *Personality and Social Psychology Bulletin, 31*, 1226–1236.

Goldstein, D. G., & Gigerenzer, G. (2002). Models of ecological rationality: The recognition heuristic. *Psychological Review, 109*, 75–90.

Grosofsky, A., Payne, D. G., & Campbell, K. D. (1994). Does the generation effect depend upon selective displaced rehearsal?. *The American Journal of Psychology, 107*, 53–68.

Hansen, J., & Wänke, M. (2008). It's the difference that counts: Expectancy/experience discrepancy moderates the use of ease of retrieval in attitude judgments. *Social Cognition, 26*, 447–468.

Hastie, R., & Kumar, P. A. (1979). Person memory: Personality traits as organizing principles in memory for behaviors. *Journal of Personality and Social Psychology, 37*, 25–38.

Hermans, D., Spruyt, A., & Eelen, P. (2003). Automatic affective priming of recently acquired stimulus valence: Priming at SOA 300 but not at SOA 1000. *Cognition & Emotion, 17*, 83–99.

Hertwig, R., Herzog, S., Schooler, L., & Reimer, T. (2008). Fluency heuristic: A model of how the mind exploits a by-product of information retrieval. *Journal of Experimental Psychology: Learning, Memory, and Cognition, 34*, 1191–1206.

Higgins, E. T. (2005). Value from regulatory fit. *Current Directions in Psychological Science, 14*, 208–213.

Hirshman, E., & Bjork, R. A. (1988). The generation effect: Support for a two-factor theory. *Journal of Experimental Psychology: Learning, Memory, and Cognition, 14*, 484–494.

Huber, D., Clark, T., Curran, T., & Winkielman, P. (2008). Effects of repetition priming on recognition memory: Testing a perceptual fluency-disfluency model. *Journal of Experimental Psychology: Learning, Memory, and Cognition, 34*, 1305–1324.

Jacoby, L., Kelley, C., Brown, J., & Jasechko, J. (1989). Becoming famous overnight: Limits on the ability to avoid unconscious influences of the past. *Journal of Personality and Social Psychology, 56*, 326–338.

Kareev, Y., Fiedler, K., & Avrahami, J. (2009). Base rates, contingencies, and prediction behavior. *Journal of Experimental Psychology: Learning, Memory, and Cognition, 35*, 371–380.

Klauer, K. C., & Musch, J. (2003). Affective priming: Findings and theories. In J. Musch & K. C. Klauer (Eds.), The psychology of evaluation: Affective processes in cognition and emotion (pp. 7–49). Mahwah, NJ: Erlbaum.

Koriat, A., & Bjork, R. A. (2005). Illusions of competence in monitoring one's knowledge during study. *Journal of Experimental Psychology: Learning, Memory, and Cognition, 31*, 187–194.

Koriat, A., & Ma'ayan, H. (2005). The effects of encoding fluency and retrieval fluency on judgments of learning. *Journal of Memory and Language, 52*, 478–492.

Kurilla, B. P., & Westerman, D. L. (2008). Processing fluency affects subjective claims of recollection. *Memory & Cognition, 36*, 82–92.

Labroo, A. A., & Lee, A. Y. (2006). Between two brands: A goal fluency account of brand evaluation. *Journal of Marketing Research, 43*, 374–385.

Lawrence, D. H., & Festinger, L. (1962). *Deterrents and reinforcement: The psychology of insufficient reward*. Oxford: Stanford University Press.

MacLeod, C. M., Gopie, N., Hourihan, K. L., Neary, K. R., & Ozubko, J. D. (2010). The production effect: Delineation of a phenomenon. *Journal of Experimental Psychology: Learning, Memory, and Cognition, 36*, 671–685.

Marewski, J. N., & Schooler, L. J. (2011). Cognitive niches: An ecological model of strategy selection. *Psychological Review, 118*, 393–437.

Miele, D. B., Finn, B., & Molden, D. C. (2011). Does easily learned mean easily remembered? It depends on your beliefs about intelligence. *Psychological Science, 22*, 320–324.

Milgram, R. M., & Arad, R. (1981). Ideational fluency as a predictor of original problem solving. *Journal of Educational Psychology, 73*, 568–572.

Molden, D. C., & Higgins, E. (2008). How preferences for eager versus vigilant judgment strategies affect self-serving conclusions. *Journal of Experimental Social Psychology, 44*, 1219–1228.

Mulligan, N. W., & Lozito, J. P. (2004). Self-generation and memory. In B. H. Ross & B. H. Ross (Eds.), *The psychology of learning and motivation: Advances in research and theory, Vol 45* (pp. 175–214). San Diego, CA: Elsevier Academic Press.

Muraven, M., & Baumeister, R. F. (2000). Self-regulation and depletion of limited resources: Does self-control resemble a muscle? *Psychological Bulletin, 126*, 247–259.

Novemsky, N., Dhar, R., Schwarz, N., & Simonson, I. (2007). Preference fluency in choice. *Journal of Marketing Research, 44*, 347–356.

Oppenheimer, D. M. (2004). Spontaneous discounting of availability in frequency judgment tasks. *Psychological Science, 15*, 100–105.

—— (2008). The secret life of fluency. *Trends in Cognitive Sciences, 12*, 237–241.

Reber, R., & Schwarz, N. (1999). Effects of perceptual fluency on judgments of truth. *Consciousness and Cognition, 8*, 338–342.

—— (2006). Perceptual fluency, preference, and evolution. *Polish Psychological Bulletin, 37*, 16–22.

Reber, R., & Unkelbach, C. (2010). The epistemic status of processing fluency as source for judgments of truth. *Review of Philosophy and Psychology, 1*, 563–581.

Rhodes, M. G., & Castel, A. D. (2008). Memory predictions are influenced by perceptual information: Evidence for metacognitive illusions. *Journal of Experimental Psychology: General, 137*, 615–625.

Schwarz, N., Bless, H., Strack, F., Klumpp, G., Rittenauer-Schatka, H., & Simons, A. (1991). Ease of retrieval as information: Another look at the availability heuristic. *Journal of Personality and Social Psychology, 61*, 195–202.

Slamecka, N. J., & Graf, P. (1978). The generation effect: Delineation of a phenomenon. *Journal of Experimental Psychology: Human Learning & Memory, 4*, 592–604.

Song, H., & Schwarz, N. (2008). If it's hard to read, it's hard to do: Processing fluency affects effort prediction and motivation. *Psychological Science, 19*, 986–988.

Stangor, C., & McMillan, D. (1992). Memory for expectancy-congruent and expectancy-incongruent information: A review of the social and social developmental literatures. *Psychological Bulletin, 111*, 42–61.

Topolinski, S., & Strack, F. (2010). False fame prevented: Avoiding fluency effects without judgmental correction. *Journal of Personality and Social Psychology, 98*, 721–733.

Unkelbach, C. (2006). The learned interpretation of cognitive fluency. *Psychological Science, 17*, 339–345.

—— (2007). Reversing the truth effect: Learning the interpretation of processing fluency in judgments of truth. *Journal of Experimental Psychology: Learning, Memory, and Cognition, 33*, 219–230.

Van Zandt, B. R., & Himelstein, P. (1961). The role of verbal fluency on a projective measure of motivation. *Educational and Psychological Measurement, 21*, 873–878.

Volz, K. G., Schooler, L. J., & von Cramon, D. (2010). It just felt right: The neural correlates of the fluency heuristic. *Consciousness and Cognition: An International Journal, 19*, 829–837.

Wänke, M., & Bless, H. (2000). The effects of subjective ease of retrieval on attitudinal judgments: The moderating role of processing motivation. In H. Bless, J. P. Forgas, H. Bless, & J. P. Forgas (Eds.), *The message within: The role of subjective experience in social cognition and behavior* (pp. 143–161). New York: Psychology Press.

Wells, G. L., Malpass, R. S., Lindsay, R. L., Fisher, R. P., Turtle, J. W., & Fulero, S. M. (2000). From the lab to the police station: A successful application of eyewitness research. *American Psychologist, 55*, 581–598.

Wicklund, R. A., & Braun, O. L. (1987). Incompetence and the concern with human categories. *Journal of Personality and Social Psychology, 53*, 373–382.

Winkielman, P., & Cacioppo, J. (2001). Mind at ease puts a smile on the face: Psychophysiological evidence that processing facilitation elicits positive affect. *Journal of Personality and Social Psychology, 81*, 989–1000.

Winkielman, P., Schwarz, N., Fazendeiro, T., & Reber, R. (2003). The hedonic marking of processing fluency: Implications for evaluative judgment. *The psychology of evaluation: Affective processes in cognition and emotion* (pp. 189–217). Mahwah, NJ: Lawrence Erlbaum Associates Publishers.

Whittlesea, B. A. (1993). Illusions of familiarity. *Journal of Experimental Psychology: Learning, Memory, and Cognition, 19*, 1235–1253.

Whittlesea, B. A., & Leboe, J. P. (2003). Two fluency heuristics (and how to tell them apart). *Journal of Memory and Language, 49*, 62–79.

Zajonc, R. B. (1968). Attitudinal effects of mere exposure. *Journal of Personality and Social Psychology, Monograph Supplement, 9 (2, Pt. 2)*, 1–27.

—— (2001). Mere exposure: A gateway to the subliminal. *Current Directions in Psychological Science, 10*, 224–228.

Zeigarnik, B. (1927). Über das Behalten von erledigten und unerledigten Handlungen [On the retention of complete and incomplete actions]. *Psychologische Forschung, 9*, 1–85.

Part IV
Final assessment

15 Thinking about "experiences of thinking"

Fluency in six principles

Christian Unkelbach and
Rainer Greifeneder

In this volume, the contributors have investigated fluency from different angles and perspectives. A diverse set of questions at the frontiers of fluency research was addressed, including the extent to which fluency is an adaptive cue when judging real-world criteria, how fluency influences subjective judgments of liking and disliking, which processes underlie the emergence and use of "experiences of thinking," and when fluency may be misleading. The chapters explored new conceptual pathways, evaluated existing methodology, and provided up-to-date summaries of entire research programs. Despite this broad spectrum, the sample of presented fluency research is (necessarily) a selective one, filtered by our own perception of the field and the relevant topics. For example, the influence of fluency on memory judgments (e.g., research by Benjamin, Bjork, & Schwartz, 1998; Koriat, 1993), or the implications of fluency for marketing were only covered in passing (e.g., research by Landwehr, Labroo, & Herrmann, 2011; Petrova & Cialdini, 2005; Pocheptsova, Labroo, & Dhar, 2010).

That the chapters constitute a selective sample may explain why there are many common themes throughout the book. Perhaps the causally more important reason is that there is a common set of tacit principles inherent in most researches' conceptualizations of fluency. We dedicate this last chapter to "unearthing" these principles, both as a means to guide future research and to construct a target for those who wish to criticize. As such, what follows is a condensed specification of the key theoretical and empirical claims spelt out throughout the book; more details are available in the individual chapters.

1. Fluency is a unitary construct

When browsing through the individual chapters, it may be surprising to see that fluency has manifold causes: from simple repetition to color contrast of written stimuli, from rhyming sentences to generating exemplars. Moreover, fluency comes in many guises: from "pure" feelings of ease to more complex experiences such as familiarity or knowing. Finally, there are multiple implications that follow from fluency; to repeat but one example, judgments about a fluently read sentence can vary from "heard before" to "factually true," from "legibly written" to "intelligent statement." These differences in source, descriptive phenomenology, and judgmental implications seem to imply a multitude of different constructs. However, investigations to what is underneath trace a clear picture of one core underlying construct, caused and specified by a finite set of mechanisms, including the way mental processing is monitored as well as the location of every mental operation on a continuum from fluent to non-fluent. Perhaps the most central conceptual feature of this unitary construct is being an experience, or more precisely, a feeling, as expressed in the book's title. Conceptualizing fluency as a feeling assigns characteristics to fluency, sets fluency apart from other constructs, and places constraints on the fluency construct—all of which guide scientific investigation. Until there is evidence to the contrary, we believe it to be fruitful and parsimonious to subscribe to this perspective of the fluency experience as a unitary construct.

2. Fluency is highly subjective

There is no deterministic relationship between what should objectively be easy and what people experience as easy; what is easy for one person might be difficult for another, what is easy in one context may be difficult in another, what is easy today may be difficult in ten years. As a consequence, it is difficult to perfectly predict whether an individual will experience fluency. More importantly perhaps, to date there is no way of objectively measuring the subjectively experienced fluency. Sometimes response latencies are used as an objectively quantifiable proxy. However, not all discrepancies in response latencies are due to fluency, so that someone might read a low contrast statement more slowly than a high contrast statement without this necessarily indexing a fluency experience. The practical implication is that in fluency research objective measures are a useful proxy, but should not be equated with the experience proper.

3. Fluency is most informative when discrepant

As with other feelings, the salience of an experience is heightened if it arises in contrast to another experience. A warm fire is most comfortable after the cold outside, and similarly, fluency is particularly informative when previous mental processes were difficult. This principle is based on the relativity of experiences and a lack of calibration with respect to what is "difficult" and what is "easy." It does not imply, however, that there are no effects when there is no discrepancy; yet these fluency effects are likely of smaller magnitude. The practical implication for researchers is that fluency effects are more easily studied in within-participant designs, where fluent and less fluent circumstances alternate and thus create respective discrepancies in the experiences.

4. Fluency's meaning is malleable

Although we believe that fluency is a feeling, and that fluency's connotation is generally positive, the meaning of this feeling is not fixed. What fluency means depends on the judgmental target it is attributed to, and on learned interpretations or available lay theories. This principle explains why fluency may have so many different implications; yet this malleability carries the danger of "anything goes." If fluency effects depend on such context variables as learned interpretations of lay theories, it is possible to recruit processing fluency *post-hoc* as explanatory construct for almost any effect. Thus, researchers must specify the context in beforehand, and manipulate the learned interpretations and lay theories *a priori*.

In addition, the process steps of attribution and interpretation open interesting pathways for future research, for example, to exemplify the rules by which fluency takes up the one or the other meaning. Does a "first come, first served" rule decide whether a specific fluency experience is used, for instance, as information for a judgment of truth or channels superficial processing of content information? Addressing questions of this type will help to predict fluency effects more precisely.

5. Fluency has informative and regulative functions

Initial fluency research focused on the feeling's informative value, that is, on fluency as an independent piece of information in judgment and decision making. For instance, experiences of fluency or disfluency may directly affect whether an instance is judged as frequent, a name as famous, or a testimony as true. Such informative influences are likely to be strongest when judgments and decisions are made immediately, and when they are feeling-based rather than based on deliberate thinking. Delays between processing and judgment alter the effects and may even reverse them. For researchers looking for fluency effects this implies that judgments are best assessed immediately or even during processing, thereby minimizing deliberate thinking and maximizing the chance that the feeling is perceived as representative of the target and relevant for the judgment.

In addition to such direct uses of fluency as information, recent investigations have focused on regulative effects, in that fluency changes downstream cognitions, similar to the impact of mood on processing styles. The most prominent conceptualization holds that fluency leads to more superficial processing, while disfluency leads to more analytic processing. Supposedly this is because fluent processing is a signal about the state of the world and the amount of energy that is needed to handle this current state. If things are going easily, less energy is invested into thinking. Yet, there is reason to assume that indirect consequences go beyond this basic distinction. For researchers, it is important to be aware of both kinds of influences when investigating the one or the other supposedly in isolation.

6. Fluency is useful

Many experiments on fluency lead people astray; they judge unknown people as famous, made-up trivia as veridical information, and rare events as frequent. Yet, these seemingly maladaptive consequences of fluency demonstrated in experimental designs are due to the fact that researchers create laboratory environments where fluency and the properties of the environment or the necessity of a strategy are uncorrelated. Outside the scientific ivory tower people are likely correct more often than not when judging a fluently perceived face to be famous, an instance that comes easily to mind as frequent, or switch to a more superficial mode when processing goes smoothly. If researchers want to decide whether fluency is useful or not, in other words, whether people should rely on this feeling or not, they need representative samples of stimuli and environments, in which the correlations of fluency with the world have a chance to manifest themselves. The orthogonal world of experimental psychology makes using fluency a poor choice by default.

Having distilled these six principles from previous research, we wish to close by looking at the horizon ahead. For sure, it is interesting to show fluency effects in different domains and their importance for real-life judgments and decisions; and we believe there is much value in such research. From a meta-theoretical point of view, however, we hope for a larger "fluency theory" that also embeds the experience into the larger architecture of the human mind. After finishing the book, it is apparent to the observant reader that none of the presented approaches cover all the bases. To give an example, Chapter 2's model primarily covers judgment processes, but omits how fluency experiences emerge, how the feeling directs thinking styles, and how fluency is intertwined with the environment. Hence, while this model fares well in regard to the question when to use fluency experiences and when not, it is far from an all-encompassing theory.

Thus, the realm of fluency research is replete with open questions. This is an asset and not a problem! The possible pathways are worthwhile of future investigation. If we compare fluency research to theories of emotional feelings (e.g., Lazarus, 1991), it is clear that fluency research is still rather in its infancy. While emotion research had more than 100 years to ripen and develop, fluency research has just taken off. However, because "having" is often not as interesting as "wanting" (i.e., an encompassing and well-established theory), it would be almost depressing if we finished this book with a sense of "all questions answered." From our perspective, it is more exciting to close with the challenge to build a larger theoretical framework and to dig deeper into the mechanisms that lead to fluency effects on judgments, decisions, and behavior. It is our sincere hope that the present volume will contribute to this endeavor.

References

Benjamin, A. S., Bjork, R. A., & Schwartz, B. L. (1998). The mismeasure of memory: When retrieval fluency is misleading as a metamnemonic index. *Journal of Experimental Psychology: General, 127,* 55–68.

Koriat, A. (1993). How do we know that we know? The accessibility model of the feeling of knowing. *Psychological Review, 100,* 609–639.

Landwehr, J., Labroo, A. A., & Herrmann, A. (2011). Gut liking for the ordinary: Incorporating design fluency improves automobile sales forecasts. *Marketing Science, 30,* 416–429.

Lazarus, R. (1991). Progress on a cognitive-motivational-relational theory of emotion. *American Psychologist, 46*, 819–834.

Petrova, P. K., & Cialdini, R. B. (2005). Fluency of consumption imagery and the backfire effects of imagery appeals. *Journal of Consumer Research, 32*, 442–452.

Pocheptsova, A., Labroo, A. A., & Dhar, R. (2010). Making products feel special: When metacognitive difficulty enhances evaluation. *Journal of Marketing Research, 47*, 1059–1069.

Author index

Subject index

Made in the USA
Middletown, DE
27 October 2020